THE INSIDERS' GAME

T0385598

PRINCETON STUDIES IN INTERNATIONAL
HISTORY AND POLITICS

*Tanisha M. Fazal, G. John Ikenberry, William C. Wohlforth,
and Keren Yarhi-Milo, Series Editors*

For a full list of titles in the series, go to https://press.princeton.edu/series
/princeton-studies-in-international-history-and-politics

The Insiders' Game: How Elites Make War and Peace, Elizabeth N. Saunders

*A World Safe for Commerce: American Foreign Policy from the Revolution to the
Rise of China*, Dale C. Copeland

*The Geopolitics of Shaming: When Human Rights Pressure Works—and When
It Backfires*, Rochelle Terman

Violent Victors: Why Bloodstained Parties Win Postwar Elections,
Sarah Zukerman Daly

An Unwritten Future: Realism and Uncertainty in World Politics, Jonathan Kirshner

Undesirable Immigrants: Why Racism Persists in International Migration,
Andrew S. Rosenberg

Human Rights for Pragmatists: Social Power in Modern Times, Jack L. Snyder

Seeking the Bomb: Strategies of Nuclear Proliferation, Vipin Narang

The Spectre of War: International Communism and the Origins of World War II,
Jonathan Haslam

*Strategic Instincts: The Adaptive Advantages of Cognitive Biases in
International Politics*, Dominic D. P. Johnson

Divided Armies: Inequality and Battlefield Performance in Modern War, Jason Lyall

Active Defense: China's Military Strategy since 1949, M. Taylor Fravel

*After Victory: Institutions, Strategic Restraint, and the Rebuilding of Order after
Major Wars, New Edition*, G. John Ikenberry

Cult of the Irrelevant: The Waning Influence of Social Science on National Security,
Michael C. Desch

Secret Wars: Covert Conflict in International Politics, Austin Carson

Who Fights for Reputation: The Psychology of Leaders in International Conflict,
Keren Yarhi-Milo

The Insiders' Game

HOW ELITES MAKE WAR AND PEACE

ELIZABETH N. SAUNDERS

PRINCETON UNIVERSITY PRESS

PRINCETON & OXFORD

Published by Princeton University Press
41 William Street, Princeton, New Jersey 08540
99 Banbury Road, Oxford OX2 6JX

press.princeton.edu

All Rights Reserved

Library of Congress Cataloging-in-Publication Data

Names: Saunders, Elizabeth N. (Elizabeth Nathan), 1978– author.
Title: The insiders' game : how elites make war and peace / Elizabeth N.
    Saunders.
Description: Princeton, New Jersey : Princeton University Press, [2024] |
    Series: Princeton studies in international history and politics |
    Includes bibliographical references and index.
Identifiers: LCCN 2023042411 (print) | LCCN 2023042412 (ebook) | ISBN
    9780691215815 (hardback) | ISBN 9780691215808 (paperback) | ISBN
    9780691215822 (ebook)
Subjects: LCSH: Politics and war—United States. | Elite (Social
    sciences)—United States. | International relations—Public opinion. |
    Government accountability—United States. | United States—Foreign
    relations. | BISAC: POLITICAL SCIENCE / Security (National &
    International) | HISTORY / Military / United States
Classification: LCC JZ6385 .S37 2024 (print) | LCC JZ6385 (ebook) | DDC
    327.73—dc23/eng/20231003
LC record available at https://lccn.loc.gov/2023042411
LC ebook record available at https://lccn.loc.gov/2023042412

British Library Cataloging-in-Publication Data is available

Editorial: Bridget Flannery-McCoy and Alena Chekanov
Production Editorial: Nathan Carr
Jacket/Cover Design: Katie Osborne
Production: Lauren Reese
Publicity: William Pagdatoon
Copyeditor: Kathleen Kageff

Jacket/Cover Credit: Sergey / Adobe Stock

This book has been composed in Arno

10 9 8 7 6 5 4 3 2 1

CONTENTS

PREFACE

WHERE DOES CONSTRAINT and accountability come from when democracies fight wars? This book challenges the prevailing answer to this question: that voter preferences and the threat of electoral punishment are the main source of democratic constraint. Instead, the book argues that elites, rather than voters, are the primary audience—and source of constraint—for democratic leaders making decisions about war and peace.

I owe this book to discussions with colleagues. The idea first arose in the seminar room of the George Washington University Department of Political Science, where I began my career as a professor and which is a place where political scientists from all subfields regularly gathered to talk about just about anything over lunch. During the 2008 primary season, as Barack Obama and Hillary Clinton vied for the Democratic presidential nomination, I listened to my colleagues who study American politics and realized that the way they talked about voting was quite different from the way international relations (IR) scholars wrote about it. Instead of going into the voting booth focused on the incumbent president's foreign policy record or the backgrounds or policy stances of the major party nominees, voters focused primarily on the economy, or their political tribe, or the candidate listed first on the ballot. Foreign policy could matter in elections—ironically, the 2008 Democratic primary may have been one of the rare cases in which it did—but generally took a back seat to other concerns or fit into a larger narrative.

As I dug into the literature on American political behavior and foreign policy, it seemed there was something missing from the American politics side, too. Scholars who approached the politics of war from a political behavior perspective tended to emphasize the role of elite cues. If elites are united, the public will generally support government policy; if elites are divided, the public will divide, usually along partisan lines, especially for those who are politically knowledgeable. This approach, articulated by John Zaller and extended by Adam Berinsky, takes a "top-down" view of public opinion about war in the United States.

The thing that was missing? Leaders. Why would a US president, for example, accept elite unity or dissent as given, without making some attempt to shape elite opinion or generate elite consensus? Additionally, as scholars of public opinion and war learned more and more about the political psychology of public preferences about the use of force, critiques of the elite, top-down approach took hold. The "bottom-up" approach reinforced that leaders cannot simply manipulate popular opinion at will during crises or wars. But democratic leaders—who know something about politics—are not powerless in the face of elite opinion about their policies.

This book attempts to bridge these perspectives and reconcile several pieces of conventional wisdom about democracies and war that, though widely accepted, are somewhat at odds. At the level of voters, for example, scholars of public opinion and war generally agree that the public is not well informed about foreign policy. Yet many scholars have noted that democratic leaders behave as if the public will hold them accountable.

At the level of political parties, several prominent studies have found few differences in the use of military force between the two major parties in the United States, even though they have very different preferences on national security, and the public perceives them to be different in their willingness to use force. The party "brands"—Democrats as weaker on national security, Republicans as stronger but overprone to use military force—have been remarkably sticky. Yet Democratic presidents have initiated or extended many wars.

And at the level of the international system, scholars continue to debate whether democracies have advantages in international conflict. Are democracies better at coercive diplomacy, selecting conflicts, and fighting and winning wars? And if so, why? After years of focus on the democratic side of this question, IR scholars turned to autocracies and have shown that some autocrats are constrained by their fellow elites and sometimes even their publics when they make decisions about war. Still, it remains unclear how to reconcile these findings with the very different constraints we observe in democratic and autocratic countries.

The path from idea to book has not been linear. Settling on how to orient and organize the book proved a major challenge. Should it be a book about democracies in general? Or a book about the United States? This tension has recurred over and over in the time I have worked on the project. Ultimately, it became clear that the book had to focus on one country. This choice was influenced by work with my friend and collaborator Susan Hyde, where we examined the nature of domestic audience constraint across regime type. Some arguments, we noticed, were about structural constraints, like domestic institutions, whether they examined democratic or autocratic settings. Other research examined sources of constraint that leaders could manage or manipulate strategically within a single country. The latter tended to focus on autocratic leaders, such as China, where Jessica Chen Weiss has shown that

Chinese leaders strategically manage popular protest to signal resolve. When examining how democratic leaders evade or manage constraint in war, scholars tended to explore secret or covert action, new technologies that reduce casualties, or even outright deception.

But democratic leaders frequently manage constraints not by resorting to secrecy or lying, but by playing regular democratic politics, out in the open. To be sure, some of this politicking happens behind closed doors, but it happens through regular channels—at the elite level. It became clear that to develop and test a theory of how elite politics shapes decisions to use force, the book had to concentrate on a single country. This approach holds domestic institutions constant and allows me to focus on how leaders play the "insiders' game."

The United States was a natural choice for several reasons. Few countries have the capabilities to make decisions about the use of force regularly. Since 1945, the United States has been the democracy that has most frequently contemplated and used force around the world. Its separation-of-powers system allows a clear distinction between the chief executive and legislative elites. And as a relatively open democracy with a long tradition of using military force, we would expect public opinion to play a significant role in choices about war and peace. The United States has much to teach us about the elite politics of war and for understanding democracies more broadly in the international arena. I point out many of these implications along the way and examine them in greater depth in the book's conclusion.

This book has been a long time in the making—far longer than anticipated. What started as an idea for a paper became a sprawling project. Along the way, life and global events intervened many times. But a benefit has been getting feedback from so many wonderful scholars and students whose questions, challenges, and suggestions have immeasurably improved the book. I am sure my records are incomplete, but my gratitude to all who helped along the way is boundless.

I owe so much to my former colleagues at George Washington University (GWU), where the American politics faculty and especially hallway neighbors Sarah Binder, Chris Deering, Danny Hayes, Eric Lawrence, Forrest Maltzman, and John Sides patiently answered my many questions. The IR faculty, especially the wonderful group in the Institute for Security and Conflict Studies led by Charlie Glaser and including Steve Biddle, Alex Downes, James Lebovic, Yon Lupu, Jo Spear, Rachel Stein, and Caitlin Talmadge, commented early and often on various stages of the project. The department fostered a collegial culture of engagement across subfields, reflecting the values of the late Lee Sigelman, from whom I was lucky to learn in the department's lunch room, and for whom the room is now named. I am also grateful to the many faculty I counted as mentors at GWU. Marty Finnemore was a constant sounding board and supportive ear in addition to serving as a sharp set of eyes on anything she read. Charlie Glaser built a strong and collaborative group of security scholars and was always generous with his feedback and advice. Jim Goldgeier has given me more of his time and wisdom over the years than I had any right to claim and read more drafts than I can count. Jim Lebovic dropped by my office almost every Friday at 5:30 p.m. to talk about the Vietnam War and any number of other things, and he gave this book its title, as well as invaluable guidance to its author. Susan Sell dispensed advice and chocolate in exactly the right proportions.

At Georgetown, where I moved in the midst of the project, many colleagues provided support and encouragement. I thank especially Rebecca Patterson and the entire Security Studies Program team; as well as Tony Arend, Laia Balcells, Andy Bennett, Dan Byman, Jenny Guardado, Lise Howard, Diana Kim, Charles King, Kate McNamara, Abe Newman, Dan Nexon, Irfan Nooruddin, Ken Opalo, Nita Rudra, Joel Simmons, and Erik Voeten, all of whom provided much-needed advice and support on many occasions; and David Edelstein and Caitlin Talmadge, who kept me sane. I also owe much to those who, in the final year of work on this book, put up with my many email replies reading, "I can't—I'm trying to finish the book," especially at the Mortara Center for International Studies, where Brittany Friedman, Sofia McGettigan, and Julio Salmeron-Perla cheerfully held down the fort, with the invaluable support of Emily Zenick.

I have been fortunate to learn from many students and scholars who enriched this book by pushing me to think differently or harder about a host of issues. My teaching and learning from my students has left its imprint on the book, and I am grateful to the many students in my US foreign policy and national security courses for their comments and questions that stuck with me long after class ended. In the time I worked on this book, I was fortunate to take on a role with the Monkey Cage (TMC) blog, now named Good Authority, helping to translate political science research into short articles for a public audience. This role introduced or reconnected me to the research of a wide community of scholars. I learned so much from the authors whom I had the privilege to edit, and this book is immeasurably better for it. I also thank the entire TMC/GA team not only for support and encouragement but also for the opportunity to learn from other editors. Special thanks to the editorial dynamic duo of E. J. Graff and Vanessa Lide, as well as Henry Farrell and Stacie Goddard on the IR beat, for taking on more TMC editing so I could finish the book.

I also thank the research assistants who helped with different aspects of the empirical work and without whom the book would not have been possible: Isabella Artaza, Gabriella Brazinski, Emily Coello, Halia Czosnek, Christina

Wagner Faegri, Jack Hasler, Nick Kodama, Kathryn Long, Julia Macdonald, Jessica McDowell, Shea Minter, Ikuma Ogura, Chaitanya Shekar, Bridget Smith, and George Zhou. They helped build the empirical evidence on which this book rests and checked and double-checked different parts of it with gusto, undoubtedly saving me from many mistakes (and all remaining errors are my own).

I am grateful to the many archivists who were generous with their expertise: Alan Houke and John Wilson at the Lyndon B. Johnson Presidential Library; Christa Cleeton and Bilqees Sayed at the Seeley G. Mudd Manuscript Library at Princeton University; Jenny Mandel, Jennifer Newby, and Gina Risetter at the Ronald Reagan Presidential Library; and David Clark and Randy Sowell at the Harry S. Truman Library.

Along the way I presented parts of this project, from germ of an idea to book manuscript, to more people than I can count who were generous with their time and feedback. I presented an early draft of several chapters at the Lone Star National Security Forum, and I thank Joshua Rovner and Eugene Gholz for the opportunity, and Richard Immerman and Alice Hunt Friend for excellent discussant comments. In the midst of the pandemic, I was lucky to have the feedback of several colleagues who generously gave their time to a virtual book workshop. Thanks to Austin Carson, Ken Schultz, and Jessica Weeks, as well as colleagues David Edelstein and Caitlin Talmadge, for their careful reading and excellent suggestions. The book is so much improved for all these participants' advice and detailed suggestions.

I also thank seminar, workshop, and conference participants for feedback at presentations of draft chapters and papers, at the Niehaus Center IR Faculty Colloquium at Princeton University, the Brookings Institution Project on International Order and Strategy, the Browne Center at the University of Pennsylvania, the MIT Security Studies Program, the University of Konstanz International Studies Seminar Series, the Center for International Trade and Security at the University of Georgia, the International Politics Seminar at Columbia, the UCLA International Relations Workshop, the Texas A&M IR speaker series, the Mershon Center conference on War, Media, and the Public at Ohio State, the University of Cambridge, the MIRTH Colloquium at Berkeley, the University of Texas–Austin IR speaker series, the Rice University IR speaker series, the Harvard IR speaker series, the Forum on International Institutions and Global Governance at Temple, the PISP series at the University of Chicago, the University of Wisconsin–Madison IR Colloquium, the Notre Dame International Security Program, the Center for International Development and Conflict Management (CIDCM) / IR Speaker Series at the University of Maryland, the Leaders and Military Conflict Workshop held at the Peace Science Society at the University of Mississippi, the Reppy Institute at Cornell, the Buffett Center at Northwestern, the University of California–San Diego IR speaker series, the Global Governance, Politics, and Security program at American University, the Georgetown University International Theory and Research Seminar (GUITARS), GWU's work-in-progress seminar at the Institute for Security and Conflict Studies, the IR speaker series at Yale, the Conference on Good Democratic Leadership held at Yale, the Wilson Center work-in-progress seminar, and many panels at the annual meetings of the American Political Science Association, the International Studies Association, the Midwest Political Science Association, and the joint International Security Studies–International Security and Arms Control (ISSS-ISAC) Annual Conference. I thank all the participants who read drafts, offered helpful feedback, and improved this project in countless ways.

For comments, advice, and patient responses to many questions, I thank the many colleagues listed above, as well as Robert Adcock, Phil Arena, Matt Baum, Adam Berinsky, Andrew Blinkinsop, Ryan Brutger, James Cameron, Steven Casey, Jonathan Caverley, Tarun Chhabra, Jeff Colgan, Rafaela Dancygier, Keith Darden, E. J. Dionne, Dan Drezner, Mary Dudziak, Alexandra Evans, Songying Fang, Henry Farrell, Tanisha Fazal, Peter Feaver, Matthew Fuhrmann, John Gans, Frank Gavin, Christopher Gelpi, Stacie Goddard, Alexandra Guisinger, Steph Haggard, Dan Hopkins, Michael Horowitz, Will Howell, Susan Hyde, Andrew Johns, Miles Kahler, John Kane, Joshua Kertzer, Ron Krebs, Sarah Kreps, Andy Kydd, David Lake, Jacqueline Larson, Carrie Lee, Ashley Leeds, Gabe Lenz, Rob Litwak, Fred Logevall, Michaela Mattes, Shea Minter, Andrew Moravcsik, Kimberly Morgan, David Nickerson, Haig Patapan, Kathleen Powers, Lauren Prather, Jeremy Pressman, Dan Reiter, Jonathan Renshon, Nicholas Sambanis, John Schuessler, Todd Sechser, Jordan Tama, Rob Trager, Jessica Chen Weiss, James Graham Wilson, Scott Wolford, Tom Wright, and Keren Yarhi-Milo. I have surely forgotten others but remain grateful to everyone who offered feedback. I also offer sincere thanks to the three reviewers, whose reviews of this manuscript were among the most helpful I have ever received: thorough, constructive, and in agreement with each other.

I have also benefited from financial and research support that enabled me to conduct the empirical research with time to focus on the theory and analysis. I thank the Woodrow Wilson Center for Scholars and the Council on Foreign Relations Stanton Nuclear Security Fellowship program for fellowships that allowed me time and space for research; and the Truman Library Institute, the American Political Science Foundation Warren Miller Fund in Electoral Politics, the George Washington Institute for Public Policy's Policy Research Scholar program, the University Facilitating Fund at GWU, the Elliott School at GWU, and the Security Studies Program and the School of Foreign Service at Georgetown for research support.

The editors at Princeton University Press have been exceedingly patient supporters of this project. Eric Crahan and Bridget Flannery-McCoy showed enthusiasm for the project that never flagged, for which I was especially grateful at the moments when mine did. Bridget, along with Alena Chekanov, offered excellent guidance, direction, and support that steered me over the finish line. At the press, I thank Nathan Carr and Jenny Wolkowicki for smoothly steering the manuscript through the production process, and Kathleen Kageff for expert copyediting. I am also grateful to Heather Kreidler, who provided excellent fact-checking. Virginia Ling prepared the index. Earlier versions of portions of chapters 2 and 5 were published in 2015 as "War and the Inner Circle: Democratic Elites and the Politics of Using Force," *Security Studies* 24(3): 466–501; reprinted by permission of Informa UK Limited, trading as Taylor and Francis Group, www.tandfonline.com. A portion of chapter 3 was published in 2018 in "Leaders, Advisers, and the Political Origins of Elite Support for War," *Journal of Conflict Resolution* 62(10): 2118–49; used with permission of Sage. And a portion of chapter 8 was published in 2014 in "Good Democratic Leadership in Foreign Affairs: An Elite-Centered Approach," in *Good Democratic Leadership: On Prudence and Judgment in Modern Democracies*, edited by John Kane and Haig Patapan, 158–77 (Oxford: Oxford University Press); used with permission of Oxford University Press. I thank the journals and publishers for their assistance.

As I completed work on this book, I learned that my dissertation adviser, Bruce Russett, had passed away. His influence is reflected throughout this book, and I will always be grateful for his support and kindness.

In academia, it often feels like your reward for mastering one opaque process is the chance to participate in another opaque process. Writing a second book proved to be a very different process from the writing of the first, and that was before the global pandemic. For their friendship in the trenches of this and so many other phases of life since graduate school, I thank Rafaela Dancygier, Alexandra Guisinger, and Susan Hyde.

The idea for this book took shape when my oldest daughter, Claire, was a baby. It was supposed to be a paper, while I figured out what my second book project would be, since I had recently come to the difficult conclusion that my original plan for a second project was not feasible. This project turned out to be a much better fit and has grown up with Claire and her sister, Sarah. I am acutely aware of how lucky I am to have them, and to have been able to work on this project in supportive environments that let me take time with them along the way. I could not have done any of it without Marceline Nganfack and Bintou Traore, to whom I will always be grateful.

On top of showing me how to navigate career and family at different stages of life and how to knit, along with countless other invaluable lessons, my mother, Catherine Nathan, taught me everything I know about good writing.

My father, John Nathan, showed me how a love of science could infuse a career in many different ways, and also how to use more power tools than a person could need in a lifetime. In addition to everything they have given me, they supported this book by throwing themselves enthusiastically into grandparenthood, as did my in-laws, Jean and Doug Saunders. While writing this book I had the opportunity to start a new project to spoil my nieces, Laura and Emma, rotten, and I thank my sister, Caroline, for her support of this important endeavor, for always being on the other end of the text chain, and for our pandemic barter system.

My husband, Tom, has been a rock through all the ups and downs and supported me in every sense while we navigated work and family. Claire and Sarah have brought more joy than I ever thought possible. Since they are both old enough to read this, I will refrain from embarrassing them further, and simply dedicate the book to them with all my love.

1

Introduction

THE HISTORY OF DEMOCRACIES and war is filled with regret. Leaders have used force and regretted it. Leaders have used force and regretted that they did not use more, or less, or that they did not use it differently. Critics on all sides have regretted that leaders used force, failed to use force, or failed to use enough force with a particular strategy.

Perhaps the most consistently puzzling regret is the failure to heed dovish warnings. Hindsight is biased, of course: perhaps doves—those who tend to advocate for less militarized ways to resolve international disputes—actually have been more effective than we realize in stopping unwise military ventures before they started, or in the case of a failed military effort, war was a prudent choice and leaders simply got unlucky. But the decisions that we know about leave many puzzles. We look back on Cold War–era hot wars in Korea and Vietnam, and post-9/11 "forever wars" in Iraq and Afghanistan—all of which had contributions from multiple democratic countries—and wonder how so many leaders started, escalated, and perpetuated war efforts that observers argued at the time were risky at best and doomed at worst, and which the public turned against long before its leaders ended the conflicts. Hawks—those who tend to view the use of force more favorably—often get the blame, whether the hawkish views originated with the leader, advisers with the leader's ear, military leaders shaping the leader's options, or legislators arguing that the leader should use force.

But the puzzling question is not really about the hawks. Reasonable people can disagree about the wisdom of war, and hawks are part of the natural diversity of views one would expect in a democracy.

The real puzzle is, What happened to the doves? In many of these cases, powerful moderates and doves, sometimes including the leader, had serious doubts or would have preferred not to use or escalate force. When hawkish leaders made decisions in these conflicts, they often had relatively dovish advisers around them. And democratic publics, while not uniformly dovish, certainly have sizable contingents of doves and choose many doves to represent them in government.

In a democracy, who constrains a leader's ability to use military force? How much leeway do democratic leaders have to start, conduct, and escalate military operations? How do democracies hold their leaders accountable for their decisions in crises and wars? These are old questions, but they have gained renewed significance in an era of populist backlash against real and perceived failures of democratic elites in the United States and Europe, after the military interventions of the early post–Cold War period, the "forever wars" of the post-9/11 period, and the Iraq War in particular. The Russian invasion of Ukraine in 2022 also tested democratic leaders, especially in the United States and Europe, whose citizens bore economic and other costs of the Western effort to sustain Ukraine's resistance to Russian aggression.

Yet citizens in democracies who want to reward or punish leaders for their decisions about war and peace often find the effort frustrating. They can vote their leader out of office, but only if the leader is not term limited. They can punish the leader's party in midterm elections, as in 2006, when Republicans suffered dramatic losses at the nadir of the Iraq War. They can damage the leader's popularity, which may be a drag on his or her ability to accomplish other policy goals. But those effects depend on other elites and institutions. The public can also protest and agitate, although the costs of such collective action are high even without the threat of punishment that citizens face in authoritarian regimes. And there is no guarantee such efforts will work: the public can protest a war they did not choose or have turned against, as they did in the United States in 1968 during the Vietnam War, and in Europe on the eve of the 2003 Iraq War, only to see their leaders carry on with their war plans.

This picture of voter frustration is at odds with the traditional view of the voting public constraining democratic leaders' choices about war and peace. In this view, democracies have advantages in choosing wars because democratic leaders are constrained by the public. Theorists going back to Immanuel Kant would argue that the public, if fully informed, would not accept many of these wars, because democratic publics want to avoid unnecessary or unwise military ventures.[1] Public constraint, channeled through institutions and the free press, makes democracies more cautious about using force and thus more peaceful. When democracies face crises, open debate and electoral accountability force democratic leaders to be more careful when choosing fights and to be more effective at using the tools of war.[2] In recent years, international relations scholars have focused on public opinion, seeking to understand what missions the public will support, whether the public rallies around the flag, or the public's casualty tolerance.[3] The rise of experiments embedded in public opinion surveys has fueled renewed scholarly interest in studying public attitudes about war.[4]

But this voter-driven approach bumps up against several stark conclusions. First, the public does not pay much attention to foreign policy, a finding backed by decades of research on political behavior. The individual citizen's knowledge of foreign affairs is slight,[5] tends not to move much in response to leaders' speeches,[6] and can be changeable on particular issues.[7] Although voters have underlying predispositions, they are often shaped by values or demographic characteristics rather than policy knowledge or material self-interest.[8] Voters are busy people, and gathering information about political issues is costly and time consuming.[9] Foreign policy is rarely important to voters in an absolute sense.[10] Rather than carefully weighing and incorporating available information about policy, voters use shortcuts to evaluate the policies they do not or cannot pay attention to on a regular basis.[11] As they do on many other issues, voters look to elites for cues about the wisdom of war.[12]

Second, rewarding leaders for successful military operations is also not straightforward, as George H. W. Bush or Winston Churchill could attest. Foreign policy issues are rarely top of mind for voters, and even issues that dominate headlines may recede by the time an election comes around. For example, the killing of Osama bin Laden in May 2011 gave Barack Obama an approval boost that lasted only a few weeks.[13]

Third, democratic leaders frequently make choices that are at odds with public opinion.[14] Democratic leaders not only start wars the public does not want but also frequently continue or escalate wars they know they are unlikely to win, as the revelations of the Pentagon Papers and the Afghanistan Papers made clear, decades apart.[15] Yet democratic leaders often act as if public opinion is important to their decision making, putting significant effort into their public message even when they make decisions they anticipate will lack public approval.

What explains this seemingly distorted decision making in democracies? Why do we see so many hawkish choices even without hawkish preferences? Why does public accountability often take so long to kick in even after widespread popular protests, as it did in the Vietnam and Iraq Wars? How are some leaders able to continue or even escalate wars in the face of strong or rising popular opposition, as George W. Bush did in Iraq and Barack Obama and other NATO leaders did in Afghanistan?[16] Why do leaders and elites risk public ire by continuing or escalating wars they know they are unlikely to win, often with halfhearted effort? Why do parties with dovish reputations on national security issues, such as the modern Democratic Party in the United States, fight or continue so many wars? In democracies, why don't doves get their way more often?

While many scholars have asked versions of the question "why hawks win,"[17] we can turn the question around and ask, "Why don't doves win?" Elite doves not only lose arguments but also frequently make or support hawkish decisions, despite having significant misgivings and significant power. Even if we make no assumptions about the public's preferences about using military force except that they want their leaders to act wisely, the muted doves pose a challenge to theories of "democratic advantage" in crises and wars that are rooted in electoral accountability. Such theories suggest that open political debate and the threat of voter punishment make democratic leaders think twice about military adventures, choosing their fights wisely, and when they use force, make them fight better and more effectively to deliver victory to voters.[18] Yet we have observed decisions about the use of force across time and space that seem contrary to what we would have expected voters to choose. If voters constrain their leaders, we would not expect to observe distorted decision making about the use of force so frequently.

Scholars and commentators have offered many explanations for distorted democratic decisions about the use of force, including information failures that keep voters from learning enough to constrain their leaders;[19] deception on the part of democratic leaders;[20] psychological bias among decision makers;[21] and what we might call "holidays from democracy," when public accountability mechanisms temporarily break down.[22] Yet none of these arguments explains the persistence of distorted decision making that takes place through regular democratic politics. Others focus on explanations specific to the United States, such as a US interventionist impulse that leads to a hawkish mind-set; a culture of "limited liability" that seeks to spread liberal ideas without committing excessive resources; or an approach that seeks to do just enough to avoid losing but not enough to win.[23] While it is true that US military power and global reach mean that it is the country most frequently able and asked to make these decisions, these questions are not confined to the United States, as illustrated by the dramatic protests in Europe on the eve of the Iraq War. Furthermore, there is significant variation across US presidential decisions about the use of force: some presidents have jumped into wars hastily, while others do so reluctantly or not at all. Many presidents have made their goal doing the "minimum necessary" to not lose, rather than seeking outright victory—an approach powerfully explained by Leslie Gelb and Richard Betts in their classic study of the Vietnam War[24]—while others do better at matching strategy to their preferred outcome, or even cut losses when they recognize failure. And in many US cases, there were plenty of doves or advocates of a more restrained approach involved in decisions to fight or extend wars.

In this book, I argue that we have been looking for the domestic politics of war in the wrong place. The theory I develop in this book posits that elites are a distinctive domestic audience with their own preferences and politics that change how we should think about democracies and war. I define elites as those with access to information and the decision-making process, and who could serve as cue givers to other elites or to the public.

While some elites represent voters, elites have a very different relationship to a leader's decisions about the use of force from that which citizens have. For example, leaders face voters infrequently, while leaders encounter at least some elites daily. Voters need to get information from other sources, usually the media, while elites have access to information and can share it with each other or directly with the press.[25] Elites and voters may also want different things, or want the same things with different intensity. Voters may want to fight and win only "necessary" wars, but they tend to have weak preferences about policy specifics. Elites, in contrast, tend to have stronger, sometimes intense preferences about specific issues that are highly salient to them.[26] And ultimately, what elites and voters can do to influence leaders' decisions also differs. Voters can throw the bums out. Elites have a much longer list of tools to impose costs on leaders: they can block a leader's future policies, they can sabotage existing policy, they can force the leader to consume political capital, they can cue other elites, and they can bring in public opinion by publicizing information about a policy or criticizing the leader's decisions.

All of this adds up to a different set of domestic constraints than we would expect if leaders responded primarily to the public's wishes. In a militarily powerful country like the United States, elites induce a hawkish bias in decisions about war and peace even when there are influential doves involved. But elite pressures do not always drive democracies like the United States to war. While elites can make it easier for democratic leaders to fight, they are also an important source of constraint and accountability. Leaders must bargain with elites or control information to secure crucial elite support for war. Even if they support war, elites can force presidents to alter military strategy or even end conflicts. Outward elite consensus can mask fierce elite politics that shape the timing, scope, strategy, and duration of military conflict.

Decision making about war and peace is thus an "insiders' game" even in democracies. While elite accountability is not as effective as some might hope, it is also not as dangerous as others might fear. Elite politics are a natural part of democratic decisions about the use of force, not a perversion of them. We cannot understand democracies at war—and the most militarily powerful democracy, the United States—without elite politics.

Argument in Brief

Public opinion on foreign policy presents a paradox. The public pays little attention to the details of most foreign policy. Even when they try to use the "bully pulpit," democratic leaders are rarely successful in changing the public's views.[27] Yet leaders frequently behave *as if* public opinion matters.[28] So why do they bother worrying about public opinion at all?

One answer is that elites lead mass opinion: citizens use elite cues as a shortcut, solving their "democratic dilemma" by getting information efficiently from those they perceive to be knowledgeable and trusted sources.[29] Many top-down approaches to American political behavior rest on similar arguments and emphasize elite leadership of mass opinion, depending on the presence or absence of elite consensus on an issue.[30] These arguments do not mean that elites can automatically manipulate the fickle masses, as classical realists like Walter Lippmann and Hans Morgenthau suggested.[31] Indeed, scholars of public opinion and foreign policy have found that the public does have coherent foreign policy attitudes and can update its views in response to events.[32] But even scholars who take a bottom-up approach to public opinion and foreign policy—that is, starting with mass public preferences— acknowledge that elite messages are often necessary to provide information or activate public attitudes.[33]

Yet the premise of elite cues as a shortcut to voter accountability—that citizens can "learn what they need to know," as Lupia and McCubbins put it—assumes that those cues point to policies that, on average, reflect what the voters want.[34] That is, democratic politics will generate good information about the wisdom of war, and that most of the time, following elite cues will lead to the kind of moderate policies that public-driven models assume the public seeks. While elites are not perfect, most theories expect elites to get it right most of the time, leading to relatively coherent and stable public preferences and responses to external events.[35]

But where does elite consensus come from? Why do some cues circulate in public debate but others do not? What explains the many instances in which elites had either knowledge or misgivings about the use of force that they did not share with citizens, or cases in which elites did not obtain relevant information to pass on to the public at all? Why does elite consensus sometimes persist in the face of rising public discontent—and conversely, why does the elite consensus sometimes fracture when public attitudes remain permissive? Why do we see so many leaders—including many from dovish parties— entering or prolonging risky wars, often fully understanding that the conflict is probably unwinnable?

I argue that the elite politics of war are the norm, not the exception, even in democracies. Elites are a distinct domestic audience for decisions to use force, and they confront democratic leaders with a different political problem than voters do. As recent international relations scholarship has shown, autocratic politics can generate both distortions in decision making when dictators use the spoils of war to keep elites happy, *and* constraints if the dictator strays too far from the elite audience's preferences.[36] I argue that the elite politics of war are different from mass politics in democracies, and that elite politics shape democratic leaders' decisions about war initiation, escalation, and termination. Elite politics are by no means the same in democracies as in autocracies, where disputes are often resolved with violence or loss of liberty.[37] But elite politics introduce their own democratic distortions into decisions about war and peace, as well as their own constraints on democratic leaders.

Why Elite Politics Are Different

If elites channel the foreign policy preferences of the public, either because voters select them to represent public preferences or because they respond to public attitudes, there would be no need for a separate theory of elite politics and war in democracies.[38] The theory must therefore address a threshold question: are elites in democracies really a distinctive audience, or are they simply what we might call "faithful intermediaries" for the voters?

The stakes of this question are high, not only for understanding democratic accountability for decisions about war and peace, but also for international relations arguments about the advantages of democracies at war. These arguments hinge on features of the public audience, such as its size, its preferences, or its attentiveness.[39] For example, in selectorate theory, developed by Bueno de Mesquita, Smith, Siverson, and Morrow, a crucial concept is the size of what they term the "selectorate," or those who have a role in selecting the leader, relative to the "winning coalition," or the subset of the selectorate whose support the leader needs to gain or retain power.[40] In democracies, where the selectorate is a very large pool of voters, leaders cannot realistically dole out the spoils of war to individual citizens in the winning coalition. In contrast, dictators, whose winning coalition is typically a small, finite number of elite supporters, can keep their audience happy with private rewards even if a war is not going well.[41] This contrast in coalition size is vital to selectorate theory's conclusion that democracies select and fight wars more effectively than autocracies, because democratic leaders, unable to parcel out rewards to individual voters, instead focus on providing public goods like effective national security. If, however, democratic leaders regularly provide private rewards to elites, their incentive to provide public goods may be reduced.

The first step is defining who I mean by "elites." I argue that in any democracy facing a decision about the use of force, three groups of elites are most likely to have systematic influence: legislators, military leaders, and high-ranking cabinet and administration officials. To keep the analysis tractable, I limit the theoretical scope to these three groups, acknowledging the importance of others, such as media elites, along the way. Even unelected elites who make decisions about war and peace are political actors, and our theories must treat them as such.

Although many elites represent or serve the public, they also have different preferences, incentives, and sources and means of power that make them capable of action independent of the voters. Elites themselves vary in how they view the costs and benefits of war, and elites are not uniformly more accepting of military conflict. But elite preferences are more specific and more informed by policy, political, or career concerns than those of the public. Elites also have policy preferences on other foreign and domestic policy issues that open up space for bargaining.

Elites can impose costs and constraints on leaders that differ from those available to the mass public. Elite-imposed costs generally take two forms. First, elites can impose resource costs, forcing a leader to expend precious time or political capital to secure elite support for preferred policies, or to abandon those policies altogether. Elites can take away or block something the leader wants (for example, legislation, policies, or personnel appointments), extract concessions that lead to policy spillover on other issues, or sabotage policies as they are implemented. Democratic elites can thus punish leaders directly. It is crucial to note that these mechanisms exist independent of public opinion, because voters do not have these tools available to them. Furthermore, elites have concentrated power that gives them outsized influence: for example, a well-placed handful of hawks can exert more leverage than legions of dovish voters.

Second, elites can impose informational costs by sharing information with other elite audience members, through either private or public communications. Sustained elite disagreement can act as a "fire alarm" that tells voters it is time to pay attention to a potential or ongoing military conflict.[42] Conversely, elite support can reassure voters that their leader's decision is sound. While public-driven models assume elites will pull the fire alarm in the service of the voters' interests, I argue that elite bargaining in the insiders' game may alter when elites pull the fire alarm, sometimes earlier than necessary, or more likely, delaying elite dissent and thus masking problems that voters might want to know about. These information costs can stay within elite circles, for example when elites cue each other and trigger some of the elite resource costs, without going public.

Thus I argue that the presence or absence of an elite consensus about the use of force is itself a political process. And as in any political process, leaders are not passive observers. Leaders have tools to shape how elites judge and what elites say about their decisions to use military force that are unavailable when dealing with voters. There are two primary mechanisms through which leaders manage elites. First, democratic leaders can use side payments to bargain with particular elites. This argument challenges the view, made prominent in selectorate theory, that democratic leaders, who face a large public audience, must provide public goods that all voters can share—like victory—to keep their audience happy, whereas leaders of authoritarian regimes can dole out private goods to a small number of supporters.[43] Second, leaders can manage information, keeping certain elites informed, choosing emissaries carefully, and cutting others out of the loop. Such information management can alter perceptions of the probability of success in war, and thus whether elites will support it. The book is thus not simply about elite leadership of mass opinion—it is also about elite leadership of elite opinion, which can be as much a part of a leader's messaging strategy as "going public."[44]

It remains possible that elites will come to a consensus in the public interest, or their sincere best estimate about what would be in the public interest. But the insiders' game can introduce democratic distortions in decisions about the use of force because leaders compromise with crucial elites and alter information flow inside elite circles. In the case studies (chapters 4–7), I look for evidence that democratic leaders are mindful of potential elite costs and that they respond by managing information and offering side payments.

Curses and Misadventures

But does this all add up to more war, less war, or different wars? I argue that what I call the "insiders' game" introduces a systematic set of distortions that lead to wars we would not expect under a public-driven model, as well as decisions about strategy and war fighting that are not part of most public-driven models at all.[45] In settings like that of the United States, these democratic distortions induce a hawkish bias in decisions related to war—even in the presence of powerful doves. One note on terminology: throughout this book I use "war" and "peace" as shorthands, but "war" can include escalation or other hawkish policies after war begins, while "peace" can mean dovish or deescalatory policies, including simply staying out of a conflict rather than making an affirmative peace overture.

To see the source of hawkish bias, we can start with a classic argument about hawks and doves. For better or for worse, hawks are more trusted on national security issues than doves, who face a larger credibility deficit when they make decisions about war and peace.[46] A dove who chooses a dovish policy has a hard time convincing a domestic audience that the policy is in the national interest, and not simply a blind commitment to dovish views. Research on this topic suggests leaders want to signal that they are moderate, giving hawkish leaders who want to avoid the "warmonger" label an advantage in peace initiatives.[47] Thus leaders can gain political benefits from acting "against type," as in the famous idea that only a hawk like Nixon could go to China.[48] Most theory, however, has been about the politics of making peace, rather than the full set of trade-offs between peace and war, for both hawks and doves. One can infer that the public-driven version of this argument is symmetric: if hawks have an advantage in making peace, doves have an advantage in making war, pulling policy toward the middle. In the public-driven model, then, the constraints on leaders are therefore symmetric if leaders want to act on their true views.[49]

Shifting to an elite view of politics alters this symmetric picture. I argue that in the insiders' game, the doves' credibility deficit generates asymmetric constraints between hawkish and dovish leaders when they want to act true to type, that is, to follow their hawkish or dovish preferences. Put simply, it is easier for hawks than for doves to be themselves.

Three mechanisms generate these asymmetric constraints in the insiders' game. First, dovish leaders face *selection pressures* that give power to elites with more intense, specific, and sometimes hawkish preferences. These pressures put at least some hawks inside dovish leaders' own governments, and these hawks can monitor decision making up close and extract a price for their support. Hawkish leaders do not face selection pressures to the same degree.

Second, doves face larger *agenda costs* if they choose or seek hawkish buy-in for a dovish policy—making the trade-off for doves between fighting and staying out of conflicts politically starker than for hawks. For doves, initiating, continuing, or escalating a war may not be their preferred policy, but choosing to fight can conserve political resources for the issues doves often prioritize, such as domestic policy. Doves therefore have incentives to make concessions on war- or security-related policies—which hawks care about intensely—to save the political capital they would have to use to get hawks to support a dovish policy (or, if they cannot or do not want to seek hawkish support, to avoid a politicized fight over whether their dovish policy is weak or harmful to national security). In contrast, hawks are more trusted and focused on national security to begin with—leaving aside whether they deserve such deference— and have lower political opportunity costs for other policy aims. Hawks can therefore obtain dovish support for military action at a lower "price," such as procedural concessions.

Third, *the costs of obtaining countertype elite support* are greater for dovish than for hawkish leaders, in part because the private benefits—including career, political, or policy benefits—to elites are greater for dovish elites who support war than for hawkish elites who support peace. Even if they are truly dovish, elites may find that supporting war or at least refraining from criticism can be better for their career or policy aims, making supporting war more attractive to doves. For a hawkish leader who wants to fight, these incentives further lower the "price" to obtain dovish elites' support for war, even if these doves are in the opposition party. Hawkish elites outside the leader's inner circle, who are more likely to gain career or policy benefits from war, do not realize the same degree of private benefits from going against type and supporting peace. To be sure, hawkish copartisans of a hawkish leader who chooses peace are unlikely to deny their own leader a Nixon-to-China moment, but the political benefits of such peace initiatives accrue mainly to the individual leader, leaving hawkish advisers or copartisans unsatisfied. Hawkish elites have much lower incentives to support dovish policies under a dovish leader—especially a dovish leader who does not share their party—and thus will provide such support only at a steep price. If dovish leaders want to get hawkish elites on board for dovish policies, therefore, they must pay those costs out of their own stock of scarce political capital.

These mechanisms lead to two ideal-typical distortions that emerge from the theory and are not expected by public-driven arguments. The first is a *dove's curse*, in which a dovish leader becomes trapped in an inconclusive military conflict. The second is the *hawk's misadventure*, in which hawks, who enjoy deference on national security and whose security priorities lower their political opportunity costs for fighting, face fewer *ex ante* constraints on initiating war. They may undertake inadvisable military ventures whose likelihood of success they have incentives to exaggerate through information management.

This hawkish bias does not inevitably lead to war. Indeed, it is theoretically possible that elite constraint can raise or lower the probability of war. Jon Western highlights an example from the George H. W. Bush administration, when the military and others in the administration framed Bosnia as the more challenging conflict and Somalia the more feasible operation, and George H. W. Bush, supported by General Colin Powell, chose to intervene in Somalia but not in Bosnia. Yet Western also notes that the military had for months insisted that Somalia would be a major challenge and shifted its stance only when it became clear that the recently elected Bill Clinton would probably try to intervene in Bosnia.[50] Elites are more likely to prevent democratic leaders from initiating conflict when the leader is already leaning against war or when the probability of success is widely perceived to be low or highly uncertain. For example, in August 2013, the British Parliament voted down Prime Minister David Cameron's proposed operation against Syria after its chemical weapons use. The unexpected outcome, widely seen as a humiliation for Cameron, influenced Barack Obama, who was already highly ambivalent about using force. Obama threw the issue to Congress to force legislators to go on the record, something most members were unwilling to risk given the very uncertain likelihood of success—thus providing Obama cover for staying out.[51]

The theory suggests that the asymmetries of elite politics make it more likely that reluctant elites will support or passively tolerate war after gaining policy concessions or after receiving an inflated estimate of the probability of success, increasing the likelihood of war initiation. It is easier for hawks to convince doves to support war than for doves to obtain hawkish buy-in for staying out. Considered in light of the bargaining model of war, elites who see benefits from fighting or who can be persuaded through side payments or information to support war can narrow the bargaining range for finding a peaceful solution with an adversary.[52] Leaders' efforts to influence perceptions of the probability of success also undermine democracies' ability to select into wars they expect to win, or to signal their intentions credibly. Thus elites need not uniformly favor war to increase the odds of conflict. In general, the lower the cost to democratic leaders to secure elite support, the greater the likelihood of initiating a war that a leader would not choose if the cost of evading constraint were higher. The ability to use relatively "cheap" side payments undermines democratic selectivity mechanisms and makes it easier for elites to slip the constraints that come with public scrutiny.[53]

But once wars begin, elite politics also contain the seeds of accountability, especially for hawks. Elites may sometimes smooth the path to war, but democratic leaders must face these elites early and often. Dovish leaders, who are subject to hawkish elite pressure, can become trapped into fighting with just enough effort not to lose in order to keep elite consensus intact—prolonging wars until the elite consensus finally reaches its limits. Hawkish leaders exhibit wider variance. They may be selective, as in the examples of Dwight Eisenhower and George H. W. Bush, who chose carefully when to fight and placed strict limits on their war aims when they did so. But hawks' lower *ex ante* constraints can allow them to pursue misadventures. What hawks seek, however, are definitive outcomes. Though they risk being seen as overly bellicose, hawks start with the benefit of the doubt on matters of war and peace, and hawkish elites want to protect their credibility on these issues. Hawkish leaders thus feel the heat from other hawkish elites if military operations go poorly. These pressures can lead hawks to pursue an outcome they can call a victory, including some form of withdrawal.

Thus the insiders' game can lead to democratic distortions in decisions about the use of military force, departing from what a fully informed and attentive public would choose. Elite politics can affect the substance of policy even if the public is not clamoring for a policy shift in the same direction or if the details remain largely out of public view, because leaders face constraints from elites that differ in their content, timing, and frequency. Elites may effectively "collude" with leaders to start a war with dim prospects. Elites can allow an unpopular war to continue, as doves seek to keep it on the back burner without losing, or as hawks gamble for a resolution. Elite politics can affect the information available to decision makers, including those in the opposition who must decide whether to lend public support to a conflict.[54] But these same elite politics can also force leaders to revisit decisions and even end wars.

It is important to stress that the insiders' game is a feature of democratic politics, not a perversion of it. I refer to outcomes like the dove's curse and hawk's misadventure as "democratic distortions" because while they are different from what we would expect from a public-driven model where voters can get the information they need to hold leaders accountable, the distortion stems from democratic politics. It is normal for elite politics in democracies to shape not only the substance of policy but also what elites say about the use of force, and thus the information available to the public. Often, these elite politics play out without entering the public arena or land there with little fanfare, precisely because leaders work strategically to keep the politics of war out of the spotlight. Leaders need not necessarily hide foreign policy or military operations from public audiences, however.[55] For example, in a military operation, leaders might make concessions on strategy to satisfy military or bureaucratic officials—a critical decision but one that the public might not know much about. Leaders can also make concessions on other foreign policy or national security issues unrelated to the conflict, leading to spillover effects the public does not necessarily view as linked to war. Insider politics also mean that elites are on the front lines of democratic accountability. The insiders' game is often the only game in town.

Why the United States? Defining the Scope of the Insiders' Game

There is a tension in studying democracies and war: do we study democracies as a group, or examine the politics of particular democracies such as those most capable of using force? Elite politics, which include the strategic behavior of leaders, are difficult to trace across institutions and national contexts, much less across changes over time like partisan polarization or shifts in the technology of war. Narrowing the focus to one country can mitigate these problems and hold many factors constant. Yet the trade-off is the risk that the findings will not generalize to the broader set of democracies.

This book examines presidential decisions about the use of force in the United States, a choice that offers many theoretical and empirical advantages, but also entails some costs given that one of the book's main motivations is to illuminate how elite politics shapes choices about war in democracies. On the plus side, studying a single country allows me to hold domestic institutions and national political characteristics constant in order to focus on the strategic behavior of leaders and elites. This strategy illuminates variation in elite constraint within one country over time to show how democratic leaders manage constraint. The long sweep of the case selection—from the dawn of the Cold War through the post-9/11 "forever wars"—tests the theory in different international environments, technological eras, and political contexts. It also holds constant factors that may be unique to a country's geopolitical or historical position. For example, in postwar Germany and Japan, antimilitarism is embedded in political culture, arguably giving doves an advantage politically.[56] In the wake of China's rise and North Korea's nuclear threats, as well as the war in Ukraine, both Germany and Japan have recently shifted away from this cautious approach. But historical factors can influence party brands and leaders' credibility on national security issues for decades at a time.

It is also the case that historically, dovish parties have been associated with the Left. Leftist parties have, of course, conducted brutal wars. But in modern democratic countries with significant military power, doves often make their home on the left. This association does not mean that all doves are left-leaning politicians, or vice versa. Indeed, as Schultz notes, the imperfect alignment of preferences and party leads to uncertainty about whether dovish parties will always oppose force, and this uncertainty allows party members to send informative signals, particularly when they support war.[57] As I discuss in chapter 4, dovish (or isolationist) elites had a strong presence in the Republican Party until the Korean War helped sort the parties more clearly. But the association between the conservative Republican Party as more hawkish and tougher on national security and the more liberal Democratic Party as more dovish and weaker predates the Korean War. This association helps make the United States a useful case through which to study the politics of hawkish and dovish elites in other settings, because parties on the left typically have more ambitious domestic programs, increasing their agenda costs when considering whether to use military force. Scholars of American politics have shown that the Democratic Party has historically had a larger domestic legislative agenda, centered on ambitious social programs, than the Republican Party, which has often pursued domestic policies, like tax cuts, that require less complex legislation.[58]

Studying the United States also has some specific advantages. First, very few democracies get to make these decisions about the use of force, and there is also much value in studying decisions about war in the most militarily powerful democracy. The United States is the democracy whose decisions about the use of force are the most potentially consequential for elites and citizens across the globe.

Second, separation of powers in the United States means that there are clearer distinctions between insider and elected elites. The presidential system allows voters to express their views directly in elections for the chief executive and legislators, with cabinet officials and other advisers appointed rather than elected.[59] Other institutional configurations muddy the waters between elected and unelected elites. For example, in a parliamentary democracy like the United Kingdom, many powerful governmental officials are also elected legislators (though civil servants and other advisers can be very powerful and can also serve as cue givers). In a proportional representation system with coalition government, defense and foreign policy portfolios may be given to other parties, imbuing disagreement between ministers with much more obvious political motives. For example, following the 2021 federal elections in Germany, the new coalition of center-left parties, led by Social Democrat (SPD) Olaf Scholz, faced the threat from Russia's military buildup on Ukraine's border. The Green Party's candidate for chancellor, Annalena Baerbock, got the foreign ministry appointment, giving the Greens considerable leverage over foreign policy. Defying her party's traditional pacifist roots, Baerbock put pressure on Scholz to shake off his dovish instincts.[60] Her position within a coalition government, however, may dilute the pressure her policy arguments put on the chancellor, because her policies can be seen as linked to her own future political ambitions and her party's electoral fortunes more directly than if she served in a US presidential administration. One could certainly account for these different institutional structures theoretically, but for theory building it is simpler to begin with a cleaner separation between the executive and legislative branches.

Even with a narrower focus on the United States, however, many aspects of the insiders' game are common across democracies. Democratic leaders in different institutional settings face many similar challenges. Democratic leaders of all stripes must manage fractious wings of their party, work with unelected policy advisers and bureaucrats, and interact with the military. Thus while extending the argument to other democratic settings is beyond the scope of the book, along the way I highlight the theory's significant implications for the broader study of democracies at war.

Implications for Theories of Democracy and War

This book challenges the voter-driven view of democracies in the international arena that has dominated international relations theory for several decades. In making this challenge, my argument is not that the public is irrelevant—especially since elites derive some of their leverage from their ability to cue the public. In recent years, many scholars have questioned the predicted effects of public accountability, such as whether democracies make more credible threats or whether democratic leaders are more likely to be punished for battlefield failures.[61] Others have examined the microfoundations of public attitudes to show how public opinion is not uniform in its response to democratic leaders' threats or conduct of foreign policy more generally.[62] But the democratic picture remains focused on leaders and voters.

The theory I develop is a more direct challenge to the nature of democratic decision making. It does not merely add an intervening variable to public opinion models. I argue that leaders must also play to an elite audience, leading to democratic distortions in decisions about war and peace. But though these distortions depart from the outcomes predicted by public-driven theories, they are nonetheless the product of democratic politics. The public remains an important, latent voice in the background, but the scope of policy that can be debated and pursued without public scrutiny is vast, and the effort required to rouse the public is large. Democratic leaders know this and try to control the composition and size of their domestic audience—a regular, normal part of politics.

This perspective echoes E. E. Schattschneider's argument that "the most important strategy of politics is concerned with the scope of conflict,"[63] where conflict here means political conflict. Schattschneider asserts that "at the nub of politics, are, first, the way in which the public participates in the spread of the conflict and, second, the processes by which the unstable relation of the public to the conflict is controlled." As he concludes, "conflicts are frequently won or lost by the success that the contestants have in getting the audience involved in the fight or in excluding it, as the case may be."[64] Thus "a tremendous amount of conflict is controlled by keeping it so private that it is almost completely invisible."[65]

Although they are part of normal democratic politics, leaders' regular use of the two main tools of the insiders' game—side payments and managing information—undermines two mechanisms that underpin several arguments that democracies are better at selecting and fighting wars: that the difficulty of buying off domestic audience members with the spoils of war causes democratic leaders to fight better and more effectively to deliver victory to voters; and that the open flow of information leads democracies to make better decisions about when and how to fight.[66] If instead the audience for many decisions about the use of force is smaller than theories of democracies and war typically assume, then an elite-driven theory of democracies and war raises the possibility of side payments and bargaining that are precluded in accounts such as selectorate theory.[67] Furthermore, elite politics may distort information flow within elite circles, and thus the efficiency of elite cues as an information shortcut for voters. Voters may still get cues, but elite politics introduces distortions in what they hear. In the insiders' game, we should expect more choices and outcomes that depart from the predictions of a public-driven model—more wars that the public appears to oppose, or more decisions not to use force when the public is permissive—as well as a wider range of outcomes, includ-ing defeats and stalemates.

Treating war as an insiders' game in democracies provides an explanation from the democratic side for findings that democracies and some autocracies exhibit similar conflict behavior, initiating and winning wars at similar rates. After decades of treating autocracies as a residual category of countries that were not democratic, scholars of autocracies and conflict have explored varia-tion in the institutional and structural features of autocracies, from personalist dictatorships, on one extreme, to relatively "constrained" autocracies where elites can hold dictators accountable, on the other.[68] This wave of research has shown that some autocracies can generate enough constraint to signal credibility in crises, and that these autocracies initiate conflicts and win them at rates similar to those of democracies.[69] Studies of autocracies and conflict highlight mechanisms of accountability, arguing that the size of the politically relevant domestic audience in some "constrained" autocratic regimes is larger than previously assumed, ranging from elites who can oust the leader to pro-testers strategically sanctioned by the state.[70] Focusing on autocratic elites, Weeks hints at an explanation that accounts for the similar conflict initiation rate between constrained autocracies and democracies, positing that "leaders of machines may find it much more difficult to massage domestic opinion when the audience consists of high-level officials—themselves often active in foreign policy and with no special appetite for force—than a 'rationally ignorant' mass public."[71]

To be sure, autocratic politics introduces its own set of elite-driven dis-tortions in decision making. Mechanisms like coup proofing, exclusionary policies toward ethnic groups, and information control undermine dictators' ability to make good decisions and to field militaries that are effective on the battlefield.[72] Dictatorships, particularly personalist dictatorships, cannot af-ford to keep competent, well-informed militaries with divided loyalties close at hand. Scholars rightly see these autocratic distortions as part of autocratic politics, as autocrats balance their own survival against the interests of the state and its people when selecting and fighting wars. There are no easy solutions for dictators, only trade-offs.

Similarly, scholarship on the domestic politics of war has come to see democratic leaders' political interests and incentives as rational, political driv-ers of crisis and conflict decisions. Some of these theories introduce distor-tions, in the sense of departures from what the public would prefer if it were fully informed and could choose policy, but the mechanisms are usually driven by public opinion and voting.[73] Others argue that political competition and partisan incentives need not distort democratic decision making and can even enhance it, if the opposition's incentives to challenge the government help uncover information that would aid public accountability and make signals more credible to adversaries.[74]

I argue that elite politics produces its own set of democratic distortions that are likewise an inescapable part of democratic politics. Democratic leaders may not take the kinds of steps to guard against violent overthrow that autocrats do, but they take plenty of political actions that can distort the choice to enter wars and how to fight them. These actions also reflect trade-offs for democratic leaders and their elite audiences—for those who want to get other things done, for those who seek to stay in or one day gain office, and for those who work to protect national security. Understanding the insiders' game allows us to see that the differences between democracies and autocracies are more subtle than existing theories suggest.

Implications for the United States

For the United States—the country with by far the most capabilities and opportunities to make decisions about the use of force—recognizing that war is an insiders' game is crucial to understanding why presidents so often seem to make self-defeating choices. There have been many attempts to explain what can seem like baffling presidential decisions in the post–World War II record of American national security decisions. Many theories explain these outcomes with a variable that hardly varies, however, including a shared ideology of hawkishness, an ideology of "limited liability" liberalism that seeks to promote values while limiting costs, or casualty sensitivity or aversion that can lead to distortions in force structure or strategy.[75] Other approaches account for variation but treat distortions as the product of psychological biases or errors that alter decision making, such as misperception and overconfidence.[76] These are distortions, to be sure, but they arise from individuals' predispositions or institutions' selection of elites with those predispositions. Yet as Gelb and Betts eloquently argue in the context of the Vietnam War, US presidents—and many other elites—often knew exactly what they were doing and that it was unlikely to succeed.[77]

In my argument, elite political incentives drive variation in when and especially how presidents decide to use military force. Outcomes like the dove's curse and the hawk's misadventure are the product of regular democratic politics, rather than mistakes or biases. The diagnosis matters for those seeking treatment. Gelb and Betts's argument that the "system worked" in the Vietnam War—that is, that the government machinery did what it was programmed to do—showed how to think about poor war outcomes as clear-eyed products of presidential decisions.[78] Such a diagnosis means that no amount of tinkering with the bureaucracy or better information from the field would have altered the outcome. Similarly, if elite politics drives the distortions I identify in this book—effects like policy sabotage, policy spillover, or asymmetric incentives to act against type—then then there are no easy fixes, only different trade-offs.

Another implication is that to understand these trade-offs, we cannot treat the major political parties symmetrically. The literature on partisanship and war in the United States treats the parties essentially the same and focuses on whether they are in or out of power. As Matt Grossmann and David Hopkins argue, even scholarship on American politics more generally has treated the parties symmetrically. Yet as they demonstrate, the two major parties have significant differences in structure, policy preferences, and ideology. Grossmann and Hopkins argue that the parties are "asymmetric," with Republicans focused on the ideology of small government, and Democrats managing a coalition while trying to pass major domestic legislation.[79] Detecting asymmetries in the observed record can be challenging, however, because of selection effects, including incentives to act against type. We know that the parties have very different priorities, generating party brands around issues that a particular party "owns."[80] These brands, in turn, generate incentives for presidents to act against type but, as Patrick Egan argues, also lead to pressure to shore up the brand for the party that owns that issue—sometimes leading to more extreme policies from the issue-owning party.[81] As I argue in chapter 2, these incentives are not symmetrical for the two parties, leading to what we can think of as an "oversupply" of war under Democratic presidents, and fewer constraints on Republican presidents' misadventures.

The parties also differ in the opportunity costs of their decisions about the use of force. For Democratic elites, who typically want to focus on domestic policy and social programs enacted through legislation, military policy is usually a lower priority, but failing to address real or perceived threats can leave them open to charges of weakness. This fear can make the short-term, private benefits of supporting war more attractive for individual elites, especially those with future career or political aspirations, lowering the cost of obtaining their support for war. For Republicans, national security is often the main event. The theory does not rely on party ideology, however—rather, it is important that elites vary in their views within parties, because this heterogeneity generates the uncertainty that underpins against-type logic, and tars all but the most extreme members of a party with the party reputation, whether they deserve it or not.[82] The theory shows that elite incentives generate asymmetries in elite selection and in the price and currency presidents must pay to secure the support of elites for their preferred policies—a process that, in turn, generates hawkish bias in US national security policy.

Both of these implications—the fundamentally political nature of democratic distortions, and the asymmetry in the parties' cost to be themselves—may seem dispiriting. Can the Democratic Party do anything to escape the dove's curse, for example, or are Democrats doomed to be prisoners of the party's reputation for weakness on national security? I return to this question in the conclusion, but it is important to note that if the elite politics diagnosis is correct, many commonly prescribed solutions will not be effective. For example, calls for more voices of "restraint" that would widen the debate are unlikely to break the dove's curse if the political incentives for elites with dovish views remain unchanged—and as the cases illustrate, there are often many doves or voices of restraint in decision-making circles already.

The effects of partisan polarization offer interesting implications for mitigating, if not necessarily escaping, the dove's curse, however. On the one hand, polarization is dangerous for US foreign policy since, as Kenneth Schultz, Rachel Myrick, and others point out, it can inhibit unity in addressing threats or prevent presidents from getting political cover for risky moves that might be necessary.[83] On the other hand, by removing some of the political upside to acting against type—because the opposition is committed to opposing the president no matter what—polarization may give dovish leaders and dovish elites more room to be their dovish selves. That President Biden could choose to exit Afghanistan, absorb significant elite and public disapproval for his handling of the withdrawal, and still go on to a string of domestic legislative successes—including the Inflation Reduction Act of 2022 and significant action on the Democratic priority of addressing climate change—illustrates the point. If Senate vote counts are rigidly partisan, Democratic presidents may perceive lower agenda costs to pursuing a more dovish course in foreign policy. Similarly, if elected Democrats are less inclined to give support up front to Republican presidents' decisions to use force, potential hawkish misadventures may face more scrutiny.

For studies of American foreign policy—and scholarship on the domestic politics of war more generally—the larger implication of the book is that we must take another step beyond the leaders-want-to-stay-in-office assumption.[84] That assumption generated important advances in the study of domestic politics and war, by treating leaders' political survival as a component of a rational leader's calculations in crises and conflict. But leaders are not the only ones with political incentives, nor are elected elites. Elite politics can have profound effects on not only when but how democracies use force.

Existing Arguments: The Missing Politics of Elites

This book is not the first to argue that the public is inattentive to the details of foreign policy or that elites shape decisions about war and peace in the United States. Its major contribution is to develop and test a theory of democratic elite politics and war. The theory bridges several literatures in international relations and American politics by focusing on features missing from each: political interactions among elites, and the political agency of leaders.

One of the book's contributions is to advance the study of elite politics in international relations. Two well-developed areas of research on elite political interactions are executive-legislative relations, which focuses on whether Congress can constrain the president in war;[85] and civil-military relations, which addresses the relationship between civilian leaders and the armed services.[86] But this work focuses on certain types of elite interactions rather than a general theory of elite politics. The bureaucratic politics perspective explicitly addresses elite bargaining, arguing that "individuals share power" and that "government decisions and actions result from a political process."[87] This emphasis on shared authority among elites echoes Richard Neustadt's arguments about presidential power as the "power to persuade" other actors to support the president's policies.[88] The bureaucratic politics approach, however, can be overly complex and strangely lacking in politics.[89] More recently, Helen Milner and Dustin Tingley explore bureaucratic politics and presidential leeway across foreign policy issues. They predict the militarization of policy because the president has a freer hand in the military arena, but given the cross-issue scope of their study, they do not explore the politics of war itself.[90] This book puts the bureaucratic politics of war on firmer footing by addressing elite politics more generally.

Some existing accounts of domestic politics and war—in both international relations and American politics scholarship—recognize the role of elite consensus or dissent but do not assess the politics that influence whether these elites decide to support war or what might sway them if they are on the fence. For example, many studies recognize the strategic behavior of opposition parties when they decide whether to publicly support the government's use of force or publicly oppose it and make a military venture politically more perilous for leaders.[91] The electoral effects of war outcomes depend critically on opposition behavior: if the opposition supported a successful war, the leader gets little political benefit, but winning a war the opposition opposed is politically exploitable.[92] Rally effects in presidential approval also depend on the presence of opposition support or criticism, an argument that accounts for Kennedy's approval bump after the Bay of Pigs, when Republicans held their fire.[93] But how does the opposition get information and decide whether supporting the government's position is wise, both for national security and for the opposition's political goals? Moreover, these accounts tend to be silent on what leaders can do to shape opposition elites' decisions.

Relatedly, in American politics research on elite leadership of mass opinion, the nature and volume of elite cues, and the presence or absence of elite consensus, are usually taken as given. The book thus contributes to the study of American political behavior by exploring the political origins of elite cues. Leaders' strategic management of elites yields variation in elite consensus and discord over time. This book joins several other recent efforts to bridge scholarship on international relations and American politics.[94]

The theory shows how leaders can intervene to shape constraints on their ability to pursue their preferred policy. Just as scholars recognize that leaders strategically engage with the public, or choose to conduct foreign policy secretly or even deceptively, I argue that leaders can intervene in the elite politics of war.[95] For example, the opposition party, whose behavior may turn on its estimate of the likelihood of victory, needs information to form that estimate—giving democratic leaders a point of leverage. It is not merely that leaders anticipate public reaction and choose messages or messengers, or even tailor policy, accordingly. Leaders also have incentives to manage the information elites receive about the war's wisdom and progress. Elites, of course, are themselves strategic. Some elites can impose greater costs than others, and the leader can offer some elites certain types of side payments, like career or prestige boosts, while others require concessions on war policy or other national security concerns. The theory developed in chapter 2 outlines when we should expect to see different forms of side payments and how that affects decisions about the use of force.

Testing the Theory: Looking for Elite Politics

Where should we look within the United States for evidence of the insiders' game? As Schattschneider observed, "in view of the highly strategic character of politics we ought not to be surprised that the instruments of strategy are likely to be important in inverse proportion to the amount of public attention given to them."[96] Elite bargaining over the use of force can look distasteful, so there may be few traces in the public record. Thus "men of affairs do in fact make an effort to control the scope of conflict though they usually explain what they do on some other grounds. The way the question is handled suggests that the real issue may be too hot to handle otherwise."[97] Furthermore, if leaders try to avoid paying the costs elites can impose on them, then there may be few instances in which we can see leaders paying these costs. As Schultz observes, it can be quite difficult to see the imprint of domestic political constraints, because "to the extent that leaders value holding office, they are unlikely to make choices that lead to outcomes with high domestic political costs. If we can observe only the domestic costs that leaders choose to pay, then we will generally miss the cases in which these costs are large."[98] This selection argument applies to many of the domestic political costs that arise in the insiders' game. For example, it is rare for advisers to resign in protest, but we cannot conclude that leaders and advisers did not struggle mightily over policy behind the scenes to avoid such a dramatic departure.

There are also challenges that arise from testing the insiders' game model against a baseline model of public constraints—what I call the "faithful intermediaries" model, developed in chapter 2. If elites lead public opinion, we would expect observed public opinion to track closely with elite opinion, and thus it will be difficult to separate them—so looking at contemporaneous polling or even polling on anticipated future policies will not be sufficient. The argument requires an empirical strategy that can combine strategic behavior at the elite level with the anticipated effects of elite cues on not only the public but also elites who are less well informed, such as legislators who are not foreign policy experts.

I therefore use a two-pronged empirical approach. I combine survey experiments, designed to show which elite cues would affect public attitudes and thus should most concern presidents if they reached the public, with case studies designed to illustrate that in the real world, presidents spend their bargaining energy—and political capital—on managing those elites whose cues would have the strongest effects on public and secondary elite opinion, as well as avoiding the political costs that elites can impose directly. Using hypotheses developed in chapter 2, the experiments focus particular attention on cues from presidential advisers in the context of group decision making and bureaucratic politics, an important topic that has long been plagued with methodological problems.

The elite-centric arguments of this book put the focus squarely on leaders and their strategic interaction with elites. Given the rarity of decisions, it is difficult to conduct a large-N test that can account for the nuances of party and insider composition within a single country. Testing the theory requires historical accounts and primary documents that can illuminate the often-hidden mechanisms of the insiders' game. This evidence can help trace strategic behavior and assess whether politicians believe that theoretically predicted domestic costs exist. Additionally, case studies allow me to expand the range of outcomes usually considered in studies of domestic politics and war: not just initiation, escalation, termination, and war outcome, but also strategy, timing, and scope—elements of war that are of intense interest to scholars and policy makers, and may have important effects on a war's progress, duration, and outcome.

As I discuss in chapter 2, both survey experiments and case studies have strengths and weaknesses. It is the combination of the experiment and the cases that makes the research design more powerful. Survey experiments can identify the costs and benefits of particular elites' support or opposition to a policy—including the costs we are unlikely to observe in the real world—and help disentangle some of the partisan and ideological effects that are often difficult to tease out in case studies. The cases, which utilize historical and archival evidence from both presidential and adviser document collections, allow me to trace the mechanisms identified in the theory.

The two-pronged empirical approach in this book also makes an important methodological point about survey experiments.[99] The real-world effects of public opinion experiments sometimes manifest not in changes in public attitudes or even in elite anticipation of such a change, but rather in elite bargaining and strategic behavior. This bargaining often occurs behind the scenes, however, so that the effects turned up by the experiment manifest not in public but rather inside the proverbial Situation Room. The theory takes a significant step beyond the implications of many survey experiments, namely, that leaders anticipate which cues will most effectively move public opinion, and then choose policies, recruit messengers, and tailor messages accordingly. Rather, the insiders' game serves as a separate interaction, distinct from leaders' interactions with foreign states and with the public.

Plan of the Book

Chapter 2 develops the "insiders' game" model and compares this elite-driven theory to a public-driven approach, or what I call the "faithful intermediaries" model. Chapter 3 tests public opinion–related hypotheses using several large-scale survey experiments. Chapters 4 through 7 examine cases of US presidential decisions to use military force across the two parties. One aim of the case selection strategy is to span multiple eras. Some arguments suggest that democratic elites have been able to escape domestic constraints more easily in more recent decades, because of technological or material developments that help insulate leaders from public scrutiny. These developments include the end of the draft, the emergence of drone warfare, advances in military medicine that reduce the number of casualties, and changes in how democracies like the United States finance their wars.[100] Some of these developments started before the fall of the Berlin Wall, but many arrived or accelerated after the end of the Cold War, decreasing accountability as the public and even members of Congress became less engaged in oversight.[101] In the post–Cold War and especially the post-9/11 era, increased presidential power relative to other elites would make it somewhat surprising to see presidents bargaining. I therefore choose several cases from the Cold War, to show that war was an insiders' game even in an era with the draft and without many of these developments.

In chapters 4 and 5, I examine two cases—Korea and Vietnam—showing that elites dominated decisions to use and escalate force in major conflicts initiated by Democratic presidents during the Cold War. These cases hold constant the Cold War context, the initiating president's political party, and the party of the president who took over at a later stage. Scholars have seen the elections of 1952 and 1968 as outliers in terms of foreign policy's influence, with rising public dissatisfaction amid mounting casualties contributing to defeat for the incumbent president's party.[102] These cases also are also central to studies that emphasize the importance of elite consensus or dissent.[103] I take these arguments a step further, showing that elite consensus was no accident but rather the product of presidential efforts to keep elites on board, thus highlighting the strategic origins of the elite consensus so central to behavioral accounts.

The Korean War mapped out the political and international hazards of limited war in the post–World War II era. Harry S. Truman was concerned about the domestic political ramifications in Congress of failing to defend Korea, as well as Taiwan, from which he had sought to disengage prior to the outbreak of war in June 1950. As the conflict unfolded, he found himself beholden to those who advocated aid to Taiwan, and to the more hawkish preferences of his well-known military commander Douglas MacArthur. Truman's attempts to contain dissent led to a "dove's curse" and culminated in his removal of MacArthur, politicizing the debate openly.[104] I briefly discuss Dwight D. Eisenhower and the armistice, noting the surprising pressure he felt from his own party.

In the Vietnam case, Lyndon B. Johnson was able to manage elites remarkably well until the early part of 1968, enabling the United States to escalate to high levels with relatively high public support. He too continually placated his hawkish advisers, in part to conserve political capital for his cherished Great Society legislation. When Nixon won the election in 1968, the public had turned against the war, but Nixon escalated significantly even as he drew down US troop levels, in search of an outcome that he plausibly could paint as honorable for the United States.

In chapters 6 and 7, I turn to Republican presidents and several very different examples of hawks' misadventures. In chapter 6, I examine another case from the Cold War: Ronald Reagan's intervention in Lebanon. For Reagan, initiating intervention was easy, but rising congressional opposition and internal administration resistance to a more aggressive strategy pushed the president to withdraw even as public opinion remained steady, in a comparatively small intervention. In chapter 7, I turn to the so-called forever wars in Iraq and Afghanistan, focusing on George W. Bush's decisions in the 2003 Iraq War, as well as the "surge" debate and decision in 2006–7. Both Reagan's decision to withdraw a small force from Lebanon under relatively permissive public opinion conditions and Bush's decision to escalate in Iraq despite the rebuke of the

2006 midterm elections illustrate the power of elite politics and the pressure they exert on Republican presidents to seek a decisive outcome. I also briefly examine successive presidents' approaches to the war in Afghanistan.

Taken together, these cases show that presidents bargain with an elite audience in ways that may force them to pay significant political costs or make policy concessions to elites, but not necessarily in a direction the public prefers. They demonstrate, across presidencies of different parties and in different time periods, both the direct effect of elite preferences and the potential costs elites can impose, as well as the effect of elite cues on public debate.

In chapter 8, I conclude the book by raising a normative question: is an elite-dominated foreign policy democratic? Answering that question requires addressing an even more basic issue: in the highly polarized, post-2016 era, is elite leadership of mass opinion—and even foreign policy—still possible? As historian Beverly Gage has noted, the word *elite* itself "has become one of the nastiest epithets in American politics."[105] Even before the 2016 election, claims that elites no longer hold sway or have lost their legitimacy abounded, particularly in the wake of the 2003 Iraq War and the 2008 financial crisis.[106] The 2016 presidential election, as well as the Brexit vote in the United Kingdom, raised fundamental questions about expertise and the limits of elite leadership.

But it is premature to conclude that elite leadership's time has passed. As Gage notes, antipathy toward elites is hardly new. Additionally, we must still reckon with the reality that the public pays little attention to day-to-day foreign policy, which is a feature to be incorporated into models of politics rather than a problem to be assumed away or fixed. Furthermore, elite cues are still remarkably potent. One powerful example is the evolution of US public attitudes toward Russia during the 2016 election campaign, when Donald Trump's comments about and alleged connections to Russia garnered widespread news coverage. Republicans' views of both Vladimir Putin and Russia shifted markedly in a more favorable direction, despite the long history of GOP hawkishness on Russia.[107] Such shifts are a dramatic illustration of the power of a single leader to shape mass opinion.[108]

The rapid polarization of public opinion on Russia in 2016 suggests a further concern: perhaps partisan polarization has become so dominant that elite bargaining of the type described in this book is no longer possible. Although politics have always permeated foreign policy—going back to the Founding era, when bitter partisanship surrounded fundamental foreign policy choices such as whether the United States should align with France or Britain—polarization in the foreign policy arena has increased.[109] Even if bargaining is more difficult in a polarized era, however, we must understand these processes if we ever hope to repair them. Given that the public is not likely to become better informed on foreign policy—nor, rationally, should it—understanding elite bargaining as a source of accountability is important even if it is eroding.

Normatively, it is somewhat unpalatable to argue that an insiders' game is consistent with popular or even some scholarly ideals of democracy. Just as Christopher Achen and Larry Bartels call for a more realistic understanding of democracy in the context of American politics, we need theories that deal with the reality of how voters delegate.[110] Robert Michels's famous "iron law of oligarchy" recognized the inevitability of elite control, which he argued was ultimately corrupting.[111] The arguments in this book are more hopeful about elite accountability but recognize that it is often a slow, flawed process.

Finally, the insiders' game also sheds light on democratic distinctiveness in international relations. Alexis de Tocqueville famously argued that aristocracies were better at foreign policy because they were stable and insulated, in contrast to the mass public, which could be "seduced by its ignorance or its passions," or a monarch, who "may be taken off his guard and induced to vacillate in his plans." Thus "foreign policy does not require the use of any of the good qualities peculiar to democracy but does demand the cultivation of almost all those which it lacks."[112]

In the last few decades, the study of war has implicitly refuted Tocqueville by putting voters front and center. I argue that Tocqueville was wrong about democracy and foreign policy, but not because the public is fickle. If democratic leaders face an elite audience, then foreign policy is an insiders' game in *both* democracies and autocracies. To be sure, the elite politics of war in democracies and in autocracies are very different. A wave of literature on comparative authoritarianism has shed light on the many ways that authoritarian regimes can mimic democracies—and yet it still concludes that the democratic regimes are fundamentally different because disputes are settled without violence.[113] In the insiders' game, however, the effects of democracy manifest primarily in the corridors of power, rather than in the voting booth.

2

Why War Is an Insiders' Game

WHO CONSTRAINS a leader's ability to make war? Scholars of authoritarian regimes have demonstrated that dictators face two distinct types of threats, from elites and from the mass public, which present very different political problems for autocratic leaders.[1] This chapter develops an elite-centered theory of democracies and war that begins from the premise that democratic leaders also face dual challenges, from elites and voters. The central question is whether introducing democratic elites as a separate domestic audience changes our expectations for when and how democracies use force, compared to a model in which elites serve as the public's "faithful intermediaries," transmitting public preferences and providing the public with information.

This chapter argues that democratic elites are a fundamentally different audience from the public, that the elite audience presents democratic leaders with a different political problem from what they face from the voters, and that elite politics induces a hawkish bias in decisions about the use of force, especially in the US context. Although this book focuses only on elites in democracies, the stakes of the argument extend to studies of regime type and armed conflict. Most comparisons of how democracies and autocracies navigate crises and wars contrast two domestic constituencies: autocratic elites and democratic voters.[2] The theory I develop here suggests that we should compare across elite audiences to understand the role of regime type in war.

In any political system, constraint requires a domestic audience that potentially wants different things than the leader wants (preferences), knows what leaders are doing (information), cares enough to judge the leader on these actions (salience), and has the ability to impose costs on leaders (coordination and tools of punishment).[3] Traditional models of democracy and war set up this accountability chain between leaders and voters. Adding elites risks unnecessarily complicating this picture, especially if they represent and channel voters' interests. To show that elites are a distinct audience in democracies, we need to know whether they can impose different costs on leaders than can voters, that they have different information, that the timing of constraint differs, and that elites have preferences that can diverge in substance or intensity from those of public audiences.

I argue that elite-imposed costs generally take two forms: resource costs, such as forcing the leader to spend time or political capital to get what they want, or to consider abandoning a policy priority altogether; and informational costs, in publicly or privately sharing information with other audience members. Leaders have tools to anticipate and manage these costs that they cannot use with the public, including side payments and information management within elite circles. From the leader's perspective, some elites are more valuable than others to have in their coalition in support of a policy. Elites have two general sources of influence: who they are (that is, their institutional position), and what they want (their policy preferences). The price and currency to get different elites on board varies across their institutional and policy positions.

It is the systematic variation in these prices and currencies—how elite costs manifest and the nature of the bargain leaders must strike to avoid them—that introduces hawkish bias into the making of decisions about whether to use force. Elites can help a leader achieve his or her goals, but striking elite bargains also shapes decisions and influences whether and how the public learns about them. Three mechanisms underpin the hawkish bias: the larger agenda costs that leaders from dovish parties face if they wish to follow a dovish course; selection effects that give hawkish elites more access to and leverage over decisions; and the larger private benefits for dovish elites of reluctantly supporting hawkish policies, relative to hawkish elites supporting dovish policies. Two ideal-typical democratic distortions emerge: the "dove's curse," which gives dovish leaders incentives to fight with just enough effort to accommodate hawkish elites, and the "hawk's misadventure," which enables hawks to initiate wars with few constraints. These outcomes are by no means automatic, but elite politics can make the path to war or escalation smoother. Yet elites are also a crucial source of constraint, especially after wars begin.

This chapter begins by narrowing the focus to three primary groups of elites that are crucial to decisions to use force. Next, I compare the two democratic audiences, voters and elites, in terms of the nature and content of the constraints they generate. This comparison yields two models: a public-driven model in which elites serve as the voters' faithful intermediaries, and the insiders' game model, where elites are independent, and often primary, agents of constraint. I elaborate the theory in general terms. Since democracies vary in their institutional and national characteristics, I then narrow the chapter's focus to more fine-grained hypotheses about US presidents and the use of force. Focusing on the United States allows me to hold formal institutions constant and examine politics within a single country. This focus sets up the empirical evidence I develop in the remaining chapters.

Who Are Elites?

As mentioned in chapter 1, I define elites as those who have access to information and the decision-making process, and who could serve as cue givers to other elites or to the public. Many elites are relevant to decisions to use force. Theory requires simplification, however, so this book concentrates on elites who consistently and directly influence decisions: legislators; high-level government officials, a group that includes cabinet officers and senior advisers; and military leaders.[4] These three groups encompass both elected and nonelected elites, a divide common to all democracies, but especially prominent in a separation-of-powers system like that of the United States.

The first group consists of elected elites, which for decisions to use force functionally means national legislators (in addition to the leader him- or herself). Legislators influence decisions to use force even if they do not vote on war directly, and they have levers to ease or block a leader's agenda or raise the political costs of national security decisions.[5] As Howell and Pevehouse demonstrate in the US context through an analysis of local news, members of Congress are key drivers of media coverage and thus act as a megaphone for cues that help shape public opinion about the use of force.[6] Legislators also have their own private costs and benefits associated with decisions to use force.

The second group, senior government officials and advisers, are a central focus of this book, in part because they have received less attention in studies of domestic politics and war. It might seem surprising to treat a leader's chosen advisers or cabinet officials as political actors.[7] One reason to do so, however, might be appointees' connections to other political interests.[8] Such outside political support presumes that there is some daylight between advisers' views, or between those of leaders and their advisers; that advisers can and do voice dissent despite the presumption of loyalty; and that such statements actually affect domestic politics.

There are good reasons to believe all three assumptions are valid. In the United States, administrations usually contain a range of views, often leading to intense debates over the use of force. The divisions within the George W. Bush administration in the lead-up to the Iraq War are well known.[9] During the Cold War, tension roiled the administrations of Jimmy Carter (Cyrus Vance vs. Zbigniew Brzezinski) and Ronald Reagan (George Shultz vs. Caspar Weinberger).[10] Intraparty divisions have also churned within governments in the United Kingdom, as illustrated by tensions over the Falklands crisis within

Margaret Thatcher's government and major resignations over the Iraq War during Tony Blair's premiership.[11]

Additionally, leaders and their inner circle drive elite rhetoric about war.[12] Media evidence bears out this view. For example, in a tabulation of *New York Times* front-page articles on "principal" uses of force from 1945 to 2004, Douglas Kriner reports that 37 percent of stories had an opinion or policy recommendation from the president, and nearly half (47 percent) contained the opinion of an administration official.[13] In a study of media coverage of the Vietnam War, Daniel Hallin argues that when there is political conflict over the use of force, the media will "continue to grant a privileged hearing particularly to senior officials of the executive branch."[14] As I show in chapter 3, these cues can have large effects on public opinion.

The third group of elites are military leaders. Scholars of civil-military relations rightfully treat the military as a political actor in domestic settings across regime types.[15] Evidence from survey experiments shows that military cues can move public opinion about the use of force.[16] Although the military's standing in the eyes of the public has varied over time, it has enjoyed unusual deference in recent decades, and it is an important contributor to public debate about the use of force.[17] To keep the analysis tractable, I bracket problems of civil-military relations and focus on military preferences.

Despite their differences, members of all three groups can be considered "insiders." Unlike voters, these elites have early and frequent access to decisions, control material or political resources, and can obtain and share information. The question is whether elites serve the voters' interests or diverge from what citizens expect decision makers to do on their behalf.

Two Models of Constraint: Faithful Intermediaries or Insiders' Game?

Are elites merely agents or faithful intermediaries of the voters, or are elites a separate audience imposing their own set of constraints, in the insiders' game? Figure 2-1 presents two contrasting models of constraint. In figure 2-1a, a reasonable model of public constraints, or the faithful intermediaries model, posits that the public is the main source of constraint on democratic leaders. Elites respond to and represent public preferences and faithfully transmit good (or at least the best available) information to voters, who do the constraining. Elites can impose some costs on the leader, but primarily by acting through the public channel.

In contrast, in the insiders' game model in figure 2-1b, elites can punish leaders independently. The public has a role in this model, but elite strategic behavior determines when and how the public is brought into debate, and the

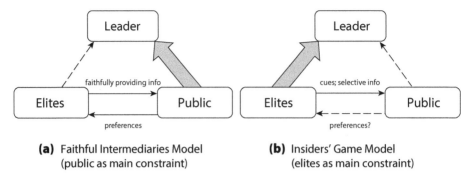

FIGURE 2-1. Two models of constraint

nature and volume of elite cues. Elite consensus or dissent is not necessarily the product of good information but rather elite bargains that can distort whether and when elites pull the fire alarm—at times that may not be in the public's interest.

I argue that these models lead to very different predictions in terms of decisions to use military force. In the faithful intermediaries model, democratic leaders face constraints from the public, but it is occasional, "lumpy" accountability that is most responsive to outcomes. The leader's task is to deliver the public good of moderate, sound foreign policy—either victory in war, or avoiding imprudent military ventures.[18] We should expect war policies to look similar across hawkish or dovish parties. Hawks and doves may have incentives to act "against type," but these incentives are symmetric, and moderating incentives should cancel out any hawkish or dovish bias. The role of elites in this model is as an intervening variable in a public-driven process of constraint. In the insiders' game model, elite bargaining induces a hawkish bias in decisions to use force because the cost of acting "true" to type—that is, choosing to act in line with their preferences—is higher for leaders from parties associated with dovishness than for leaders from hawkish parties, lowering constraints on hawks who want to fight, and incentivizing doves to fight when they otherwise would not. We would also expect few differences between the parties in terms of how often they fight or escalate—but that convergence is at a more hawkish point on the spectrum compared to the faithful intermediaries model.

Comparing Public and Elite Constraints

To reach these conclusions, I first show that the constraints that democratic elites impose are very different from public constraints, as summarized in table 2-1. The first two differences are relatively straightforward. One simple

TABLE 2-1. Comparing Public and Elite Constraints

	Public Constraints	**Elite Constraints**
Timing	Elections every 2–4 years; infrequent protests	Frequent encounters
Information	Information takers Elite cues based on good, available information Fire alarms in public interest	Information makers, can share or withhold information Elite cues based on selective information Fire alarms affected by private interest
Tools	Vote leader out of office Protest	Drain time or political capital (resource costs) Block policies (agenda costs) Extract policy concessions Policy sabotage Cue other elites Cue public opinion (fire alarm)
Preferences	Want moderation, good performance Weak preferences, low salience	Want specific policies Stronger preferences, higher salience
What can the leader do about it?	Select "good" wars, win wars, persuade elites and/or voters in public sphere	Side payments (political or procedural benefits, war policy concessions, other policy concessions), manage information, disrupt coordination

difference is *timing*: elites can exert constraints earlier and more often than voters. The public has only one regularly scheduled way to express its views on its leaders: in elections. In democracies, the timing is usually out of the voters' hands—whether through fixed election timing or leader control of election timing in parliamentary systems. Between elections, voters must exert effort to become informed and coordinate on an issue if it is to be salient in a politically meaningful way between elections (for example, through protests).[19] In contrast, elites have frequent opportunities to constrain leaders, through regular bureaucratic or consultative processes, or through ad hoc encounters. The shadow of elite monitoring is nearly constant.

A second difference between elite and public constraint is *information*. Voters are information takers. A challenge for the public is to get information about their leader's performance without spending its limited time and attention gathering that information. In the US context, as Ole Holsti notes, even the research on the coherence of foreign policy attitudes does not challenge "the overwhelming evidence on one important point: the American public is generally poorly informed about international affairs."[20] This strategy is rational: voters naturally seek shortcuts to make sense of a complex world.

The traditional answer to this "democratic dilemma" is that voters can use cues from knowledgeable and trusted sources to gather information efficiently.[21] This view of elites and the cues they provide fits the faithful intermediaries role. Even foreign policy scholars who argue that constraints come from the public (a bottom-up approach) acknowledge that elite messages are often necessary to provide information or activate public attitudes.[22] This informational role is one of the main ways theories of democracies and war incorporate elites. Opposition elites, for example, can inform the electorate about foreign policy mistakes.[23] The opposition's behavior affects the electoral salience of crises and wars, because voters care about outcomes, and the opposition's support for a failed outcome can blunt its salience.[24] Elites can also help leaders reduce the domestic cost of changing course in crises.[25] In a long war, the public has more opportunity to gain information through media reports.[26] In these arguments, elected elites have domestic political motivations separate from national security concerns. Indeed, those political motivations give the opposition's cues their bite, because politicians are unlikely to support a president from the other party without good reason. But although there are impediments to gathering and transmitting information, this view of elites is still that of reasonably faithful intermediaries for the voters.

In contrast, if we look at elites as an independent set of actors, the difference in information as an input to constraint becomes clearer. Elites can generate new information, access information not available to voters and many other elites, and choose whether to share information with other elites or the public. Elites can disseminate information strategically or in response to elite bargaining, potentially distorting the open flow of information essential to public-driven theories of democracies at war. Crucially, knowledgeable, informed elites serve as information conduits not only to voters, but also to other, less informed elites, whose preferences and interests may diverge from the voters. Information variation occurs within the executive branch, where some insiders have earlier or more privileged access to information. Within legislatures, some members have expertise or positions that give them access to information, while others who do not specialize in foreign policy may be looking for their own cue to provide information or political cover.[27] Thus cuing *within* elite circles is as important as the elite cuing of voters.

Elites are especially interested in information to help them form an estimate of the probability that the leader's course of action is likely to be successful. Even if they have privileged access to information, elites, particularly legislators, may be at the mercy of the government to share what it knows. Thus leaders are especially tempted to shape, manage, or conceal information related to the probability of success, and in turn, leaders' actions may distort elites' ability to serve as the information conduit expected in public opinion models.

The remaining differences between public and elite constraints in table 2-1— the *tools* of constraint and the nature of public and elite *preferences*, which inform what Weeks calls the "content of constraint"—require further elaboration.[28] Ultimately, all these differences shape what leaders can do about elite and public constraints, as shown in the final row of table 2-1 and elaborated below.

The Constraint Toolbox: How Can Audiences Punish Leaders?

Voters: Constraint at the Ballot Box

What can voters do to their leaders? For citizens, the *tools* of constraint are limited. First and foremost, they can throw the bums out. Although they differ in the details, many theories of democracies and war rely on the shadow of voter punishment, through retrospective voting on a leader's past record; contemporaneous approval, where leaders seek to follow popular sentiment at the time of a decision to use force; or anticipated public reactions in upcoming elections.[29] For example, Dan Reiter and Allan Stam argue that democracies tend to win the wars they fight as "a direct result of the constraining power of political consent granted to the leaders and the people's ability to withdraw it."[30] James Fearon posits that democratic foreign policy is "made by an agent on behalf of principals (voters) who have the power to sanction the agent electorally or through the workings of public opinion."[31] As Tomz, Weeks, and Yarhi-Milo argue, leaders can be responsive to public opinion about the use of force, or voters can select leaders who share similar preferences.[32]

Voters face uphill battles to wield their limited tools, however. Although elections can serve a coordinating function to channel voters' voices, it is difficult for voters to coordinate on war as a reason to select candidates or sanction incumbent leaders. Even if they have sufficient information, there is no guarantee that informed citizens will attach enough importance to an issue to base their approval or vote on this knowledge.[33] Not only is foreign policy typically not salient in elections, but candidates have incentives to "trespass" on the other party's issues and take moderate stances.[34] If candidates do strategically adopt similar positions on an issue, then the voters cannot use it as a basis for selection. Indeed, a paradox of the 1968 election is that it came at a turning point for the public's view of the Vietnam War, but the similarity of the positions of the major party nominees, Richard Nixon and Hubert Humphrey, meant the war was not central to vote choice.[35]

What about the "workings of public opinion" between elections? As Tomz and coauthors point out, public disapproval can make it harder for leaders to generate political capital for other international and domestic priorities—what I have called political opportunity costs.[36] It is theoretically unclear, however, how public opinion about the use of military force exerts constraint in this way. One mechanism certainly could be that unpopular policies diminish a leader's political capital, or relatedly, that disapproval of how the leader handles crises and wars could be a drag on a leader's ability to pursue other priorities—what Gelpi and Grieco call "competency costs."[37] But if perceptions of sound policy and perceptions of success in crises depend on elite discourse, then a second, alternative mechanism is that elite displeasure reduces the leader's political capital for other projects and generates public disapproval in the process. Additionally, if, as discussed below, leaders' actions are measured against the expectations of their hawkish or dovish reputations, can we assume that the effect of perceived success is uniform across leaders? A third possibility is that the leader pursues other policies as a way to shore up public approval given public displeasure with a decision about the use of force. A fourth is that the decision about the use of force is not particularly salient to voters, and thus unpopular policies do not drag down the leader's other prospects.

But which mechanism dominates? To make matters more complicated, Douglas Foyle argues that individual leaders vary in their views of whether and how public opinion matters.[38] It is also unclear how long a mismatch between public opinion and the leader's decision must last to seriously affect political capital. As Zaller argues, leaders sometimes act against current public opinion because they anticipate "latent" public opinion that will exist in the future—making it perfectly rational for leaders to sometimes ignore the polls.[39] It is thus difficult to discern what the "workings of public opinion" predict about the connection between public attitudes and the use of force.

Protests provide another, albeit more costly, way to for voters to coordinate on an issue. Although the politics of protest is beyond the scope of this book, it is worth noting that it is somewhat difficult to disentangle some protests from elite support, especially when elites provide signals or resources that help or hinder protesters' ability to coordinate. Furthermore, even grassroots protests face the prospect that they might coordinate around a position so well that they can be easily labeled and politicized as "fringe" or "unpatriotic," especially if they oppose war. Finally, although citizens of a democracy ostensibly enjoy greater protections for freedom of speech and assembly, protesting in a democracy is not free of the risk of violent crackdowns, as antiwar and civil rights protestors are all too aware.[40] Though information-gathering and collective-action costs in a democracy are not remotely comparable to the cost of enduring direct repression, they are politically relevant because they make replacing a leader on foreign policy grounds difficult.[41]

The Tools of Elite Constraint

In contrast to voters, the political features of elites give them a much larger array of tools to impose costs on leaders. Very simply, elites are smaller in number than voters. Even a large group of elites is still a finite group with proper names. Smaller groups can more easily monitor and coordinate sanctions against a leader than can large coalitions, as scholars of autocratic accountability and war emphasize.[42] Additionally, many elites have concentrated power. Institutions may disproportionately empower some elites with different preferences from those of the median voter (for example, a member of the US Senate). Elites also have earlier and wider access to information than voters do, as discussed above. And elites control resources the leader needs to achieve policy goals, including those unrelated to war. These political features allow elites to impose two types of costs that voters cannot: elites can deplete a leader's finite pool of resources, and they can impose informational costs.

RESOURCE COSTS. Elites can force the leader to expend scarce resources. One precious resource is time, which must be parceled out to different priorities, foreign and domestic. Scarce time-related resources include not only the chief executive's time but also legislative floor time,[43] as well as procedures in international institutions, such as seeking UN resolutions, that can slow down decision making. Elites can also force the leader to spend political capital that the leader might prefer to use for other goals. Elites that control material resources, such as military assets, diplomatic or civilian infrastructure or personnel, and budgets, can diminish the resources at a leaders' disposal by withholding access, or imposing a cost for access, to those resources. Elites can stymie progress on other policy priorities, for example through legislative tactics, or in the executive branch, by dragging their feet on policy implementation or withholding resources in interagency coordination. Elites can also impose related personnel costs, delaying confirmations or nomination processes that leave important posts vacant.

These resource costs can affect not only the crisis or war at hand, but also other priorities or goals on the leader's agenda. Elites can raise the *policy costs*, that is, the political or material cost of pursuing leaders' preferred decision about the use of force, whether that is war or peace, or escalation or deescalation.[44] Once a leader makes a decision, elites in the military and executive branch can engage in *policy sabotage* that undermines the outcome leaders want. Such sabotage might include fighting a war with the elites' preferred strategy, or alternatively, taking actions that prolong conflict, provoke escalation by adversaries, or undermine diplomacy when the leader would prefer to limit the use of force. Policy sabotage can have spillover political effects, potentially damaging a leader's reputation.[45]

Elites can also impose *agenda costs*, or the political opportunity costs to the leader of pursuing his or her course. The threat of agenda costs may force the leader to spend political capital on a war-related policy choice that the leader would prefer to conserve for other priorities. Elites can also extract policy concessions the leader would prefer not to give, such as escalation or a costly military strategy, that depletes material resources available for other national security programs. If the concessions are on issues unrelated to the crisis or war, the result is *policy spillover* into other areas.

Some elites can threaten policy or agenda costs with small numbers and little coordination, because the shadow of these elites' "anticipated reactions" may be enough to make the leader think twice about pursuing his or her preferred policies.[46] Other elites, particularly those without control of resources, have to overcome a more significant coordination problem, since individual elites may fear being the first to take a stance against the leader. It is important to note that the leader may still achieve his or her preferred outcome, but at higher cost than in the absence of elite-imposed resource costs.

INFORMATIONAL COSTS. In addition to these direct costs that elites can impose—largely independent of the public—the second set of costs elites can impose on leaders are *informational* costs, imposed by cuing either other elites or the public directly. These informational costs are different from the informative role that elite cues play in public-driven theories. Elites can be the gatekeepers who determine whether the public is brought into debate at all—whether the "scope of conflict" is expanded. Even if immediate foreign policy outcomes are not salient, elites can wrap a leader's decisions into simpler narratives, such as weakness or toughness, or define limits on when the use of force is acceptable, highlighting when leaders transgress those boundaries.[47]

As informational theories suggest, elites with authority and knowledge can cue the public, but that same authority and knowledge also give certain elites more leverage over the leader. We know from theories of elite cues that there are two ways that cues can be credible, though they are rarely discussed jointly. A cue can be *institutionally* informative if it comes from an elite with a credible or surprising institutional position.[48] The media, in search of juicy stories, oversamples surprising cues like same-party criticism or opposition-party support of the leader.[49] Below, I extend this logic to members of the leader's team within government. Second, cues can be *substantively* informative if they run counter to expectations of what the cue giver wants.[50]

As noted, information transmitted via elite cues has a place in the faithful intermediaries model. The role of elite cues in the insiders' game differs, however, in terms of both substance and timing. Elites with strong views that diverge in substance or intensity from the voters' preferences can put a cue into circulation that amplifies or competes with the government's line. Such cues can shape other elites' estimates of the probability that the use of force will be successful, for example. Elites can also alter the timing of when information reaches the public domain. Instead of fire alarms based on elite monitoring of the public interest, the alarm can come earlier or later as a result of elite politics. The voters may not get a fire alarm in time to avoid disaster, as occurred in the 2003 Iraq War, discussed in chapter 7. Alternatively, they might get an early or false alarm that turns them against a policy before leaders have time to fully deliberate its value. For example, President Jimmy Carter made an ill-fated attempt to withdraw US troops from South Korea. Carter ultimately abandoned the proposal, which was widely opposed within his own administration and members of Congress. Along the way, Carter removed the military's chief of staff in South Korea, General John Singlaub, from his position after the general told the *Washington Post* that Carter's plan would "lead to war."[51] As discussed in chapter 7, the 2009 leak of General Stanley McChrystal's report on Afghanistan to the *Washington Post* can be seen as an early fire alarm that put pressure on Obama, then reviewing policy in Afghanistan, to send more troops.

What Audiences Want: Comparing Public and Elite Preferences

None of this would matter if elites and the public wanted the same thing—and in the faithful intermediaries model, they effectively do. This view, going back to Kant, is that in a representative democracy, elites are drawn from the citizenry and thus are cautious in starting wars because citizens bear the costs of conflict.[52] An alternative view is that elites generally have more hawkish preferences, whether they stem from a disconnection from or lack of consideration of the costs to citizens or society; from a commitment to interventionism that may be well intentioned but misguided; or from psychological biases.[53] I argue that both of these perspectives take an overly simplistic view not only of the public but also of elites, whose preferences are not necessarily more hawkish and yet differ in important ways from those of the voters.

Public Preferences and the Use of Force

Trying to characterize public preferences about the use of force raises a chicken-and-egg question at the heart of the book: which comes first, elite preferences or mass preferences? Much research suggests that public opinion about foreign policy shapes the incentives and selection of elites, from the bottom up.[54] Theories of elite leadership of public opinion argue the arrow points the other way: that elite opinion shapes public opinion from the top down.[55] In between these views is the idea that elites anticipate what V. O. Key called "latent" opinion, that is, future public opinion rather than current attitudes.[56] There is no perfect way to resolve this debate, and both sides acknowledge that effects can run both ways.[57] Elites may be responsive to public opinion, yet the state of public opinion depends on prior elite messages—or the absence of messages.[58] As Berinsky argues, public preferences may be shallow or lack an elite message to latch onto, resulting in many "don't know" responses in surveys.[59]

There are also reasons to doubt that public opinion derives from issue-based preferences related to the use of force. Recent research reinforces long-standing findings that psychological or demographic traits strongly shape public attitudes.[60] Foreign policy preferences can also derive directly from political preferences. In the American context, Gabriel Lenz finds that when informed of a party's or candidate's position on an issue, individuals do not switch their vote to the party or candidate that shares their position; rather, they internalize their preferred party or candidate's position on an issue as their own.[61] This leadership effect was powerfully illustrated by the change in Republican voters' views of Russia after Trump won the 2016 Republican nomination, as well as by the switch in their views about withdrawing from Syria and Afghanistan.[62]

Thus it is difficult to identify a single view of "what the public wants" in terms of the use of military force. But for purposes of theory testing, we can still make useful simplifications to form the strongest possible baseline case for the faithful intermediaries model. Much theoretical and empirical work suggests that in the aggregate, the public wants moderate national security policies.[63] More specifically, citizens are "pretty prudent" and want their leaders to be neither too hawkish nor too dovish, to fight necessary wars well, and to avoid misadventures, particularly those involving the internal affairs of other countries.[64] Nincic argues that during the Cold War, the public engaged in the "politics of opposites," acting as a kind of thermostat to favor whichever position—hawkishness or dovishness—it felt was lacking.[65] In their study of peace initiatives, Mattes and Weeks show that hawks who offer the olive branch have an approval advantage over doves who take the same action, and that such against-type action makes the leader seem more moderate.[66] As

Schultz points out, a "moderate" public does not mean a dovish public, but rather that voters are willing to revise their policy preferences in response to new information.[67] Thus I assume aggregate public opinion is moderate in the sense that it wants security without unreasonable risk, and prefers favorable outcomes to unfavorable outcomes, although this assumption can be tricky since elite cues can shape the public's view of success.[68] Below, I address alternative possibilities, such as a hawkish or dovish public.

Moderation is not the only mechanism that shapes how the public judges decisions about the use of force, however: voters also want some credible signal that the policy is the right one.[69] Theoretical and empirical evidence shows that doves have an uphill battle in sending such signals; that is, doves have a credibility gap. When a dovish leader makes a dovish policy decision—a peace proposal, or declining to fight, or ending a war—how do voters know the leader made this choice out of a well-informed judgment that the policy is in the national interest, rather than acting out of a commitment to dovish policies? A hawk's decision to seek peace is more credible because it is surprising.[70] It is also consistent with the idea of politicians "trespassing" on traits that other candidates "own," such as stronger leadership or compassion.[71] While most of the literature exploring credibility in the context of national security policy has focused on the so-called Nixon-to-China question—that is, whether a hawk is advantaged in making peace—it can be extended to decisions for war. For example, Trager and Vavreck find that hawks face the opposite credibility problem when choosing to fight, because their image is one of bellicosity and the public does not know whether to trust that war is really in the national interest.[72] But when a dove chooses to fight, the public has more confidence in the wisdom of war because it is surprising. They find that independent voters, who lack partisan attachments, reward Democrats for engaging in war and punish Republicans who fight.

One question is whether the credibility problems faced by hawks and doves are symmetric, and if not, whether public opinion could account for any asymmetry. Theories of against-type behavior suggest that the rewards and penalties should be reciprocal, that is, that doves have an approval advantage when they fight and that hawks reap the approval benefits of making peace, and that these advantages are symmetric.[73] This argument is also consistent with the findings in public opinion studies that show that Democratic presidents, branded as doves, are less punished for unsuccessful wars, and that hawks are less punished for peace initiatives that fail.[74] The implication is that leaders who act against type can more credibly signal they chose the right policy, and get some credit for trying, regardless of the outcome.

Is there a case for asymmetric constraints on hawks and doves under a public-driven model? One could argue that the credibility gap generalizes to all national security choices, so that hawks will be more trusted not only

Belief in Military Competence

"Looking ahead for the next few years, which political party do you think will do a better job of protecting the country from international terrorism and military threats, the Republican Party or the Democratic Party?"

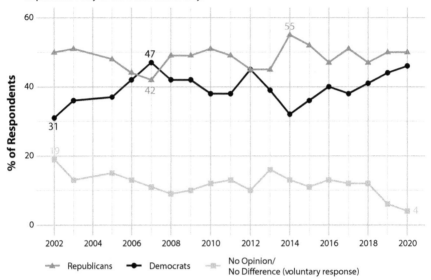

FIGURE 2-2. Public perception of parties' military competence, 2002–20 (Gallup polls)

to make peace but also to conduct wars.[75] On its face, this view seems plausible. In the United States, for example, the Republican Party has had an advantage on national security issues since at least 1949, when the "who lost China?" debate following the Communist victory in the Chinese Civil War plagued Harry Truman and haunted successive Democratic presidents.[76] This party image of weakness has been remarkably sticky. For example, figure 2-2 shows responses in Gallup polls over the period from 2002 to 2020 when respondents were asked which party would "do a better job of protecting the country from international terrorism and military threats." The Democratic Party led only once, at the nadir of the Iraq War in 2007, and never broke the 50 percent mark. Perhaps doves, or elites from parties associated with dovishness, have to work harder to convince voters they are not weak than hawks have to work to avoid the "warmonger" label.

Yet even in this scenario, there are reasons to doubt that public opinion generates more than a mild asymmetry. First, several studies of peace initiatives find that both the credibility and the moderation mechanisms operate when a hawk initiates peace.[77] If these findings apply more generally, moderation may thus act as a brake on excessive against-type behavior, pulling policy toward the middle, as so many public-oriented theories argue. Furthermore, leaders considering their electoral prospects balance against-type actions with tending to the expectations of their own type. As Danny Hayes argues, "trait owner-ship" generates expectations that candidates have to manage—they may have incentives to "trespass" on the opposite traits, but they will suffer if they do not meet the expectations for the traits they own.[78] This argument is the converse of findings that leaders get some credit for trying when they act against type: when they act true to type, their policies had better be successful.[79] Lastly, as Egan argues, while the public favors the *priorities* that are associated with the parties' issue ownership—favoring "consensus" issues like defense spending and education—they often do not favor the individual *policies* that party lead-ers enact, such as torture as a tool in the war on terrorism.[80] Egan argues that party activists pursue ideologically extreme policies that prove unpopular with voters, suggesting a disconnect between the moderate preferences of voters and elite priorities. We would expect that incentives to signal moderation to voters limit the asymmetries arising from policy credibility.

Elite Preferences and the Use of Force

How do elite preferences compare to voter preferences? The components of elite preferences can be theoretically simplified by considering the benefits of victory (i.e., the stakes), the costs and benefits of fighting irrespective of the outcome (which influence the costs of defeat), and the probability of suc-cess.[81] Elites weigh the costs and benefits of using military force in terms of not only their policy preferences, but also their institutional or political prefer-ences. Compared to voters, elites likely have more specific views of the benefits of fighting, the stakes of conflict, and the probability of war success. Even if they are not hawks, these features leave their preferences more finely balanced and thus open to persuasion or bargaining.

In addition to how they view these costs and benefits for the nation, elites also consider the *private costs and benefits* of using force. Office-seeking officials would like not only to be (re)elected or help their party, but also to further their careers and reputations. Political appointees or bureaucrats want to get, keep, and improve their jobs. Existing theories have explored how partisan incentives conflict with the public or national interest,[82] but my argument includes indi-viduals' motivations, sometimes at the expense of other copartisans.

Elite institutional or political preferences can point in the same direc-tion as policy preferences, or they can pull in different directions, generating cross pressure. Considering both these facets of elite preferences opens space for bargaining between leaders and elites over benefits that are targeted at particular elites rather than enjoyed by all citizens. A prerequisite for the theory is that elites have a range of preferences, from which the leader can try to build an elite coalition. As the following discussion makes clear, we should expect a range of policy preferences within parties, and inside governments.

POLICY PREFERENCES. Elites naturally have sincere differences in how they view the national stakes in a given conflict. Elites who share broadly similar worldviews can still differ in their views of the stakes of conflict, variation that can arise from individuals' backgrounds or psychology, experience, and prior diplomatic or military service. Elites may also have different causal beliefs about the security benefits of victory.[83] Even within governments of a single party, we would expect a diversity of views of national security stakes. Stakes also vary across bureaucratic departments or the military, for example, if the outcome of a conflict affects the ease of future military operations (such as base or sea-lane access).

There are good reasons to expect that among elites who are involved in decisions to use military force, hawkish elites have more specific and intense preferences, and sometimes more extreme preferences, than do dovish elites. We do not need to assume that elites are necessarily more hawkish overall than the public to reach this conclusion. But we would expect that as a group, hawkish elites have a larger proportion of those with strong and specific preferences—analogous to what scholars of political parties call "intense policy demanders."[84] Hawks who are in positions to influence decisions about the use of force, or to manage or control resources related to military conflict, are more likely to have intense policy views that they work to promote within their institutional positions. These views may or may not be more extreme, but they are likely to be well formed and more firmly held. This argument does not mean that all elites who lean hawkish seek war every time they have the chance, nor does it mean that there are not passionate activists for peace among doves. But selection effects mean that even dovish leaders deal with and appoint officials whose preferences are stronger and more hawkish than average.

In the three categories of elites on which this book focuses, there are reasons to expect a disproportionate number of elites with intense policy preferences relevant to decisions about war and peace. Executive-branch officials or civil servants may develop strong preferences about a country or region for which they have day-to-day responsibility, which may lead to hawkish preferences if the country or region is under attack.[85] Insider elites may also hold different views about the benefits of fighting, irrespective of victory. Some insider elites may see demonstrating resolve or bolstering reputation as a benefit of fighting, as Yarhi-Milo has shown.[86] A second motive for fighting may be the urge to take action in cases of humanitarian crises, a motive ascribed to those who urged the Obama administration to intervene in Libya in 2011, since many of them served or advised the Clinton administration, which failed to take action during the 1994 genocide in Rwanda.[87]

The military's policy preferences are another source of insider preference diversity. Scholars have long debated the nature of military preferences. In a unique study of civilian elites and military officers, Feaver and Gelpi find that those in the military are more reluctant to initiate the use of force compared to civilians or those who have not seen combat, but once engaged in conflict, military officers prefer to use higher levels of force, without constraints.[88] Others argue that the military favors hawkish solutions.[89] For present purposes, it is not necessary to resolve this debate; rather, we should expect military officers to have a distribution of views, just as civilians do. There are reasons to expect, however, that when we consider the military and civilian insiders who control the tools of military force, the pool of those with access to decisions skews hawkish or at least permissive of the use of force even if individuals are not especially hawkish. On the military side, research in the US context suggests that the top echelons of the military tend to be much more Republican and male—demographics with more hawkish preferences—although the views of the US Army overall tend to reflect the political attitudes of the civilian population.[90] Even if the military is reluctant to initiate conflict, this preference may be finely balanced. On the civilian side, domain-specific expertise likely leads to more hawkish appointments in defense-related posts, even under a leader with dovish views. Although dovish presidents may prefer cooperation and diplomacy, they must fill defense ministry and military positions responsible for preparing for and managing the use of force. The supply of candidates is not likely to include many true doves.

What about legislators' policy preferences? Even when parties are "branded" as hawkish or dovish, parties have a range of views on the use of force. In the US context, both parties have hawkish and more restrained wings that are often at odds.[91] For example, during the Cold War, geography played an important role, with Southern Democrats generally more hawkish—and overrepresented in the Senate.[92] Legislators who are more authoritative on national security and foreign policy issues, such as those who serve on the relevant committees, generally have more hawkish predispositions, regardless of party.[93] Linda Fowler finds that the Senate Armed Services Committee (SASC) generally advocates for the military, with muted partisanship.[94] There is also a long tradition within both types of parties of those who support using force for humanitarian reasons.[95]

INSTITUTIONAL OR POLITICAL PREFERENCES. Elected and non-elected elites alike are political actors who have institutional or political preferences. These preferences can stem from collective membership in a party, agency, or organization, or they can relate to individuals' career or political incentives. Some of these private benefits do not depend on the outcome of the leader's decisions. Additionally, institutional or political incentives can pull in the opposite direction of elites' policy views, opening up the distribution of elite preferences even inside administrations in ways that might surprise voters.

For elites championing bureaucratic or organizational interests, war may yield benefits even without victory, and even if those same elites would not necessarily choose war if they were in charge. For example, military conflict affects the future tasking of a military services or civilian agencies involved in aid or diplomacy. Individual elites also have their own political or career incentives: to keep their jobs, earn and maintain their reputations, forge relationships with other elites, get promoted, and in the case of political appointees, stay in good standing with a political party. Civilian advisers who want to stay on their party's foreign policy "bench" have incentives to stay loyal and support their leader. Individual elites may see career benefits from war irrespective of the outcome, for example, if they earn a reputation for competence. For example, then-general David Petraeus earned praise and promotion for his stabilization of parts of northern Iraq while the rest of the war was going poorly.[96] Elites must also consider the political opportunity costs of the leader's decisions. Insiders with responsibility for protecting the leaders' agenda and political interests, or those who work on nonsecurity or domestic issues, must weigh whether war would crowd out progress on other issues, or conversely whether military action would neutralize critiques of weakness.

It is important to note that these pressures do not automatically mean supporting more hawkish policies. Sometimes those who want to use force are frustrated by a leader's inaction, or worry most about the risk that war will overshadow a leader's agenda. And of course, bureaucratic and military elites also face particularized costs of war. Even if they do not risk injury or death, they may face mental health or other human costs of war that affect their well-being.

Turning to elected elites in legislatures, in the US context, while divided or unified government is an important feature of congressional interactions with the president, it is not the most important for my theory, for several reasons. First, individual members of Congress may be sufficiently influential or powerful that they can bring along many others even if they are in the minority party. Party leaders, committee chairs or influential committee members with national security expertise, or "pivotal" legislators, such as those at the filibuster point, have concentrated power.[97] Second, congressional rules, particularly in the Senate, protect the minority by allowing members to block nominations or legislation, or through the threat of a filibuster. Third, since the early 2000s, partisanship and partisan polarization dominate the effects of party control of the legislature.[98] Fourth, the president's own party can be an important source of constraint, as is true in parliamentary systems as well.

Legislators share some institutional incentives that generalize across democratic systems. Legislators care about their standing in the party and will not want to buck their party's position unless they are among the few with independent standing on an issue. Elected legislators generally seek success for their party and its "bench" of fellow members and staff. Those with foreign and defense policy expertise can benefit from involvement in military conflict (even if they do not desire it in specific cases). For rank-and-file members without strong foreign policy views, the costs and benefits of military ventures are more diffuse. Nonetheless, if they are on the "right" side of a decision about the use of force, they may share the partisan benefits.[99]

Beyond these commonalities, incentives differ for members of the leader's party versus opposition parties. For the leader's copartisans in the legislature, loyalty to the chief executive is a very important motive. As Howell and Pevehouse argue in the US context, the president's copartisans should fall in line because of shared worldviews, trust in the signals sent from presidents of their own party, shared electoral fortunes, and the need to curry favor.[100] If copartisans disagree with the leader on policy grounds, they feel cross pressure to support the chief executive not only out of loyalty, but also because the media overreports same-party criticism of the leader, which is surprising and newsworthy.[101] Even if individual members disagree with the leader, their party as a whole may benefit from a leader's efforts to act against type to diffuse lines of attack—especially for doves, whose party may benefit from dampening accusations of weakness on national security and who are likely to prefer focusing on other domestic priorities.

The opposition party's motives are more complex, because the party as a whole has strategic incentives to support a successful war and oppose a war they think will go poorly. Cross-nationally, Philip Arena finds that whether the opposition party disagreed with a democratic leader shapes whether the leader is punished or rewarded for the war's outcome.[102] This strategic incentive for the opposition, in turn, gives leaders incentives to manipulate information about the probability that their chosen course will be successful.

But individual legislators also have career or political incentives that can lead them to support a decision that departs from their party and seems at odds with their personal policy preferences. Aspiring or current foreign policy or national security leaders have reputational costs and benefits to consider. Legislators who want to run for higher office may wish to go against their party's stereotype, perhaps to signal they are moderate. Here, however, estimates of the probability of success are crucial. If legislators end up on the "wrong" side of a war—opposing a war that goes well, or supporting a war that goes poorly—their reputation on national security may take a hit. As discussed in chapter 7, this dynamic affected how Democratic presidential hopefuls in the Senate voted in 2002 on the authorization to use military force in Iraq. Legislators' private, individual incentives are reflected in the variation we observe in opposition-party behavior. As Howell and Pevehouse note, in votes to authorize force before a US troop deployment that were not unanimous, a substantial fraction of the opposition party supported authorization. In the 1991 Gulf War, for example, nearly one-third of House Democrats (86 of 265) supported authorization, and nearly one-fifth of Democratic Senators (10 of 56) did the same. In the 1999 Kosovo vote, Democrats fell in line behind Bill Clinton, with 90 percent of House Democrats and 91 percent of Senate Democrats voting to authorize force, but Clinton also had 20 percent of House Republicans and a third of Senate Republicans. In the 2002 Iraq War authorization, crossover was even higher, perhaps unsurprising given the attack on US soil. In the House, nearly 40 percent of Democrats voted to authorize Bush to use force, while 42 percent of Senate Democrats did the same.[103]

It is important to note that some legislative incentives reduce the attractiveness of war. Party leaders can face agenda costs if war crowds out other business. Kriner documents how the Iraq War eventually began to swamp Bush's other priorities, for example.[104] War also injects uncertainty into elections, which helps explain why members generally do not like to take risky votes on war, as their relief at not having to vote on a Syria authorization in 2013 shows.[105] However, as I discuss later in this chapter, incentives vary for hawkish and dovish leaders and elites, but there are reasons to expect that incentives push in the direction of supporting hawkish policies.

What Can Leaders Do? Facing Public and Elite Constraints

Thus far we have established that leaders face two audiences that have different tools (usable at different times), different information, and different preferences. To understand how these audiences affect the domestic politics of war, we need one more piece of the puzzle: comparing how leaders can respond to public and elite constraints.

Facing Voters and Their Faithful Intermediaries

In the faithful intermediaries model, leaders have limited tools for addressing voter-driven constraints. They can select "good" wars; they can make the best effort to win the wars they fight; and they can try to persuade voters, channeling messages through elites. Elites influence the politics of war through open debate that generates the presence of elite consensus or disagreement, which,

TABLE 2-2. Elite Discourse, Outcomes, and Electoral Consequences

	Successful War	Failing or Failed War	Stay Out
Elite consensus	Salience: high but short-lived (rally effects) Electoral consequences: low (opposition supported) Example: 1991 Gulf War	Salience: low–medium depending on scale of war Electoral consequences: low (opposition cover) Example: Vietnam War (prior to 1968)	Salience: low Electoral consequences: low (opposition supported) Example: 2013 Syria Crisis
Elite division	Salience: high Electoral consequences: possible electoral rewards (opposition opposed) Rare because opposition strategic	Salience: high; rising? Electoral consequences: possible electoral punishment (opposition opposed and can exploit), especially for hawkish leaders Example: Lebanon 1984	Salience: possibly high, especially for dovish leaders Electoral consequences: possible

Note: Shading indicates greater political risk to leaders.

in turn, serves as a conduit for information and can raise or lower the salience of conflict in elections.

Table 2-2 illustrates how the configuration of cues interacts with outcomes to affect potential electoral consequences. Table 2-2 makes clear that it is safer for the leader to be in the top row, with elite consensus. If the war goes well, there may be a rally effect, but political benefits may be short-lived, because opposition parties are strategic and will support wars they think are likely to be successful.[106] If the war goes poorly or the leader decides to stay out, opposition support for the government provides political cover.

The bottom row, with elite dissensus, is riskier. In the lower-left corner, elites are divided about a war that is successful—an outcome the leader would presumably like to make highly salient, but that is unlikely to occur because the opposition is strategic. Furthermore, war is a gamble, so it is useful for leaders to have some political cover. In the lower middle box, however, elites are divided, and the war is not going well. This configuration is the most risky for any leader, but especially so for those from parties whose brand depends on military competence. The opposition is likely motivated to raise the salience of the conflict, and the risk of political or even electoral consequences are real. Finally, in the right-hand column, leaders must consider the risks of staying out of a conflict, or choosing to limit the scale of further commitments. The opposition can politicize the conflict for political advantage (the case of elite division, in the lower-right corner). If there is elite consensus, however, as in the top-right column, then leaders have political cover to avoid conflict, as in Obama's choice in the 2013 Syria crisis.

The faithful intermediaries model makes three crucial assumptions about the politics of war. First, it assumes that democratic elites have relatively unfettered access to information, even if they are in the opposition party.[107] Second, it assumes leaders do not have agency to try to generate consensus. Third, it assumes the main (if not only) costs elites impose on leaders is publicizing information. If these assumptions hold, then the public can get the information it needs to hold leaders accountable. But if elites do not have good information, then the information they transmit to the public may be distorted. If elites can impose other costs on the leader, then they can reward or punish decisions about the use of force at different times, for different reasons. And if leaders can manage the consensus the public sees—that is, can shift from the bottom to the top row of table 2-2 through bargaining—the public will get a picture that reflects elite politics, rather than the efforts of their faithful intermediaries.

Playing the Insiders' Game

The insiders' game model starts from the premise that leaders do not have to accept the presence or absence of elite consensus as given. A key question is how leaders get to the top row of table 2-2. For example, is it worth the cost to secure consensus, even if it means choosing war or escalation as a risky gamble versus staying out? Is bringing political antagonists into a coalition worth the risk of giving them information and leverage? The answers depend on how costly it is for leaders to bargain with elites. Democratic leaders can make use of the finite nature of the elite audience in two main ways: side payments and information management.

SIDE PAYMENTS AND THE USE OF FORCE. Public-driven theories of democracies and war often assume side payments away, because democratic leaders cannot dole out private goods to voters to make up for military misadventures or poor war performance.[108] Persuading voters, however, presents its own challenges, reflected in evidence from the United States that the "bully pulpit" is not very effective.[109] It may be simpler for democratic leaders to convince other elites, who are a smaller, finite audience, to support a decision about the use of force.

Typically, we think of side payments as a benefit that compensates the recipients for their support of a policy. As Riker argues, a threat can also be a form of side payment, which "consists of a promise not to carry out the threat and the gain of the follower is simply escape from misfortune."[110] Similarly, Milner argues that side payments encompass a broad array of tactics, including both explicit transfers and logrolls as well as implicit deals, and promises of benefits as well as threats such as party discipline or other forms of future reprisals.[111] As Milner notes, all varieties of side payments have the common feature that "an actor gives up value on one issue of lesser importance in order to gain value from others on an issue of greater importance."[112] What makes side payments possible, then, is that "individuals have different preferences or different intensities of preferences across issue areas."[113]

One might reasonably ask why side payments do not wreck the credibility of elite cues about the advisability of war, if leaders seem to be "buying" support. One reason is that elites who are less-informed about an issue may look to those with better information—and if the side payment is large enough but not too large, and the better-informed elite accepts, then the side payment can convey information about whether the policy is wise.[114] Another reason is that leaders can obfuscate or distribute side payments to make them less obvious, or make an implicit bargain.[115] For example, as Betts describes, promotions and "lateral transfers" are a common tool presidents use to "move unwanted officers out of Washington or out of field commands," because such a "maneuver minimizes the embarrassment of the rejected general and forestalls protests by suspicious members of Congress." Betts notes that "such transfers are, in effect, bribes."[116] The public likely pays more attention to the substance of cues rather than process.

The politics of the use of force suggest three main categories of side payments. The first are broadly political, requiring leaders to pay in scarce political resources, such as political support (or opposition), patronage (or lack of it), or procedural concessions involving time and political capital. For elected elites, examples include campaign support, the threat of electoral harm that is then removed, forced votes on war resolutions, or reputational or career benefits or damage. Elites of all types can receive appointments, promotions, or the leader's favor. Leaders can usually frame these moves as necessary for national security. Legislative consultation and procedural votes can be political goods that further some members' reputations. Alternatively, elites may seek the blessing of an international organization (IO) like the United Nations as a source of legitimacy, but such a move could be time-consuming.[117]

A second form side payments can take is conflict-related policy concessions. For those with strong views about when and particularly how to use military force, concessions on the size of deployments or the choice of strategy can make supporting war more attractive. These concessions ultimately affect war effort and the probability of success, a point I return to later in this chapter.[118] If the decision is to avoid conflict, leaders may substitute policies such as sending security assistance or military "advisers," a tactic that can increase the chances of having to make another decision about using force later (as successive presidents found during the Vietnam War, discussed in chapter 5).

A third form of side payment is a policy concession on an issue not directly related to the crisis or conflict, which can lead to policy spillover. If the issue relates to foreign policy or national security, it can more easily be framed in national security terms, or folded into overall security policy. Budget increases—which Feaver reports were part of Bush's strategy to keep the military on board with the Iraq surge—allow organizations to pursue other projects.[119] Other policies can be logrolled into the decision, as occurred with Taiwan policy at the start of the Korean War, discussed in chapter 4. Side payments on domestic policies are possible, but less likely, because leaders want to avoid such explicit trades. Leaders can effectively smuggle domestic priorities into elite bargaining, however, by making security-related side payments that save political capital and time to pursue those priorities.

INSIDER INFORMATION MANAGEMENT. Elites cannot constrain what they don't know about. The second tool leaders can use to manage elites is the strategic control of information within elite circles. Many theories of democracies and war assume that elites, including the opposition, have good access to information and that there is robust debate in the "marketplace of ideas."[120]

The marketplace of ideas is not straightforward in democracies contemplating war.[121] Judgements about the advisability of war turn on estimates of the probability of success, and many elites must estimate the probability of success with little information. Seeking out information on the likelihood of war success can be time consuming for elites who do not regularly focus on foreign policy or national security, making them functionally more like members of the public awaiting cues from other elites. Assessing new information that affects estimates of the probability of success, such as information about military operations or details about the capabilities or internal politics of other countries, requires domain-specific knowledge.[122]

Leaders thus have incentives to target estimates of the probability of success as they try to shape elite constraints for or against the use of force. These incentives apply especially to presidents who seek opposition-party support. Schultz notes that the opposition must "choose its battles wisely," because there "is no benefit in presenting an alternative to a policy that is popular or widely regarded as successful."[123] As Zaller shows, members of Congress during the 1990–91 Gulf War wanted to be on the "right" side of the conflict, but "the most politically relevant aspect of the decision, the outcome of the war, was unknown."[124] In the 2003 Iraq War, the Bush administration exerted significant effort to frame the probability of success as very high, as discussed in chapter 7.

Just as elite cues can alter the substance and timing of information that reaches the voters, leaders' ability to manage information at many different stages of decision making can distort the flow of information that voters need to impose constraints. Inside government, leaders manage who gets access to information in executive-branch meetings. Leaders can set the agenda for what information the bureaucracy gathers or seeks out, and they can manipulate or politicize intelligence, as Joshua Rovner has documented.[125] Leaders can shape information transmission by controlling which executive-branch military and civilian elites consult with or testify before the legislature. Opposition parties are therefore likely to see only a selective sample of information. The surprising (and therefore credible) nature of dissent from the leader's own party also means the leader must be careful to manage information even with copartisans. All this can occur before leaders disclose decisions publicly. Leaders can use information management to alter how the public perceives the likely odds of success in war, and prevent elites from pulling the fire alarm when the public might wish to hear it. They can also use these tools to dampen the salience of war without using secrecy.

These tools enable democratic leaders to disrupt the formation of a coalition that opposes their preferred policy. Punishing or ousting a leader in any regime requires coordination, a process dictators are skilled at disrupting through the tools of authoritarian control such as coup proofing.[126] Elites in democracies face different coordination challenges, but they are challenges nonetheless. For example, opposition critics fear political punishment if not enough like-minded people support an effort to impose costs on or punish the leader. Side payments and information help the leader raise the costs of coordination for policy opponents.

The Sources of Hawkish Bias: The Price and Currency of Elite Support

We can now generate hypotheses and observable implications from the insiders' game model. I assume that parties are branded as hawkish or dovish, and that dovish parties have a credibility deficit—that is, the democracy is not one like Germany or Japan where hawks are mistrusted for historical reasons. I outline these first in general terms and then make them more concrete in the US case, setting the stage for testing the theory.[127]

A democratic leader's strategy for building support for war policy depends on the value of having certain elites in the coalition—as Lyndon Johnson said of J. Edgar Hoover, better to have them "inside the tent pissing out, than outside pissing in"—and the price of gaining their support.[128] Both the absolute cost of obtaining support and how those costs manifest—the currency—matter to the leader. Different leaders may wish to pay in different currencies. The price and currency of elite support depend on both what elites think and their power to inflict costs on the leader. Table 2-3 illustrates two policy

TABLE 2-3. Elite Policy and Institutional Preferences

	Escalatory Action		Deescalatory Action	
	Hawks	Doves	Hawks	Doves
Copartisan/ Insider	Natural allies	Cross-pressured	Cross-pressured	Natural allies
Opposition	Reluctant allies	Natural opponents	Natural opponents	Reluctant allies

Note: Darker shading indicates larger costs for leaders to gain elite support for their chosen action (escalatory or deescalatory).

choices, one escalatory, such as initiating the use of force or escalating a conflict in progress, and one deescalatory, such as staying out of a conflict or choosing not to escalate. The columns capture elites' policy preferences, that is, hawkish or dovish. The rows capture institutional positions: in the top row are elected copartisans, as well as military and civilian insiders. In the bottom row are elected elites in the opposition party.

Table 2-3 shows when policy and political preferences point in the same direction, and when they conflict. For example, hawks favor escalatory action on both policy and political grounds when they share the leader's party or serve in government, making them natural allies if the leader chooses escalatory action. If hawks are in opposition, however, they have countervailing instincts: they favor escalatory action and want to avoid looking unpatriotic, but they do not want to hand the leader of the other party a political victory, especially if they estimate the probability of success to be low. Escalatory action makes opposition hawks reluctant allies who face cross pressure but are likely to support the leader's choice. Similarly, copartisan or insider doves are natural allies for a leader who chooses deescalatory action, and reluctant allies if they are in the opposition. In contrast, copartisan or insider doves are cross-pressured when the leader escalates and the leader's task is to keep them loyal; the same is true for copartisan or insider hawks if the leader chooses deescalatory action. When doves are in the opposition, they are natural opponents of leaders who escalate, and opposition hawks are natural opponents of leaders who choose deescalatory action. Looking across columns of table 2-3, hawks need convincing to support deescalatory action, and doves need persuading to support escalatory action. Across rows, opposition elites are more reluctant to support the leader than are copartisans or insiders.

Under the faithful intermediaries model, we would expect that leaders face similar costs to get or keep hawks and doves inside the tent. For example,

TABLE 2-4. Mechanisms of Hawkish Bias

	Leaders from Dovish Parties	Leaders from Hawkish Parties
Countertype selection pressure	**High:** appoint hawks to close credibility gap	**Low:** hawkish party more credible on national security
Agenda costs	**High:** dovish parties prioritize nonsecurity issues	**Low:** national security central to hawkish party's agenda
Cost of countertype elite support	**High:** hawkish elites get little private benefit from supporting dovish policies, difficult to co-opt	**Low:** dovish elites get private benefits from supporting hawkish policies, easier to co-opt

getting opposition doves to support escalatory action should about as difficult as getting opposition hawks to support deescalatory action. In contrast, in the insiders' game model, the price and currency of elite support varies, as indicated by progressively darker shading in table 2-3 that reflects larger costs for leaders to gain elite support. Leaving the leader's own preferences aside for the moment, the most difficult "get" for a leader is convincing opposition hawks to accept deescalatory action, because their institutional preferences are squarely against the leader and their policy preferences are more intense and specific than those of opposition doves. Likewise, hawks inside government are harder to keep loyal for deescalatory action than doves are to keep loyal for escalation. These differences do not mean that doves do not care at all about these issues, but rather that there are differences—opening space to bargain. This logic leads to the following hypotheses:

- Leaders face higher costs to get hawkish elites to support peace / deescalatory action than to get dovish elites to support war / escalatory action.
- Leaders face higher costs to obtain opposition support than to keep cross-pressured copartisans or insider elites in their coalition.

When we consider the preferences and incentives of leaders from hawkish and dovish parties, the asymmetry in constraints only grows more pronounced, pushing more in the direction of hawkish bias. These asymmetric constraints stem from three mechanisms: selection pressures, agenda costs, and the cost of countertype elite support, which in turn depends on elite political incentives, including private benefits of war. These mechanisms are summarized in table 2-4, showing how leaders from dovish parties face greater constraints as a result.

Selection Pressures

Leaders have wide discretion to choose advisers and officials who share their policy preferences and worldview. Typically, leaders staff their government with members of their party's "bench" of foreign policy and national security experts. But leaders also appoint advisers and cabinet officials for competence, loyalty, expertise, and experience, as well as relations among different advisers. Leaders may actively seek out diverse views—what Alexander George called "multiple advocacy."[129] Leaders also have political motives to appoint advisers, such as appeasing a wing or faction of their party, as in the case of William Jennings Bryan's appointment as secretary of state under Woodrow Wilson, and Hillary Clinton's appointment under Barack Obama.[130] We should thus expect a range of views inside most governments. This distribution of views generates some uncertainty over just how hawkish or dovish the government really is, because, as Schultz points out, it is not clear whether moderate or extreme views dominate the government, or whether the leader must cater to these factions.[131] Such uncertainty is an important prerequisite for elite cues to carry information about policy credibility, because if there were perfect overlap, signals would not be informative.[132]

A leader from a dovish party, however, faces selection pressures to include hawkish voices in government. A dovish party's credibility deficit affects its affiliated leaders and elites no matter their true preferences. In the US context, Democratic presidents have a history of appointing hawkish advisers, including installing Republicans as secretary of defense. The crossover has never gone in the other direction.[133] Aside from the credibility deficit, dovish leaders need military and civilian appointees to manage military resources, planning, and personnel, and those qualified are more likely to have hawkish views, or at least are unlikely to have truly dovish views. In general, dovish leaders are likely to face greater challenges because there are many more senior conservative military officers available to appoint (that is, an undersupply of those who might have more dovish views).[134] Because cues from within government have institutional credibility—a member of the leader's own team speaking out is surprising and newsworthy—and because dovish leaders face a credibility deficit that hawks can confirm if they go public, hawkish elites in a dovish leader's government have significant leverage and have more intense and specific preferences the leader must consider accommodating. In the US context, for example, although presidents of both parties have found it difficult to replace military service chiefs with whom they disagree because of the political costs, presidents like Kennedy and Johnson have felt this pressure more acutely. As Betts notes, Kennedy and Johnson both wanted to replace hawks like Curtis LeMay but "felt too vulnerable to charges of stifling military experts."[135] Kennedy did replace other chiefs but with appointments (i.e., side payments) to give them a soft landing, such as Chief of Naval Operations George W. Anderson, who became ambassador to Portugal.[136]

Hawks from the party associated with national security policy face less pressure to make dovish appointments. To be sure, hawkish governments also contain diverse views and are by no means spared internal disagreements. The range of views inside hawkish administrations is more likely to run from a more restrained view of the use of force, such as the skepticism of foreign interventions exhibited by many military or former military leaders like Colin Powell, to moderate hawks, to more extreme hawks. Overall, selection pressures lead to the following hypothesis:

- Leaders from dovish parties face stronger pressure from hawks inside their governments than leaders from hawkish parties face from doves inside their governments.

Agenda Costs

Agenda costs are an important source of the asymmetry in constraints on hawkish and dovish leaders. The difference in how leaders and elites prioritize the outcome of a decision to use force generates leverage for elites in a position to impose agenda costs. If the potential costs of appeasing these elites are sufficiently high, even a leader who would prefer not to fight or escalate may calculate that the agenda costs are too high to avoid war.

In general, dovish leaders and dovish elites, who tend to come from left-leaning parties, have a larger domestic policy agenda than do hawks, who have a greater focus on foreign affairs and national security. Again, this argument need not mean doves do not care at all about national security. Doves may care a great deal about reducing military budgets or reforming national security institutions, for example. Nor does it mean that hawkish parties have no domestic agenda. But doves likely care more about domestic priorities than national security issues. In the US context, scholars of American politics have provided a wealth of evidence to support this asymmetry in priorities and the size of the parties' domestic legislative agendas.[137] Left-leaning governments are associated with a larger welfare state.[138] Left governments also tend to have policy goals that require complex legislation to build new government systems, rather than downsizing them or cutting taxes.[139] In the context of the United States, Grossmann and Hopkins argue that the Democratic Party, "composed of a coalition of social groups making specific programmatic demands on government," pursues "large-scale legislative and administrative programs to address a variety of social problems." In contrast, Republicans, who are "agents of an ideological movement . . . skeptical of the assumption that government action can ameliorate social problems," tend to talk about policy "in general terms" and are "more content than Democrats with inaction or legislative gridlock."[140] One implication is that the nature of a party skeptical of government leaves room for the intense policy demanders on foreign and defense policy.

The extent of this difference varies across democracies, but theoretically it makes sense that leaders from left-leaning parties "need" more out of both the legislature and the government itself to execute their policy priorities— leaving doves with more agenda cost exposure in matters of war and peace. At the level of individuals, hawks, particularly those with national security roles or portfolios, care more about decisions to use force as well as other national security issues that do not relate to the military crisis. A dovish leader who prioritizes other issues may find it expedient to appease hawkish demands, which are likely to encompass either war policy concessions or policy concessions on other national security issues, leading to policy spillover.

Additionally, hawkish elites, many of whom will have ready access to the leader in times of crisis or conflict, can threaten agenda costs with less coordination, or overcome coordination issues more easily than dovish elites, who face higher hurdles to gaining the leader's ear in debates about military force. A dovish leader is hardly likely to deny hawkish voices a hearing when making a decision about the use of force. For dovish elites challenging a hawkish leader, coordination problems loom larger. Unless they are committed doves, elites with dovish preferences might be reluctant to challenge a hawkish leader, lest they bear the blame for undermining the president's coercive diplomacy or an ongoing war effort. Dovish leaders may fall back on procedural or process-based demands, which are less likely to run these risks—but are also cheaper for hawkish leaders to satisfy.

These arguments about agenda costs and agenda exposure lead to the following hypotheses:

- Hawkish elites can more easily threaten to impose agenda costs on dovish leaders than dovish elites can threaten to impose agenda costs on hawkish leaders.
- Leaders from dovish parties are more likely to pay costs in terms of war policy concessions or concessions on other national security issues, rather than in terms of agenda costs.

Cost of Countertype Elite Support

The third mechanism of hawkish bias is the asymmetry in the costs of gaining countertype elite support. As discussed above, dovish elites can gain private benefits from supporting a war even if they have misgivings. These can be agenda benefits (i.e., pursuing a favored priority) or career benefits (e.g., supporting a war they believe will be successful, especially if they have future plans to run for office). Private benefits need not be enormous, but they can make supporting war more attractive for doves, lowering the cost for hawkish leaders to obtain their support. Furthermore, the side payments doves can extract are more likely to be procedural or political, rather than costs that directly tax the hawk's main priority. Doves are unlikely to win concessions on military spending or national security reforms in times of crisis or war. Given the higher costs dovish elites face in challenging a hawkish leader's choice to use force, extracting procedural or political concessions may seem like a win for dovish elites and a relatively low price for hawkish leaders to pay.

In contrast, hawkish elites do not reap the same benefits from supporting peace, although copartisan hawks may do so out of loyalty. The benefits of peace may accrue more to the leader than to elites in the party or bureaucratic institutions as a whole. As intense policy demanders—whose policy views may not match what the public wants—hawks do not gain much from a hawkish leader's decision to pursue a dovish course.[141] Going to China might have made Nixon look like a statesman, but many hawks were left as reluctant, unsatisfied allies, especially concerned with the abandonment of Taiwan.[142] Under a dovish leader, hawkish elites, particularly those in the opposition party, have little incentive to support peace or deescalatory action unless they are well compensated, especially knowing how valuable their endorsement will be for the dovish leader. The hawks' price is likely to relate to national security, their more highly prioritized issue area. For example, in the ratification negotiation for the New START nuclear arms reduction treaty between the United States and Russia, the Obama administration agreed to a massive nuclear modernization plan to secure Republican support.[143]

The asymmetric private benefits of war lead to the following hypotheses:

- Dovish elites have more potential for private gain from supporting war than hawkish elites have from supporting peace.
- Leaders from dovish parties face higher costs to obtaining hawkish elite support for peace than leaders from hawkish parties face in obtaining dovish elite support for war.

Informational Costs and Benefits

Although it is not a mechanism of hawkish bias per se, these three mechanisms have important effects on the informational costs and benefits of elite cues about the leader's policies. Elite bargaining can enable or dampen these cues in ways that distort information flow to other elites or to the public. Cues can be effective for three reasons: institutional credibility (who cue givers are); substantive surprise (what cue givers say, i.e., a statement that goes against the cue giver's type, such as a hawkish adviser opposing war); or as reinforcing or countering party brands (e.g., a hawkish adviser opposing war under a dovish president, or a dovish adviser supporting war under a hawkish president). The latter builds on Trager and Vavreck's finding that opposition-party support is most useful for true-to-type actions.[144] These hypotheses are elaborated and tested in chapter 3 using survey experiments but can be summarized as follows:

- **Institutional Credibility Hypothesis:** Insider or copartisan cues that oppose the leader will have stronger effects on support for war and leader approval than will same-party or insider support or opposition-party criticism.
- **Countertype Signal Hypothesis:** Insider or copartisan cues that run counter to the cue giver's type (e.g., dovish adviser supporting war, or hawkish adviser supporting peace) will have a greater effect on support for war and leader approval than will cues that are expected based on the cue giver's type (e.g., dovish adviser opposing war, or hawkish adviser supporting war).
- **Countertype Signals and Party Brands Hypothesis:** Adviser cues that run counter to party brands will have larger effects on support for war and leader approval than those that reinforce the brand. For leaders from a dovish party, a hawkish adviser's support for a decision for peace will have a larger effect than a hawkish adviser supporting a decision for war. For leaders from a hawkish party, a dovish adviser supporting war will have a larger effect than a dovish adviser supporting peace.

Given these hypotheses, we would expect that for leaders from dovish parties, the most valuable cue is a hawkish adviser who supports peace or deescalatory action, while for a leader from a hawkish party, it is a dovish or more restrained adviser endorsing war, as in the case of Colin Powell in the George W. Bush administration, discussed in chapter 7. Per the discussion above, we need not assume that there are asymmetries in the effectiveness of cues on public opinion for hawkish and dovish leaders, because incentives to appear moderate act as a brake on asymmetries arising from public opinion. But even if the cues are equally effective, the price to obtain or suppress them is not. A dovish adviser's support for war benefits a hawkish leader but is less costly to obtain. It is important to reiterate that the possibility of bargaining makes these cues potentially less useful to voters because they will not necessarily be connected or timed to the public interest. For example, as discussed in chapter 7, the leak of General Stanley McChrystal's report on Afghanistan can be thought of as an "early" fire alarm that put hawkish pressure on Obama in the public sphere and may have led him to a more hawkish choice than he would have liked, because the leak raised the price to satisfy hawks through bargaining.

Democratic Distortions:
The Dove's Curse and the Hawk's Misadventure

We come now to the democratic distortions introduced by the insiders' game. The mechanisms of hawkish bias do not determine the leader's choices, but they lead to very different political trade-offs for leaders from hawkish and dovish parties. As noted, even when parties are strongly branded there is uncertainty about whether a given leader is truly hawkish or dovish, or represents an extreme or moderate wing, and thus all leaders from the party feel the effects of party brands. For simplicity, unless otherwise noted, I refer to "hawkish" and "dovish" leaders as shorthand for leaders from hawkish and dovish parties. Table 2-5 summarizes the asymmetric trade-offs dovish and hawkish leaders face when they make a decision about whether to fight or take escalatory action, or stay out of conflict or take deescalatory action. Leaders have their own policy preferences and can act "true to type" or "against type."

Consider first the trade-off for dovish leaders, in the top row. A dovish leader can choose peace or deescalatory action but has to pay a high, elite-driven political price. Leaders can make this "dove's choice," of course, choosing to absorb the cost and staying out of war. President Obama's decision in the 2013 Syria crisis, for example, was to hold a vote in Congress to get congressional buy-in for any decision to use force or to stay out.[145] Notably, Obama was a second-term president during this crisis, with less to lose on the domestic legislative front. But throwing the decision to Congress also chewed up legislative time, increased salience, and gave the opposition a talking point. In addition to paying the costs directly, another route to a "dove's choice" is to avoid insider hawkish pressure through selection, a case illustrated by President Biden's decision to withdraw from Afghanistan. As discussed in chapter 7, Biden came into office with strongly held views on withdrawing from Afghanistan and chose advisers who would support that effort.

A dovish leader can instead choose to fight, with the against-type action lowering the price to keep elites inside the tent, at least initially. To be sure, some elites will oppose fighting on policy or political grounds, but loyalty and the private benefits for dovish elites who support hawkish policies make it easier for dovish leaders to placate disgruntled doves. The political trade-off between fighting and staying out is stark for leaders from dovish parties.

This seemingly clear trade-off can be a trap for dovish leaders, however, leading to the "dove's curse." Having faced greater selection pressures to appoint hawkish advisers to mitigate the dovish party brand, dovish leaders face

TABLE 2-5. The Elite Politics of War and Peace

	Peace / Deescalatory Action	War / Escalatory Action
Leader from dovish party	*Dove's choice* (act true to type) High cost	*Dove's curse* (act against type) Low cost
Leader from hawkish party	*Hawk's advantage* (act against type) Moderate cost	*Hawk's (mis)adventure* (act true to type) Low to moderate cost

Note: Shading indicates the outcomes predicted by the insiders' game model to be the most likely; faithful intermediaries model would predict the against-type actions on the diagonals would be most likely.

monitoring and pressure from those same hawkish advisers as the war goes on. If dovish leaders meet insider hawks at the point where they are willing to support the leader's policy choice, they may end up compromising on military strategy in a way that leads to protracted, indecisive conflicts. The dove's curse acts as a ratchet effect where placating insider hawks prolongs a war that seemed like a more politically palatable option at the time.

Turning to leaders from hawkish parties in the bottom row of table 2-5, on the left we see the familiar "hawk's advantage" in diplomacy, where hawks are advantaged in making peace overtures as in the case of Nixon going to China. On the right, however, is the "hawk's (mis)adventure," when hawks act according to their true type—that is, they follow their hawkish policy preferences and choose to fight or escalate. As I have argued, the insiders' game predicts that this true-to-type behavior is easier politically for hawks than for doves, because the cost of dovish elite support that neutralizes the hawkish stereotype is lower. The outcome need not be a misadventure in the sense of a risky military operation known to be ill fated from the outset. The theory does not preclude a hawk from acting selectively and cautiously when choosing whether to fight. But hawks can more easily pursue such military ventures because the deference hawkish leaders enjoy on national security and the relative ease with which they can secure elite support reduce the *ex ante* constraints on going to war.

Table 2-5 offers one way to see the hawkish bias in the insiders' game: the two most likely outcomes are war or escalatory policy, by both hawkish and dovish leaders, as indicated by the grey shading. The trade-off between war and peace is much starker for dovish leaders, while hawkish leaders can more easily obtain the backing to dampen their "warmonger" image and spread the political risk of war. This conclusion is in stark contrast to the faithful intermediaries model, under which we would expect the diagonals in table 2-5 to be the most likely outcomes, with similar incentives for leaders of both types to act against type.

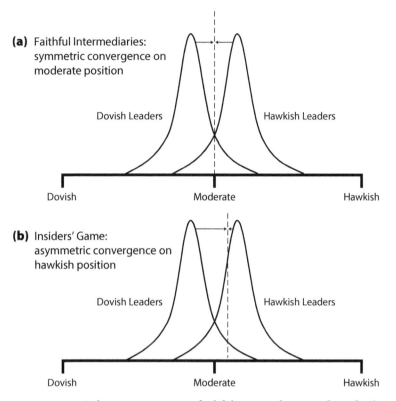

FIGURE 2-3. Policy convergence in faithful intermediaries and insiders' game models

Figure 2-3 illustrates another aspect of the insiders' game: the hawkish bias disproportionately affects dovish leaders. In the top panel, figure 2-3a, the faithful intermediaries model suggests symmetric convergence around a moderate policy—there is no bias one way or the other. In the bottom panel, figure 2-3b, we see asymmetric convergence, where both types of leaders move toward a similar policy, but at a more hawkish point on the spectrum. Dovish leaders have further to go to reach this point and end up deviating further from their preferences. None of this implies that war or escalation are inevitable. The dove can make a dove's choice, and bias is a tendency, not a deterministic force. There is also some dovish pull on hawkish leaders, although we would expect this to be smaller in magnitude. The asymmetry illustrates the incentives that make dovish preferences insufficient for avoiding war.

One question that arises from this argument is what happens if the voters are more dovish, or more hawkish. Democracies have seen shifts in aggregate opinion in the wake of events, such as more hawkish sentiment after the 9/11 attacks, or more dovish sentiment associated with war weariness in the wake of the Iraq War.[146] As discussed in chapter 7, however, many of these shifts were relatively brief, with aggregate opinion reverting to a somewhat moderate stance, in the sense of receptivity to new information.

But even if the public is not moderate in the aggregate, we can still expect the hawkish bias of the insiders' game to manifest, even if its magnitude is smaller. Following arguments about the value of surprising signals,[147] as well as shared values between sender and receiver, we would expect that a dovish public would respond to surprising signals from dovish elites—that is, that if a dovish leader or dovish elites choose or support war, even doves will be persuaded. This scenario is perhaps not especially interesting in the real world, since after all, if dovish elites support war in a democracy with a dovish median voter, events must be so dramatic that nearly all elites see the necessity of conflict. In the wake of Russia's 2022 invasion of Ukraine, for example, even progressive Democrats in Congress, who had ardently sought reductions in military spending, supported US military assistance to Ukraine, while in Germany, the normally pacifist Green Party became more confrontational.[148] Still, we would expect that cues from doves supporting war or escalation would persuade some dovish voters, shifting policy in a more hawkish direction even if only slightly.

In the case of a hawkish public, the effect of the insiders' game is more difficult to separate from the faithful intermediaries model. Yet the nature of these two explanations can be very different. If we assume that voters in a democracy are culturally or historically disposed to hawkishness—for example, a belligerent American culture that embraces war—then we would expect long periods without much systematic variation in the nature of that country's decision making, whereas the insiders' game predicts such variation. Even if hawkish public attitudes are more transitory, however, elites can still make surprising judgments that constrain leaders. As Schultz argues, signals can still be informative if they are surprising.[149] With hawkish voters, there may be less room for a dove's surprising embrace of force to boost public support for war, but the signal from hawkish elites who *oppose* war would still be informative. One observable implication would be that hawkish leaders, who are sensitive to war outcomes, are even more subject to early *ex post* elite constraints if the war goes poorly.

Observable Implications and Cases from the United States

I now turn the theory's lens more directly on the United States, developing hypotheses and observable implications that can be tested in the empirical chapters, while holding domestic institutions and other national-level factors

TABLE 2-6. Cross-Party Hypotheses

	Faithful Intermediaries Model	Insiders' Game Model
War initiation	Symmetric convergence on moderate position, symmetric acting "against type" by presidents of both parties	Asymmetric convergence on hawkish position; "oversupply" of Democratic wars
Escalation	Presidents of both parties seek victory	Democrats: minimum necessary Republicans: gamble for decision or deescalate
Duration/ termination	Similar across parties	Democrats: longer, inconclusive wars Republicans: higher variance (short or long wars, seek decisive outcome)

constant. I also discuss case selection, as part of the overall two-pronged empirical strategy outlined in chapter 1. The main source of variation is across parties that are associated with either dovishness or hawkishness. While the two dominant parties in the United States have both hawkish and dovish wings, since the "who lost China?" debate the Democratic Party has struggled to escape its dovish image, and Republicans have been viewed as more hawkish. This variation generates expectations for the pattern of conflict we would expect to observe across parties. The theory also generates within-case predictions for presidents from each party about which insiders will have the most leverage, what kinds of bargains presidents and elites will strike, and how they affect war.

Cross-Party Expectations

Table 2-6 summarizes the hypotheses across parties, contrasting the faithful intermediaries model with the insiders' game. While we expect the parties to converge in terms of war initiation in both models, the faithful intermediaries model predicts no particular bias one way or the other as the parties have similar incentives to act against type and converge around moderate policies. We would expect both parties to seek victory if they fight, because their main audience is the voting public. We would likewise expect similarities across parties in terms of duration and war termination.

In contrast, under the insiders' game model, we would expect against-type pressures to affect Democratic presidents more strongly, because the trade-offs between fighting and staying out of a conflict are starker for Democratic

TABLE 2-7. Presidents, Parties, and Decisions about the Use of Force, 1945–2021

President (Party)	Interventions	Major Noninterventions
Truman (D)	Korea, 1950	Chinese Civil War, 1948; carrying Korean War into China
Eisenhower (R)	Lebanon, 1958	Indochina, 1954; Suez, 1956; Iraq, 1958
Kennedy (D)	Vietnam counterinsurgency, 1962	Cuba, 1961 (overt); Laos, 1961; Cuba, 1962
Johnson (D)	Vietnam, 1965; Dominican Republic, 1965	Panama crisis, 1964
Nixon (R)	Vietnam escalation, 1969; Cambodia, 1970	Yom Kippur War, 1973
Ford (R)		Angola (overt), 1975
Carter (D)		Nicaragua, 1978–79; Afghanistan, 1979; Iran, 1979–80
Reagan (R)	Lebanon, 1982; Grenada, 1983	El Salvador/Nicaragua (overt), 1980s
George H. W. Bush (R)	Panama, 1989; Gulf War, 1991; Somalia, 1992	Carrying Gulf War to Baghdad, 1991; Bosnia, 1992
Clinton (D)	Somalia (escalation), 1993; Haiti, 1994; Bosnia, 1995; Kosovo, 1999	Rwanda, 1994
George W. Bush (R)	Afghanistan, 2001; Iraq, 2003	Darfur, 2004
Obama (D)	Afghanistan "surge," 2009; Libya, 2011; Iraq (counter-ISIS), 2014	Syria, 2013
Trump (R)		Iran (overt escalation), 2020
Biden (D)		Afghanistan (continuation), 2021

Note: Interventions defined as overt deployments with ground troops (see Saunders 2011, ch. 1 for discussion).

presidents than for Republican presidents. We would thus expect more Democratic-initiated conflicts than we would anticipate based on the party's dovish image and base of support.

This prediction helps resolve a puzzle about US presidents and war. Why have the most dovish political leaders—Democratic presidents—initiated and escalated so many of America's wars? Despite the persistent charge of weakness, Democratic presidents have fought and escalated many wars (defined as overt deployments with ground troops) since 1945, as shown in table 2-7.

TABLE 2-8. Within-Case Observable Implications for Democratic Presidents

	Side Payments	Information
War initiation	To insider/opposition hawks: • Policy spillover: concessions on other foreign policy issues • War policy concessions To copartisan doves: • Procedural/political concessions or benefits • Attention to domestic priorities	Fear early fire alarm from hawks Dampen salience of war
Escalation	To insider/opposition hawks: • War policy concessions (minimum necessary)	Cut extreme hawks out of the loop Manage testimony Dampen salience
Duration/ termination	Prolong inconclusive wars	Fire alarm too late to stop escalation Delayed accountability from insiders or copartisan Democrats

Indeed, in their study of Congress and the use of force, Howell and Peve-house find that Republican and Democratic presidents use force at similar rates.[150] This pattern should surprise us, given the Democratic Party's tradi-tionally more restrained view of military force. I argue that it represents an "oversupply" of wars under Democratic presidents, relative to what the faithful intermediaries model would expect.

The insiders' game also generates cross-party expectations for differences in how presidents pursue escalation and decide when and how to end wars. Democratic presidents are more likely to escalate with the minimum level of force necessary to placate hawkish insiders, while Republicans are more likely to gamble for a decision or deescalate. These differences suggest that Democratic presidents will fight longer yet inconclusive wars, as Gelb and Betts describe, knowingly choosing a strategy of doing what is "minimally necessary" to avoid losing, rather than winning.[151] In contrast, Republicans will have higher-variance outcomes, that is, short or long wars.

To see these latter cross-party implications, it is useful to unpack the within-party observable implications we would expect to observe in the cases, sum-marized in table 2-8 for Democratic presidents, and table 2-9 for Republican presidents. The faithful intermediaries model does not expect these systematic

TABLE 2-9. Within-Case Observable Implications for Republican Presidents

	Side Payments	Information
War initiation	To insider doves: • Patronage/career benefits • Procedural concessions To opposition doves: • Political pressure or benefits • Procedural concessions	Shape perceptions of probability of success
Escalation	To insider doves (and hawks?): • War policy concessions • Seek a decisive outcome To opposition doves: • Political threats • Domestic policy concessions	Cut insider doves out of the loop Manage testimony (especially on war progress or success)
Duration/ termination	Short or long; Accountability from opposition Democrats	Fire alarm too late to stop initiation Threat from insider doves or opposition Democrats can constrain escalation

differences in how elite politics unfold under presidents of different parties, because elites are merely conduits of public preferences.

Within-Case Expectations for Democratic Presidents

If a Democratic president chooses to act against type and take escalatory action, the theory generates expectations about how Democratic presidents will bargain with elites and the consequences of those bargains for the course of the war. At the war's outset, the costs of dovish opposition will be muted, because doves are expected to oppose the use of force. Insider or copartisan doves would also have political incentives to support the president, and the escalatory action itself provides private benefits to many of them. Keeping these doves on board should require a relatively small side payment, such as a procedural or political concession, like an authorization from an international organization (IO) like the United Nations, which can also reassure the Democratic base.[152]

Once involved in a war, however, Democratic presidents risk the ratchet effect of the "dove's curse." Their war-related decisions are subject to monitoring by the very insider hawks that enhance their national security credibility.

Democratic presidents likely want to keep war limited, to dampen salience and press on with other priorities, while hawks with intense and specific policy preference may demand larger commitments or a wider conflict. We would expect to see side payments to insider or opposition hawks in terms of concessions on the hawks' other foreign policy priorities (for example, Truman's concession on Taiwan at the outset of the Korean War, discussed in chapter 4), as well as concessions on war policy itself.

Why do Democratic presidents pursue this course? Appeasing insider hawks means it is less likely that hawks will complain to members of Congress or go public with concerns. Furthermore, these war-related side payments to insiders have some attractive properties. First, they are relatively easy to frame as militarily necessary. Second, to the extent that attentive members of Congress follow debates about strategy, these policy concessions, if large enough, may help with the Democratic president's credibility problem. Third, war-related policy concessions to insiders do not require the president to spend political resources that may be required for other priorities. The details of war strategy are unlikely to make sustained headlines since neither voters nor most members of Congress follow war policy closely, and both insiders and the president have incentives to package them in a favorable light.

For Democrats, information management in war is about dampening salience. The dove's credibility gap means that Democratic presidents fear early fire alarms from hawks that generate escalatory pressure, as the examples of Carter in South Korea and Obama in Afghanistan illustrate. We should expect Democratic presidents to try to mute hawkish pressure, and leave room for other domestic issues.[153] We would therefore expect information management within government and especially limits on information flow from the White House and the military to Congress. Democratic presidents who fight are graded on a curve, so their goal is to keep the conflict in the background by dampening its salience in order to pursue other priorities, rather than to trumpet a wartime message.

We should thus expect Democrats to choose "just enough" military strategies to keep hawks satisfied enough to stay onside, at the price of leaving hawks with scope to return with more demands, leading to potentially prolonged and inconclusive conflicts. We should also expect that these wars will last longer than they would under the faithful intermediaries model, because elite accountability will take longer to kick in. Elites risk opposing a president at war, and if they call for a larger military effort, more restrained US action may look reasonable in contrast. Because so much of the Democratic president's coalition of support is inside the fold, then, tensions within a Democratic president's own administration and party are likely to be a crucial source of elite accountability. By prolonging wars while devoting less overall effort than would be expected by a democracy aiming for victory, however, Democratic presidents risk making the war outcome itself a casualty.

Within-Case Expectations for Republican Presidents

While scholars often focus on the "hawk's advantage" in making conciliatory diplomatic moves or peace initiatives, one could argue the real advantage for a Republican president is in the lower price for acting true to type. Republican presidents face fewer initial constraints on using force because they have more elite coalition-building options and, where there are constraints, more options to maneuver around them.

Insider doves, or those with more restrained views on the use of force inside Republican administrations, are of concern to Republican presidents who wish to use force. But the selection pressures on Republican presidents are lower and thus the distance between the president's and the most dovish adviser's views is not especially large. Augmenting the ties of loyalty to keep insider doves onside should be feasible through procedural concessions or patronage, such as promotions or other career benefits. In Congress, Republican presidents can obtain opposition Democratic support for the use of force with relative ease compared to the cost Democratic presidents must pay for hawkish Republican support of a dovish policy. Republican presidents can offer some Democrats political patronage (or political threats if they do not support the war). Procedural side payments may be attractive to Democrats who believe that supporting the commander in chief is good for their party, as House Speaker Thomas "Tip" O'Neill Jr. calculated when he struck a deal to extend Reagan's Lebanon intervention under the War Powers Resolution (discussed in chapter 6). Republican presidents also have lower agenda costs relative to Democratic presidents since their domestic agenda is less complex. The time and capital spent obtaining elite support carries less opportunity cost.

A "hawk's misadventure" is by no means inevitable even if Republicans choose to fight. Since they come from the party that "owns" national security issues, however, Republican presidents should be more sensitive to war outcomes. Thus we would expect Republican presidents to exhibit higher variance in their decisions about the use of force: choosing to stay out or initiate wars under strict limits, or initiating risky wars. Regardless, Republican presidents will want to distribute responsibility by obtaining opposition support. The apparent ease of gaining opposition or insider support can prove double-edged, however. Many Republican presidents have had prior national security or foreign policy experience and have been quite selective in choosing when and how to initiate the use of military force. In some cases they have declined to do so, as in the case of Eisenhower in Dien Bien Phu or George H. W. Bush in Bosnia. In other cases they put strict limits on the scope of operations, as in Eisenhower's 1958 intervention in Lebanon or George H. W. Bush's intervention in Somalia and decision to eject Saddam Hussein from Kuwait but not to pursue regime change in Iraq.[154] In other cases, Republican presidents have been unfettered, or have seen a path around constraints, as in the case of Reagan's intervention in Lebanon and George W. Bush's initiation of the war in Iraq. The risk for Republicans is that they will initiate a risky war that turns into a "hawk's misadventure" because *ex ante* constraints were weak.

Information management can reinforce this dynamic. While Democratic presidents try to dampen overall war salience, information control under Republican presidents is likely to take a different form. For Republican presidents, obtaining the support of insider doves and opposition Democrats requires some assurance that the use of force is likely to be successful. We should expect, then, that Republican presidents are more likely to engage in information management that shapes perceptions of the probability of success before initiating war, rather than downplaying the size or scope of US involvement overall. One need not assume nefarious motives on the part of the president.[155] But limiting information about risks and framing the public case to support a high probability of success will be tempting for Republican presidents.

Once war is underway, Republican presidents may feel constraints acutely if the trajectory of the war is not smooth—and these constraints will kick in at the elite level before they reach the public. While the public can receive and interpret bad war news, pressure to support the president and coordination problems can delay the fracturing of elite consensus. Elites, therefore, are on the leading edge of ensuring that "reality asserts itself."[156]

Elite concerns likely generate cross-cutting pressures on Republican presidents. Insider and copartisan hawks, whose careers and policy preferences are tied to the war most directly and who can monitor the war up close, will want to shift resources or strategy in the hope of victory. Insider doves, however, can impose costs from within and put pressure on Republican presidents to reverse course. Additionally, Republican presidents are more likely to fight a war with the opposition as a crucial part of their coalition. The challenge for leaders to maintain their coalition rises as wars continue, and as the pace of elite scrutiny increases.[157] Negative information about the ongoing war may point elites who supported war reluctantly or as a result of bargaining back to their predispositions.[158] Since side payments to congressional Democrats will tend to take the form of political benefits, those Democrats' ears will prick up if the war appears to be going poorly enough. Indeed, Fowler argues there are some structural features of the major oversight committees that disproportionately affect Republican presidents. As Fowler notes, "the imbalance in party reputations meant that oversight would be more costly to Republican presidents, while the payoffs from calling Democratic presidents to account for their management of crises might be relatively modest."[159]

Thus while the *ex ante* constraints are lower for Republicans, allowing them an easier path to acting on hawkish instincts, the politics of war embed risks for *ex post* constraints in later stages of war. Republican presidents may thus engage in "gambling for resurrection," or more precisely, gambling for an outcome they can claim as a victory.[160] Nixon's Vietnamization strategy and Bush's surge in Iraq can be seen in this light. Alternatively, if the probability of success seems low for continuing or escalating the war, Republican presidents are more likely to end US military action. This can mean terminating the war without adding additional war aims that are appealing to some of the president's team, such as overthrowing Saddam Hussein in 1991. It can also mean cutting losses even when the president's preferences are to continue fighting, as in the case of Reagan's withdrawal from Lebanon in 1984.

When accountability arises, it should come from Democratic opposition in Congress, fed by insider skeptics. But of course, these constraints are not automatic. Republican presidents have tools to divide opposition to the war, such as raising the political costs of opposition and making some war concessions. Chapters 6 and 7 illustrate these incentives in two Republican-initiated uses of force, when Ronald Reagan ultimately terminated a small war and George W. Bush escalated a large and by-then unpopular conflict.

Case Selection

As I elaborated in chapter 1, I use a two-pronged empirical approach to address the many research design challenges that arise from a theory of elite politics that involves strategic behavior. I combine survey experiments with case studies to test the theory's implications. The two approaches are directly connected: the adviser experiments in chapter 3 identify effects that are often selected out of the real world because leaders work hard to avoid them, and the cases trace the mechanisms of bargaining between leaders and elites, focusing on the cues that the experiments identify as most effective. In addition to this substantive connection between the experiments and the cases, the combination of methods helps harness the strengths and address the weaknesses of each. Survey experiments offer researchers the ability not only to control what factors vary, but also to observe how respondents view outcomes that may be rare in the real world because of strategic behavior.[161] Survey experiments come with their own limitations, however, in terms of whether they adequately reflect the real world and whether they capture how citizens would behave in a foreign policy crisis rather than how they would answer survey questions.[162]

Qualitative case studies can help illuminate the strategic behavior of elites, trace the mechanisms the theory identifies, and tease out the observable implications. But case studies, particularly those focusing on the domestic politics of war, have challenges of their own. How can we know whether presidents make concessions to advisers in response to anticipated domestic political costs or benefits, rather than events, or even a leader's own preferences? Leaders often do not admit, even in private, when they make policy concessions or side payments for political gain. Demonstrating that there would be political effects via public (or by extension, less-informed elite) opinion through the experiments bolsters the case that leaders are motivated by political factors when bargaining with elites over decisions to use force.

To give the theory an especially difficult test against the faithful intermediaries model, the case studies examine decisions not only to initiate military operations but also to escalate those ongoing, since the public is already informed about American involvement in a conflict and thus the deck is stacked in favor of the public having a more direct role.[163] In several cases, new presidents took over, and we would expect the easiest path to be ending an unpopular war for which they are not "culpable."[164] Where possible, several chapters therefore examine how different presidents handled the same ongoing conflict. As the cases of Nixon in Vietnam and Obama in Afghanistan show, however, elites can still put obstacles in these leaders' path.

Selecting cases to test both the cross-party and the within-case expectations is an additional challenge. As I have written elsewhere, it is important to consider not only decisions to go to war, but decisions not to fight.[165] Examining these noninterventions is difficult, however, especially when we need evidence from within wars to establish that the mechanisms of the theory operate. Given the level of detail required to trace the mechanisms, I choose cases of war to focus on the within-case variation and use the evidence from the survey experiments, which by design include scenarios in which presidents of each party decide to stay out of a conflict. As discussed in chapter 1, I choose cases that span the Cold War and post–Cold War periods to ensure that the findings are not merely the product of technological or geopolitical developments. For each party, I choose two cases to examine in depth, illuminating the within-case expectations for presidents from both parties. I also address other cases in less detail along the way for comparison purposes. Viewed as a whole, the cases demonstrate that Democratic presidents made concessions to hawks that exacted a steep price, while Republican presidents could more easily co-opt doves at the outset of war, but often found themselves facing elite constraints once war began.

For Democratic presidents, I examine the Korean War (chapter 4) and the Vietnam War (chapter 5). These cases are both examples of a dove's curse. To be sure, in the Korean War case especially, factors external to the insiders' game influenced Truman's decision making, not least the shock of North Korea's invasion in June 1950. Korea is also an important case because it shows what happens when the president ultimately fails to contain hawkish pressure and a hawkish elite pulls the fire alarm, as MacArthur did. Truman's firing of MacArthur triggered public backlash against Truman. But the course of the war up to that point had been heavily influenced by elite politics, including policy spillovers like the placating of the pro-Taiwan faction in Congress, which had both short-term effects on the war and long-term effects on US policy in Asia. Additionally, Truman's repeated concessions to MacArthur and attempts to dampen the salience of the war arguably delayed fire alarms that the public might have wanted to hear and, instead, enabled MacArthur to conduct risky operations that ultimately contributed to the Chinese intervention in 1951.

The Vietnam case is one that more clearly demonstrates a presidential choice for war initiation. While conserving his political capital for the legislative battles over the Great Society may not have been Lyndon Johnson's only motivation, he himself considered it a strong one. As Gelb and Betts argue, his efforts to contain elite dissent were remarkably successful, in the sense that he could pursue a middle-of-the-road strategy—the real goal of US policy in Vietnam being to not lose.[166] The war reached staggering levels of US involvement with even further escalation a real possibility until the shock of the Tet Offensive in January 1968 finally fractured Johnson's elite consensus—a fire alarm long delayed by Johnson's skill at the insiders' game. The Korea and Vietnam cases show how Democratic presidents during the Cold War—when any US military venture could be rhetorically tied to the superpower conflict and the draft and the economic consequences of the wars loomed over domestic society—could maneuver around public constraints, but at the cost of prolonging inconclusive and deadly conflicts.

Chapters 6 and 7 turn to Republican presidents. I choose two interventions with permissive but wary public opinion, one small scale (Ronald Reagan's intervention in Lebanon, explored in chapter 6) and one large scale (George W. Bush's invasion of Iraq). The course of these wars illustrates the higher-variance expectations for Republican presidents: elites constrained Reagan's war in Lebanon before public opinion turned against it, while Bush turned away from the public (and elite) rebuke in the 2006 midterm elections and instead cobbled together an elite coalition for a risky surge of troops into Iraq. Given its close connection to the Iraq War in terms of the domestic politics of the post-9/11 environment, I conclude chapter 7 with a discussion of how successive presidents managed the war in Afghanistan, from Bush's declaration of victory to Biden's choice to accept the costs of withdrawal—a "dove's choice."

In the Korea, Vietnam, and Lebanon cases, I draw on material from presidential archives as well as smaller archival collections for key actors in the cases, and published document collections such as *Foreign Relations of the United States*, published by the State Department. Where relevant, I refer to historiographical debates and point out where the insiders' game theory fits or adds value to existing accounts, as well as differentiating the findings from the expectations of the faithful intermediaries model. The Iraq and Afghanistan cases are too recent for archival records, but I rely on the available contemporaneous sources and retrospective accounts.

The theory, of course, makes probabilistic arguments. Outcomes like the dove's curse and hawk's misadventure are ideal types, and the real world is more complex. I do not suggest that public opinion never matters, or that other factors do not contribute to presidential decisions. A hawkish bias is just that—an increased likelihood, but not a sure thing. The evidence in the following chapters, however, clearly shows the imprint of this hawkish bias when we examine both the mechanisms and the trends across the cases as a whole. Presidents can keep public constraints at a remove through elite bargaining, which introduces its own, very different constraints that can smooth the path to war and yet also restrain leaders, if not as rapidly as the public might prefer.

3

Evidence from Public Opinion

THE THEORY OUTLINED IN CHAPTER 2 presents many challenges when we turn to seeking evidence in the real world. If elites lead mass opinion, public opinion polls may reflect elite leadership, and there is not likely to be much daylight between elite and public opinion—particularly at moments of high salience. Thus surveying elites and the public cannot directly address the dynamics raised in this book. A different approach is to triangulate the evidence from many sources, as the remainder of this book attempts to do. In this chapter, I present data from a set of original surveys and survey experiments conducted between 2008 and 2022.[1] Individually and collectively, these surveys paint a picture of how the public reacts to information about US military actions.

The survey data are designed to do four things. First, I present evidence about the public's knowledge of foreign policy issues and personnel. Second, using data from experiments that vary across contexts and real-world conditions, I show that presidential advisers' statements can affect public attitudes about the use of force. Third, the data show which adviser cues matter most in the insiders' game, testing the public opinion hypotheses developed in chapter 2. Fourth and finally, I report the results of an experiment that shows how elites set the terms of debate about *how* force will be used.

Although this analysis again focuses on advisers, it has implications for congressional and military elites. I focus on advisers for both theoretical and practical reasons. Scholars of public opinion and media have shown that the executive branch drives elite rhetoric about war, with the power to set the framing of military operations.[2] It follows that the politics inside an administration are crucial, and shape cues from further down the elite chain. Yet public opinion research has focused primarily on congressional and military cues.[3] Given the robustness of prior findings on congressional and military cues, I concentrate my efforts on advisers.

It is important to stress several features of the evidence presented in this chapter. First, the findings do not mean that the public is irrelevant or incompetent. On the contrary, the data are consistent with a public rationally delegating to elites. Second, they are consistent with the view that the state of the public's general views or "mood" is an important background constraint any leader would be foolish to ignore.[4] The 2014 survey experiments, conducted against a backdrop of war weariness, and a 2022 replication of the main adviser experiment, first conducted in 2016, illustrate this point. Third, the public opinion evidence in this chapter links to the qualitative evidence presented in the chapters that follow. The experiments help identify which cues would matter most under controlled conditions, while the cases help uncover evidence that presidents bargain over those cues in the real world. Some of the cues in the experiments may therefore never see the light of day or may be significantly muted in congressional and public debate—selected in or out of public discourse as a result of strategic presidential behavior. Fire alarms may occur earlier or later than we would expect under a faithful intermediaries model. Pairing experimental and qualitative evidence shows that we may observe the effect of the elite cues not in public opinion polls, but rather behind the scenes.

Public Knowledge, Foreign Policy, and the Use of Force

One basic question is what the US public knows about the politics of military force, including the actors who make the decisions. Table 3-1 provides summary data from knowledge questions I asked on the preelection waves of the Cooperative Congressional Election Study (CCES) in five different years: 2008, 2012, 2014, 2016, and 2022.[5] These studies, all fielded by the same survey firm (YouGov) on nationally representative samples, provide a snapshot of public opinion in the month leading up to three presidential elections and two midterm elections.

The top portion of table 3-1 summarizes questions about foreign policy personnel. The secretary of state is the cabinet official that gets the most news coverage.[6] The name recognition of the incumbent matters greatly, however: in 2008, 79 percent could correctly identify Condoleezza Rice, who had been prominent in the George W. Bush administration since 9/11, as the current secretary, and in 2014, 56 percent could identify John Kerry, a former presidential candidate. In 2022, only 27 percent could correctly identify Antony Blinken's position as secretary of state. Other national security positions are similarly low: 33 percent correctly identified the secretary of defense in 2012, while 20 percent correctly placed Lloyd Austin in the role in 2022; inside the White House, 14 percent could place Susan Rice as the national security advisor in 2014, while 19 percent could do so in 2016. Economic policy actors do not seem to fare much better: only 24 percent could identify Janet Yellen's job as chair of the Federal Reserve Board of Governors in 2016, while 33 percent could identify her when she was in the role of treasury secretary. These findings do not mean that voters consider these officials unimportant. Respondents may be receptive to cues

TABLE 3-1. Knowledge of US Foreign Policy Personnel and Issues, 2008–22

Year		Correct Answer	% Correct
	Personnel Questions		
2008	Who is currently the secretary of state?	Condoleezza Rice	79%
2012	Who is currently serving as the US secretary of defense?	Leon Panetta	33%
2014	Who is currently serving as the secretary of state?	John Kerry	56%
2014	Who is currently serving as the national security advisor?	Susan Rice	19%
2016	What position in government does Susan Rice currently hold?	National security advisor	14%
2016	What job in government is now held by Janet Yellen?	Chair, Federal Reserve	24%
2022	What position in government does Lloyd Austin currently hold?	Secretary of defense	20%
2022	What position in government does Antony Blinken currently hold?	Secretary of state	27%
2022	What job in government does Janet Yellen currently hold?	Secretary of the treasury	33%
	Issue Questions		
2008	What is currently the main point of conflict between the United States and Iran?	Iran's nuclear program	67%
2012	Which country is the United States' largest trading partner?	Canada	11%
2016	The Trans-Pacific Partnership, or TPP, is a trade agreement between the United States and several countries in Asia and the Pacific Rim. Is China a part of the TPP agreement?	No	28%
2016	In June, voters in Great Britain were asked to decide in a referendum whether to remain in the European Union or leave the European Union. What did they decide?	Leave	74%
2022	Is the United Kingdom currently a member of the European Union?	No	48%
2022	To the best of your knowledge, does the United States have a defense agreement with Taiwan that obligates the US to intervene militarily to help Taiwan if the Chinese government were to attack or invade the island?[a]	No	21%

Note: All percentages calculated with module weights from each CCES. Samples sizes for all surveys were n = 1,000 except in 2012, which combined two modules for n = 2,000. All percentages calculated with non-responses (i.e., missing rather than choice of "don't know") included; average frequency of non-responses was 28, or less than 2.5 percent of each sample, with no substantive differences if the non-responses were excluded.

[a] This question contained a map and introductory text: "The mainland Chinese government (officially the People's Republic of China but commonly referred to as China) regards Taiwan as a breakaway province that is part of China."

when foreign policy officials speak out, but information about their role and views or reputation provided in the cue will be informative.

In the bottom portion of table 3-1, consistent with prior research, the data show that the public can acquire knowledge of foreign policy issues that have been in the news. For example, in 2016, 74 percent of respondents correctly identified the outcome of the Brexit vote, which had taken place a few months earlier. By 2022, after the United Kingdom had officially left the European Union, 48 percent correctly said the UK was not in the EU, although 29 percent responded that they did not know. They also have basic knowledge of US relations with adversaries: 67 percent correctly identified the nuclear program as the main point of conflict between the United States and Iran in 2008.[7]

There is a significant drop-off as the questions become more specific. For example, as table 3-2 shows, in four surveys between 2012 and 2022, no more than 18 percent of respondents can correctly identify the approximate number of combat troops the US had in Iraq at the time of the survey. For comparison, knowledge about trade is also low: in 2012, only 11 percent of respondents correctly chose Canada as the largest US trading partner; in 2016 only 28 percent of respondents correctly answered that China was not part of the Trans-Pacific Partnership (TPP).

It is worth examining the Iraq questions in more detail, given the scale of the war and its salience in American politics during the Bush administration and after 2014 when the United States returned combat troops to the country. As shown in table 3-2, in 2012, 2014, 2016, and 2022, I asked respondents "How many combat troops does the United States currently have in Iraq?"[8] In the 2012 and 2014 versions, the scale was identical, ranging from zero to 100,000. In 2016 and 2022, I provided a range that ended at 50,000 but included a response option of 500, and in 2022 I replaced the response option of 1,000 with 2,500 (the number of noncombat troops that remained). In 2012, nearly a year after the official withdrawal of American troops, the correct answer was zero, a figure only 8 percent of respondents correctly identified. One might think that some respondents considered those remaining at the US embassy and might have chosen a number like 1,000, but only 4 percent did so. A combined 32 percent chose 50,000 or 100,000, and 37 percent chose "Don't know." In 2014, following a string of brutal actions like beheadings by ISIS and after Obama made a national address in September, the percentage who could correctly answer was only 14 percent, although the percentage who choose either 50,000 or 100,000 dropped to 14 percent, with 39 percent choosing "Don't know." In 2016, with the response scale limited to 50,000 at the high end, the percentage of correct responses was 18 percent, and 34 percent chose "Don't know." In 2022, when the number of combat troops was back to zero, 16 percent answered correctly, and only 10 percent chose 2,500, with 52 percent answering "Don't know."

TABLE 3-2. Knowledge of Iraq Troop Levels, 2012–22

		% Correct
2012 CCES (n = 2,000 combining two modules)		
How many combat troops does the United States currently have in Iraq? (Correct answer: 0)	**0**	**8%**
	1,000	4%
	10,000	18%
	50,000	22%
	100,000	10%
	Don't know	37%
	No response	2%
2014 CCES (n = 1,000)		
How many combat troops does the United States currently have in Iraq? (Correct answer: closest to 1,000)	0	14%
	1,000	**14%**
	10,000	18%
	50,000	10%
	100,000	4%
	Don't know	39%
	No response	2%
2016 CCES (n = 1,000)		
How many combat troops does the United States currently have in Iraq? Please choose the closest number. (Correct answer: closest to 5,000)	0	3%
	500	4%
	1,000	11%
	5,000	**18%**
	10,000	18%
	50,000	9%
	Don't know	34%
	No response	4%
2022 CCES (n = 1,000)		
How many combat troops does the United States currently have in Iraq? Please choose the closest number. (Correct answer: 0; 2,500 noncombat troops remained)	**0**	**16%**
	500	6%
	2,500	10%
	5,000	6%
	10,000	5%
	50,000	2%
	Don't know	52%
	No response	3%

Note: Correct answer in bold. All percentages calculated with module weights from each CCES, with nonresponses included in total (average frequency of nonresponse was 29, with no substantive differences if the nonresponses were excluded). Percentages may not sum to 100 because of rounding.

These questions by no means cover the foreign policy waterfront, but they are consistent with a general picture of a public that understands the basics of US friends and foes, can take in salient information, and leaves the details to others—a rational way for most people to navigate a complex world.

Leaders, Advisers, and the Politics of Using Force

How do debates about using military force inside an administration affect the politics of military ventures? In chapter 2, I generated hypotheses for how insider and copartisan cues affect public opinion; here, I refine those hypotheses to focus more directly on presidential advisers. There are three mechanisms through which advisers could send informative signals to other elites, and ultimately to the public, based on their institutional status as advisers and the substance of the cue. Many decisions to use force unfold after a process of debate. We can thus consider how adviser cues affect support for war *ex ante*, as well as approval of the president once he or she announces whether force will be used. I develop hypotheses for support for war and approval of the president's actions; later, I discuss perceptions of competence and success.

First, advisers have institutional credibility from their position on the president's team. A supportive statement from an adviser should have relatively little effect on elite or public opinion, however, because advisers are expected to support the president.[9] But if an adviser opposes the proposal, support for force is likely to decrease even before a decision in announced, because opposing a proposal under discussion is surprising and can be costly to advisers. If the president ultimately acts against the recommendation of advisers, either for or against force, presidential approval should be lower than if the president had made the same decision with full support, or at least no dissent.

> H1A: *Adviser statements opposing the use of force will reduce support for war (prior to the president announcing a decision).*
>
> H1B: *Presidents who act in opposition to their advisers will have lower approval than those who have their advisers' support.*

The effect of adviser cues may also depend on the adviser's own reputation or the substance of what the adviser says. If an adviser makes a statement that is counter to his or her own type—an adviser from the hawkish end of the spectrum coming out in opposition to a war, or a dovish adviser coming out in favor—then the statement will be surprising. Furthermore, presidents who act against countertype signals may risk a greater hit to their approval than if they buck advice from advisers who are conforming to type.

H2A: *Adviser statements that run counter to type (e.g., a dovish adviser supporting the use of force, or a hawkish adviser opposing the use of force) will have a greater effect on public support for the use of force than true-to-type adviser statements, before a decision is announced.*

H2B: *Presidents who act in opposition to advisers who make countertype statements will suffer a greater approval penalty than those who act against the advice of advisers who conform to type.*

The third mechanism draws on party brands. Advisers with a hawkish reputation who support the use of force may make it harder for a Democratic president to stay out of a conflict, for example, because the hawkish adviser's support for war may signal that the war is necessary and reinforce the stereotype of a Democrat as overly dovish if the president decides not to fight. Similarly, a relatively dovish adviser who opposes a Republican president's decision to fight could confirm the image of a Republican as too eager to use force.

The adviser's type and party brands can thus interact. When presidents wish to act according to type—that is, when a Democratic president wants to avoid the use of force, or a Republican president wishes to fight—the most beneficial endorsement would be from a countertype adviser: an adviser known to be hawkish endorsing a Democratic president's decision to stay out (or to choose a lower-level military option), or a dove endorsing a Republican president for escalating. Even when presidents act counter to type, a hawk endorsing a Republican president's decision to stay out or a dove endorsing a Democratic president who uses force would also be somewhat surprising. The costliest criticism would be from a like-minded adviser—an adviser known to be dovish criticizing a Democratic president, particularly for staying out, or a hawkish adviser criticizing a Republican president, especially for escalating.[10] These scenarios, however, are rarer, since if a dovish adviser advocates that a Democratic president should use force, for example, presumably other elites have already agreed that force is necessary. But the risk of such scenarios has concerned presidents, as in the Iraq "surge," which many military commanders and top Bush advisers opposed.[11]

H3A: *Countertype adviser cues that counteract the party brand will have larger effects on* ex ante *support for war than those that reinforce the brand. Under a Democratic president, a hawkish adviser's support for a decision not to use force will have a larger effect on support for war than a hawkish adviser supporting a decision for war. Under a Republican president, a dovish adviser supporting war will have a larger effect on support for war than a dovish adviser supporting a decision not to use force.*

H3B: *Democratic presidents who stay out of a conflict will get greater approval benefits from securing the support of a hawkish adviser. Republican presidents who fight benefit most from a dovish adviser supporting the use of force.*

Testing Advisers as Cue Givers:
Main Adviser Experiment, 2016

To test the effects of adviser cues, I conducted a survey experiment, fielded online in March 2016 through the survey firm Survey Sampling International (SSI). The survey uses a large national American sample of approximately 3,000 respondents.[12] The experiment, whose structure is depicted in table 3-3, employs a vignette mirroring a standard vignette on crisis bargaining.[13] The vignette focuses on a cross-border attack by a foreign state against a smaller neighbor; the US president must decide whether to send troops to repel the invaders.[14]

While many experiments provide all the information in a single stage, this experiment unfolds in two stages. The two-stage approach allows the initial step to unfold under some uncertainty, which more closely resembles real-world cases in which the decision plays out amid debate and ambiguity. In the first stage, the president considers whether to use force; in the baseline condition, there is no statement from an adviser, but in the other four adviser treatment conditions, a key adviser, who can be either hawkish or dovish, makes a statement supporting or opposing force; respondents are then asked whether they support or oppose sending troops. The first stage is thus a 2×5 design, reflecting two conditions for the president's party (Democratic or Republican), and five adviser speech conditions (a baseline with no speech, a hawk supporting a troop deployment, a hawk opposing troops, a dove supporting troops, and a dove opposing troops). In the second stage, respondents learn whether the president sent troops or stayed out of the conflict, potentially with the support of or over the objection of an adviser; they also learn the outcome. Respondents are then asked whether they approve of the president's handling of the situation. The second stage is thus a $2 \times 5 \times 2$ design. The large sample ($n = 3,000$) yields roughly 300 respondents per condition in the first stage, and 150 respondents per condition in the second.

The structure of the vignette is as follows (table 3-4 summarizes the treatments).[15] First, respondents read an introductory prompt (similar to those in other experiments),[16] with an admonition that the scenario is hypothetical—a choice designed to avoid priming opinions about ongoing wars. Next, respondents read that "a country sent its military to take over a smaller neighboring country. The country that has been attacked is important to US economic and security interests." Respondents are then told that "the US president, who is a [Democrat | Republican], debated extensively with his advisers about whether to send the military to push back the invaders, or stay out of the conflict." In all conditions, respondents are told that "Best estimates suggest that if the United States intervened, most of the territory could be secured, but the US

TABLE 3-3. Structure of the Main Adviser Experiment

Stage 1 (2 × 5): Support for War, Prior to President's Decision

---

President's Party (2)

Democratic   Republican

Adviser Speech (5)

| No speech | Hawkish adviser supports war | Hawkish adviser opposes war | Dovish adviser supports war | Dovish adviser opposes war |

Stage 1 Dependent Variable: Support or oppose sending US troops to push back the invaders

---

Stage 2 (2 × 5 × 2): Approval, after Learning President's Decision and Outcome

---

Decision (2)

Send troops   Stay out [over objection of adviser | with support of adviser]

Stage 2 Dependent Variable: Approve or disapprove of the president's handling of this situation

---

would face significant armed resistance." These statements hold constant expectations about the likelihood of success and expected costs.[17] The mention of resistance tests whether adviser cues can move public opinion even in the face of potentially high costs.

Respondents are then randomly assigned to an "adviser speech" condition that tests the effect of a hawkish or dovish adviser's support or opposition to the use of force, plus a control "no speech" condition. In all conditions, including the control, the vignette mentions that the president "debated extensively with his advisers," to hold the possibility of debate constant. In the condition where a hawkish adviser opposes using force, respondents are told that "one of the president's key advisers, who usually takes a hawkish approach to foreign policy and has advocated the use of force in the past when many other advisers did not, opposed the use of force in this case." In the condition in which a usually dovish adviser supports force, respondents are told, "One of the president's key advisers, who usually takes a dovish approach to foreign policy and has opposed the use of force in the past when other advisers did not, supported the use of force in the case." These two conditions—in which a usually hawkish adviser opposes force and a usually dovish adviser supports it—also constitute surprising or costly conditions. In the remaining two conditions, a usually hawkish adviser supports force, and a usually dovish adviser opposes. Although these adviser statements are more in line with expectations, they may still be effective given the institutional

TABLE 3-1 Experimental Conditions, 2016 Adviser Experiment

Scenario (after introduction that situation is hypothetical)
A country sent its military to take over a smaller neighboring country. The country that has been attacked is important to US economic and security interests.

President's Party

Democrat	Republican
The US president, who is a Democrat . . .	The US president, who is a Republican . . .

Hawkish/Dovish Adviser

Hawkish Adviser	Dovish Adviser
One of the president's key advisers, who usually takes a hawkish approach to foreign policy and has advocated the use of force in the past when many other advisers did not . . .	One of the president's key advisers, who usually takes a dovish approach to foreign policy and has opposed the use of force in the past when other advisers did not . . .

Adviser Stance

No Adviser Speech	Supports the Use of Force	Opposes the Use of Force
	. . . supported the use of force in this case.	. . . opposed the use of force in this case.

President's Decision

Send Troops	Stay Out
. . . decided to send troops to push back the invaders [if no adviser speech: nothing | with the support of his hawkish / dovish adviser | over the objection of his hawkish / dovish adviser].	. . . decided to stay out of the conflict and did not send troops [if no adviser speech: nothing | with the support of his hawkish / dovish adviser | over the objection of his hawkish / dovish adviser].

source of the speech and the effects of the party brands.[18] At the end of the first stage, respondents are asked, "If the attacker cannot be talked into withdrawing, would you support or oppose sending US troops to push back the invaders?"

In the second stage, respondents learn the president's decision to either send troops or stay out; the vignette notes whether this decision came "with the support of" or "over the objection of" the hawkish or dovish adviser. Respondents also learn the outcome, which in all conditions ends with "the attacking country taking control of 20 percent of the contested territory."[19] If the president sent troops, the vignette specifies that "the US suffered just under 100 casualties in the effort." After summary bullet points, respondents are asked if they approve or disapprove of the president's handling of the situation, with responses on a 7-point scale.[20] For stage 1, I report the percentage of respondents who support a troop deployment (including those who lean toward support), and for stage 2, I report the percentage who approve of the president's handling of the situation (with the scale collapsed so that those who strongly approve, somewhat approve, or lean toward approve are coded as approving).

Results

First, consider the overall effect of adviser cues, and thus *H1*, which examines whether adviser support or opposition affects support for war in the first stage (*H1a*) and approval once the president announces a decision (*H1b*), regardless of the president's partisanship or the adviser's hawk/dove reputation. The top panel of table 3-5 shows the effect of adviser statements on support for war in stage 1, before the decision. An adviser's opposition to sending troops results in a 9 percentage point decrease in support for the use of force, compared to the condition in which advisers support sending troops, a highly statistically significant difference given the aggregated cell size. An adviser's explicit statement of support is substantively and statistically indistinguishable from the baseline condition in which advisers say nothing. This result holds across the analysis: support does not boost support for war or approval compared to silence, suggesting that advisers are expected to support the president most of the time.

As shown in the bottom panel of table 3-5, once the president has announced the decision (*H1b*), approval depends on whether he acted with the support of or over the opposition of his advisers. We cannot simply examine the effect of adviser support or opposition for a particular action, however, because differences in approval could arise from either the adviser statement or views about the choice to use force. Rather, assessing the effect of adviser support requires the difference in approval between sending troops and staying out across both adviser support and adviser opposition.[21] This "effect of fighting"—the approval premium or penalty for sending troops versus staying out—is the quantity of interest for much of the analysis below. Mathematically, this difference in differences can be expressed as:

[Approval (send troops | adviser supports)–Approval (stay out | adviser supports)]–[Approval (send troops | adviser opposes)– Approval (stay out | adviser opposes)]

As the right side of the bottom panel in table 3-5 shows, this difference in differences, that is, the effect of sending troops versus staying out with adviser support versus without, is a highly significant 19 percentage point gain in approval. Presidents who decide to stay out of the conflict when their advisers opposed sending troops see 9 percentage points higher approval (and

TABLE 3-5. Effect of Adviser Statements on Support for War and Presidential Approval

Stage 1 (Decision under Debate)	Support for War
Baseline: no speech	59%
Adviser supports troops	61%
Adviser opposes troops	52%***
Adviser support vs. opposition	**+9%***

Stage 2 (After Decision Revealed)	Approval: Stay Out	Approval: Send Troops	Effect of Fighting (Send Troops– Stay Out)
Baseline: no speech	46%	55%	9%**
Adviser supports troops	44%	57%	12%***
Adviser opposes troops	53%*	46%**	−7%**
Adviser support vs. opposition	**−9%***	**+10%***	**+19%***

Note: Percentages are rounded. Asterisks denote the following p-values: * ≤ .10, ** ≤ .05, and *** ≤ .01 (two-tailed test) for all tables and figures.

over the 50 percent mark) compared to those who stay out when an adviser supported sending troops. When presidents send troops, nearly the mirror image occurs in approval, with 10 percentage point higher approval for those who send troops with their adviser's support, compared to opposition (both results are again highly statistically significant). Table 3-6 aggregates the conditions in which the president acted according to his adviser's recommendation (sending troops when the adviser supported troops, or staying out when the adviser opposed troops) and those in which the president acts against the adviser. Acting against advisers results in a 10 percentage point drop in approval compared to following the adviser's recommendation.[22]

What about the content of the adviser's statement and how it interacts with the president's partisanship and the adviser's hawkishness or dovishness? Direct tests of *H2a* and *H2b*, aggregating across the president's party and the costly or expected nature of the adviser's statement, do not show significant differences in the effect of advisers making expected versus countertype statements. But these results could mask differences across the adviser's statement and the president's party.

Consider first the stage 1 results, broken down by party and adviser reputation in table 3-7 (hawkish adviser in the top panel, dovish adviser in the bottom panel). The first feature of interest is that in the baseline condition, with no adviser speech, there is more support for sending US troops when

TABLE 3-6. Effect of Action after Adviser Statements (Stage 2)

	Approval
Baseline: no speech	51%
Action with adviser rec	55%*
Action against adviser rec	45%***
Action with vs. against adviser rec	**+10%***

TABLE 3-7. Support for a US Troop Deployment (Stage 1)

Hawkish Adviser	Democratic President	Republican President	Partisan Difference
Baseline: no speech	63%	55%	−7%*
Hawk supports troops	67%	56%	−11%***
Hawk opposes troops	53%**	47%**	−6%
Hawk swing (support vs. oppose)	**+14%***	**+9%**	**−5%**

Dovish Adviser	Democratic President	Republican President	Partisan Difference
Baseline: no speech	63%	55%	−7%*
Dove supports troops	62%	58%	−4%
Dove opposes troops	56%	52%	−5%
Dove swing (support vs. oppose)	**+6%**	**+6%**	**+1%**
Difference in hawk swing vs. dove swing (difference in differences)	**+9%**	**+3%**	**−6%**

the president is a Democrat (63 percent) rather than a Republican (55 percent, p = .07, two-tailed). This partisan difference in support for using force also appears in the full sample (60 percent support for a Democratic president, 53 percent for a Republican) and is highly statistically significant (p = .0001) given the large sample size.[23]

The next two conditions explore the effect of a hawkish adviser's speech. Again, however, we cannot simply compare supportive statements from two different types of advisers (hawkish vs. dovish), because this comparison would not disentangle respondents' views of hawkish or dovish elites, or the fact of support. The most relevant comparison is the difference between a given adviser's support for the use of force and opposition to it. We can think of this difference or "swing" as the "price" of obtaining the support of that adviser, or the upside to preventing that adviser from making a statement opposing the use of force. We can then compare these differences across adviser types.

In the upper half of table 3-7, if a usually hawkish adviser supports using force, the effect as compared to baseline is neither large nor statistically significant for either a Democratic or a Republican president, but the 4 percentage point increase in support for sending troops under a Democratic president widens the gap between support for a deployment under a Democratic and that of a Republican president to 11 percentage points, a gap that is now highly statistically significant ($p = .004$). Per *H2a*, if a usually hawkish adviser opposes using force in this case, however, support for sending troops drops to 53 percent for a Democratic president, a drop of 10 percentage points from baseline ($p = .02$). The "swing" in support for sending troops from a hawkish adviser who opposes a deployment to a hawkish adviser who supports is 14 percentage points ($p = .0004$). Put differently, a president who wants to avoid sending troops can substantially reduce support for using force by convincing a hawkish adviser to oppose a deployment. The effect of a hawkish adviser who comes out against using force is expected to be large, especially for a Democrat, because all three mechanisms are in place: the hawk is engaging in surprising speech; opposing a potential presidential initiative from within the inner circle; and counteracting the president's party brand, giving a Democratic president cover for staying out. Interestingly, and in contrast to *H3a*, under a Republican president, a hawkish adviser who opposes using force in this case also has a negative, statistically significant effect (-9 percentage points, $p = .03$) on support for sending troops, which helps account for the fact that the partisan gap when a hawk opposes war remains 6 percentage points, although it is no longer statistically significant. Hawks who oppose using force can still affect support for war under a Republican president.

The lower half of table 3-7 reports similar comparisons when dovish advisers support or oppose the use of force. Even against-type statements from dovish advisers, however, do not appear to have large effects on support for war. A usually dovish adviser who favors force does not appreciably affect support for war, although the baseline partisan gap falls below statistical significance. A dovish adviser who opposes war has slightly larger, negative effects on support, illustrating that any opposition from an adviser can depress support (per *H1a*). The swing from dovish support to dovish opposition does not result in a statistically significant change in support for a president of either party. In the very bottom row of table 3-7, the difference in differences between the hawk swing (support-oppose) and the dove swing (support-oppose) is 9 percentage points for a Democratic president and just misses the threshold of statistical significance at the $p = .1$ level. The difference in differences in adviser swings for a Republican president is a (nonsignificant) 3 percentage points.

TABLE 3-8. Approval for Democratic Presidents, by Decision and Adviser Statement (Stage 2)

Democratic President	Stay Out	Send Troops	Effect of Fighting (Send Troops–Stay Out)
No speech	47%	59%	+12%**
Hawk supports troops	41%	61%	+21%***
Hawk opposes troops	54%	43%***	−11%*
Hawk swing (support vs. oppose)	**−13%***	**+18%****	**+31%****

Democratic President	Stay Out	Send Troops	Effect of Fighting (Send Troops–Stay Out)
No speech	47%	59%	+12%**
Dove supports troops	45%	54%	+10%*
Dove opposes troops	48%	50%	+2%
Dove swing (support vs. oppose)	−3%	+5%	+8%
Difference in hawk swing vs. dove swing (difference in differences)	−10%	+14%*	+24%**

Overall, the first stage results suggest that advisers matter even when taking partisanship into account; that hawkish advisers have a larger effect than dovish advisers for presidents of both parties; and that hawkish advisers are particularly important under Democratic presidents (in line with $H3a$). If a Democratic president wants to avoid sending troops—that is, play to type—convincing a hawk to move from supporting to opposing a deployment results in a larger reduction in public support for using force—a swing from two-thirds support to just over half supporting—than a similar shift in a dovish adviser's stance.

The importance of advisers persists in the second stage, once the president's decision and the conflict's outcome are announced. Table 3-8 and table 3-9 present the results in terms of approval. Looking across the tables, from the "stay out" decision to the "send troops" decision, reveals how adviser speech affects the political incentives to send troops; looking down the columns shows the effect of adviser speech for each decision. Results for Democratic presidents, in table 3-8, again reflect a baseline gap between sending troops and staying out. Approval for Democratic presidents who send troops is 59 percent, whereas Democrats who stay out get 47 percent, a statistically significant gap ($p = .04$). This gap also holds in the full sample: across all conditions for Democrats, there is a smaller gap (53 percent approval for sending troops vs. 46 percent for staying out, $p = .006$). As shown in the table's top set of results, which report the effects of hawkish adviser speech, when a hawkish adviser explicitly supports sending troops, the gap in approval between staying out and sending

troops—the effect of fighting, or the fighting premium—for a Democratic
president widens to 21 percentage points, with 41 percent approval at the stay-
out decision and 61 percent if there is an intervention.

In contrast, if a hawkish adviser opposes sending troops, the gap is reversed: 54 percent approve of a Democratic president who stays out if a hawkish adviser opposed sending troops, while 43 percent approve if the president
sends troops over the hawkish adviser's objection. The gap between staying
out and sending troops swings to 11 percentage points in favor of staying out
in the hawkish adviser opposing force scenario (and a significant and negative 23 percentage point reduction in the gap favoring a troop deployment,
as compared to the no-speech baseline). The difference in differences in the
stay-out versus send-troops gap when the hawk supports versus opposes force
is a highly significant 31 percentage points. A hawkish adviser who comes out
against a deployment can provide cover for a Democratic president in terms
of approval, per H3b.

Similar comparisons for dovish advisers do not yield effects nearly as large
or significant for Democratic presidents. The right-hand side of the very bottom row of the table reports the difference in differences between the effect
of a hawk shift in support for using force versus opposition to it and a similar
dove shift in support versus opposition on the overall approval gap between
staying out and sending troops. The hawkish adviser's swing to supporting
force has a much larger effect on the approval gap (31 percentage point increase
in the approval gap, favoring sending troops) than the dove's swing (8 percentage point increase in the approval gap); the difference in differences is
24 percentage points in the effect on the approval gap favoring force (p = .04).

Looking down the columns of table 3-8, at the stay-out decision—where
a Democratic president acts according to type—there is, as mentioned, a statistically significant swing of 13 percentage points in approval when the hawk
shifts from support for force to opposition, but no similar effect for a dovish
swing (the difference in differences at the stay-out decision, in bottom row on
the left-hand side, is not statistically significant). Interestingly, hawkish advisers also significantly affect approval if a Democratic president sends troops. If a
Democratic president sends troops over the objection of a hawkish adviser,
approval dips to the low forties, almost indistinguishable from staying out
over the objection of a hawkish adviser.[24] At the send-troops decision (middle
column, very bottom row), the difference in differences for the effect of a shift
from support to opposition for a hawkish versus dovish adviser is 14 percentage points (p = .08). A hawkish adviser can affect approval of Democratic
presidents for any decision.

The pattern for Republican presidents, in table 3-9, is somewhat different. Approval for Republican presidents exhibits a smaller baseline gap of

TABLE 3-9. Approval for Republican Presidents, by Decision and Adviser Statement (Stage 2)

Republican President	Stay Out	Send Troops	Effect of Fighting (Send Troops–Stay Out)
No speech	46%	52%	+6%
Hawk supports troops	47%	51%	+4%
Hawk opposes troops	57%**	47%	−9%*
Hawk swing (support vs. oppose)	**−10%***	+4%	+14%*

Republican President	Stay Out	Send Troops	Effect of Fighting (Send Troops–Stay Out)
No speech	46%	52%	+6%
Dove supports troops	46%	60%	+14%***
Dove opposes troops	54%	46%	−8%
Dove swing (support vs. oppose)	**−8%**	**+15%***	+22%***
Difference in hawk swing vs. dove swing (difference in differences)	−2%	−11%	−8%

6 percentage points in approval between the stay-out and send-troops decisions (the gap is not significant in either the baseline, no-speech condition or the full sample). For a Republican president with a hawkish adviser who opposed the use of force in this case, the gap flips to 9 percentage points ($p = .09$) in favor of staying out, with 57 percent approval for staying out and 47 percent for sending troops. The effect of a hawk swing (support vs. opposition) on the overall approval gap across decisions is 14 percentage points ($p = .09$). A hawkish adviser helps a Republican president who wants to stay out, but the explicit support of a hawkish adviser does little to influence approval for Republicans who intervene.

Republican presidents see larger effects, however, from a dovish adviser ($H3b$). A dovish adviser who supports war widens the approval gap in favor of war to 60 percent approval for a Republican president who sends troops versus 46 percent for staying out ($p = .01$). The swing in a dovish adviser's position (support-oppose) results in a 22 percentage point difference in the approval gap when the dovish adviser supports force versus opposes force ($p = .006$). Although the difference in differences in the bottom row of table 3-9 does not reveal significant differences in the effect of a hawkish adviser swing versus a dovish adviser swing, looking at the send-troops decision column, a dovish adviser can significantly influence approval for a Republican president who intervenes (supporting $H3b$). If a Republican president sends troops, approval is 60 percent if a dovish adviser supports it but 46 percent if the decision to

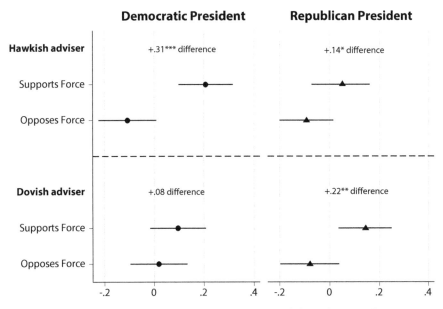

FIGURE 3-1. Differences in predicted probability of approval
(send troops vs. stay out)

send troops was over the dovish adviser's objection (p = .013). In contrast, a change in a hawkish adviser's position does not result in a significant change in approval for Republicans who intervene.

It is notable that the effect of a dovish adviser's swing from support to opposition to intervention for a Republican president who fights is substantively similar to the effect of a hawkish adviser's swing from support to opposition for a Democratic president who makes the same decision. Figure 3-1 plots the differences in predicted probability of approval for sending troops versus staying out (a measure of the political incentive to fight) for presidents of both parties, in the four conditions where advisers speak. The graph illustrates that changes in hawks' statements have a larger effect on the political incentives for Democratic presidents to fight, while the swing in a dovish adviser's statements is most important for Republican presidents.

Overall, the results suggest, first, that advisers can significantly affect public support for war and approval of the president (H_1), even in the presence of casualties. Second, presidents who wish to play to their party's type would do well to persuade an adviser of the opposite stripe to support their position (H_3). Third, the effects of different types of advisers are asymmetric. When sending troops is under consideration, cues from hawkish advisers are the most important for presidents of either party, suggesting that hawks are the most trusted to signal the wisdom of intervening. In the second stage, there are asymmetric effects for Democratic and Republican presidents. For Democratic presidents, acting in accordance with a hawkish adviser's view is beneficial and acting over the objection of a hawkish adviser is damaging, for either decision. The effects of advisers on the Democratic side are concentrated among hawks, while for Republican presidents, advisers of both types can have significant effects, although relatively dovish advisers have the largest effects on approval. Finally, the similarities between the no-speech and support conditions suggest that respondents assume advisers support the president (even before an initiative is announced), suggesting that the silence of an adviser whose opposition would be damaging is almost as good as that adviser's explicit support.

Perceptions of Competence, Success, and Party Brands

Thus far, we have seen how adviser cues can affect public support for war and approval of the president's actions, and that partisanship shapes these effects. Other follow-up questions in the experiment allow me to explore how these cues can affect perceptions of the president, of the parties, and of the outcome of the conflict. These effects can contribute to narratives that presidents may want to exploit or avoid.

First, consider perceptions of the president's competence.[25] Again, the effect of elite statements may not manifest because leaders work to avoid them; observing such effects in the real world may require sustained elite discourse that fits a larger narrative. But the experiment can illuminate what would happen if the cues reached the public's ears. Thus, after asking about approval of the president's handling of the situation, respondents are asked, "In this scenario, how would you describe the president's competence?" with responses on a 5-point scale from "very competent" to "very incompetent."[26] For ease of exposition, this discussion focuses on either a 3-point scale or a binary variable for competence.

Focusing on the same quantity of interest, the effect of sending troops, is there a "competence premium" for sending troops, or a "competence penalty" for staying out of a conflict? There is a small but only borderline significant effect on perceptions of competence if the president decides to intervene. On a 3-point scale of competence, sending troops results in a 3 percentage point increase in the probability of rating the president as "competent" ($p = .08$), but the change in perceptions of competence is not particularly meaningful, from 45 percent to 48 percent (with a corresponding decline in perceptions of incompetence). Of course, this result could be masking variation depending on internal consensus or dissent. Breaking down the effect of troops by whether or not an adviser supported or opposed it, there is a slightly larger competence

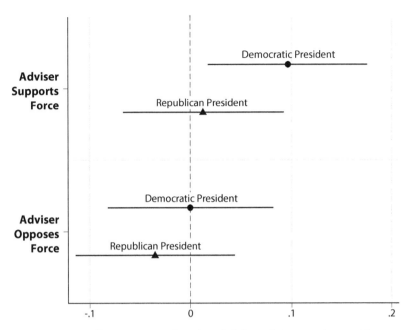

FIGURE 3-2. Differences in predicted probability of viewing the president as
competent (send troops vs. stay out)

gap favoring sending troops when an adviser supports rather than opposes, but
significant only at the p < .1 level (3-point scale). Further analysis suggests that
a hawkish adviser's opposition can make a difference compared to the baseline
of no speech, pushing perceptions of the president's competence to 52 percent
if the decision is to stay out (significance hovers around p = .05).[27]

But the effect of the decision on perceptions of the president's competence
emerges more clearly when examining the effects by party. Averaging over
the adviser conditions, the effect of fighting for a Democrat—that is, the difference in the predicted probability of viewing the president as competent
between sending-troops and staying-out decisions—is 5 percentage points,
shifting from 45 percent to 50 percent (p = .05, two tailed), while there is no
effect on perceptions of a Republican president's competence (46 percent
view a Republican president as competent no matter what the decision). In
the baseline condition, with advisory debate but no explicit adviser statement,
sending troops is favored for presidents of both parties, but the effects are
not statistically significant. As depicted in figure 3-2, however, for a Democratic president, when an adviser speaks in favor of sending troops, a highly
significant 10 percentage point gap opens up in the effect of fighting (p = .02,
two-tailed), with 52 percent viewing the president as competent if he decides

to intervene and 42 percent if the president decides to stay out. Again, for a Republican president, there is no effect of fighting on competence at all. When an adviser opposes force, for Democratic presidents, competence reverts to nearly equal perceptions no matter the decision, while for Republicans staying out is slightly favored, but the effect is not statistically significant. In a regression framework, for Democratic presidents, the difference in differences between sending troops and staying out, when an adviser supports versus opposes using force, is a weakly significant 9.6 percentage point increase in the probability of a respondent viewing the president as competent ($p < .1$) (and if the adviser supports force, the competence premium for sending troops versus staying out is highly significant at $p = .02$). Cell sizes become too small to detect meaningful difference in differences between the parties on this score, but there is no statistically significant effect for Republican presidents.

We can further investigate the drivers of these effects by looking at the adviser's type. Again looking at the effect of fighting (i.e., sending troops versus staying out) on the probability of perceiving the president as competent, a Democratic president sees no effect from a dovish adviser's support versus opposition, but a nearly 15 percentage point difference in the effect of fighting on the odds of looking competent if a hawkish adviser supports versus opposes ($p = .07$). Viewed another way, opposition to the use of force from a hawkish adviser versus a dovish adviser diminishes a Democratic president's competence premium for sending troops by 16.5 percentage points ($p = .047$). Republicans see no such effects from either adviser.

Thus internal debate about the use of force can affect perceptions of the president's competence—but mainly for Democratic presidents, and again mainly from the hawkish side. Democratic presidents who wish to avoid a competence penalty *and* stay out of a conflict get meaningful political benefits from a hawkish adviser's opposition to using force versus support for sending troops. To the extent that competence is an important focal point for voters to coordinate around, the results show that how presidents manage their advisers can affect the link between the use of force and competence.

What about perceptions of the operation's success? Recall that the experiment explicitly attempts to hold the outcome constant—the invading country takes 20 percent of the contested territory regardless of whether the president decides to send troops—with the only difference that in the intervention condition, there are casualties, to ensure that respondents consider the costs of fighting. In the context of the Iraq War, scholars debated whether the expectation of success was a crucial ingredient of public support for war, or instead another indicator of generalized war support.[28] This debate hinges on whether expectations of success are an independent influence on generalized war support, or instead another measure or component of that support. One challenge in adjudicating this debate in the Iraq War context is that scholars had to measure expectations of success in an ongoing war, about which survey respondents already held views.

The experiment here cannot adjudicate the debate, and in some sense it does not matter for my argument whether success is an input of war support or a reflection of it. Either way, if elite cues can affect perceptions of success, the president's room for maneuver may change.[29] But this experiment has several advantages. First, it can show how elite cues from inside the administration affect perceptions of success. Importantly, any such effects matter not only for their influence on public opinion directly, but also because they illuminate incentives for other elites to contribute cues that alter perceptions of success and failure. Presidents may have incentives to prevent these cues from cascading to other elites who can turn war into a wedge issue for the opposition party, for example. Second, the experiment is hypothetical, which presents its own challenges but avoids some of the specific problems of asking about the likelihood of success in a real, ongoing war.[30] The success question asks about the outcome, rather than expectations about future success. Furthermore, this experiment is a cross-border intervention involving territory, a scenario where success and failure should be relatively clear compared to the more amorphous peacekeeping and counterinsurgency interventions of the post–Cold War era. If elite cues can move perceptions of success in such a case, we would expect them to exert similar if not stronger effects in other scenarios where success is even more amorphous. And the casualties in the intervention condition should decrease the likelihood that respondents will perceive the operation as a success, making it a tougher test for elites to move perceptions toward success. In this experiment, respondents were asked, "In this scenario, how would you describe the outcome?" with response choices as "Successful outcome for the United States"; "Unsuccessful outcome for the United States"; or "Neither successful nor unsuccessful."[31]

First, consider the effect of sending troops—the continued quantity of interest—on perceptions of success. As figure 3-3 shows, sending troops—which yields the same outcome on the ground except that the US incurs casualties—increases the share of those who consider the outcome successful, from 29 percent with no troops to 37 percent if the president sent troops, while decreasing the share who consider it neither successful nor unsuccessful from 42 percent to 36 percent. The percentage viewing the outcome as unsuccessful is stable at 29 percent versus 28 percent.

When broken down by adviser statement, however, a different pattern emerges. I use multinomial logit to analyze these results so as not to assume that "neither" is a middle category. As shown in figure 3-4, the effects of an adviser opposing versus supporting force results in a 12 percentage point increase in

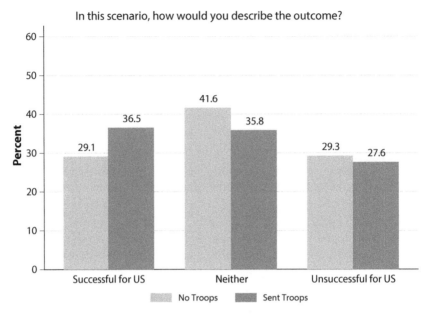

FIGURE 3-3. Effect of fighting on perceptions of outcome

the effect of sending troops on the probability of viewing the outcome as *unsuccessful* (p = .001, multinomial logit). That is, the difference in respondents' views of the outcome when the president sends troops versus stays out of the conflict shift significantly when the adviser supported sending troops rather than opposed a deployment. The differences are not enormous, but they do shift perceptions of success at the decision nodes. For example, if the president declines to send troops, the predicted probability of viewing the *same substantive outcome* as unsuccessful shifts from 33 percent if the adviser supported force to 25 percent if the adviser opposed it (p = .005). In the multinomial framework, there is a discernible, but smaller and less significant, effect on the probability of viewing the outcome as neither successful nor unsuccessful. The shift from a quarter to a third of respondents viewing the outcome as unsuccessful may not seem large but is effectively the difference between a solid minority viewing the outcome as unsuccessful and indifference between successful and unsuccessful.

In contrast to views of competence, both Republican and Democratic presidents feel the effects of adviser statements on perceptions of success.[32] Looking first only at the effect of troops (not depicted), presidents of both parties see a nearly identical, highly significant increase of about 7 percentage points in the probability of the outcome being seen as successful if they send troops versus stay out (p = .005 for Democrats, p = .001 for Republicans), so

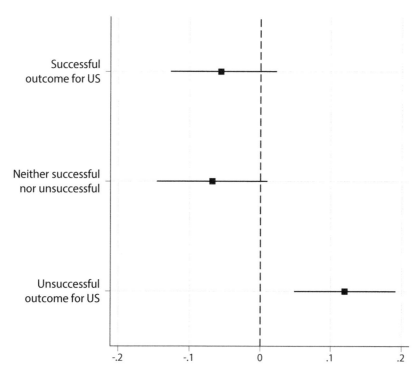

FIGURE 3-4. Difference in predicted probability of viewing outcome as (un)successful (adviser oppose vs. support, send troops vs. stay out)

there is no overall partisan advantage for fighting.[33] As figure 3-5 shows, when we look at the effect of adviser opposition to force versus support on the fighting premium, presidents of both parties have a nearly identical and highly significant 12 percentage point increase in the probability of viewing the outcome as unsuccessful ($p = .02$). Republican presidents do therefore face some effect on views of success, in contrast to competence.

There are, however, intriguing differences in how adviser statements affect presidents from the two parties, especially as compared to the baseline of no speech. For a Democratic president, an adviser expressing support for using force has a significant effect on views of success. For presidents of both parties in the control condition of no adviser speech, the distribution of views of success when the president chooses not to send troops is nearly identical: a clear plurality of 40 percent view the outcome as neither successful nor unsuccessful, with the remaining 60 percent evenly split between successful and unsuccessful. When the president sends troops, however, this distribution is effectively unchanged for Republican presidents, while for Democratic presidents, there is a 10 percentage point gap in the share viewing the outcome

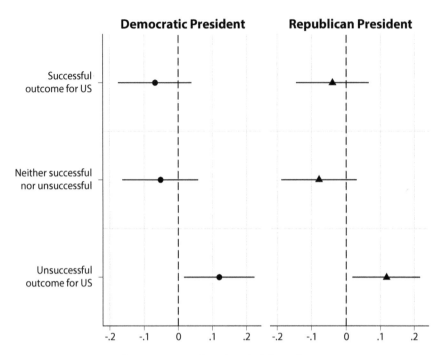

FIGURE 3-5. Differences in predicted probability of viewing outcome as (un)successful (adviser oppose vs. support, send troops vs. stay out), by president's party

as a success (versus staying out), with a plurality (40 percent) viewing the outcome as successful if the president sends troops. This increase comes out of the share viewing the outcome as neither successful nor unsuccessful, where the share for Democratic presidents drops from a plurality of 40 percent for no troops to 29 percent if there is a troop deployment.

When we consider adviser statements against this baseline, it is the surprising statements, along the lines of *H2a* and *H2b*, that affect views of success. For Democratic presidents, an adviser's opposition to the use of force has little effect on the gap in views of success by the effect of fighting. But an adviser's statement of support for the use of force erases the gap in the "neither" category and opens up a 10 percentage point gap in those who view the outcome as unsuccessful, with 35 percent deeming the outcome unsuccessful if the president decides to stay out versus 25 percent if there is a deployment. In contrast, Republican presidents see small changes in views of success across the troop decisions when an adviser supports force as compared to the control, no-speech condition. But when an adviser opposes force, a large gap opens up in the "neither" category, whereas it was evenly split at 40 percent in the control condition. Fully 47 percent view the outcome as neither successful nor unsuccessful, a clear plurality, if a Republican president does not send troops and an adviser opposed a deployment, while 34 percent take this "neither" view if the president sends troops (a 12 percentage point drop in the probability of taking the "neither" view, p = .06). Interestingly, the successful and unsuccessful categories are not significantly affected by this shift, although there is a nearly 10 percentage point increase in the odds of seeing the outcome as unsuccessful that misses conventional significance levels (p = .13) but is similar in magnitude to the decrease in the probability of viewing the outcome as "neither."[34] Although we must be careful in reading too much into these results, they suggest that surprising cues—advisers who take the opposite view of what one might expect given that they serve a president of a particular party—are important to how the public interprets outcomes.

The number of respondents per condition becomes smaller and smaller the more we subset the data, so it is perhaps unsurprising that there few differences between hawkish and dovish advisers on the relationship between whether the president fights and perceptions of success. In general, the effect of an adviser's support or opposition swamps these differences. But a few comparisons are suggestive. For Democratic presidents, this is a case where dovish advisers who support war make a difference to the fighting premium: if a dovish adviser supports using force versus opposing it, there is a 14 percentage point reduction in the odds of viewing the outcome of a deployment as unsuccessful compared to staying out (p = .07). Hawkish advisers have a similar effect in terms of magnitude, a 10 percentage point reduction in the probability of viewing the outcome as unsuccessful across the decisions, but the effect misses conventional significance levels (p = .16). The similarity of the effects, however, means the difference in differences is not significant given small cell sizes, and again, these effects may reflect the mere fact of adviser support rather than the identity of the adviser. But the importance of doves here is bolstered by the comparison of a dove's support for force compared to the control condition for Democratic presidents, where the probability of viewing the outcome as unsuccessful drops 14 percentage points if the president sends troops rather than staying out (p = .06). This drop goes almost entirely into an increase of 20 percent in the probability of respondents seeing the outcome as "neither successful nor unsuccessful," highly significant at p = .01, and perhaps reflecting some ambivalence about what sending troops means for Democratic presidents.

For Republicans, hawks who support force have no effect compared to the control condition (p = .09), but hawks who oppose force lower the probability of viewing the outcome as "neither" by 13 percentage points compared to the control condition and raise the probability of viewing it as unsuccessful by 11 percentage points (just missing significance at p = .11). Doves who support force under a

Republican president increase the probability of viewing the outcome as successful for the deployment versus staying out by 13 percentage points ($p = .08$) and lower the odds of viewing the outcome as "neither" by a nearly identical amount ($p = .11$). In a direct comparison of adviser support versus opposition across the decisions, only the hawkish adviser has a significant effect, reducing the probability of seeing the outcome as unsuccessful by 15 percentage points ($p = .03$) and increasing the probability of "neither" by nearly the same (16 percentage points, $p = .04$). But comparing a dovish versus a hawkish adviser's support for force across decisions to deploy or stay out, the dovish adviser's support increases the odds of viewing the operation as a success by 12 percentage points, the only comparison to meaningfully shift views of success across the decisions (although the difference misses conventional levels of significance at $p = .13$, understandable given the smaller cell sizes). In contrast, the effect of dovish versus hawkish adviser support for Democratic presidents is mainly absorbed by the "neither" category, even as the probability of viewing the outcome as unsuccessful drops.

When we compare across parties, the effect of a dovish adviser supporting force versus a hawkish adviser supporting force is significantly stronger for Republican presidents across the decisions. When we look at the difference in differences across the parties and decisions to send troops, a dove's support compared to a hawk's increases the probability of viewing the outcome as a success by 21 percentage points ($p = .05$) and decreases the probability of viewing it as "neither" by 30 percentage points ($p = .007$).

Overall, all presidents seem sensitive to their adviser's statements in terms of framing the operation as a success or failure, especially surprising statements that cut against what we might expect. Republican presidents seem especially sensitive, consistent with the argument that a successful outcome matters more for Republican presidents, whereas merely fighting does much for Democratic chief executives. Of course, we must be careful not to go too far in interpreting these results, since the outcome contains ambiguity.

Finally, do the president's actions affect views of the party—which may affect how copartisans view the costs and benefits of war? One risk in assessing such effects is that the experiment itself may alter views of the party, so we need some measure of how respondents view the party before the treatment.[35] Here, we can exploit a feature of the experimental design. The experiment contains a block of questions about how respondents view the parties' militarism (as well as their own); half of respondents see this block before the experiment and half afterward. Those (randomly assigned) respondents who answer the questions before the experiment can therefore serve as a benchmark in a placebo test of the effect of the experiment on these views.[36] Focusing again on the effect of sending troops, those who answer the militarism questions before the experiment have no exposure to the scenario or decision, but we can still compare across the random assignment of the conditions in which they later find themselves. We should expect no effect from this comparison, and it provides a benchmark of respondents' views in the absence of any treatment. We can then compare this to the effect of the treatments on those who answer the militarism questions after the experiment. Given that analyzing the data by the order of questions halves the sample size, I focus here on the effect of troops and not adviser statements.

The question for party placement is drawn from the American National Election Study (ANES) and asks respondents to place themselves as well as the two parties on a scale from most likely to use diplomacy to solve international problems to most willing to use force, on a 7-point scale.[37] The most important result is that there is no effect of a Republican president's action—sending troops or staying out—on views of the Republican Party, but there is a shift in views of the Democratic Party when Democratic presidents use force. Among those who answered before and after the experiment, the actions of a Republican president do not move the needle on views of the Republican Party. For simplicity, if we collapse the scale to be on the "force" side, the "diplomacy" side, or in the middle, roughly 60 percent of respondents put the Republican Party on the "force" end of the spectrum whether or not a Republican president uses force (and whether respondents answer this question before or after the experiment).

As shown in the left panel of figure 3-6a, for Democratic presidents, an average of 50 percent of those who answer before the experiment put the Democratic Party on the "diplomacy side" while (again using averages) 41 percent put them on the "force" side and 9 percent in the middle (and, as should be the case, no significant difference between those who subsequently get the troops and no-troops treatments). For those who answer after the experiment, however, a significant gap opens up in views of the Democratic Party depending on the Democratic president's actions, as shown in the left panel of figure 3-6b. If the president declines to send troops, the share who put the party on the "diplomacy" end of the scale remains 50 percent, with a slight increase in the percentage of those who put it in the middle (13 percent) and a corresponding decrease in those (37 percent) who put it on the "force" end. But if the Democratic president sends troops, the distribution is reversed, with a plurality 48 percent putting the Democratic Party on the "force" end, 15 percent in the middle, and 37 percent on the "diplomacy" end.

As shown in figure 3-7, in an ordered logit framework (given the clearly ordered nature of the data), there is a nearly 10 percentage point drop in the probability of putting the Democratic Party on the "diplomacy" end of

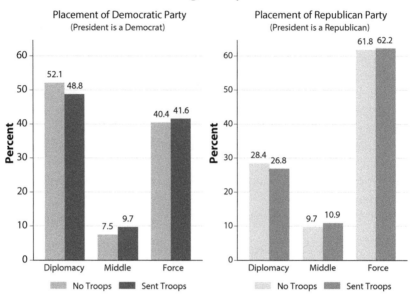

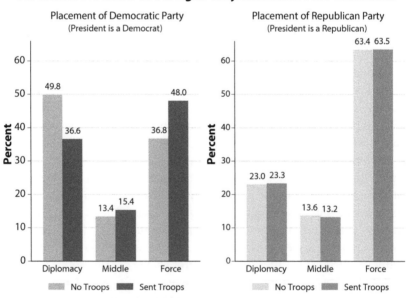

FIGURE 3-6. Placement of president's party, measured (a) pre-treatment and (b) post-treatment

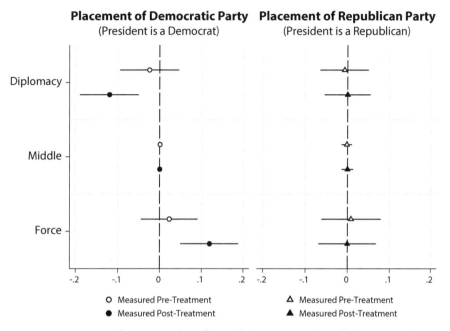

FIGURE 3-7. Differences in the effect of fighting on predicted placement of president's party (pre- and post-treatment)

the scale (p=.06) if a Democratic president sends troops vs. stays out, and a corresponding 10 percentage point increase in the odds of putting the party on the "force" end (p = .05), when compared to the placebo, before-experiment respondents. Looking just at those who answered after the experiment, the effect of fighting makes the gap slightly larger—a 12 percentage point drop and matching rise in the odds of putting the Democratic Party on the diplomacy and force ends of the spectrum, respectively—and highly significant (p < .0001). Interestingly, these effects appear to be driven by Republican respondents, whose views of the Democratic Party undergo apparently large shifts if a Democratic president uses force, although these results must be interpreted with caution given smaller cell sizes.[38] Still, no other combination of respondent and presidential party identification yields a shift in views of the party.

Such a shift in views may be fleeting. These results, however, shed interesting light on a puzzling question: why are party brands on national security so sticky? The results reinforce the idea that Democratic presidents have incentives to use force based on the Democratic Party brand, and that for Democratic presidents and their copartisans in Congress, even a short-term shift in views of the party may be politically relevant and affect their overall preference for using force. But a Republican president's decision to send forces or not does not move views of the Republican Party, even though voters' views of how successful the outcome is depends on elite statements even for Republican presidents. As Egan argues, brands are very difficult to shift if parties make the issues they "own" a priority, and the brands can withstand disapproval of a particular president's policies.[39]

Generalizability: Replications and Extensions

The main adviser experiment reflects both deliberate design choices, such as holding the outcome constant, and the particular context in which the experiment took place, in 2016. As is true of any experiment, these features limit what the experiment can tell us about the real world. To assess the generalizability and external validity of the experiment, I report results from several additional experiments that help fill in the picture beyond these limits. I discuss the main takeaways here, with results available in appendix B.[40]

Pilot and Replication of Main Adviser Experiment

First, I consider variations on the main adviser experiment. I conducted a pilot experiment run in August 2015 on Amazon's Mechanical Turk (MTurk) platform, using nearly the same vignette described above, with four main differences. First, the pilot unfolds all in one stage, giving respondents information about the advisers' statement, the president's decision, and the outcome, and then asking about approval of the president's decision. Second, the pilot omits the discussion of expected armed resistance and holds actual costs constant at zero casualties. This approach follows Kertzer and Brutger in specifying zero casualties even when the president sent troops.[41] Third, the sample size (n = 1,690) is just over half that of the 2016 adviser experiment. Fourth, consistent with the literature on MTurk samples, the 2015 pilot study undertaken via MTurk skews more liberal than the 2016 adviser experiment undertaken via SSI.[42] Despite these differences, main results for adviser effects were broadly similar though with higher approval levels, as might be expected given the lack of costs.

Second, what about the effect of the background politics of the time when the 2016 adviser experiment was in the field? To address this question, I replicated the main 2016 experiment, using the same survey firm (now called Dynata, formerly SSI) and a similar sample of 3,000 American respondents, in a preregistered experiment in January 2022.[43] The background context for this experiment shares some features with the 2016 adviser experiment—notably, a Democratic president, and proximity to a crisis in Ukraine—but also some major differences. In 2016, the Russian seizure of Crimea was two years in the past, and while the invasion of Ukraine continued in the Donbas region, it faded from public view. In January 2022, the Russian buildup on the Ukrainian border was in the news, though not yet dominant as it would be after the invasion began in late February. The Biden administration had also received major criticism for its handling of the US withdrawal from Afghanistan in August 2021, damaging Biden's reputation for competence in national security matters. Additionally, the political environment of 2022 was even more polarized than 2016. According to Gallup, Biden's first-year approval was second only to Trump's final year in office as the most polarized, with Trump's second through fourth years and Biden's first year as the most polarized in Gallup's history.[44] Under these conditions, as noted in the preregistration, I expected adviser cue effects in 2022 to be significantly smaller than in 2016, and in the wake of the withdrawal from Afghanistan, a particularly difficult test for an argument that administration insider cues could affect public opinion about the use of military force.

As expected, the 2022 context yielded significantly different results for the 2022 version of the adviser experiment. Many of the main results from 2016 results are not significant in 2022. Most surprisingly, the effect of hawkish adviser cues for Democratic presidents was quite different, with hawkish support for war leading to *lower* approval if a Democratic president sent troops. Cues have almost no effect on war support in stage 1, with approximately 60 percent of respondents favoring a move to send troops in all conditions, across the president's party.[45] Despite these changes, however, several results show that adviser cues could, in fact, still move public attitudes significantly. Unlike in the 2016 case, however, $H2b$, the effect of countertype rather than true-to-type adviser cues—that is, as noted in the vignette, a hawkish adviser opposing force, or a dovish adviser supporting force—receives strong support in the 2022 data. In an environment increasingly skeptical of expertise and perhaps of hawks in particular, advisers offering advice that goes against their own reputations carries more weight. These effects appear to be driven in partly by the persuasive cues of doves when they support the use of force, particularly for Democratic presidents.[46]

Focusing on approval to assess $H2b$, table 3-10 shows there is a significantly different approval penalty for presidents who act against the recommendation of a countertype adviser statement (that is, a dovish adviser supporting force or a hawkish adviser opposing force). The approval penalty is not huge, a roughly 6 percentage point reduction in approval for acting against a countertype adviser recommendation versus a true-to-type recommendation, but it is both highly significant ($p = .03$) and substantively significant. The swing, which shows up in both approval and disapproval, is enough to shift the majority toward approval if the president acts according to the countertype

TABLE 3-10. Approval by Adviser Statement Type, 2022 Adviser Experiment

Stage 2 (After Decision Revealed)	Baseline (No Speech)	Adviser True to Type	Adviser against Type	Difference (Against vs. True to Type)
Baseline: no speech	46%			
Action with adviser rec.		48%	52%	+4%
Action against adviser rec.		53%	47%	−6%**
Action with vs. against adviser rec		*−5%**	*+5%**	*+10%****

signal. In contrast, acting against a true-to-type signal actually increases the president's approval and decreases disapproval. These effects are driven partly by dovish advisers supporting force, but also by backlash against hawks, whose support for war is not persuasive in this experiment. Instead, it is the president listening to those who speak against type that is most relevant, in line with Calvert's theory of biased advise. These results are similar for both Democratic and Republican presidents.

Whether the adviser speaks counter or true to type also affects perceptions of success in the 2022 adviser experiment (which, as in the 2016 adviser experiment, held the outcome constant with the attacking country taking control of 20 percent of the contested territory). As table 3-11 shows, acting against a true-to-type adviser statement versus acting as a true-to-type adviser recommended yields a slight (but not significant) boost in the share of respondents who see the outcome as successful. Acting against a countertype adviser statement, however, compared to following the countertype statement, decreases the proportion perceiving the outcome as successful by 6 percentage points (p = .03). The difference in differences of 7 percentage points is significant at p < .05. Perhaps more ominously, acting against a countertype adviser statement versus following a countertype statement increases the likelihood that respondents will see the outcome as unsuccessful (p = .03), while bucking a true-to-type statement versus following it decreases the share of those who perceive an unsuccessful outcome by a similar 5.5 percentage points (p = .04). The difference in differences is 11 percentage points in the share seeing the outcome—which is, again, fixed—as unsuccessful (p = .009). While these differences are not especially large, they again have substantive meaning in shifting the balance of perceptions of the same outcome. As with approval, this effect is driven by the signal from doves supporting the use of force. Results are similar for presidents of both parties.

Overall, then, in an intensely polarized environment, in the wake of a widely perceived foreign policy failure and on the brink of a potential major war in Europe, elite cues could still affect presidential approval and perceptions of

TABLE 3-11. Perception of Outcome, 2022 Adviser Experiment

In this scenario, how would you describe the outcome?		Successful Outcome for US	Neither Successful nor Unsuccessful	Unsuccessful Outcome for US
Action with adviser rec.	Baseline: no speech	34%	36%	30%
	Adviser true-to-type statement	31%	37%	33%
	Adviser against-type statement	36%	36%	28%
	Action with true vs. against type adviser rec	*−5%**	*0%*	*+5%**
Action against adviser rec.	Adviser true-to-type statement	32%	40%	27%
	Adviser against-type statement	30%	37%	34%
	Action against true vs. against type adviser	*+2%*	*+4%*	*−6%***
	Difference in differences	*−7%***	*−4%*	*+11%****

the outcome. While partisan attitudes may have hardened, unexpected adviser statements, per *H2b*, can still shape how respondents view the president's decisions to use force.

Varying the Outcome: October 2021 Naval Scenario Experiment

The main adviser experiments in 2016 and 2022 deliberately held constant the outcome and left ambiguity about whether it should be considered a success. While this approach has many benefits, it ignores the shadow of the crisis or war outcome. To address this question, in September 2021 I conducted another experiment that varied the outcome. Given the heightened salience of conflict after the Biden administration withdrew from Afghanistan in August 2021, I chose a vignette involving naval forces to avoid confounding.[47] The design is similar to the 2016 adviser experiment and unfolds in two stages. After a preamble noting that the scenario is hypothetical, respondents are told,

> A country sent its navy to block access to a strategic sea route. The sea route is crucial to the economy and national security of a US ally.

> The US president, who is a [Democrat | Republican], held many discussions with his advisers about whether to send US Navy ships and planes to

reopen the sea route, or stay out of the conflict. Officials estimate that if the United States intervened, there would be a significant risk of an armed clash at sea.

Respondents are then told that "during the deliberations," an elite actor either "strongly supported" or "strongly opposed" the use of force in this case, where the elite actor could be a hawkish or dovish adviser, or a hawkish or dovish member of either party in Congress.[48] For example, in the condition where the elite cue comes from hawkish members of Congress, respondents would read, "During the deliberations, several prominent [Democrats | Republicans in Congress], who usually take a hawkish approach to foreign policy and have advocated the use of force in the past when others in their party did not, [strongly supported | strongly opposed] the use of force in this case." The cue for advisers takes the same form as the prior experiment; for example, "one of the president's key advisers, who usually takes a dovish approach to foreign policy and has opposed the use of force in the past when other advisers did not, [strongly supported | strongly opposed] the use of force in this case." Respondents then learn the president's decision (to send US naval forces or not) and are reminded whether that comes with the support of or over the objection of the elite mentioned in the experimental condition. At this stage, respondents are asked if they approve of the president's decision.

If the president sends naval forces, respondents are randomly assigned to one of two outcome conditions. In the "war success" outcome, respondents learn that "there was a clash and the US sailors and pilots suffered just under 100 casualties. US forces successfully got the attacking country's navy to return to home waters. The sea route reopened." In the "war failure" condition, respondents read that "There was a clash and the US sailors and pilots suffered just under 100 casualties. US forces failed to get the attacking country's navy to turn back and the sea route remained blocked." If the president decides not to send naval forces, again the outcome can take one of two forms. In the "stay out / failure" outcome, respondents simply learn that "the sea route remained blocked." I included a fourth condition to compare a diplomatic response to reopen the sea route but added US concessions so that it was clear the resolution of the crisis comes at a cost to the US and its ally. In this "stay out / success" outcome, respondents read that "after several months, the US and its ally negotiated with the attacking country and agreed to some concessions about control of the sea route. The sea route reopened." After this outcome stage, respondents are asked their approval of the president's handling of the situation, as well as several questions related to competence and leadership.[49]

In the interest of brevity, I focus on the effect of the outcome and aggregate all the elite cues into either support or opposition for sending naval forces.

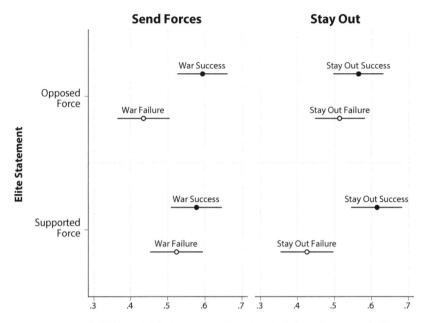

FIGURE 3-8. Effect of fighting on predicted probability of approval of a Democratic president, by elite statement and outcome

Figure 3-8 shows the effect of elite support or opposition to sending naval forces on the predicted probability of approving a Democratic president's handling of the situation, broken down by the outcome. For Democratic presidents, elite statements have a significant effect on the political incentives to send naval forces. If elites support force, then the action that is a gamble for Democratic presidents is to stay out of the conflict (lower right). In contrast, if they send forces, approval is above 50 percent and not significantly different no matter whether the war is a success or failure (lower left). If elites oppose force, then staying out is similarly a politically safe choice no matter the outcome (upper right), but sending forces becomes a gamble dependent on the outcome (upper left). Elite support for war thus incentives Democratic presidents to fight, while elite opposition provides cover for staying out. In contrast, for Republican presidents, as shown figure 3-9, approval depends more directly on the outcome, except when elites oppose war.

Varying the Mission: Intervention in Civil Conflicts

Another consideration is the nature of the mission. In the main adviser experiments and the naval scenario experiment, the mission was an international confrontation between the United States and a foreign country on behalf of

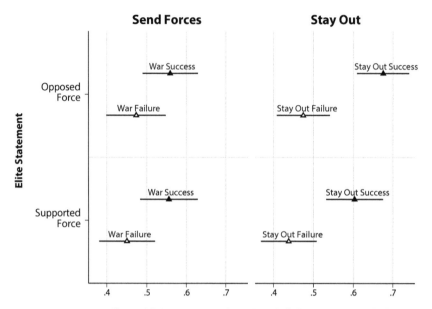

FIGURE 3-9. Effect of fighting on predicted probability of approval of a Republican president, by elite statement and outcome

an ally or partner. I also conducted three experiments where the scenario vignette is about an ongoing US intervention in a civil war, where the United States already has 30,000 troops and the president must decide whether or not to send more.[50] These experiments vary the party of the president as well as whether advisers criticize the president for doing too much or too little. None of the experiments, however, identifies the hawkishness or dovishness of the adviser, nor do they include support conditions (so we cannot directly compare insider support and opposition). Given evidence that public opinion is generally more supportive of military operations aimed at restraining other countries' foreign policies, rather than internal political change, we would expect support for using military force to be lower on average than for the cross-border invasion scenario.[51] Additionally, I conducted all three experiments in the second half of 2014, a challenging time to assess public attitudes about military intervention. This period saw the rise of ISIS and the series of beheadings that began in the summer of 2014, all in the shadow of the official end of the US commitment of combat troops in Iraq in December 2011 and the August 2013 chemical weapons crisis in Syria, when Obama clearly signaled reluctance to intervene.

Given this climate and a scenario involving an ongoing war, it is notable that adviser cues can still move attitudes. All three experiments show an overwhelming preference for presidents of both parties not to escalate US involvement. Nonetheless, in all three, Republican presidents face greater disapproval if they escalate, especially if they do so with advisers criticizing them for doing too much. Democratic presidents in two of the experiments do not see significant effects from hawkish criticism, but in one experiment, conducted in October and November 2014, hawkish criticism increases the disapproval penalty for Democratic presidents who decide not to escalate (although dovish criticism also affects a Democratic president). It is difficult to know whether the lack of movement for Democratic presidents is the result of real-world conditions; the closeness of the scenario to the Iraq and Afghanistan Wars, begun under a Republican president; or strong views of a Democratic incumbent's recent decisions in those wars. But it is notable that Democratic presidents are less subject to these pressures in an ongoing war than Republicans.

These additional experiments vary not only the internal conditions of the experiment, such as the mission or the outcome, but also the background conditions in the real world. The latter, in turn, shape the prior landscape of elite messages and thus the baseline distribution of public attitudes.[52] It is not surprising that the results vary across these contexts. But results as a whole show that adviser cues affect public views of the use of force in a wide variety of settings.

Extension: Public Opinion and the Size of Deployments

The experiments up to this point have focused on initiating or escalating the use of force. There is a vast set of important military decisions in between the beginning and end of wars, however. These decisions significantly affect the course of the war and the outcome but rarely play out in the public domain. Of course, that could be because leaders want to keep such debate behind the scenes. The *how* of war is usually presented to the public as a fait accompli. Of all the aspects of war fighting, one might expect the size of deployments to be the most politically salient and the most likely to attract public interest.[53] In most cases when decisions to use force are debated publicly, the range under discussion can anchor the debate. For example, in late 2009, the Obama administration debated whether to send an additional deployment to Afghanistan ranging from 10,000 to 40,000. The public thus reacts to a range set by elites.

I therefore conducted an experiment in which I randomly varied whether the proposed deployment under debate is in the 1,000–4,000 range or the 10,000–40,000 range. I then can examine public support and approval of the president's ultimate decision conditional on deployment size. I fielded this experiment in summer 2018 on a sample of 1,000 respondents via YouGov. In this experiment, as summarized in table 3-12, the scenario was a cross-border invasion rather a civil war, very similar to the scenario in the main adviser

TABLE 3-12. Experimental Conditions, 2018 Troop Level / Consensus Experiment

Scenario (after introduction that situation is hypothetical)

The year is 2029. A country sent its military to take over a smaller neighboring
country, which is important to US economic and security interests. The US
president debated extensively with his advisers and military leaders about
whether to send the military to help push back the invaders, or stay out of the
conflict. Best estimates suggest that if the United States intervened, the fighting
could be stopped, but the US would face significant armed resistance.
White House advisers and military leaders debated whether the United States
should intervene and how many troops would be required.

Troop Level

Low	High
These officials considered options ranging from 1,000 troops to 4,000 troops, and unanimously agreed that if the president deployed US forces, the mission would require 2,500 troops.	These officials considered options ranging from 10,000 troops to 40,000 troops, and unanimously agreed that if the president deployed US forces, the mission would require 25,000 troops.

Advisory Stance

Dissensus	Consensus
But many officials involved in the debate opposed the use of force in this case and believed the president should not send troops.	All officials involved in the debate supported the use of force in this case and agreed that the president should send troops.

Decision

Stay Out	Send [2,500 | 25,000] Troops
In the end, the president decided to stay out of the conflict and did not send troops. After several months, there was a cease-fire, but sporadic fighting continued in parts of the country.	In the end, the president decided to send [2,500 | 25,000] troops to restore peace. The US suffered just under 100 casualties in the effort. After several months, there was a cease-fire, but sporadic fighting continued in parts of the country.

experiment described above. The troop-level condition randomized the same
ranges (1,000–4,000, settling on 2,500, or 10,000–40,000, settling on 25,000).
In all conditions, I specified that there was unanimity among officials on the
size of the troop deployment required (either 2,500 or 25,000), and the con-
sensus/dissensus conditions focused only on whether officials involved in

TABLE 3-13. Support for War (Stage 1), 2018 Troop Level / Consensus Experiment

Stage 1 (Support for War), Main Effects

Troop Level Condition	Support for War	Consensus Condition	Support for War
High troop level (10,000–40,000)	57%	Consensus	58%
Low troop level (1,000–4,000)	60%	Dissensus	59%
Difference	*–4%*	*Difference*	*–1%*

Stage 1 (Support for War), Interaction Effects

Consensus, by Troop Level	Support for War	Dissensus, by Troop Level	Support for War
High troop level (10,000–40,000)	59%	High troop level (10,000–40,000)	62%
Low troop level (1,000–4,000)	60%	Low troop level (1,000–4,000)	54%
Difference	*–1%*	*Difference*	*+9%**

the debate supported or opposed the troop decision. This wording eliminates confusion over whether officials' support or opposition stemmed from the size of the deployment or the operation itself.

As shown in the top half of table 3-13, there is no direct effect of either the troop-level treatment (i.e., going up an order of magnitude in the size of the deployment under debate) or consensus on support for deployment. Setting the issue of consensus aside, these results imply that public opinion about intervention in this scenario is not particularly sensitive to an order of magnitude difference in the size of a troop deployment. Interestingly, when we examine interactions (shown numerically in the bottom half of table 3-13 and depicted graphically in figure 3-10), if there is dissensus, there is significantly more support for a higher-level troop deployment. In the consensus condition, the troop-level treatment has no effect, suggesting that if the president has a consensus, a deployment of either magnitude will have similar support.[54] It is unclear why respondents are more supportive of a deployment at a higher order of magnitude when there is disagreement. One possibility, consistent with the findings of Herrmann, Tetlock and Visser, is that specifying the support or opposition to the use of force, coupled with unanimity of the size of the proposed deployment, means that the latter signals something about the stakes or seriousness of the threat.[55] Still, these differences are not substantively large, and in all cases support for a deployment is over 50 percent.

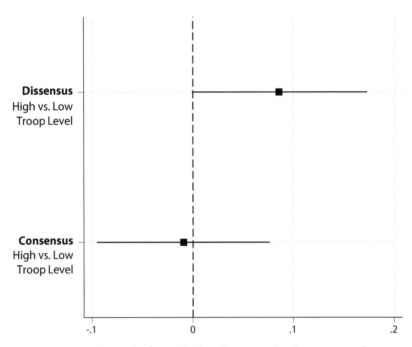

FIGURE 3-10. Marginal effect of high vs. low troop level on support for war,
by level of consensus

In the second stage, as shown in table 3-14, we see a strong preference for
sending troops, and again no main effect of troop level or consensus. But consensus has a similar effect on approval in this stage: while sending troops is
associated with significant increases in support and decreases in opposition
under both the consensus and the dissensus conditions, the magnitude and
significance are much stronger under consensus. Sending troops with consensus is associated with a 14 percentage point increase in approval (p = .0001)
and a nearly 10 percentage point decrease in disapproval (p = .001). Smaller
but significant effects in the same direction under dissensus mean there is no
significant difference in differences in the effect of fighting under consensus
versus dissensus. The larger effect of consensus, however, is driven by greater
approval benefits for fighting under consensus at the higher troop level and
lower penalties for staying out if there is dissensus. Indeed, consensus at the
high troop level opens up a 21 percentage point gap in approval between
sending troops and staying out (62 percent versus 41 percent, p = .0002), and
leads to a 15 percentage point gap in disapproval (32 percent to 16 percent,
p = .0005). There is a smaller, significant approval benefit from fighting even
if there is dissent, but no disapproval penalty for staying out. In the low troop

TABLE 3-14. Support for Presidential Approval (Stage 2), 2018 Troop Level / Consensus Experiment

Stage 2 (Approval), Main Effects

Condition	Approval	Difference
Decision: send troops	60%	+13%***
Decision: stay out	47%	
Troop level: high (10,000–40,000)	52%	+4%
Troop level: low (1,000–4,000)	56%	
Consensus	51%	−5%
Dissensus	56%	

Stage 2 (Approval), Effect on Fighting Premium

Condition	Approval: Stay Out	Approval: Send Troops	Effect of Troops
High troop level, consensus	41%	62%	+21%***
High troop level, dissensus	53%	66%	+13%**
Low troop level, consensus	47%	55%	+8%
Low troop level, dissensus	47%	57%	+10%

condition, consensus has no significant effects. Cell sizes are too small for meaningful difference-in-differences tests here. But the results suggest that consensus can generate greater benefits from fighting at high levels, as well as a penalty for staying out. Looking only at the stay-out decision, over both troop-level treatments, consensus generates a significant penalty if the president goes against officials' recommendations and declines to send troops.[56]

This experiment illustrates that insider elites can affect public support or opposition for military operations, and that the public is relatively impervious to the size of the deployment (although elite cues can affect views of deployment size). Since these experiments do not vary partisanship or adviser views, and conflate military and civilian advisers, it is interesting to compare these results with those from the main adviser experiments discussed earlier in the chapter. Despite imperfect knowledge of the particular national security figures involved in decisions to use force—as suggested by the political knowledge data—the results from the 2016 adviser experiment suggest that when presented with the adviser's general hawkish or dovish stance, respondents use that information to weigh the cue. In the absence of that information, dissent is less powerful. While I leave further testing to future research, the results imply that the information provided in a cue from the White House—not just noting the dissenter or endorser, but providing information about their type, per $H2$ and $H3$—is important.

Takeaways

While no experiment or group of experiments can conclusively test the theory, these surveys, taken together, provide a wealth of evidence that adviser and insider elite cues shape how the public views the use of military force. The results show that advisers influence how the public views decisions to use force; that presidents can use their advisers' type to their advantage or suffer penalties from the statements of particular advisers; and that these cues affect presidents of the two parties differently. Elite cues also define the parameters for how the public views the size of military deployments.

These results also set up expectations for how presidents will engage with elites in debates and decisions about military operations. Presidents can seek supportive cues and dampen or eliminate those that are politically dangerous. I turn now to the case studies that show the insiders' game at work.

4

The Korean War

DEFINING THE INSIDERS' GAME

ALTHOUGH FOREIGN POLICY and US involvement in conflicts abroad have been partisan since the bitter disputes between Jefferson and Hamilton in the Washington administration,[1] the modern landscape of elite politics and war, in the era of nuclear weapons and modern communications, arguably dates from the conflict in Korea.[2] This chapter shows how the Korean War marked out the parameters of elite war politics in the United States that continued to shape presidential decisions to use force long after the Cold War ended. Truman's dealings not only with his commander in the field, Douglas MacArthur, but also with key administration and congressional insiders, trapped him in a "dove's curse."[3]

Truman was the first president to attempt a limited war in the nuclear age while trying to define the domestic and international terms of the post–World War II era. In doing so, Truman pushed up to, and on several occasions, past the limits of the international and domestic constraints he faced, showing future presidents where those limits were as well as the costs and benefits of his approach. Starting with insider appointments before the war that contributed to the "dove's curse," Truman found that maintaining consensus and conserving political capital for other priorities required making concessions to elites. Truman regretted some of these concessions on policy grounds. Other concessions only ratcheted up hawkish pressure as the war went on.

North Korea's invasion of South Korea in June 1950 presented Truman with a series of decisions. Perhaps the most straightforward was whether he would send US forces to Korea. But there were more complicated questions about how and to what extent the United States would intervene. The compromises Truman made from the very outset of the war—compromises that were the direct result of elite bargaining—pushed Truman's policies in a more hawkish direction than we would expect under the faithful intermediaries model. These hawkish policies related not only to battlefield decisions, but also to spillover effects on other aspects of US foreign policy, notably the US stance toward Taiwan. A public-driven model would not expect the risky and often-reluctant choices Truman made, but the insiders' game can explain the direction of those compromises and why elite politics trapped Truman in a "dove's curse."

The Korean War also illustrates the limits of the insiders' game because it offers a case in which the president ultimately failed to contain elite dissent, with dramatic results that put the politics of the war squarely in the public domain. Truman's firing of MacArthur in April 1951 dramatically politicized the acrimonious disagreement over war policy between the president and his commander in the field. In his seminal study of public opinion and war, John Mueller compared the effects of the Korean War and those of the Vietnam War on presidential popularity, concluding that "the single event that best differentiates the impact of the Korean and Vietnam Wars on presidential popularity was President Truman's dismissal of General Douglas MacArthur. That move was a major factor in the politicization of the war as Republicans took the General's side and echoed his complaints that it was the president's meddling in policy that was keeping the war from being won."[4] In his study of presidential power, Richard Neustadt concurs that the firing of MacArthur was a "marked failure," and that up until that point, Truman had answered MacArthur's challenges to presidential authority by seeking "means to keep the general both contained and on the job."[5]

My contention is not that public opinion played no role in the Korean War. But I argue the insiders' game is essential to understanding the course of the war up to that point, and indeed the timing of MacArthur's fire alarm. Truman's need to meet hawks at the point where they would be minimally satisfied resulted in a series of choices that pushed US policy in a more hawkish direction, and this hawkish tilt spilled over into other areas of US policy. This claim does not mean that other factors, such as the emerging geopolitical conflict and the internal dynamics of both North and South Korea, were not important to the course of the war. But compared to a faithful intermediaries explanation—which might have tolerated US intervention but not the more risky, aggressive campaign Truman allowed MacArthur to wage—the evolution of US policy in Korea reflects the insiders' game under a Democratic president. Table 4-1 compares the expectations for the two models in cases under a Democratic president and applies to both this chapter and the following chapter on Johnson and Vietnam.

This chapter concentrates on the facets of the Korean War over which the theory provides the most leverage, that is, the period up to MacArthur's firing. I examine not only Truman's initial decision to send US troops under the auspices of the United Nations, but also his deployment of the Seventh Fleet to the Taiwan Strait—a fateful decision that scholars of China's involvement

TABLE 4-1. Comparing Within-Case Expectations for Democratic Presidents

	Faithful Intermediaries Model	Insiders' Game Model
Side payments	None; careful selection of conflict; insiders act in concert to seek victory if not too risky	War policy concessions to insider hawks (minimum necessary) Concessions to insider/opposition hawks on other national security issues (policy spillover) Procedural concessions to copartisan doves Policy sabotage from dissatisfied hawks
Information	Open flow within government Fire alarm when appropriate	Limited flow to those who could damage agenda Dampen salience of war Avoid/delay hawkish fire alarm
Expectations	Send forces only if not too risky; commit necessary effort; do not prolong war unnecessarily	Limited, indecisive war; policy sabotage; prolonged war Delayed hawkish fire alarm

in the war see as pivotal, and which I argue was the result of bargaining with Taiwan hawks inside the administration and in Congress. Once the war began, Truman's bargaining with MacArthur resulted in risky escalation choices. The decision to cross the thirty-eighth parallel was complex, and MacArthur's preference for a decisive victory was not the only factor, but the pressure it put on Truman was an important contributing influence. Although the politics of the war after MacArthur's firing are more complex, I briefly discuss how Truman managed to use some elite politicking to get his Cold War rearmament program through despite his historic unpopularity, and how even Truman's successor, Dwight Eisenhower, faced elite constraints as he sought an armistice in Korea.

Throughout the chapter, I emphasize the mechanisms of hawkish bias identified in chapter 2. After the Chinese Communists prevailed in the Chinese Civil War, Truman faced a credibility gap, and his Asia policy in particular came under heavy fire from Congress. As the theory expects for leaders from parties associated with dovishness, Truman faced selection pressures to try to close the credibility gap; high agenda costs, not only from his domestic "Fair Deal" agenda but also from his own security and foreign policy team, which produced the famous National Security Council (NSC) document known as NSC-68, outlining a rearmament program focused on Europe rather than

Asia; and the high costs to obtain the support of hawkish elites for a more dovish approach in Korea. He made major concessions to insider and opposition hawks on the war and on other policies and relied on the private and political benefits the war could provide reluctant doves.

Why Revisit the Korean War?

The Korean War is well-trod historical ground whose domestic politics have been analyzed by political scientists and historians alike, so it is worth enumerating the value of the case for an elite theory of democracies and war. First, starting with this case demonstrates that the elite-driven framework applies long before the technological, technocratic, and political changes that give presidents more tools to evade public scrutiny. Second, the Korea case is also useful because it is an example of a conventional conflict, illustrating that elite coalition dynamics apply beyond counterinsurgency wars—where we might expect that the less obvious signs of progress would make elite leadership of mass opinion even more likely. The Korean War was nothing if not a dramatic series of events: the surprise attack from the North on June 25, 1950; the UN forces' successful stabilization of the Pusan perimeter; MacArthur's risky and unexpectedly successful landing at Inchon in September 1950, turning the tide back in the UN's favor; the crossing of the thirty-eighth parallel in October 1950; the initiation of MacArthur's "end-the-war" offensive in late November 1950, contrary to suggestions for more limited options that would keep American soldiers away from the most sensitive northern border regions; the massive Chinese intervention in November 1950 that ultimately pushed the front back to the thirty-eighth parallel; MacArthur's dismissal in April 1951; and finally, the subsequent years of stalemate.

In addition, historians have reconsidered how Truman aimed to "sell" the Korean War in the context of generating domestic support for his approach to containing Communism.[6] The Korean War is frequently seen through the prism of the mobilization strategy the Truman administration used to build domestic support for the major recommitment to Europe that NSC-68 represented. Caught between threats in Asia and Europe, Truman effected a "logroll," as Jack Snyder describes, to meet an overt threat from communism in Asia while confronting the looming threat in Europe.[7] Truman—a budget balancer who was a reluctant convert to a major rearmament program in the first place—was caught in between. Most existing accounts of the domestic politics of the Korean War focus on the mobilization of public support for the war or for the larger rearmament.[8] Korea, in this view, was part of an effort to "scare the hell out of the country," as Republican Senator Arthur Vandenberg had told Truman in the context of debate over aid to Greece and Turkey a few years earlier.[9] In recent reconsiderations, however, historians have cast doubt on this interpretation. In a history of the Truman administration's efforts to sell the Korean War, for example, Steven Casey argues that the scare tactics frame misses actions Truman took to manage public and elite opinion, as well as Truman's desire not to ratchet up but rather to tamp down public war hysteria lest it exert too much hawkish pressure.[10]

Previous accounts also emphasize public constraints or presidential imperatives but have not explored the mechanisms of elite bargaining systematically.[11] Political scientists have been interested in the determinants of public attitudes toward the war, as well as the effect of casualties on public opinion, long the most famous of Mueller's findings.[12] Mueller also highlights the striking finding that after a significant drop in public support when China entered the war, public support remained remarkably steady for the remainder of the conflict despite many dramatic events.[13] Casey argues this public support was partly the product of the Truman administration's improved elite interactions, as "the government found ways to redefine its objectives, while also improving its relationships with key mediating voices in the polity."[14]

Among those who have examined elite politics, Victor Cha explores US elite views about the Korean War but focuses mainly on the choice of alliance structure in Asia.[15] Jack Snyder posits that the politics of national security in the early Cold War period were scrambled across party lines and thus were "cartelized," and later subject to the scrutiny of the median voter.[16] Snyder argues that this pattern of cartelization was only "temporary," however, and makes the "claim only that coalition dynamics contributed to the intellectual and domestic political underpinnings of a Cold War consensus favoring global containment of communism."[17] Relatedly, Benjamin Fordham argues that elite bargaining rooted in the politics of domestic economic concerns explain the emergence of the Cold War consensus around rearmament, in which the Korean War played a central role.[18]

My argument is that the patterns observable in Korea, at least prior to MacArthur's firing, fit a stronger claim: that the insiders' game pushed policy in a more hawkish direction, and as illustrated in subsequent chapters, these patterns were far from temporary. Throughout the conflict, Truman used the side payment and information strategies laid out in chapter 2. As summarized in table 4-2, Truman attempted to co-opt and accommodate hawks who could provide political cover, notably by including Republican John Foster Dulles as a State Department adviser, and by repeatedly attempting to keep MacArthur happy enough on the battlefield. Truman also tried to manage information flow within and among elite circles to dampen salience and attempted to keep debate from spilling into the public domain. These efforts largely succeeded until MacArthur reached intolerable levels of insubordination and Truman

TABLE 4-2. Within-Case Evidence for Korean War

	Side Payments	Information
War initiation (June 1950)	To insider hawks: 7th Fleet to Taiwan Strait To copartisans: act through UN	Dampen salience (act through UN, limited White House speech, control of bureaucratic statements)
Escalation Pre-Inchon	War policy concessions to MacArthur	Removal of Louis Johnson (secretary of defense)
Post-Inchon	War policy control to MacArthur, change in war aim to unification (risky escalation) Internal security program	Attempts to limit MacArthur's public statements
Duration/ termination	Prolonged by bargaining with hawks (dove's curse) Resolution at 38th parallel (Eisenhower)	Delayed fire alarm (MacArthur firing)

fired him. In the process, Truman chose more hawkish policies that elites cared about but about which the public knew little. These policy concessions were a high price to pay to maintain elite consensus. They prolonged the war and enabled a risky and aggressive effort to unify the peninsula—and led to spill-over effects on US policy toward Taiwan, as well as internal security policy in the United States—only to result in Chinese intervention and ultimately the return to the original stalemate.

Truman's Domestic Political Landscape

Truman faced an elite landscape that seems unusual from the perspective of familiar Cold War domestic politics. For Truman, the peculiar feature of elite politics was the cross-cutting coalitions that favored or opposed his two sets of priorities. On foreign policy, there was a significant divide between Europe-first internationalists led by Secretary of State Dean Acheson, on the one hand, who focused on building a multilateral architecture in Europe to confront the Soviet threat, and nationalists, on the other hand, led by Ohio Republican senator Robert Taft, whose real beliefs were closer to isolationism, but who latched on to "Asia-first" (or "Asialationist," as they became known) critiques of Truman and Acheson's approach to containment.[19] As Casey notes, "in terms of raw numbers . . . the nationalist wing of the GOP was not terribly potent, with only between ten and twenty Republican senators habitually voting against the administration's foreign policy," but they made plenty of noise, especially on the issue of support for the Chinese nationalist regime in Taiwan.[20] This problem of intense and specific preferences, coupled with concentrated power, was particularly acute on Asia policy. Since "Congress as a whole displayed an almost complete indifference to Asia," the field was left to a small group of congressional elites.[21] The Republicans also had a significant internationalist wing led by Vandenberg.

Truman's problem, as Neustadt summarizes, was that "the internationalist coalition, which supported Truman's foreign policy, existed, cheek by jowl, with a 'conservative' coalition," which opposed his domestic program. The Southern Democrats, who tended to be hawkish, joined with the internationalist Republicans to support his foreign and oppose his domestic policies, "side by side, through issue after issue, Congress after Congress."[22] Thus "a coalition of southern Democrats and Republicans might at any time jeopardize key pieces of foreign policy legislation."[23] As would be true for Lyndon Johnson, then, the position of Southern Democratic hawks meant that Democratic control of Congress did not necessarily translate into easy legislative victories for Truman, and decisions about the war had to be taken with other priorities in mind.[24] As a Democrat, Truman also faced criticism that his overall stance in the Cold War was insufficiently tough, especially in the wake of the perceived failure to stop the Chinese Communist victory. The "who lost China?" debate trained particular fire on Secretary of State Dean Acheson, who became the target of direct attacks from Senator Joseph McCarthy.[25] These domestic political cleavages shaped politics before the outbreak of the Korean War and set the stage for the elite bargaining that would take place at the outset of the conflict and during the escalation. The politics of this period led Truman to make policy concessions and generated selection pressures for insider appointments that shaped subsequent elite bargaining.

Public opinion is more difficult to characterize. It is challenging to develop a counterfactual version of the US response to the invasion of South Korea and subsequent wartime decisions under a faithful intermediaries model, because the prewar elite attacks on Truman's Asia policy and the elite cues during the war shaped the observed public attitudes we see in polls. But scholars of Truman's approach to public opinion suggest he was concerned both about mobilizing public support for a recommitment to international confrontation, and about stoking excessive hawkish sentiment that would increase escalatory pressure.[26] In a detailed study of Truman's public opinion strategy during the war, Casey notes that the State Department was especially concerned by data suggesting that public opinion was "especially volatile, oscillating rapidly between calls for disarmament and budding support for a preventive war."[27] Only five years after the end of World War II, the public was not eager for another conflict with potential nuclear escalation, but the concept of limited war was also "difficult to square with the enormous national effort used in World War II."[28] Casey thus documents how Truman and many in the administration were skeptical of a "scare campaign" to mobilize support for rearmament, for fear that public opinion would be *too* enamored of a buildup, especially in the wake of a crisis.[29] If the United States were to fight, however, the public would presumably wish to pursue victory while avoiding unnecessary or excessive risk. Policy makers might justifiably argue that these goals were incompatible, and the events of the war would bear out this view. But decision makers attempting to anticipate public opinion would have to make do with the public's seeming desire to have its cake and eat it too.

What seems clearer in terms of public opinion is that it was largely silent on many of the other policy areas that would prove essential to the course of the war. For example, the faithful intermediaries model would not expect the spillover effects into Taiwan policy that would have such important consequences. As the data on Taiwan policy discussed below suggest, the public knew little about the controversy, which was instead driven by the intense preferences of a small group of elites.

Mechanisms of Hawkish Bias

When North Korea invaded South Korea on June 25, 1950, Truman quickly returned to Washington from Missouri and met with his top military and civilian advisers at Blair House. The emerging dynamics of the international environment were the most important factor that led Truman to take a stand in Korea, and within days he had committed US forces to aid South Korea. But from the very outset, the nature of the intervention reflected elite politics, which embedded hawkish bias into the decisions of a Democratic president who was hesitant to use force, had only reluctantly come around to the need for rearmament in Europe, and wanted to resist hawkish escalatory pressure. In this section, I discuss the three mechanisms of hawkish bias and how they affected Truman's response to the crisis.

Selection Pressures

When war broke out in June 1950, Truman was not starting with a blank slate. He had already faced McCarthy's attacks on the State Department and its China experts, which led Truman to try to diffuse criticism of his Asia policy by co-opting and enlisting erstwhile critics. Selection pressures also tied Truman's hands with existing appointments.

Two examples illustrate that the these selection pressures pointed in a decidedly hawkish direction. First, John Foster Dulles's appointment in April 1950 was a direct attempt to shore up Republican support in Congress for Truman's policy in Asia. Acheson sought Republican support in the form of a "distinguished Republican to become a roving Ambassador in Japan and the Far East," and in correspondence, Arthur Vandenberg made clear to Acheson that anyone who favored recognizing Beijing would be "entirely ineligible."[30] Vandenberg followed up two days later with a strong personal endorsement of Dulles.[31] Snyder comments that "Dulles's coercion of Acheson in this context was breathtaking," with Dulles essentially threatening to mount what would be his second campaign for Senate in New York in the fall of 1950, having lost a special election the previous year and having criticized Truman's foreign policy during the campaign.[32]

Truman, who was clearly aware of Dulles's comments in his prior, unsuccessful Senate run, was reluctant to appoint the Republican but sought some way to include him, as long as he was not named "Ambassador-at-Large."[33] Acheson engaged in a delicate dance to get Dulles to sign on without the appearance of a deal to preempt another Senate run. The mere need for this discussion, however, suggested that the threat of political retaliation loomed over his appointment. Dulles haggled over his title, suggesting ambassador-at-large, which Acheson had to awkwardly reject. Dulles "said that he had been in touch with Senator Vandenberg and Senator Smith, who along with Governor Dewey felt that the Republican Party was selling out awfully cheap."[34] In a meeting with Truman to clear the air when Dulles arrived in Washington, the new State Department counselor raised the past Senate campaign history, complaining, "the opposition had said some rather vicious things about me." In his memorandum of the conversation for Acheson's benefit, Dulles recounted that he warned Truman:

> the mere fact that I had a desk in the State Department did not in any way automatically assure bi-partisanship in foreign policy or protect the State Department against Republican criticism. I said that as I worked on foreign policies, and as there developed foreign policies that I could wholeheartedly support, I had confidence that they would receive sympathetic consideration by Republicans on the Hill, and that in the main Republicans would not attack such policies merely on partisan grounds. A good deal would, of course, depend on whether I was in a position to help to work out policies that I could genuinely endorse.[35]

Dulles thus clearly signaled to Truman that his endorsement came at a price. Dulles mentioned "some early affirmative action . . . to deal with the Communist menace," ideally in the "East," which would help drive McCarthy to the background. As discussed below, it soon became clear that the "action" Dulles had in mind was making a commitment to Taiwan.

The second example of selection pressure was Truman's understanding that he was stuck with MacArthur, still commanding allied forces in Japan and the obvious choice to lead the effort in Korea. Privately, Truman was candid in his views of MacArthur's record and future ambitions. On July 1, Truman talked with his press aides about MacArthur,

> for whom the President has little regard or respect. He feels, as do most others, that MacArthur is a supreme egotist, who regarded himself as something of a god. The President commented on MacArthur's departure from Manila and Corregidor, when the Japanese besieged the Philippines early in the war, and his escape to Australia, leaving General Wainwright to be captured. Wainwright has never recovered from the experience while MacArthur has become a hero and dictator in Japan.[36]

Truman wasn't finished. He told his aides that they

> should have heard John Foster Dulles and what he had to say to the President about MacArthur when he came in to see him this week after returning from Tokyo. . . . Dulles, the President indicated, would like to have MacArthur hauled back to the United States but the President pointed out to him that the General is involved politically in this country—where he has from time to time [been] mentioned as a possible Republican Presidential candidate—and that he could not recall MacArthur without causing a tr[e]mendous reaction in this country where he has been built up, to heroic stature.[37]

As Casey concludes, not only would failing to appoint MacArthur to the UN command be politically dangerous, but "if he were given command, this would send out a strong signal to Republicans that the administration meant business."[38]

Even Dulles recognized that MacArthur might act more aggressively or recklessly than Republicans would prefer. Dulles expressed his concerns to Acheson in writing on July 7:

> In view of the extreme delicacy of the present situation; the importance of preventing the Korean fighting from developing into a world war; the importance of maintaining the confidence of the other members of the Security Council that their resolutions will be scrupulously complied with; and in view of the factors which you and I discussed with the President, I suggest that the President might want to emphasize by personal message to General MacArthur the delicate nature of the responsibilities which he will now be carrying, not only on behalf of the United States but on behalf of the United Nations, and the importance of instructing his staff to comply scrupulously with political and military limitations and instructions which may be sent, the reasons for which may not always be immediately apparent but which will often have behind them political considerations of gravity.[39]

These examples do not mean that Truman was a hapless prisoner of partisan circumstance when choosing advisers. He held the line against calls for a war cabinet that included Republicans, for example.[40] Truman was also unafraid to fire politically troublesome advisers who proved incompetent. For example, a different source of pressure on Truman came from the Pentagon, where Secretary of Defense Louis Johnson was such a thorn in the president's side that Truman took the costly step of firing him in wartime. Although known as an "economizer" and thus not hawkish in the traditional sense, Johnson soon associated himself with the Asialationist perspective. Politically, he also represented a danger to Truman, not only because he had presidential ambitions of his own, but also because he was a habitual leaker with direct and close connections with key Republicans in Congress. Johnson was known for passing information to the administration's critics in Congress—for example at the Mayflower Hotel, where he and Republican Owen Brewster of Maine both lived. Brewster joined McCarthyite attacks on Acheson, "doubtless aided by inside information from the Pentagon."[41]

Johnson's opportunistic aid to the Asialationists while undermining mobilization efforts at home ultimately pushed Truman too far. In September 1950, Truman replaced him with George Marshall, whose standing, though somewhat diminished by the "who lost China" debate, nonetheless provided cover. Casey notes, however, that "in practical political terms," Marshall's appointment was "probably a mistake, for it meant passing over the chance to appoint a leading Republican who could shield the cabinet against partisan attacks."[42] Perhaps the Dulles experience led Truman to be cautious about including Republicans, particularly when the smooth functioning of the war machine was paramount.

Selection pressures therefore mattered, but they were not determinative. Nonetheless, Truman arrived at the critical decisions in June 1950 with hawkish pressure built in to his decision-making circle. These officials, already critical of Truman's Asia policy, would also have access to information, continuous opportunities to monitor and criticize policy, and the power to impose significant costs on the president.

Agenda Costs

Given the timing of his presidency, Truman had an unusual constellation of priorities for a Democratic chief executive: he had to chart the US course in the Cold War that later presidents could take for granted, while dealing with the domestic aftermath of World War II. As a Democrat, he had a long list of domestic priorities that the coalition of Southern Democrats and Republicans could (and did) threaten. As David Mayhew summarizes, the Fair Deal was not merely an extension of the New Deal but rather "largely stood on its own base," adding civil rights, education, and health insurance as issue areas not covered by the New Deal.[43] Ultimately, Mayhew concludes, LBJ's Great Society "seems to have been chiefly a fulfillment of the Fair Deal, not the New Deal."[44] Although the outbreak of war in Korea led Truman to shelve formal pursuit of some of his major domestic priorities, Neustadt notes that he continued to press them rhetorically and, where he could, legislatively, ultimately "preparing new positions for his party," on which later Democratic presidents could and did build.[45] Thus Neustadt argues that even after the United States became bogged down in Korea, "Truman kept asking for all of it and getting none of it."[46]

If Truman was a typical Democrat with a large domestic social agenda requiring legislative action, however, he was atypical in that he also had a large foreign policy agenda requiring the same. Once Truman decided on a major rearmament program, encapsulated in NSC-68, he had not one but two major legislative programs to shepherd. As Fordham argues, the foreign and national security policies that emerged from these years were not inevitable responses to international imperatives, nor were the linkages across policies, such as the connection between Cold War containment and the anticommunist crusade at home.[47] Instead, Fordham argues that they were the product of elite bargaining, although he sees these elites as rooted in societal interests that shaped their preferences over national and domestic policies, at a time when the basic direction of the country's containment strategy was still unsettled.

Cost of Hawkish Elite Support

The theory posits that for Democratic presidents, the price of hawkish elite support for a more limited or cautious approach will be steep, and the cost of hawkish opposition very high. I develop this evidence in the discussion below, but recall that the theory expects that Democratic presidents will need to make side payments to insider and opposition hawks on war policy as well as other foreign policy issues, while they can more easily placate copartisan doves with political coattails or private benefits, as well as the benefits of attention to domestic priorities copartisan doves likely favor. In terms of information management, we would expect that Democratic presidents fear an early fire alarm from hawks, who will increase escalation pressure—something Truman was quite fearful of, as noted. They will seek to dampen salience, playing down the war while trying to get on with other priorities. Democratic leaders in Congress did generally support Truman, going so far as to advise the administration against a formal congressional authorization, as discussed below.

War Initiation: Truman's Response to the Invasion of South Korea

Initial Side Payments: Taiwan Policy

A remarkable feature of Truman's elite bargaining at the outset of Korean War was its close connection to Taiwan policy. To a remarkable degree, the early internal discussions about how to respond to the Korean crisis repeatedly involved Taiwan. The internal debate reflected long-standing divisions within the administration and reinforce the arguments from chapter 2 that politics pervades the executive branch.

The administration's internal and external battles over Taiwan policy started long before the outbreak of war in Korea. Earlier in 1950, prior to the North Korean invasion, the Truman administration had had to placate the Republican right, especially the China bloc, to get a measure for economic aid to South Korea through Congress by extending aid to Chiang Kai-shek's regime in Taiwan through June 30. Aid to Taiwan had emerged as a necessary side payment to smooth the path for other key administration initiatives, including those in Europe.[48]

The January 1950 debate over aid to South Korea occurred against the backdrop of Truman's January 5 speech announcing that the United States would essentially stay out of the Chinese Civil War and the US position that Taiwan, also known as Formosa, was part of China.[49] The speech was the culmination of an intra-administration battle. On one side was Acheson, who favored disengagement from the conflict in the hope of encouraging closer ties between the US and mainland China (including US recognition of the Communist regime). Both Acheson and Truman were also highly skeptical of Chiang Kai-shek.[50] On the other side were military and Pentagon officials, including the Joint Chiefs of Staff (JCS), Defense Secretary Louis Johnson, and MacArthur (still overseeing the rebuilding of Japan at that point).[51] Even some internationalist Republican senators were unhappy with the administration's apparent willingness to accept the loss of Taiwan, and they told Acheson so in a long and tense meeting on January 5.[52] The split within the administration over Taiwan policy had been detailed by James Reston in the *New York Times*, which noted the administration's preference for recognizing the Communist regime in Beijing but that Truman "needs the support in Congress of anti-recognition Senators whose votes are felt to be necessary on other projects."[53] Thomas Christensen notes that Reston "almost certainly had been granted briefings by someone in the administration . . . to counter damaging leaks by Johnson and MacArthur."[54]

Soon after his appointment as a State Department adviser, Dulles met with Republican Senate leaders in May 1950. On Taiwan policy, they agreed they would "start no 'fireworks' until Dulles has a chance to move in on this with Acheson."[55] Dulles had already drafted a memo for Dean Rusk, then serving as assistant secretary of state for East Asian and Pacific affairs, parts of which Rusk adopted verbatim in a memo to Acheson on May 30. The Dulles/Rusk memo, as transmitted to Acheson, stated that a "series of disasters can probably be prevented if . . . we quickly take a dramatic and strong stand that shows our confidence and resolution." Of all places "where such a stand might be taken, Formosa has advantages superior to any other."[56] In a meeting the same day, an aide reported Rusk's view that "Formosa presents a plausible place to 'draw the line' and is, in itself, important politically if not strategically, for what it represents in continued Communist expansion."[57] As Tucker notes, though Dulles had no "special love" for Chiang's regime, he was well aware of his political position within the administration and served as a conduit for a particular set of Republican congressional views.[58]

The outbreak of war in Korea did not change Acheson's mind about Taiwan, which he had mentioned with Korea as being outside the US "defensive perimeter" in his famous January 1950 speech to the National Press Club.[59] Remarkably, however, when Truman and his top advisers convened at Blair House on June 25, Taiwan was the first item discussed. Secretary Johnson asked JCS chairman Omar Bradley to read a letter from MacArthur dated June 14 on the importance of keeping Taiwan out of Communist hands.[60] Acheson "recognized this as an opening gun in a diversionary argument that Johnson wished to start with me. Evidently another did also, for when Bradley had finished, the President announced that discussion of the Far Eastern situation had better be postponed until after dinner when we would be alone."[61] In these meetings, the JCS expressed hesitation about sending US forces to Korea (as Dulles would also when he arrived back from the Far East), illustrating that their concerns were more narrowly focused on Taiwan and not simply aimed at fighting in Asia.

Snyder argues that Acheson, who was no dove on overall national security policy but formerly an advocate of disengagement in Asia, "stands out as the most hawkish of the advisers in the Blair House meetings," largely as a result of the domestic political pressure he and the administration had suffered generally for its China policy.[62] Along with his initial recommendations to address the North Korean invasion, Acheson also recommended sending the Seventh Fleet to the Taiwan Strait "to prevent an attack on Formosa from the mainland. At the same time operations from Formosa against the mainland should be prevented."[63] As Cha describes, sending the Seventh Fleet "was as much about avoiding entrapment by the client state as it was about containment of the adversary."[64] Yet the shift in Taiwan policy clearly had a domestic angle: as Snyder argues, it was Acheson's attempt to "preempt the inevitable in order to implement it in the least damaging way."[65] That Truman and Acheson were unenthusiastic about the decision—pulled off their ideal point—was evident in the June 26 Blair House meeting at which the president authorized orders for "the Seventh Fleet to prevent an attack on Formosa." As Truman mused about possibilities for Taiwan's future, Acheson said it was "undesirable that we should get mixed up in the question of the Chinese administration of the Island." Truman added that "we were not going to give the Chinese 'a nickel' for any purpose whatever."[66]

The decision to send the Seventh Fleet to the Taiwan Strait would turn out to have far-reaching consequences for the war. Although it somewhat diffused the Taiwan issue politically—affording Truman some leeway on that front, despite MacArthur's subsequent efforts to reengage it—the decision also had important international ramifications. First, although it was partly designed to keep hostilities confined to Korea, it made US allies very nervous.[67] Second, and more importantly, it also generated a strong reaction in China and may have helped undermine US hopes to reassure China of its limited aims when UN forces regained their footing and then crossed the thirty-eighth parallel. As Chen Jian writes, "the eruption of the Korean War . . . did not take Beijing's leaders by surprise, but Washington's decision to intervene not only in Korea but also in Taiwan did." The US move not only stopped momentum for Mao's invasion of Taiwan but also threatened China with a two-front war and played into an image of "U.S. imperialist aggression" that Mao could confront and thereby consolidate his position at home.[68] As Christensen argues,

> For both political and strategic reasons, Truman's June decision to protect Chiang intensified Mao's sense that any long-term American presence in North Korea would threaten his new nation's security. The possibility of a future two-front war against the United States not only led Mao to fight but also counseled him to adopt an extremely offensive strategy designed to drive the Americans completely off the Korean peninsula.[69]

Although Christensen sees these politics as driven by public opinion, I argue that they were the result of accommodating elites with more intense, specific, and, in this case, extreme preferences. As William Stueck argues, "it is difficult to avoid the conclusion that the State Department could have achieved its objective of deterrence without announcing an increase in aid to Taiwan and Indochina," and might have instead "issued a general statement that attacks by Communist forces in areas other than Korea would have serious consequences." Acknowledging the elite pressures, Stueck also concludes that the Truman administration could likely have convinced the public of the wisdom of avoiding further entanglement on Taiwan, since "a public campaign had been waged before—and with a large measure of success—to avoid direct involvement in the Chinese Civil War. Had it been waged again," he argues, the administration "probably would have suffered no greater embarrassment on the Taiwan issue, both at home and abroad, than it actually did as the summer of 1950 progressed."[70]

Indeed, under the faithful intermediaries model, there would be little reason to expect the Seventh Fleet commitment. Nancy Bernkopf Tucker argues that public opinion was not a major constraint on Truman's approach to China and Taiwan. As she notes, while polls in this period "on any specific question might suggest strong popular convictions, government analysts found the most dominant characteristic was the consistently large percentage of people with 'no opinion.'" Even the release of the China "White Paper" in 1949, intended in part as a public relations effort, resulted in a poll showing 64 percent of respondents had not heard about it.[71] Polling also found ambivalence about and ignorance of Chiang Kai-shek and Taiwan policy.[72] She concludes that "American public opinion did not prevent United States recognition of the Chinese Communist regime," and that "official assessments of public views showed that the American people had few firmly held ideas about China policy."[73]

A third consequence of the decision, important from the perspective of the theory, is that the decision to send the Seventh Fleet to the Taiwan Strait made it difficult to reverse course and extricate the United States from Taiwan, and indeed served as a lever for hawks as the Korean War unfolded. Truman and Acheson had not intended this commitment to last beyond the end of the Korean War, but almost inevitably, it took on a life of its own. Furthermore, MacArthur used the Taiwan issue as he tugged at the leash Washington found it increasingly difficult to keep him on. Chiang offered thirty-three thousand nationalist troops for the Korean effort, which tempted Truman. Even after he rejected the plan, "it remained in place to plague Acheson and the State Department during subsequent stages of the conflict."[74] MacArthur visited Taiwan in July 1951 in a move halfheartedly condoned by the JCS but without the State Department's input, "reflecting the poor relations between State and Defense in this policy area," and made public statements with Chiang that suggested close future coordination.[75] By May 1951, with the signing of NSC 48/4—which put Asia front and center in terms of US security threats and made a clear commitment to Taiwan—"the Republican policy toward China was adopted by the Truman administration virtually intact."[76]

Though insider hawks extracted this side payment, it was also aimed at Republicans from both wings of the party since support for Taiwan was a common preference. And it illustrated that for a Democratic president, national security support from that quarter, even in wartime, would necessitate long-lasting policy concessions on other national security issues. Still, that Truman could frame the policy as a necessary preventive measure in a crisis context may have helped the administration gloss over its pivot from Truman's public stance in January that the US would not aid Taiwan. Thus the shadow of the direct costs that a concentrated group of elites could impose on his national security program directly influenced how Truman approached the Korean War and contributed to the costly trap the war would ultimately become.

Initial Side Payments: Rearmament Policy and Domestic Priorities

Truman also bargained with members of Congress at the outset of the war over national security and domestic policy. This process took the form of "tacit bargaining," as Fordham puts it, because it is less palatable to admit these trade-offs publicly, whereas a "tacit bargaining process can be explained in a variety of ways to different audiences."[77] The bargaining that took place at the beginning of the Korean War set the tone not only for the escalation but also for the direction of US policy in the Cold War itself. That Truman, a Democrat with a full slate of domestic priorities, was willing to give up these priorities and reluctantly preside over the enactment of an internal security program he detested reflects both the unusual elite landscape he faced and the unsettled nature of early Cold War policy. Truman's bargaining with Congress, then, is an exception that proves the rule.

Fordham argues that the linkage between Korea and rearmament was a deliberate and by no means inevitable political strategy.[78] Indeed, he argues the decision to intervene in Korea was not obvious, an argument bolstered by the initial hesitation of many top advisers, including anti-rearmament Secretary Johnson and Secretary of the Army Frank Pace, as well as, more surprisingly, MacArthur, the Joint Chiefs of Staff, and Dulles, all of whom expressed reservations about using US ground forces.[79] MacArthur quickly became more enthusiastic once placed in command, and Dulles seemed to oppose ground forces specifically but had openly called for US involvement as well as linking Korea and Taiwan.

Fordham argues that the decision to intervene was part of the domestic bargaining process.[80] Support for the war made opposition to rearmament more difficult, although not impossible. The nationalists' support for the war was fragile, however, making further concessions to the Republican Asialationists politically advisable. Thus Fordham argues that Truman supported, with great reluctance, the harsh internal security program ostensibly targeted at domestic subversive activities but ripe for abuse in the name of anticommunism.[81] Given these realities, Truman had to give up asking Congress for the Fair Deal and instead pushed forward on the internal security front. Fordham argues that it was not budget constraints, the distraction of Korea, or time constraints in Congress that led Truman to stop putting legislative effort into the Fair Deal, to which he was still personally and rhetorically committed. Instead, the end of the Fair Deal as a legislative priority, and the administration's affirmative efforts on internal security, were specific policy concessions to the nationalist Republicans, who had wanted the former for a long time and who were increasingly committed to the latter.

It was the need to get rearmament through Congress that led Truman to make this trade-off. The Korean War allowed Truman to force through rearmament by putting pressure on the nationalist Republican skeptics to support military spending in wartime—even though the spending went well beyond Korea—but at the price of the Fair Deal.[82] Even after the war began, "the decision to make these concessions still made sense because it offered a way to attract some Republican support and to reduce the chance that they would turn against intervention in Korea and attempt to force a coalition with others who opposed the rearmament program."[83] Policy concessions on internal security, an issue that predated the war and was largely unconnected to it, also made sense as a way to prevent Republican nationalist defections.

The Korean War thus provided a powerful example for future Democratic presidents of the cost of obtaining congressional support—even without an official authorization for war—at the expense of other priorities. The circumstances of the Korea question were certainly different from many later Cold War decisions because for Truman, the very terms of American Cold War policy were at stake. Future presidents would not have to legislate basic commitments as Truman had had to do, nor did they face a strong isolationist wing of the Republican Party, making it possible for Lyndon Johnson to even contemplate pursuing the Great Society while prosecuting the Vietnam War.

But the concessions on Taiwan policy and on internal security showed that opposition Republicans of different stripes could extract difficult-to-reverse policy concessions on other national security issues, even when they did not control either chamber. Indeed, the Taiwan commitment stuck, and the internal security concessions became harder to roll back as they became more institutionalized through bureaucracies like the Federal Bureau of Investigation (FBI).[84] It is no surprise, then, that Democratic presidents made these concessions much more rarely, preferring to bargain with their insider and copartisan hawks over war policy. For Truman, facing a Republican Party with real and potent internal divisions over the direction of US national security policy, some bargaining with Congress made sense. Later Democratic presidents would not need Republicans or other hawkish elites to pass large increases in military spending; on the contrary, they would need to make that kind of spending a side payment to get more dovish policies like arms control through the Senate.[85]

War Initiation: Audience and Information Control

In addition to side payments, Truman sought to control the size and composition of his domestic audience, and specifically to avoid hawkish constraints from both Congress and the public. Truman used several tools to control information flow within and outside elite circles and to limit the possibilities for debate. His most well-known decision, and arguably the one with the most far-reaching consequences for executive power in the United States, was to take advantage of the Soviet delegate's absence from the United Nations to seek UN authority for the action in Korea, rather than congressional authorization.[86] The UN decision was made quickly, but over the next two weeks, Truman considered and ultimately declined to seek a congressional resolution, lest it devolve into an opportunity for partisan debate.[87] Given the efforts Truman had already made to diffuse opposition to his Asia policy, one might see this move as curious—after all, despite the intraparty cleavages on foreign policy, the Democrats controlled both the House and the Senate in 1950, and a vote could generate elite consensus and political cover. Recent historical accounts see this move as avoiding escalation pressures at a time when Truman was acutely aware of the dangers of a nuclear war, given the Soviet acquisition of the bomb a year earlier.[88]

Instead of a congressional address or vote, Truman consulted select congressmen quietly. In a meeting on July 3, Acheson proposed a congressional message and for friendly members to propose a resolution, going so far as to present a draft to the group. Although several advisers suggested that Congress would want to weigh in, Senate majority leader Scott Lucas "frankly questioned the desirability" of delivering a message to Congress, arguing that the "President had very properly done what he had to without consulting the Congress," and that "many members of Congress had suggested to him that the President should keep away from Congress and avoid debate." Truman decided against seeking a resolution, especially since Congress was not in session and he did not want to call them back, instead proposing further consultations with the Democratic leaders with whom he met regularly.[89]

To be sure, Truman had national security reasons to manage information flow to Congress, as illustrated by his handling of the highly sensitive issue of Soviet involvement in the war. As Austin Carson has demonstrated, the United States and the Soviet Union effectively colluded to conceal Soviet involvement in the Korean War, a strategy that suited Truman's hope to keep the war limited and avoid hawkish pressure for escalation.[90] From the earliest days of the crisis Truman was very careful to manage discussion of Soviet involvement, going so far to as to ask members of Congress, at a June 27 meeting, not to openly connect the Soviets to the war in Korea. As Acheson turned to Moscow's role, "the President called for attention and said that he wanted everyone to be attentive to what Mr. Acheson was saying." Acheson "said this Government is doing its best to leave a door wide open for the Soviet Union to back down without losing too much face. The Secretary said it would be very helpful if the Members of Congress would avoid any reference to Soviet participation or involvement in the Korean crisis." Otherwise, he warned, "we will find ourselves with a really tough scrap on our hands."[91] The administration's desire to tamp down international tensions and keep the conflict contained led it to minimize its own public statements but left a vacuum that MacArthur and the Republicans could exploit.[92]

One question, however, is why Truman did not see *political* value in congressional authorization, which might have spread the blame. Looking retrospectively, several historians have concluded that authorization would not have helped much on this front. Truman biographer Alonzo Hamby, for example, argues that Truman "became the visible father of a failure; to assume that one or more congressional resolutions would have protected him from his enemies is to wander into a historical theater of the absurd."[93] In a history of Truman's relations with Congress during the Korean War, Larry Blomstedt agrees with Hamby, arguing that "Republicans may have tempered their attacks on 'Truman's War' had they endorsed it, but a congressional war resolution would not have saved the president much political grief in 1951–1952."[94] The blazing intensity of the MacArthur firing makes this assessment clear in hindsight.

But from the perspective of June and early July 1950, when Truman actually considered congressional authorization, there is another important piece of the political puzzle: the political cost of not using force, and the political upside of fighting. While Truman was reluctant to go to war, it was not clear how staying out of Korea would have played politically, as Hamby notes.[95] And a public debate, as the congressional leadership reminded him, might have led to further airing of Republican attacks on the administration's Asia policy, as well as on the State Department and Acheson. Once Truman had decided to fight, taking a tough stance took some of the sting out of this line of attack and diminished the political value of a formal authorization. As the theory predicts, for a Democratic president who fights, authorization from Congress for war is not particularly prized, especially when a procedural alternative like the United Nations is available, and the president still needed Congress for other priorities.

In addition to cutting Congress out of the authorization process, the White House also moved to control how information flowed within elite circles— with mixed success. Truman kept an especially close eye on two potentially troublesome insiders from the very start of the crisis: MacArthur and Defense Secretary Louis Johnson. The two men posed potential problems not only because of their policy views but also because of their outside base of political support, potential future ambitions, and tendency to speak to the press, either through leaks or simply by speaking publicly. Both Johnson and MacArthur took actions that impeded the administration's preferred flow of information and actively sabotaged policy.

Truman was well aware of Johnson's ambitions and leaky habits—and their consequences. At the very start of the war, Johnson leaked information about the June 25 and June 26 Blair House meetings to the press. According to Undersecretary of State James Webb—who later recalled that he reported this to Truman on June 27—"Johnson was feeding stories to the reporters that Acheson had been 'soft' on Formosa and he, Johnson, was responsible for the President's order that Formosa was to be neutralized."[96] Johnson also withheld information from the State Department, stymieing cooperation between the State and Defense Departments, which became "two warring powers."[97] Johnson's conduct led the White House to maneuver around him. When White House aides realized that "a Presidential speech or Message to Congress was inevitable" and would need to contain budget specifics, they "began to do some homework." Aware that Johnson was a leaker who opposed rearmament, Truman's aides talked instead to Secretary of the Army Frank Pace, in meetings that Truman aide George Elsey called "off-the-record . . . because we were short-circuiting the secretary of defense."[98]

Assistant White House press secretary Eben Ayers recalled in his diary that on June 29, in a preparatory session for Truman's news conference, the group discussed the stories in the press: "All of these the President labeled as untrue. There was some mention of differences between Acheson and Secretary of Defense Johnson and stories have charged that Acheson opposed action. The President said the fact was they had had trouble getting the defense establishment to move. . . . 'If this keeps up,' the President commented, 'we're going to have a new secretary of defense.'"[99] On July 3, ahead of the afternoon Blair House meeting to discuss whether to make a speech or statement to Congress, Truman recounted to his press aides an "incredible story" relayed to him a few days prior by a "whitefaced and upset" Averell Harriman, then serving as a special assistant to the president. Harriman said "he had been in the office of Secretary of Defense Johnson and, in his presence, Johnson talked to [Republican] Senator Taft of Ohio on the telephone and congratulated Taft on a speech he made a few days ago, criticizing the President for not consulting Congress before acting in the Korean crisis, and calling for the resignation of Secretary of State Acheson." After the call, "Harriman said Johnson turned to him and told him that if they could get Acheson out he (Johnson) would see that Harriman was made secretary of state." As press aide Eben Ayers recounted in his diary, the aides knew Johnson "apparently is ambitious for power and has his eyes set on the presidency. . . . Johnson, we know, talks too much, leaks things to newspapermen and feeds stuff to columnists." Truman also told his aides a rumor about Johnson talking to "some Republicans" about his willingness "to be a Republican presidential conservative candidate."[100]

Nor was Truman under any illusions about MacArthur. The concern he displayed with Congress on the issue of Soviet involvement also applied to MacArthur. In a June 29 meeting, at which the president discussed a draft directive to MacArthur, Truman interrupted Johnson's reading of the draft and "stated flatly: I do not want any implication in the letter that we are going to war with Russia at this time. . . . We must be damn careful. We must not say that we are anticipating a war with the Soviet Union." When Pace expressed "considerable reservations about putting any limitations in the directive to General MacArthur," Truman reiterated that "some reservations were necessary. . . . He only wanted to restore order to the 38th Parallel. . . . You can give [MacArthur] all the authority he needs to do that but he is not to go north of the 38th parallel."[101] Truman also recognized the need to make sure information was flowing properly *to* him from the field. At the end of the June 29 meeting, after Acheson asked Louis Johnson "if it would be possible to get General MacArthur to report what was going on," Truman "instructed Mr. Johnson to order General MacArthur, in the name of the President, to submit complete daily reports. The President remarked that it was just as hard to get information out of MacArthur now as it had been during the war." After some apparent grumbling, Truman "concluded the meeting by stating that he had no quarrel with anybody. . . . He just wanted to know what the facts were, and, he concluded, 'I don't want any leaks.'"[102]

War Escalation: The "Dove's Curse" in Korea

As the military reversals unfolded up and down the Korean Peninsula—first with the near total loss of the UN position, then with MacArthur's surprising success at Inchon—Truman had to manage hawkish pressure already embedded within his decision-making team.

Side Payments: Accommodating MacArthur and the Thirty-Eighth Parallel

No "insider" required more co-opting than MacArthur. MacArthur's forays into public debate, as well as his influence on information flow, were important in explaining Truman's reactions. There were clear national security reasons to rein in MacArthur: as Leffler notes, from the outset of the war Truman's major concern was not Congress but "to see that MacArthur's behavior was monitored closely so that the Russians would not be provoked into a wider conflict."[103] But as noted, Truman was well aware of the general's standing and the political risk, particularly to a Democratic president, of a public battle with MacArthur.

This is not the place to adjudicate fully claims about shifts in the war, such as the crossing of the thirty-eighth parallel or the approach to the Yalu River, nor every episode of tension between MacArthur and Truman.[104] But from the perspective of the theory, the political considerations that clearly tinged Truman's dealings with MacArthur are an important factor behind the "dove's curse" that afflicted Truman. MacArthur was often out in front of Truman's policies, or in some cases actively sabotaging them. At several points, these considerations led Truman to accommodate MacArthur's preferences for the strategy and scope of the conflict.

There is not universal agreement about the extent of MacArthur's influence on the course of the war. In a reappraisal of the war, Bruce Cumings writes that "MacArthur made no decision that was central to the war, except his fateful one to split his army corps as they marched into the North."[105] But Stueck, in his own reappraisal, argues that domestic political factors were important, especially after the Inchon landing, which was a "very personal victory for General MacArthur. . . . The Washington brass approved his plan but only with great reluctance. When the Inchon operation proved a brilliant success, they were unlikely anytime soon to again question his judgment."[106] Furthermore, "MacArthur was a highly political general," who had allowed himself to be entered in the 1948 Wisconsin Republican primary and "held views that were of great interest to Republicans intent on attacking the Truman administration's policies toward East Asia."[107] In a staff meeting on the day of the MacArthur firing, Truman said of his ousted general, "He's going to be regarded as a worse double-crosser than McClellan. He did just what McClellan did—got in touch with minority leaders in the Senate. He worked with the minority to undercut the Administration when there was a war on."[108] MacArthur was also in contact with Democrats who supported stronger action, such as Congressman Frank Boykin of Alabama, who had worked back channels on behalf of Chiang Kai-shek. In December 1950, Boykin sent MacArthur his view that Korea could be temporarily given up while the United States instead chose to "arm to the teeth," and meanwhile, "from our Pacific ramparts, we can strike back at the Chinese Communists."[109] MacArthur replied appreciatively from Tokyo, blaming the press for "such extravagant superlatives as 'decimated divisions', 'military debacle' and such nonsense," and calling recent fighting efforts a successful operation to flush out intelligence on Chinese military movements.[110]

It is certainly true that before the Inchon landing, the administration discussed the possibility that UN forces might cross the thirty-eighth parallel under limited circumstances.[111] Dan Reiter argues that the classic problem of credible commitments—specifically, the likelihood that North Korea would renege on any settlement that divided the peninsula—led Washington to raise its war aims in the hope that Korea could be unified and the conflict settled permanently, without the need for a long-term US troop presence. An important caveat, of course, is that the United States would attempt to cross the parallel only if it could avoid a confrontation with the Soviets and Chinese.[112] Notably, in the pre-Inchon discussions in Washington, Dulles expressed clearly his view that "the 38th Parallel was never intended to, and never ought to be, a political line. . . . If we have the opportunity to obliterate the line as a political division, certainly we should do so in the interest of 'peace and security in the area,'" per the UN resolution. Dulles consistently argued that to preserve flexibility, the United States should not publicly declare its intention to go north; he also consistently referenced the risks of provoking wider conflict with the Chinese and Soviets. But he "believe[d] strongly that we should not now tie our hands by a public statement precluding the possibility of our forces, if victorious, being used to forge a new Korea which would include at least most of the area north of the 38th Parallel."[113]

The State Department as a whole was split, with Rusk and John Allison in the Bureau of Far Eastern Affairs taking the more hawkish line against the more restrained Policy Planning Staff, which had been urging orders to MacArthur not to cross the thirty-eighth parallel since at least July 5. Policy Planning went through several drafts of a policy paper on the thirty-eighth parallel in the ensuing weeks of July.[114] Allison wrote to Rusk several times expressing strong disagreement with the Policy Planning drafts, arguing, like Dulles, that no public statement should be made in favor of crossing but also urging no statements that implied the acceptability of the "*status quo ante bellum.*"[115] After a July 25 revision, Allison wrote Rusk saying that Far Eastern Affairs could support the Policy Planning document, noting that although the conclusions and recommendations "do not go as far as I personally would like, nevertheless I believe they do go as far as we can reasonably expect at the present time."[116] Dulles, however, wrote director of policy planning Paul Nitze on August 1 to say that he "did not agree with much of the body of the [July 25] paper," and that "there is every reason to go beyond the 38th Parallel except possibly one," that is, the military risk of a war with the Soviets and Chinese.[117] After Inchon, when the focus turned to whether the UN would pass another resolution enshrining a new war aim of unification, Dulles continued to press this line as well as allowing the South Korean government to talk in terms of Korean unity, since that was a popular issue for the government.[118]

Thus even before Inchon there was internal pressure from hawkish voices pushing for at least the option to go past the thirty-eighth parallel. In addition to this Washington-based debate, many historians see MacArthur's political standing as an influence on American strategy after Inchon, and partisan politics as a strong tailwind at MacArthur's back. Notably, US allies, particularly the British, were nervous about the conflict-widening potential of a move across the thirty-eighth parallel.[119] Stueck notes that "after Inchon any effort to halt MacArthur was sure to generate a public response from the imperious general and sharp Republican attacks under conditions disadvantageous to the Democrats."[120] Casey concurs, arguing that "if going north promised political gains at a time when Republicans were accusing Truman and the Democrats of excessive softness toward Asian communism, then a presidential order halting the advance into North Korea pointed toward political catastrophe."[121] Truman could be in no doubt that MacArthur would go public if halted at the thirty-eighth parallel, "buttressed by highly vocal support from the Republican right and the China lobby."[122]

Historians Campbell Craig and Fredrik Logevall also argue domestic politics were essential to understanding Truman's wartime decisions, including the choice to go north of the thirty-eighth parallel. Craig and Logevall consider Truman's decision to give "MacArthur free rein in Korea for several months, triggering a Chinese counterattack and a great intensification of the war" as an "overreaction."[123] The domestic political impetus stemmed not only from the rise of strong anticommunism as a winning political issue, but also from the pressure on Democrats, who "would have felt especially vulnerable to the 'soft on communism' charge" after the loss of China and the Soviet gain of the atomic bomb.[124] Craig and Logevall argue that "the United States had a clear opportunity after the invasion of Inchon, and then again after the counterattack against the Chinese, to secure a ceasefire and restore the antebellum border" at the thirty-eighth parallel, and that this would have been consistent with George Kennan's strategy of containment.[125] Thus, domestic politics led Truman to press forward, rather than taking the Kennan-esque path.

In this period, Truman consistently sought opportunities to conciliate MacArthur and even bask in his reflected glory, while privately growing increasingly frustrated with his insubordination and policy sabotage. As discussed below, in August 1950, MacArthur issued a public statement in the form of a letter to the Veterans of Foreign Wars (VFW) about the importance of Taiwan to US policy beyond the Korean conflict. Truman rebuked MacArthur by demanding the statement's withdrawal. But he was quick to add, in a letter to MacArthur, that he found the most recent reports from the JCS after their visit to Korea "most satisfactory and highly gratifying to me."[126] In October 1950, after the dramatic Inchon success, Truman took a more visible step, flying to Wake Island to confer with MacArthur personally. With the midterm elections approaching, the trip was an opportunity to "underline his role as commander-in-chief now that U.S. forces were on the offensive."[127] There was no substantive breakthrough, and Truman had to stifle his displeasure at MacArthur's somewhat imperious behavior in order to get his photo opportunity.[128] But Truman kept a publicly cheerful gloss on the episode.

More important than the photo opportunity was keeping MacArthur himself happy, or as happy as could be expected given his evident distaste for his civilian leaders' Europe-first and conflict-limiting preferences. Though the crossing of the thirty-eighth parallel may have had a momentum of its own after Inchon, there was still significant concern about Chinese intervention, and discussion about how far into North Korea UN forces should proceed. Officials also debated whether only Korean troops should be used in the border regions where the Chinese were most likely to feel threatened. Not long after Wake Island, MacArthur first began to encounter Chinese troops but, through a combination of intelligence failures and willful blindness, missed their significance and pressed for an offensive that would end the war.[129]

Christensen argues that after UN forces crossed the thirty-eighth parallel, none of the proposals for some restraint short of a full march to the Yalu— such as stopping south of the Yalu, using Korean troops in the sensitive border regions, or even a buffer zone in the north—would have prevented a large-scale Chinese intervention.[130] But Stueck argues that the way the UN offensive unfolded affected the subsequent course of the war, and that the United States would have been better off with a more limited approach:

> What we now know about Mao's intentions in Korea in mid-October demonstrates the momentous nature of MacArthur's decision to continue an all-out offensive and Washington's decision to permit him to do so. Had non-Korea forces stopped at the narrow neck [of the peninsula], only ROK [Republic of Korea, i.e., South Korean] units would have confronted the Chinese during the fall and winter. Those units would have been badly mauled, and whatever was left of them would have retreated behind UN lines, which would have been solidifying well south of the Yalu. Thus UN forces could have dug in over the winter and prepared for enemy offensives in the spring. Meanwhile, the United States could have searched for a diplomatic solution.[131]

There was debate over the nature and extent of MacArthur's offensive, but in the end, Washington did not restrain MacArthur, even after the November 7 midterm elections (which had brought Republican gains). The JCS suggested to MacArthur that he stop south of the Yalu, but the hesitant tone of their communication conveyed that they deferred to the general.[132] MacArthur, in turn, retorted that "any failure on our part to prosecute the military campaign through to the achievement of its public and oft repeated objective of destroying all enemy forces south of Korea's northern boundary as essential to the restoration of unity and peace to all of Korea would be fraught with most disastrous consequences." Not least, it would be taken "by the Chinese and all the other peoples of Asia as weakness reflected from the appeasement of Communist aggression."[133] MacArthur proceeded, and the massive Chinese intervention soon pushed the UN forces to the brink.

What about the role of public opinion? Was the Truman administration merely channeling the public's desire for victory, as faithful intermediaries? An interesting thread played out in the various drafts and discussions about thirty-eighth parallel policy in July 1950, before MacArthur's Inchon triumph. The July 22 draft contained a numbered paragraph noting that

> public and Congressional opinion in the United States might be dissatisfied with any conclusion falling short of what it would consider a "final" settlement of the problem. Hence, a sentiment might arise favoring a continuation of military action north of the 38th parallel. The development of such a sentiment might create serious problems for the execution of United States policy.[134]

The July 25 draft removed the last sentence but kept the prior two.[135] Allison wrote Rusk suggesting changes to "to bring it into line" with what he saw as the "true situation," that is, that opinion was already shifting.[136] In the meeting at the State Department to discuss the paper on July 28, the participants agreed to modify the paragraph "to indicate that U.S. public and Congressional opinion would not now be satisfied with a restoration of the *status quo ante*, but on the other hand that they would probably not desire to make elimination of the 38th parallel a U.S. war objective."[137] By August 1, the language shifted: "sentiment favoring a continuation of military action north of the thirty-eighth parallel already is arising. On the other hand, there may well develop a contrasting sentiment against U.S. military forces to help establish an independent Korea."[138] Casey notes that public opinion, monitored in the State Department, indicated strong sentiment for crossing the thirty-eighth parallel in early October, after Inchon.[139]

But there are good reasons to doubt that this expressed public sentiment played an important role in the decision to go north. For one thing, those like Allison who argued the public would not tolerate stopping at the thirty-eighth parallel were also those who favored going past it. The subsequent editorial changes in the policy paper show that policy makers were not confident the public's preference for removing the thirty-eighth parallel as a political border would last, and the public was not clamoring for a change in war aims. In the absence of strong elite cues suggesting that crossing the thirty-eighth parallel would be very dangerous, little wonder public opinion polls showed enthusiasm about taking the war into North Korea and taking care of the problem once and for all. More likely, the public responded to the momentum after Inchon, just as Truman had. If an elite consensus settled on some alternative course, it might have blunted the fallout from halting at the prewar status quo. Furthermore, as Douglas Foyle argues, Truman did not think his decisions should take much account of current public attitudes, both as a normative matter and as a practical belief that "temporary public sentiments were irrelevant to achieving the long-term objectives of the nation."[140]

Still, the theory predicts that a Democratic president will not seek outright victory but instead will kick the can down the road, an expectation that does not square easily with Truman's decision to change the war aims. It is trickier to assess this prediction against the faithful intermediaries model, because it is difficult to say what a fully informed public would want. If it were a matter of putting adequate resources behind a push for victory, one could argue the public would clearly be in favor. But it is possible to make the case that a public with preferences for moderate policies would not see the decision to expand the war aims as prudent, especially given that there was the alternative of returning to the prewar status quo (which is ultimately where the armistice ended up). The decision to cross the thirty-eighth parallel was particularly risky because of North Korea's border with China, and the public had shown uneasiness with the prospect of escalation in the era of atomic weaponry. Gallup polling showed that despite initially high support for the war, throughout the Korean conflict roughly half of US respondents thought the United States was "now actually in World War III."[141]

As ever, it is difficult to know what the public would want, especially given that the elite cue environment could have been different; furthermore, the definition of a "moderate" policy in the shadow of nuclear escalation is often unclear. What seems clearer is that without strong cues about the risks or outright arguments against going north, the public did not like the limits on the war. The government's information vacuum, ironically aimed at limiting hawkish pressure, left Republicans and MacArthur room to apply just that kind of pressure by arguing that Truman was not doing enough to win. But while it is difficult to construct the counterfactual of what the public would want, making an aggressive move without properly assessing the risks was not likely to be popular.

So why did Truman do just that? Like the public, Truman probably saw the change in war aims as a relatively risk-free chance to obtain victory—and break the dove's curse. Why risk-free? MacArthur confidently discounted the risk of Chinese intervention, dismissing it in his conference with Truman at Wake Island, allowing Truman to feel he could avoid the political costs of reining in MacArthur with little military risk.[142] Most of official Washington ignored the few warnings that arose. Neustadt argues that the unification of Korea was essentially gravy to Truman and that his decision to shift US war aims to include the unification of Korea—an aim he resisted for months—was colored by the failure to properly assess the risks to his other priorities. In doing so, he "gambled with his own ability to get done many things far more important to him than the unification of Korea," including the Fair Deal and his other foreign policy goals, and he quickly dropped the unification goal after the Chinese intervention.[143] Truman did allow MacArthur to go north, but he also had made the choice to give "MacArthur, of all people, the initiative in calculating costs. . . . The greatest risk that Truman ran lay in MacArthur's capability to magnify all other risks."[144]

Instead, Truman moved the goalposts of US war aims, deeming that less risky than letting MacArthur pull the fire alarm at the thirty-eighth parallel, with Republicans of many stripes ready to pounce and deny him his other priorities. The dove's curse was more dramatic in Truman's case than for future Democratic presidents, perhaps because it was a conventional war whose geography invited the gamble MacArthur took. There were moments when Truman might have adjusted MacArthur's orders, before his final march in the north, but instead "the general, not the President, became the judge and arbiter of White House risks."[145] Civil-military dynamics undoubtedly also played a role in Truman's deference.[146] But while he did approve the change in US policy, his priorities and liabilities as a Democrat left him vulnerable to hawkish pressure.

Escalation: Information Management and Public Spillover

As Truman navigated MacArthur's demands and the need to avoid an escalatory spiral, information management became even more challenging, especially with respect to disgruntled insiders. These challenges culminated in the firing first of Johnson, and later, of course, MacArthur. Truman accepted the costs of ousting Johnson since they came with the benefits of a more competent administrator in a time of not only war but also long-term mobilization. But the specter of MacArthur's fire alarm led him to avoid confronting MacArthur and make policy concessions to keep him in the fold. Ultimately, despite all the insider politicking to postpone the fire alarm, Truman could not avoid a dramatic spillover of internal divisions into the public sphere—and paid a high political price when he recalled MacArthur.

Throughout his time in command, MacArthur used his position to speak directly to both Congress and, in turn, the public. MacArthur's August 1950 address by letter to the VFW—a document he did not send to the White House—was a remarkable case in point. He put Taiwan front and center, arguing for a long-term US commitment and laying out an argument for a

Pacific-focused American foreign policy. He also attacked the State Department's diplomatic approach to Taiwan, calling "fallacious" the

> threadbare argument by those who advocate appeasement and defeatism in
> the Pacific that if we defend Formosa we alienate continental Asia. Those who
> speak thus do not understand the Orient. They do not grant that it is in the
> pattern of the Oriental psychology to respect and follow aggressive, resolute
> and dynamic leadership—to quickly turn on a leadership characterized by
> timidity or vacillation—and they underestimate the Oriental mentality.[147]

Truman was understandably livid and ordered Johnson to have MacArthur
withdraw the message. MacArthur used this tactic repeatedly, however, often
communicating directly with the US press.[148]

As the situation in Korea began to stabilize and UN forces clawed back
toward the thirty-eighth parallel, US war aims reverted to the more limited
goal of maintaining South Korea in essentially the prewar status quo, keeping
the conflict limited, and even letting Korea go if circumstances necessitated
that American troops be deployed elsewhere.[149] MacArthur chafed at what he
saw as Truman's unwillingness to fight the proper fight in Asia. He continued
to make public and private statements that undermined Truman's policies,
including a public threat to expand the war and bring "imminent military collapse" to the Chinese in late March 1951 despite knowing that Truman planned
a peace initiative.[150] Truman kept his anger mostly under control, at least in
terms of public statements, the product of a desire to contain tensions and the
public sidelining of the politically compromised Acheson State Department.

Behind the scenes, however, both international developments and political
concerns made continued hawkish pressure from MacArthur increasingly intolerable in the weeks leading up to his recall in early April 1951. In addition to
signs of further expansion of the war in Korea, there were fears in Washington
that the Soviets were preparing a major move. Although the administration
had not approved MacArthur's statements calling for expansion of the war,
Washington began to make contingency plans to meet the perceived international challenges. On April 5, House minority leader Joseph Martin Jr. (R-MA)
read on the House floor MacArthur's famous "no substitute for victory" letter,
a reply to an invitation from Martin to air his views.[151]

Although this letter triggered the sequence of events that led to Mac-
Arthur's firing on April 11, there was more than just another incident of insubordination and political meddling behind the events that unfolded. Even as
Truman debated whether to recall MacArthur, he also apparently approved
new orders to be sent by the JCS, "if and when the enemy launches from outside Korea a major air attack against our forces in the Korean area," authorizing MacArthur to bomb positions in China.[152] But the JCS did not send the

order to MacArthur, because, as JCS chairman Omar Bradley recalled, he was "now so wary of MacArthur" that he "deliberately withheld the message and all knowledge of its existence from him."[153] In the midst of deliberations over what to do about MacArthur and this withholding of information from the commander in the field, Truman also decided to send crucial nuclear bomb components to Asia.

Cumings argues that the desire for a reliable commander to handle the potential use of nuclear weapons was the real reason Truman chose this moment to remove MacArthur.[154] Roger Dingman asserts that Truman's deployment of nuclear weapons was "essential to winning the joint chiefs' support for his decision to relieve General MacArthur," which they were initially reluctant to do. The deployment, which can be considered a war-related side payment, allowed Truman to make "clear the distinction between his disapproval of MacArthur's public statements and his acceptance of the strategic concepts underlying them." Dingman also notes that Truman disclosed the deployment of nuclear bombers to the Joint Committee on Atomic Energy, so that on the day before MacArthur's firing became public, "eighteen legislators, including some of the sharpest critics of administration East Asian policies, knew that Truman was sending nuclear weapons abroad for the first time since 1945."[155] Though it could not blunt the effect of one of the most politically explosive moments of Cold War national security policy, Truman still used information to ensure that his nuclear policies were well understood by those who needed to know.

MacArthur's return to the United States, his address to a joint session of Congress, and the subsequent hearings irrevocably put the details of Korea policy in the political domain. MacArthur had pulled the fire alarm (or, seen another way, Truman had finally decided that he could no longer pretend that his top general had not been tugging on it for years). As the American politics scholars George Belknap and Angus Campbell found in survey data from June 1951, the public was deeply split along partisan lines in its views of the MacArthur controversy. Respondents were asked, "In the disagreements between President Truman and General MacArthur about how to carry on the war in Korea, who do you think was most nearly right?" Democratic respondents favored Truman 47 percent over MacArthur at 42 percent, while Republican respondents backed MacArthur overwhelmingly, 82 percent to only 7 percent for Truman. Belknap and Campbell argue that respondents' views "reflected the positions held by the leadership of the two parties."[156] As Mueller notes, the politicization of the war, driven by the MacArthur firing, contributed to the large negative effect of the war on Truman's popularity.[157] But even as Truman's own popularity was broken, public support for the war remained intact, perhaps because the signals from Republican critics were for continued firmness in Korea.

The delayed fire alarm raises the question of what kind of alarm the public would have liked to hear and when—that is, what the faithful intermediaries model would predict. If we again assume the public wants moderate decisions and good outcomes, then earlier elite cues alerting them to the risks of Chinese intervention would have been useful. Truman's efforts to keep the war out of the arena of public debate, especially in Congress, not only delayed such a signal but also seems to have blinded even the president to prudent risk assessment. Alternatively, the public might have wanted to know earlier that the war, and especially the unification of Korea, was not as important to Truman, to many of his advisers, or to the national interest as elite rhetoric made it seem, sparing several years of costly, tragic war effort. The insiders' game under a Democratic president, however, drove Truman to worry most about appeasing the hawkish calls for doing more, not less, in Korea.

After MacArthur: Truman, Eisenhower, and War Termination

The MacArthur Hearings

It is important to note that the theory does not expect that leaders are always successful at maintaining elite consensus. Some leaders will fail at maintaining elite consensus, a prospect that gives the threat of public spillover bite. Battlefield events or other international factors can also push the consensus to the breaking point, as arguably happened in Vietnam after the Tet Offensive. Truman's continual concessions to MacArthur not only failed to contain his dissent and the dramatic politicization of the war but also resulted in terrible human and material costs for no gain beyond what he might have settled for in late 1950. In some sense, then, the politics of the war after MacArthur's firing represent an entirely different game, one played in the public domain.

While not attempting to stretch the theory beyond recognition, however, the aftermath of MacArthur's recall provides some interesting evidence on the effect of elite cues on a hawkish, strongly anti-Truman public. Ironically, as Casey argues, the MacArthur hearings finally provided the missing cues that had been silenced by Truman's strategy of maintaining elite consensus with a hawkish slant.[158] The goal now was to protect Truman's primary policy objective: rearmament. Truman began to talk about the administration's Cold War strategy, including in Korea, as avoiding another world war. But he faced an uphill battle given his shredded popularity, public displeasure with the firing of MacArthur, and the voters' apparent receptivity to a more aggressive posture that would take the war to the Chinese.[159]

The administration was not without allies, however, including the JCS, as well as Senator Richard Russell, a key Southern Democrat who took charge of the hearings in the hopes of controlling them. Russell's effective management of the hearings, coupled with strong testimony by the JCS in rebuttal of MacArthur's claims, blunted the power of MacArthur's testimony.[160] Foot describes the administration's presentation as "an impressive show of solidarity" among the main witnesses.[161] The substance of the military testimony unequivocally painted MacArthur's calls for widening the war as unnecessarily risky and likely to lead to a global war, or as JCS Chairman Omar Bradley famously put it, "the wrong war, at the wrong place, at the wrong time, with the wrong enemy."[162] In a climate where the public might be primed to respond to hawkish elite cues, the countertype testimony from the JCS, in a hearing led by a Southern Democrat who was not close to Truman, helped blunt the damage and drove down support for MacArthur.

Casey concludes that while historians have typically seen the MacArthur controversy as further constricting Truman's governing flexibility as his approval ratings sank to levels from which they could not recover, in reality Truman emerged from the hearings with unexpected room to maneuver, at least in terms of his rearmament program. Moderates could conclude that Truman's "fundamental strategy, both in Korea and in Europe, remained sound."[163] Many internationalist Republicans even refused to sign the minority Republican committee report on the MacArthur episode. It is also notable that although Truman bowed out of the 1952 presidential race, the Republican nominee that emerged was not MacArthur, nor the Asialationist Taft, but rather the internationalist Eisenhower.[164]

While Truman was not able to keep the politics of the war contained within the Beltway, Casey concludes that "the government did have some power to salvage a degree of popular support even when the fighting dragged on, in part because officials at all levels of the government had the astuteness to learn from their mistakes."[165] The MacArthur firing serves as a dramatic illustration of the costs presidents pay for failing to contain public spillover, but the post-MacArthur success of Truman's mobilization program also illustrates that "Truman and his advisers were able to convince those elites that mattered."[166] In contrast, direct public "education" did not work, but neither did mounting casualties undermine public support.[167]

Eisenhower and the Armistice

One of the tragedies of the Korean War is not only that it ended where it began, but that the armistice Eisenhower signed in 1953 was essentially the one Truman had nearly reached in 1951, and yet so many more suffered and died in the intervening two years. Political scientists have been especially interested in the end of the war and its domestic politics. Dan Reiter eschews domestic political arguments, arguing that information and commitment problems were central to the timing of peace.[168] Elizabeth Stanley argues that wars end when domestic coalitions shift.[169] Similarly, Sarah Croco argues that war termination depends on a "non-culpable" leader, that is, a leader elected from another party, coming to power.[170] Although Eisenhower was not culpable for the Korean War and was able to end active US involvement, Republicans have not always chosen peace when confronted with a failing war, as later chapters show.

The theory has less to say about inherited wars, particularly one already stalemated along a clear and familiar line of demarcation. It is interesting to note, however, that despite his nonculpable status and his unique standing given his war record, even Eisenhower faced domestic political pressures. As Stueck notes, the partisan landscape was complicated for Eisenhower: despite Republican control of both houses of Congress, the president's party remained deeply split and not yet unified around the internationalist position that Eisenhower and Dulles would later consolidate, forcing them to act "with a wary eye toward Capitol Hill."[171]

Most historians agree that the atomic threats Dulles later boasted as crucial to ending the war were neither serious nor effective.[172] But after taking office, despite his campaign pledge to "go to Korea," Eisenhower had no clear plan for how to end the war and briefly considered whether another attempt at going north might be worthwhile.[173] He was under some pressure from within his own party to do so. The record of the months until the armistice shows repeated pressure from the right and the challenges of managing both the Republican Party and South Korean president Syngman Rhee.[174] As Casey notes, "Eisenhower and his senior advisers made a concerted effort to brief and consult the congressional leadership" and "even revealed the threats they had recently transmitted to the enemy."[175] Of particular concern was the China bloc, still led by California Republican senator William Knowland, who would soon take over as Senate majority leader with the illness and death of Robert Taft. Eisenhower and Dulles repeatedly enlisted Knowland to help pressure Rhee and to publicly endorse an armistice that accepted Korea's division.[176] They pledged not to recognize Mao's regime, while resisting pressure to make aggressive moves like blockading the Chinese coast. Of course, Eisenhower had unique strengths in beating back challenges from Knowland and others who pressed for further action in Korea and Asia, but the attacks kept coming.

In considering his course in Korea, Eisenhower had the "hawk's advantage" if he chose to make peace, giving him leeway to conclude the armistice that had eluded Truman. But he also had room to consider a renewed military effort in the north with the aim of reunifying Korea by force, despite all the arguments now in the public domain against such a course. With pressure from his party to be more aggressive in Asia, Eisenhower could consider both options. The public also gave him some leeway: Rosemary Foot observes that public opinion, while favoring an end to the war, was "malleable" about the path to getting there, and a plurality even favored increasing military action.[177] According to Gallup, public views that the war was a "mistake" peaked at 50 percent in February 1952 compared to 37 percent who saw it as not a mistake, but almost as soon as Eisenhower took office, attitudes rebounded, with 50 percent saying it was not a mistake compared to 36 percent agreeing it was a mistake.[178]

In the end, Eisenhower delivered on his promise to end the war. That Eisenhower signed the armistice with few changes from his predecessor's policies is perhaps not surprising but also reflected a judgment that becoming politically culpable for it was unwise. His decision is also consistent with his preexisting views and tendency to be highly selective in choosing military operations.[179] As Berinsky notes, Eisenhower "never embraced the war after his election," so public opinion did not polarize along party lines during his term—but the data from Gallup and from Belknap and Campbell show this would have been a real risk had he chosen otherwise.[180] Eisenhower's vice president, Richard Nixon, would make a different choice when he inherited the Vietnam War. For Eisenhower, however, ending the war with an armistice, rather than escalating or continuing a simmering conflict was the preferred option and one he had the political leeway to pursue.

Conclusion

Despite the shock of the initial North Korean invasion, the Korean War was a distant conflict for most Americans. Snyder argues that eventually the median voter constrained Truman (and later, Johnson in Vietnam).[181] But this chapter has shown that in the case of Korea, Truman spent considerable effort managing and making concessions to hawkish elites—trapping him in a dove's curse. This chapter has also shown that elite bargaining was crucial to a conventional conflict fought not long after World War II, illustrating that these elite dynamics are not confined to post–Cold War "surgical" military operations. Nor were these elite dynamics a temporary phenomenon stemming from now-bygone cross-party cleavages on foreign policy, as the patterns identified in the following chapter illustrate. This account is therefore more consistent with an elite-dominated framework that sees public opinion as long dormant and hard to mobilize. The battle for opinion and presidential approval in Korea was really a battle that began—and for a long time, remained—at the elite level.

5

The Vietnam War as an Insiders' Game

OF ALL POST–WORLD WAR II uses of force by the United States, the Vietnam War stands out for the high human and societal costs policy makers chose to incur despite widely shared misgivings and pessimism in the innermost circles of decision making. The documentary record of the war clearly shows American policy makers and military leaders with their eyes wide open about the difficulty of fighting in Vietnam. In their classic study, Leslie Gelb and Richard Betts argue that "the system worked" in Vietnam, because successful US presidents made their war aim not victory, but the avoidance of loss.[1]

In this chapter, I argue that the Vietnam War was an insiders' game. Many analysts have noted the elite consensus that helped keep public support for the war intact for much of Lyndon Johnson's tenure.[2] Most accounts do not explore the elite bargaining that underpinned this consensus, however. Furthermore, the connection between the Great Society and Vietnam—Johnson's fear that his failure to act in Vietnam would cost him his signature legislative achievements—has received significant attention but lacks theoretical grounding in debates about domestic politics and war. Consistent with the theory, despite the presence of dovish voices Johnson's fears were asymmetrically focused on hawkish criticism—in part because of the shadow of what had happened to Truman. One White House official remembers Johnson saying, "If he had a problem, it was the hawks, not the doves, whom he dismissed as a band of 'rattlebrains.'"[3]

Given the extensive record of scholarship on Vietnam, I focus this chapter on episodes that highlight mechanisms and implications derived from the theory—in this case, another Democratic president trapped in a dove's curse. First, I examine the onset of the major American commitment under Lyndon Johnson. As in other cases, there are many factors at play, and the theory does not claim to explain all of them. Although Kennedy certainly escalated US involvement (decisions I have written about elsewhere), Johnson made the most consequential initiation decisions in what Fredrik Logevall calls "the long 1964."[4] Johnson's own views on Vietnam are complex: he preferred to focus on domestic policy at home but had genuine impulses to act tough and disagreed with the Kennedy approach of focusing on governance in South Vietnam.[5] Even if we do not consider Johnson a "dove," however, he himself was well aware that as a leader from a party with a dovish reputation, he would be politically vulnerable to charges of dovish weakness.

Nonetheless, like Truman, Johnson's decision making in Vietnam reflected the hawkish bias baked into the incentives facing Democratic presidents. The discussion gives special attention to his decision to co-opt political and legislative opponents. Johnson's congressional strategy highlights the elite landscape facing Democratic presidents, heightened in this case by Johnson's desire to press forward with a major, sweeping domestic legislative program, the Great Society. Johnson was the rare Democratic president who took pains to secure congressional authorization for war in advance, but his position was also unusual in that his own party held a significant majority in Congress yet was geographically and at times ideologically divided. Although the Tonkin Gulf episode has been extensively studied, the politics of the congressional resolution itself usually receive only passing analysis.[6] I situate Johnson's actions in his larger strategy to fight quietly while legislating loudly. I also highlight specific side payment and information dynamics as Johnson placated hawks while controlling the level and volume of elite debate.

Second, I look at the remarkable—though in many ways pyrrhic—success Johnson had in maintaining outward elite consensus. Although Johnson feared intervention by the Chinese or Soviets, his personal concern with credibility required, from his perspective, strong demonstrations of resolve.[7] The order of battle controversy in 1967, just as his own party began to turn on him in the Senate, shows the lengths presidents can go to keep consensus intact. This period also included policy spillover to other national security areas as Johnson worked to keep the consensus from breaking completely.

Third, I look briefly at Richard Nixon's escalation of the war after taking office, promising that he had a secret plan to end it. Nixon's actions complicate the story of his trip to China and the "hawk's advantage" in making peace. His hawkish actions, aimed at what he called his hawkish base, were crucial to his later conciliatory moves, which in turn were important to his putting pressure on North Vietnam to negotiate. The "decent interval" idea—that the loss of Vietnam must be postponed until after Nixon's reelection—illustrates that once he took ownership of the war, Nixon felt he had to reach something that could be framed as a decisive outcome.

These arguments generate a friendly amendment to Gelb and Betts's classic and enduring argument.[8] It is undoubtedly true that successive presidential administrations of both parties perpetuated the American commitment to Vietnam, knowing that victory was unlikely if not unattainable and seeking instead merely to avoid defeat. But the picture is a little more complicated. The two Republican presidents faced with a decision about initiating or escalating US combat, Eisenhower and Nixon, took quite different approaches from those of the Democratic presidents. Although the circumstances on the ground and in the international arena evolved, it is notable that Eisenhower chose not to fight in 1954 (even while recommitting the United States to Vietnam), while Nixon chose to expand the war even while withdrawing some US troops.[9] Kennedy and especially Johnson, in contrast, followed the Gelb and Betts's "system worked" argument nearly to the letter.[10] These dynamics affected all presidents to some degree in Vietnam, but asymmetrically across parties.

As in the other cases, it is challenging to assess the insiders' game against the faithful intermediaries model, because we cannot undo the effects of the elite cues that reached the public. We have extensive scholarly evidence, however, that public attitudes about the war were outwardly supportive but also ambivalent, reflecting the dominance of prowar cues and the absence of dovish elite messages for much of the period of dramatic escalation.[11] Johnson's consensus ultimately shattered after a dramatic battlefield event: the Tet Offensive in 1968. Until then, the consensus remained frayed but intact, as did public support for the war.[12] In this case, we would expect that the public, which was not especially enthusiastic about the war even if it was supportive, would have wanted a much earlier fire alarm to alert them to the ineffective, "just enough" strategy Johnson deliberately employed. Instead, his concessions to hawks prolonged that strategy and allowed him to generate the illusion of meeting dubious benchmarks for success. As in Korea, some in the public wanted Johnson to do more, not less, in Vietnam, even after Tet—and voters expressed both views in the 1968 New Hampshire primary, which helped spur his decision not to seek reelection.[13] There is not room in this chapter to address all the Vietnam decisions or even all the presidential administrations that faced choices in Vietnam, but this chapter highlights how the insiders' game drove the logic of the war—a logic that is illustrated poignantly by the public protests of 1968 and the continuation of the war for another seven years. That Johnson reached that point, and even contemplated adding more troops, reflects the power of the insiders' game to move policy in a more hawkish direction.

Elites, Voters, and Vietnam

As with the Korean War, the documentary and historiographical record of the Vietnam War is by now well developed. Many factors that had little to do with domestic politics contributed to Johnson's choices, including his own personal obsession with credibility; the tendency to see Vietnam, like other nationalist conflicts, through the lens of the Cold War; the real and prudent fear of Soviet and Chinese intervention; and the general and unquestioned consensus shared by successive US presidents, as Gelb and Betts argue, that defending South Vietnam was a vital interest.[14] But domestic politics had a profound effect on the decisions Johnson in particular made, at nearly every step and at every level.

This chapter's contribution is to specify more clearly the nature of Johnson's domestic political concerns. One could argue, as outlined in chapter 2, that voters would prefer a prudent choice to either avoid escalation in the first place, or escalate enough to win, as theories of democracy and war generally predict. In this view, voters would not approve of a strategy that prolongs the war in the full knowledge that the strategy will not achieve victory. They would want their faithful intermediaries to provide them with fire alarms that could alert them to the dubious strategy early enough to express their concerns about it, and for their leaders not to take unnecessary and knowingly pointless risks. As table 4-2 in the previous chapter summarizes, the faithful intermediaries model does not predict the patterns of side payments and information management that the insiders' game predicts for Democratic presidents.

Instead, I argue not only that Johnson's domestic political concerns about Vietnam were primarily focused on the elite level, but also that they were asymmetrically focused on hawkish elites, and that his concessions and compromises pushed policy in a more hawkish direction than a moderate median voter would want. The within-case evidence is summarized in table 5-1. Having decided to escalate the war, Johnson found it relatively easy to make procedural and patronage-related concessions to skeptics and doves, such as giving Under Secretary of State George Ball a forum to air his dissent, or giving his friend and ally J. William Fulbright, chair of the Senate Foreign Relations Committee, prestige and access in the early part of the escalation. He worked far harder to continually appease hawks, first on war policy, and later spilling over into other national security policies, such as missile defense. As discussed below, his concerns about passing the Great Society led him to preempt the costs he believed hawkish elites could impose on his domestic legislative agenda. To be sure, there were some important defections along the way, notably Fulbright's break with Johnson and the start of hearings in Congress, and later, Defense Secretary Robert McNamara's turn against the war. But Johnson was able to contain the fallout, and instead we observe Johnson staving off the major fire alarm until an external event, the Tet Offensive in January 1968, proved too loud for his political skills to silence.

Of course, the above argument is based on the idea of voters wanting moderate, prudent policy, in the aggregate. Some scholars offer an alternative public-driven perspective: that we can explain Johnson's compromise military

TABLE 5-1. Within-Case Evidence for Vietnam War

	Side Payments	Information
War initiation ("Long 1964," Tonkin Gulf Resolution)	To insider hawks: Retaining/ accommodating Ambassador Lodge; war concessions To insider/copartisan doves: Prestige and access (to Fulbright, Ball); procedural concession (Congressional resolution)	Limit information to/from insider doves (e.g., limit discussion of 1965 George Ball paper) and congressional hawks Dampen salience (no debate on Tonkin Gulf, initial 1965 deployments done quietly)
Escalation	War policy concessions to JCS Policy spillover to ABM system McNamara to World Bank	Containment of controversy Removing McNamara
Duration/ termination	LBJ: Accountability begins from copartisans (e.g., Fulbright hearings) Nixon: Vietnamization (to doves) Cambodian incursion (to hawks)	Secrecy of Cambodian incursion

strategy, which he knew would not result in victory but was instead aimed at not losing and minimizing the war's impact on domestic society, as a direct appeal to voters' preferences for a "free lunch," that is, to save Vietnam at low cost. Zaller, for example, argues that in Vietnam, both Kennedy and especially Johnson responded to what they saw as latent public sentiment that would not tolerate Vietnam's loss, but also would not support a lengthy military effort to prevent it.[15] This argument suggests that the median voter might affirmatively prefer compromise strategies that escalate at relatively low cost, as we observe in Vietnam case.[16] A policy that appears to push policy in a (mildly) more hawkish direction, then, could be seen as an appeal to this voter preference.

It is difficult to argue that the ambiguous and lengthy war that unfolded in Vietnam, at troop levels and casualty totals that would boggle the minds of most voters in the 1964 election, represented a "free lunch." Additionally, one important question is whether latent public opinion is an underlying prefer- ence of the mass public, or instead would require an elite cue to trigger public disapproval of the president, as Zaller himself hints.[17] In the latter case, we would expect to observe a leader who is trying to appeal to an affirmative voter preference for a compromise strategy to build a coalition of moderate elites to counter calls for more hawkish policy. Instead, Johnson tried to pla- cate both hawkish and dovish elites, and by the time elite opinion fractured in 1968, Democratic voters in the New Hampshire primary were more likely to be angry with Johnson for not doing enough in Vietnam, rather than for doing too much.[18] Still, one can view the middle-of-the-road strategy as an alternative public-driven argument.

How can we distinguish between this version of the faithful intermediaries model and the insiders' game? In addition to the expected pattern of side payments, which the insiders' game predicts should be larger and more frequent to hawks than to doves and should thus generate more than a mild asymmetry, we can look at patterns of secrecy and internal elite debate. If the public had a more direct preference for a middle-of-the-road escalation strategy, one might expect that information would still flow relatively openly within government in the service of this basic strategy. If the goal is simply not to lose and informed elites understand this approach, then the incentives to mislead elites and manage intra-elite information channels should not be as strong. Furthermore, leaders and insider elites would presumably not feel as strong a need to keep the escalation hidden, whereas Johnson made major decisions in 1964 and 1965 out of public view and deliberately tried to dampen their salience.

Johnson's Domestic Political Landscape

During the period when Johnson made major decisions about sending troops to Vietnam, in 1964 and 1965, the Democrats controlled both houses of Congress with significant majorities. These majorities, however, masked internal divisions between the Southern Democrats, who opposed Johnson's civil rights reforms, and liberals from northern states, who were more traditionally dovish. A further complication was that many Southern Democrats, while hawkish in general, opposed getting further involved in Vietnam. Johnson's mentor and chair of the Senate Armed Services Committee, Richard Russell of Georgia, was an important case in point. As noted in chapter 4 and emphasized by historian Steven Casey, Russell had been instrumental in steering the Truman administration through the MacArthur hearings in 1951, and Southern Democrats in general were supportive of Truman and his rearmament program.[19] But in the case of Vietnam specifically, Russell and many of his Southern Democratic colleagues did not support greater involvement. On the other hand, once committed, they supported using the full force of US power to achieve victory, and many criticized Johnson for holding back the military effort.[20] In the next section, I discuss how Johnson thought about this constituency and why he believed it presented such a conundrum for him on the Vietnam question. The more traditional Democrats were not naturally supportive of the war but were also loyal to the president. Fulbright, although a southerner, was more aligned with this group on foreign policy as the powerful chairman of the Senate Foreign Relations Committee and an internationalist in outlook.

An interesting feature of the political landscape was the strange position of the Republican Party, which typically does not feature much in the historiography of Vietnam in the Johnson years, except for 1964 Republican presidential nominee Barry Goldwater. As Andrew Johns writes in a history that corrects this imbalance, many Republicans were dovish on the war even as their party nominated an extreme hawk.[21] They might have been a useful constituency to provide cover for Johnson had he chosen a different path.

A major difference between Johnson and Truman, however, is that Truman had another set of national security goals for which he needed Republican support—rearmament—while Johnson inherited the fruits of that labor and already had the basic national security architecture in place. To bargain with Republicans, then, he would have to make concessions on other foreign policy or national security issues. Johnson did not have the same cross-cutting coalitions available, shifting most of the bargaining action to his copartisans and insiders.

What about public opinion? Though Johnson attempted to keep the initial escalation as low profile as possible, by the end of 1965 there were nearly 185,000 American troops in Vietnam, on the way to a peak level of over 500,000 in 1968.[22] Yet he was remarkably successful at maintaining public and elite support until early 1968. Scholars who have examined the pattern of elite and public opinion on the war generally conclude that elite leadership of mass opinion was highly significant. Both Zaller and Berinsky, for example, demonstrate that public opinion took its cue from elite unity in the period of escalation and, up through at least 1968, was largely supportive of the war.[23] While overall public support dropped as the war progressed, support for withdrawal did not rise above 19 percent until after November 1968, and support for escalation actually peaked at 55 percent in November 1967, when troop levels were near half a million.[24] Mueller finds that Vietnam had no independent effect on Johnson's approval rating.[25] Among elites in the Vietnam case, Republicans were generally (though not universally) supportive of the war, while Democratic opinion began to fracture earlier, particularly when Fulbright held hearings in 1966.

This elite consensus was not an accident but rather was actively shaped by presidential management. Johnson's forging of an elite consensus was distinct from direct public "education," which he avoided. Indeed, Jacobs and Shapiro find that "thousands of pages of White House public opinion analysis provide no evidence that Johnson . . . tracked public opinion to move policy in the public's direction."[26] George Herring notes that Johnson did not make a major public relations effort on Vietnam until 1967.[27] Instead of undertaking a direct effort to educate the public, Johnson shaped the message through elite management behind the scenes.

Mechanisms of Hawkish Bias

Selection Pressures

Like Truman, Johnson faced selection pressures that embedded hawkish pressure on his decision making from the outset. The circumstances of Johnson's accession to the presidency following Kennedy's assassination complicated an already-complex elite landscape. Johnson inherited Kennedy's team but had not been in the trusted inner circle for many of the crucial decisions Kennedy made about Southeast Asia. Johnson distrusted and replaced many Kennedy advisers but relied heavily on a few holdovers including Defense Secretary Robert McNamara and National Security Advisor McGeorge Bundy, both hawkish on the war at the outset.[28] While Johnson shared their frustration with Kennedy's unwillingness to make a stronger military commitment to South Vietnam, these advisers steered him in a more hawkish direction and, in internal administration debates, consistently rejected diplomatic solutions that would have allowed Johnson a way out.

Another inherited Kennedy appointee who put hawkish pressure on Johnson was Henry Cabot Lodge Jr. A Republican, Lodge had been the 1960 Republican vice presidential candidate and Kennedy's (losing) opponent in the 1952 Senate race in Massachusetts. Kennedy appointed Lodge as ambassador to South Vietnam. Arthur Schlesinger reports that Kennedy saw political advantage in "implicating a leading Republican in the Vietnam mess."[29] Andrew Johns argues that Lodge's party affiliation was a "decisive" reason he got the ambassador position in Saigon and that Secretary of State Dean Rusk "convinced Kennedy that Lodge was to the Republican Party in 1963 what John Foster Dulles had been in 1950."[30] After Kennedy's death, Fulbright told Johnson he believed Lodge "was put there partly to conciliate the opposition."[31] The appointment proved to carry real risks, however. While Kennedy was eager to put pressure on South Vietnamese president Ngô Đình Diệm and was involved in the high-level consideration of Diệm's ouster, Lodge encouraged a coup on a faster timetable and more strongly than Kennedy might have liked, with a result Kennedy did not desire: Diệm's death, rather than exile.[32] But Kennedy recognized that Lodge was "there and we can't fire him so we're going to have to give him directions."[33] As discussed below, Johnson took this perspective quite literally.

Agenda Costs

Much scholarship on Vietnam accepts that domestic politics played a role in Johnson's decision to escalate. As Alexander Downes succinctly puts it, "Johnson feared political punishment if he withdrew from Vietnam more than if he engaged in war."[34] Yet there remain significant questions about exactly what type of political punishment Johnson feared. As Vice President Hubert Humphrey wrote Johnson in early 1965, "It is always hard to cut losses," but "1965 is the year of minimum political risk for the Johnson administration."[35]

Despite his landslide victory in 1964 over the extremely hawkish Goldwater, Johnson feared that failing to act in Vietnam would derail the Great Society legislation he sought in Congress.[36] There has been significant historical debate over these propositions, particularly the role of the Great Society. Johnson's deputy national security advisor, Francis Bator, argues that "Johnson believed—and he knew how to count votes—that had he backed away in Vietnam in 1965, there would have been no Great Society. . . . It would have been stillborn in Congress."[37] Bator asserts that "Johnson thought that hawkish Dixiecrats and small-government Republicans were more likely to defy him—by joining together to filibuster the civil rights and social legislation that they and their constituents detested—if he could be made to appear an appeaser of Communists who had reneged on Eisenhower's and Kennedy's commitment of U.S. honor."[38] Bator goes so far as to argue that Johnson had "no good choices" and could not have backed away from Vietnam. Fredrik Logevall, however, convincingly argues that especially after the 1964 election, Johnson had a dominant political position and there were many members of Congress in both parties who opposed escalation.[39]

The key, however, is that Johnson *believed* he would suffer politically. In arguing against Bator's thesis, Logevall acknowledges that Johnson "worried about the harm that failure in Vietnam could do to his domestic agenda."[40] Though Logevall discounts the Great Society as the primary motive for initiating the escalation, he nonetheless sees it as essential to understanding the nature of Johnson's war.[41] H. R. McMaster calls the Great Society the "dominant political determinant of Johnson's military strategy."[42]

Cost of Hawkish Elite Support

Vietnam was not the clear-cut invasion scenario that led Truman to decide to intervene quickly in Korea. Perhaps the lack of such a dramatic scenario might have led Johnson to seek a way not to escalate the conflict further. But to Johnson, the cost of obtaining hawkish elite support for deescalatory policy in Vietnam apparently seemed enormous. In an often-quoted line, he asked his Senate mentor and ally Richard Russell, "Well, they'd impeach a President though that would run out, wouldn't they?" He followed this rhetorical question with a discussion of congressional opinion, noting that "outside of [Democratic war opponent Wayne] Morse, everybody I talk to says you got to go in . . . including all the Republicans. . . . And I don't know how in the hell you're gonna get out unless they tell you to get out."[43] Johnson put it more colorfully in another discussion: "If I don't go in now and they show later that I should have, then they'll be all over me in Congress. They won't be talking about my civil rights bill, or education, or beautification. . . . They'll push Vietnam up my ass every time."[44]

To be sure, Johnson was concerned about Republican criticism; indeed, recent scholarship makes clear that Kennedy, Johnson, and Nixon were "preoccupied with the fear of a right-wing backlash if Vietnam 'fell' to communism."[45] Johnson faced a particularly difficult version of this problem, however, because there were powerful congressional hawks in his own party, concentrated in the South and deeply opposed to civil rights, who were also critical to the success of his legislative program. As Randall Woods notes in a response to Bator, Johnson wanted these Democrats to at least "refrain from obstructing" key civil rights bills and vote for other parts of the Great Society, and "he could not at the same time ask them to acquiesce in the neutralization of Vietnam."[46] In addition to the damage these members of Congress could do to the Great Society, criticism from within his own party would be particularly credible. Johnson reached across the aisle to gain Republican support for his civil rights program, working with Senate minority leader Everett Dirksen—who was also a staunch backer of the war and who frequently worked to quell dissent from other Republicans with both hawkish and dovish criticism of the president.[47] But Johnson clearly believed he would use up his political capital by staying out of Vietnam and that his political opponents would use it against him, even if many had their own misgivings about the war.

War Initiation: The "Long 1964"

When Johnson took office and contemplated what to do in Vietnam, he saw his trade-off between escalation and some kind of deescalatory or diplomatic policy as particularly stark. But once he chose to fight, he was continually confronted with demands from insider hawks to add more troops. Hawkish elite sentiment therefore had a magnified role—especially given its representation among Southern Democrats in the Senate—as contrasted with public opinion more generally. As Downes notes in an analysis of public opinion before the Tonkin Gulf incident in August 1964 and the initiation of bombing in early 1965 (when rally effects were confounding), the public did not know much about Vietnam, and those that did were split among many options.[48] Berinsky argues that polling understated dovish sentiment early in the war, because the dominant elite messages in this period were pro-escalation and the "don't know" respondents were more likely to be "uncertain doves" with no elite message to give their sentiments voice.[49] Johnson understood the lack of public attention to Vietnam and focused on the elite threat. In a May 1964 conversation, Johnson told his former mentor and Senate colleague Richard Russell that the public did not "know much about Vietnam and I think they care a hell of a lot less."[50] This basic fact underpinned Johnson's strategy to keep the war quiet—certainly before the 1964 election, but even afterward—so as not to make it a salient issue, and so that he could focus on the elite political costs. As this section illustrates, the muted dovish elite discourse—despite many elites with dovish views or concerns about the war—was no accident.

This section also shows that electoral politics are insufficient to explain Johnson's choices. What is remarkable about the elite bargaining in 1964 is that while it clearly took place in the shadow of the election, the particular form it took related directly to Johnson's agenda, his identity as a Democratic president, and the preferences and power of the elites around him. He placated specific elites, weighted heavily toward the hawks. He backed away from the congressional resolution they wanted, however, until a low-cost opportunity to seek one arose. Elites shaped his policies long before, and well after, the voters had their say.

Initial Side Payments: 1964–65

Johnson's policy concessions to insider hawks, including McNamara and Mc-George Bundy, have been thoroughly documented by historians and are discussed below in the context of information management.[51] A strikingly explicit example of Johnson's concern with hawkish insiders is his remarkable preoccupation with Lodge, a potential opponent in the 1964 election who favored wider US military action against North Vietnam.[52] From the earliest days of his presidency, Johnson sought to neutralize Lodge, still serving as ambassador in Saigon, by accommodating him within the fold. Immediately after Kennedy's assassination, Johnson had to meet with Lodge, who was in Washington following a conference of US officials in Honolulu. McNamara and Rusk sent him memos and briefing papers on November 23, 1963, in preparation for the meeting on November 24.[53] It was in this meeting that Johnson declared, "I am not going to be the President who saw Southeast Asia go the way China went."[54] In the meeting, CIA director John McCone noted that Lodge's tone was "optimistic, hopeful, and left the President with the impression that we are on the road to victory," whereas intelligence estimates were much less optimistic. Johnson expressed "misgivings" about the coup that had overthrown South Vietnamese president Ngô Đình Diệm only a few weeks earlier, an effort Lodge had supported. Johnson expressed his strong displeasure with the "dissension and division" in the US effort in Vietnam and insisted twice that the "Ambassador was the Number One man and he, the President, was holding the Ambassador personally responsible."[55] Bundy later reported to Averell

Harriman that "Lodge didn't distinguish himself in his interview with the President. . . . He thought Lodge may know that the President never thought much of him," later adding, "he doesn't have the operation going."[56]

Indeed, Johnson complained privately about Lodge just days after the November 24 meeting, telling Donald Cook, the president of the American Electric Power Company, that Lodge was "just about as much an administrator as he is a utility magnate."[57] In his May 1964 call with Russell, Johnson complained that Lodge was "one of our big problems" and "ain't worth a damn. He can't work with any-*bodd*-y." But when Russell suggested Johnson "get somebody who's more pliant than Lodge, who'd do exactly what you said, right quick," Johnson retorted that "he'd be back home campaigning against us on this issue, every day."[58]

Johnson's political concerns about Lodge seeped into the policy realm. In the early months of 1964, amid relentlessly pessimistic assessments of the situation on the ground in Vietnam, Johnson repeatedly stressed that he wanted Lodge's recommendations followed—almost as his highest priority. On February 4, the NSC's Michael Forrestal wrote Bundy that "if Lodge must remain, the military commander must be changed. The President might publicly load Lodge with full responsibility for the whole U.S. effort in South Vietnam, giving him as deputy the ablest, most modern-minded 3-star general we can find," going on to suggest General William Westmoreland.[59] Later in the month, Johnson prodded Lodge for a report after delivering the president's personal message to General Nguyễn Khánh, the new prime minister, two weeks earlier. Lodge replied with a short and upbeat summary that "current civil and military plans will bring victory" and that there was enough US economic aid except for funds to increase pay to the army and paramilitary. Johnson replied the next day that this request "would be addressed immediately."[60] Lodge's assessment was at odds with those of others, including that of his own deputy, David Nes, sent to Washington on the same day.[61] When Johnson met with his top advisers on February 20, he directed that "any requests for assistance or other Washington action from Ambassador Lodge should be given prompt and sympathetic response. Such staff work as may be required to back up such requests in Washington should be given the highest priority, so that decisions can be reached quickly."[62] Lodge sent another telegram that same day urging more pressure and retaliation against North Vietnam in response to "terrorism against Americans in Saigon."[63] Bundy made sure to get Lodge's message and a draft reply, which looked favorably on a greater effort in North Vietnam, to Johnson in California, where he was on vacation, noting that the rush was "because of the President's desire to be very quick and effective in responses to Lodge's messages."[64]

In private conversations, Johnson made clear his motives were not simply to back up his man on the scene—they were political. In a discussion with

McNamara, Johnson noted that if the administration backed Lodge's recommendations "we're not in too bad a condition politically," but if they did not, they could be "caught with our britches down." Accordingly, he wanted McNamara to "make a record on this thing," wiring Saigon "nearly every day" and "either approving what Lodge is recommending" or "trying to boost them up to do a little something extra"—in other words, keeping a paper trail of support for Lodge so the Republican could not use administration foot dragging as a political issue in a potential campaign.[65] Johnson followed up with Rusk later the same day, arguing that Lodge was "thinking of New Hampshire" and that he wanted to respond to Lodge's cables with immediate cables back "complimenting him and agreeing with him . . . if it's at all possible. . . . I think that we got to build that record. . . . I think we've got to watch what that fellow says."[66] Johnson had some reason for concern, since news reports had suggested in December 1963 that Lodge was Eisenhower's favored choice for the Republican nomination in 1964. Lodge publicly professed no interest in running and a commitment to his duties as ambassador but made moves privately.[67] Johnson kept up the emphasis on the track record of support for Lodge, again raising it in a meeting prior to McNamara's March 1964 visit to South Vietnam. Johnson asked if it "was true that all recommendations made by Ambassador Lodge had been dealt with without exception—promptly and generally favorably."[68]

That the president would suggest out loud, several times, that for partisan political reasons the administration should uncritically support an ambassador he thought was incompetent, in a country supposedly as important to US national security as South Vietnam, speaks to Johnson's desire for political cover from hawks (even a moderate hawk like Lodge). Lodge was a particular concern not just as a Republican with presidential ambitions, but as a moderate favored by the likes of Eisenhower, rather than a hard-line conservative such as Goldwater. Of course, Lodge's very willingness to serve in the Kennedy and Johnson administrations made him suspect to conservatives—who dubbed him "Henry Sabotage" for implicating and dividing the party—dooming his presidential hopes.[69]

Still, Johnson continued to look over his shoulder where Lodge was concerned—and a surprise fluke victory for Lodge in the Republican New Hampshire primary in March 1964 did not help. Lodge was not on the New Hampshire ballot and had not campaigned at all, but supporters in New Hampshire, neighbor to Lodge's home state of Massachusetts, had organized just enough write-ins to deliver a victory in a state that would not endorse Goldwater. The *New York Times'* Arthur Krock noted the highly unusual circumstances that lit the "little candle which New Hampshire Republicans lighted" for Lodge but thought it was unlikely to burn for long in the primary season.[70] In addition to Lodge's unpopularity among conservatives, Krock noted the very thing Kennedy and

Johnson had hoped for in appointing Lodge: that his service as ambassador would not only provide cover but also neutralize him as a candidate. When Lodge resigned in June 1964, Robert Kennedy offered to serve as ambassador, but Johnson did not want to deal with another political rival and "worry hourly that Kennedy might resign the job in protest over his Vietnam policies."[71] Instead, over the objections of key White House aides, Johnson appointed Joint Chiefs of Staff (JCS) chairman Maxwell Taylor to the Saigon post, arguing that he "can give us the best protection with all the forces that want to make that a political war."[72] While one might chalk up Johnson's concerns with Lodge to the looming 1964 election, only a year later, Johnson would reappoint Lodge. Michael Beschloss argues this appointment was largely to "maintain Republican support for his actions in Vietnam."[73]

From the beginning, Johnson used include-and-appease tactics with the military, partly with an eye on what military displeasure would mean on Capitol Hill. In a meeting with the JCS on March 4, 1964, he "directed a check made on all requests from" General Paul D. Harkins, Military Assistance Command, Vietnam (MACV), "for help since November to see if any have been rejected or significantly curtailed. He anticipates queries from Congress on this score."[74] On November 14—nearly two weeks after the election—Jack Valenti, a special assistant to the president who managed contacts with Republicans in Congress, recommended that "before you make final decisions on the problems in Viet Nam, you 'sign on' the Joint Chiefs in that decision." Thinking ahead to the "possible future aftermath of the decisions," Valenti argued that if "something should go wrong later and investigations begin in Congress, it would be beneficial to have the Chiefs definitely a part of the Presidential decision so there can be no recriminations at these hearings, should they be held." He invoked the MacArthur hearings and the helpful back up from General Omar Bradley, "who had been in on the Truman decision." Valenti was remarkably blunt, concluding his memo with recommendations for face-to-face meetings with the Joint Chiefs of Staff so that "they will have been heard, they will have been part of the consensus, and our flank will have been covered in the event of some kind of flap or investigation later."[75]

As the war expanded in 1965, the divergence between strategy in the public interest and Johnson's elite-driven approach to do just enough not to lose South Vietnam became more and more apparent, especially in his war policy concessions to the military. Johnson needed the support of the JCS, which was in turn crucial to the effort to keep the escalation from upsetting Congress and the public.[76] Although there were interservice differences, the military favored a more aggressive approach.[77] As Herring describes, Johnson knew that his limited war approach would not please the military, but the president also "made enough concessions to their point of view to keep them on board, and he left the impression that more might be obtained later."[78] Keeping hawks minimally satisfied was costly, but less costly than risking the elite consensus. McGeorge Bundy later reflected that Johnson "conceived of military strategy as a function of political calculations, particularly the need to sustain a consensus among General Westmoreland, the Joint Chiefs of Staff, and the civilian leadership of the Pentagon on the scope of the troop escalation in the summer of 1965."[79]

In one key meeting in July 1965, Johnson stood directly in front of the chairman of the JCS, Earle Wheeler, known to be unhappy with the failure to call up the reserves, and obtained his nodded agreement for the escalation plan, leading one observer to call it "an extraordinary moment, like watching a lion-tamer dealing with some of the great lions."[80] Johnson's attempts to adjust policy so that he could simultaneously circumvent and appease the military had real consequences. As Herring notes, "sharp divisions on strategy were subordinated to the tactical necessity of maintaining the façade of unity," and even when the military approach was obviously failing, there was no high-level discussion of a change in strategy for fear of triggering debate.[81] The military continued to demand more resources, leading to a gradual but steady increase in the US commitment—another "dove's curse."

Conserving Political Capital: The Tonkin Gulf Resolution

The incident in the Tonkin Gulf in August 1964 is well-trod historical ground, because of the administration's disingenuous handling of the facts and the subsequent resolution that provided Johnson with a virtual blank check to use force.[82] But scholars usually gloss over the politics surrounding the resolution itself, which are interesting on their own terms and reinforce the connection between Vietnam and the Great Society.

Recall from chapter 2 that the theory expects Republican presidents to be more likely than Democratic presidents to seek formal approval, in part because Democratic presidents are more likely to want to conserve political capital for future fights and because Republicans can more easily co-opt Democratic doves. Democratic presidents also have less need for formal approval since if they choose to fight, they are acting against type, dampening hawkish criticism, and they can reassure their dovish base through other means, such as getting approval from international organizations. In the Vietnam case, even before the 1964 election, Democrats had large majorities in both chambers, including sixty-six seats in the Senate, so perhaps Johnson sought authorization because he could. Yet the United States was already bound to South Vietnam through a collective defense treaty as a member of the Southeast Asia Treaty Organization (SEATO), ratified 82–1 by the Senate in 1955. So what do we make of Johnson's decision to ask Congress for authorization to use force in the wake of the August 1964 Gulf of Tonkin incident, which the administration greatly exaggerated?

To see how unusual the Tonkin Gulf Resolution was, it is useful to take a short digression. Table 5-2 shows the authorization pattern for major US military conflicts since World War II, including the Taiwan Straits crisis of 1954–55, which did not escalate to war. The table shows that presidents of both parties have used force with and without congressional authorization, in wars large and small. Beneath the surface, however, another pattern emerges. Democratic presidents have used alternative sources of authorization on numerous occasions, starting with Truman's UN-led "police action." Republican presidents turned to Congress to strengthen their hands in wars large (both the 1991 Gulf War and the 2003 Iraq War) and small (Lebanon 1982–84). Democratic presidents often ended up with congressional action for other reasons. Bill Clinton sought authorization for using force, but as Schultz notes, by the 1990s, international organizations like the UN were far more viable options as alternatives to congressional authorization.[83] As Ryan Hendrickson notes, Clinton generally did not reach out to Congress, although his 1998 impeachment resulted in some effort to consult and repair channels.[84] In the case of Syria in 2013, Obama used Congress as a way to essentially call the hawks' bluff, but it is notable that this was not a case of the president wanting to fight and seeking congressional cover.[85] Furthermore, Obama was in his second term with little prospect of major domestic legislation.

That leaves us with two resolutions from the Democratic presidencies of the Cold War that stand out: the Tonkin Gulf Resolution, and the quarantine of Cuba. In the case of Cuba, however, Congress was the impetus for a resolution prior to the actual crisis. Republicans, joined by some Democrats, wanted to put pressure on the Kennedy administration and highlight its perceived weakness on Cuba, especially after the Bay of Pigs debacle.[86] On September 12, 1962, Senate majority leader Mike Mansfield wrote Kennedy that at a meeting of top Senate Democrats, there was "a great deal of concern . . . over the Cuban situation— its domestic-political and international implications," and that "the feeling was much more general than might have been anticipated that at least a 'do-something' gesture of militancy is necessary," with talk ranging from a resolution to "all out war, at least with Cuba and perhaps with Russia as well." Mansfield told the president that "there was some talk that those Democrats running for re-election in November would have to leave you on this matter unless something were done." With concern about the "intensity of the expressions on this issue," Mansfield warned of the pressure on Democrats to "engage in an attempt to outdo Republicans in militancy on Cuba" and expressed his concern about "where it might end," urging prompt action to "cut off this tendency."[87]

TABLE 5-2. Congressional Authorizations in US Crises and Interventions, 1945–2020

President (Party)	Crisis/Intervention	Congressional Authorization
Truman (D)	Korea, 1950	No (UN-led)
Eisenhower (R)	Taiwan Straits, 1954–55[†]	Yes
	Lebanon, 1958	Yes (Middle East Res., 1957)
Kennedy (D)	Quarantine of Cuba	Yes (Repub.-driven, precrisis)
	Laos, 1961	No
	Vietnam counterinsurgency, 1962	No
Johnson (D)	Vietnam, 1964 (Tonkin Gulf)	Yes (Tonkin Gulf Resolution)
	Dominican Republic, 1965	No
Nixon (R)	Vietnam escalation, 1969	No
	Cambodia, 1970	No
Ford (R)		
Carter (D)	Iran hostage rescue, 1980	No
Reagan (R)	Sinai multinational force, 1982	Yes
	Lebanon, 1982	Yes (via War Powers Res.)
	Grenada, 1983	No
George H. W. Bush (R)	Panama, 1989	No
	Gulf War, 1991	Yes
	Somalia, 1992 (UNITAF)	Yes (in Feb. 1993)
Clinton (D)	Somalia (escalation/ UNISOM II), 1993	Partial (House)
	Haiti, 1994	No
	Bosnia, 1993	Partial (Senate)
	Kosovo (air strikes), 1999	Partial (Senate)
George W. Bush (R)	Afghanistan, 2001	Yes
	Iraq, 2003	Yes
Obama (D)	Afghanistan "surge," 2009	No
	Libya, 2011	No
	Syria, 2013[†]	No (vote called off)
	Iraq (counter-ISIS), 2014	No
Trump (R)	Syria (2017 and 2018)	No
	Iran Soleimani crisis, 2020	No

Note: Cases adapted and extended from Schultz 2003, table 1 (cases of minor clashes, e.g., Mayaguez incident, omitted).
[†] = no US military force used.

Kennedy asked Congress for authorization to call up the reserves, as he had previously for Berlin. He was far more skeptical, however, of various resolutions expressing Congress's view of what to do about Cuba. Kennedy signed the legislation, but the record makes clear he did so reluctantly. As he told House Speaker John McCormack and the chairmen of the House Foreign Affairs and Armed Services Committees in a call on September 13, 1962, Kennedy wanted to "dispose of it" quickly, to "head off their giving us something much worse." Kennedy also specifically asked if the language "mentions 1958," a reference to the authorization that Eisenhower relied on for his 1958 Lebanon intervention, "because that puts it back on them," that is, Republicans.[88] Congress thus brought Cuba to Kennedy, rather than the other way around.

Johnson's pursuit of congressional authorization in Vietnam is therefore something of an outlier. The somewhat tortured backstory of the congressional resolution, however, shows the Tonkin resolution as an exception that proves the rule: Johnson pursued it only at a moment when it would cost him little in terms of political capital or open debate. The administration alternately viewed a congressional resolution as essential and impossible, until the moment arose to push it through at low cost.[89]

There was a general electoral and public dimension to Johnson's domestic political concern. Johnson was preoccupied with the November election and wanted to delay major action on Vietnam until the election was over. In a call with McGeorge Bundy on March 2, 1964, Johnson said, "I just can't believe that we can't take 15,000 advisers and 200,000 [South Vietnamese] people and maintain the status quo for six months."[90]

But as he and his administration explored options for future US involvement in Vietnam, he also believed having Congress on board was important. Walt Rostow floated the idea of a congressional resolution in February 1964.[91] Over the next few months, as Johnson and his administration struggled to get a handle on the facts in South Vietnam, many of his advisers favored a resolution for its signaling value to North Vietnam and its morale-boosting effect on South Vietnam.[92] Johnson's advisers worked on a draft congressional resolution and considered it in the context of a larger set of options for Vietnam and the political strategy required to implement them.[93]

The problem was that Johnson was also still quite unsure of his own course in Southeast Asia. Like Truman, he feared the effect of a long congressional debate that would focus public attention on a war that was still very much on the back burner for most Americans. He chastised those who spoke out of turn, even when he was inclined to agree with them: for example, in March 1964, he took Rostow to task over the phone for giving a *Washington Post* columnist the impression that Johnson had plans to expand the war to North Vietnam.[94] At the same time, Johnson obsessed over what senators said about Vietnam, telling Ball earlier the same week that he thought "somebody out to brief the Foreign Relations Committee pretty quick on North Vietnam . . . on the Vietnam situation. I notice about four senators this morning raising hell about the uncertainty and everything, and I think we ought to go over the alternatives with them and try to let them see we're doing the right thing."[95] Having given a speech at UCLA in late February widely interpreted as a threat to North Vietnam, Johnson was torn between explaining himself to Congress and avoiding a divisive debate.[96]

Underneath these general political themes, then, were specific concerns about the elite politics of a potential resolution. A major question was the timing—when exactly would Johnson seek a resolution? Unlike the Korean War, which had started with a dramatic invasion, the nature of the war in Vietnam did not offer an obvious moment. Interestingly, the discussion centered around the legislative calendar more than the electoral calendar. Johnson planned to make a major push for civil rights legislation in 1964—which would require expending considerable political capital—and then seek his own mandate in November. His party was already split on the war; as William Bundy noted in his analysis of the problem of a congressional resolution, Johnson had "doubtful friends" on the Hill.[97] Mansfield had expressed his doubts in several strongly worded letters from the beginning of Johnson's presidency; Johnson allies Fulbright and Russell had expressed skepticism about getting in as well.[98]

From the other direction, however, Johnson faced Republican critics who wanted him to clarify the US position. As Johns describes, Johnson's national security team was debating the prospect of a congressional resolution on Vietnam just at the moment Johnson was managing the fight over his civil rights bill in the spring of 1964. Republicans introduced a resolution in late May that was "essentially a demand to win or get out."[99] Johnson's advisers were well aware of the timing. As they worked on a draft congressional resolution alongside planning for expanding the war, they had an eye on the congressional calendar. In late May, McGeorge Bundy updated Johnson on the planning by a "small, tightly knit group," noting that "the preliminary consensus is that such a resolution is essential before we act against North Vietnam, but that it should be sufficiently general in form not to commit you to any particular action ahead of time. Our hope is that you might be able to persuade Dick Russell to accept a three-day truce in Civil Rights on straight patriotic grounds."[100] Several days later, Bundy sent Johnson a paper, "Basic Recommendation and Projected Course of Action on Southeast Asia," advocating "selected and carefully graduated military force against North Vietnam." The group recommended a congressional resolution, but they differed on the timing:

> We agree that no such resolution should be sought until Civil Rights is off the Senate calendar, and we believe that the preceding stages can be

conducted in such a way as to leave a free choice on the timing of such a resolution. Some of us recommend that we aim at presenting and passing the resolution between the passage of Civil Rights and the convening of the Republican Convention. Others believe that delay may be to our advantage and that we could as well handle the matter later in the summer, in spite of domestic politics.[101]

Johns notes that "the desire to focus administration efforts and expend political capital on the domestic agenda overrode any possible discussion of an immediate resort to Congress over Vietnam."[102]

By June 10, Bundy wrote a memo outlining "alternative public positions" the administration could take, noting that it was "agreed that the best available time for such a move is immediately after the Civil Rights bill clears the Senate floor. Finally, it is agreed that no such resolution should be sought unless careful Congressional soundings indicate rapid passage by a very substantial majority." He did not shy away from noting that "a Congressional resolution would require a major public campaign by the Administration. A very important element in such a campaign would be early and outspoken support by leading members of Congress. This is not a small undertaking, and it would have heavy implications." He concluded that unless there were an "acute emergency," a "strong case can be made that we do not now need to commit ourselves so heavily. . . . It appears that we need a Congressional Resolution if and only if we decide that a substantial increase of national attention and international tension is a necessary part of the defense of Southeast Asia in the coming summer."[103] When Johnson's top advisers met later that day and discussed the paper, however, they raised many questions about the challenges and risks of going to Congress without a clear decision about the US course of action.[104]

Although this group discussed a draft of a congressional resolution on June 15, by this point there were so many doubts that Bundy included in the papers for discussion a document outlining what could be done *without* a resolution, concluding that many avenues for increasing the use of force remained open.[105] And indeed, Johnson backed off. Having used considerable political resources to push through his civil rights bill, Johnson did not want to fight with his own party in Congress, nor did he want to appear a warmonger. As Johns concludes, "Johnson's finely honed political senses warned him to back away from the resolution in June and avoid it if possible before November, relying instead on actions that would be less public."[106]

The Tonkin Gulf incident in August offered the administration the opportunity to get a resolution without much prior political spade work. Notably, Johnson tasked Fulbright, his longtime ally, to get the resolution passed overwhelmingly, knowing that many doubting Democrats "respected Fulbright and would listen to him."[107] Fulbright himself was skeptical of the escalation but served Johnson faithfully, partly because he trusted Johnson and wanted to maintain his close relationship with him—that is, Johnson could offer him continued access and prestige.[108] Johnson saw co-opting skeptical doves as simpler than absorbing the wrath of hawks if he deescalated in Vietnam.

Thus the Tonkin Gulf Resolution was not the culmination of a carefully considered campaign to gain congressional backing. Rather, having rejected planning for such a campaign, Johnson responded to external events and seized the opportunity. Johns assesses bluntly the rapid shift from the clear rejection of a congressional resolution in June: the events in the Tonkin Gulf "provided Johnson with the perfect pretext to submit a resolution to Congress and avoid divisive debate as a matter of patriotism and expediency."[109] This was a strategy to conserve political capital for other legislative fights, to prevent public spillover, and to diffuse Vietnam as a campaign issue given Goldwater's hawkishness. The one thing Johnson could not give his insider hawks—who favored a resolution for its value in shoring up South Vietnam and projecting toughness to North Vietnam—was a forceful resolution that required debate.[110] As a result, dovish public sentiment had few if any elite messages to latch onto, leading to opinion bias in favor of the war in reported polling.[111]

Managing Elite Information Channels: Suppression of Information and Dissent

In the early phases of the escalation, Johnson also worked to manage the flow of information among elites, a process that included concealment of information not only from the public but also from key elites. Although Johnson wanted to avoid major decisions on Vietnam until after the 1964 election, Mitchell Lerner has noted that Johnson did not exactly hide his intentions from the public in the course of the campaign, stating clearly that he would not back down from US commitments in Vietnam.[112] After the election, during key decisions in the late fall and early winter of 1964, Johnson concealed the escalation from both Congress and the public, issuing directions to his advisers on this score. After a key set of decisions in December 1964, for example, Johnson wrote to Secretary of State Rusk, Secretary of Defense McNamara, and CIA director John McCone: "I consider it a matter of the highest importance that the substance of this position should not become public except as I specifically direct." He ordered them to "take personal responsibility" for ensuring that information was "confined as narrowly as possible to those who have an immediate working need to know."[113] As John Schuessler describes, Johnson engaged in outright deception in the course of the escalation, to shift blame onto the Communists and to preempt debate within the United States.[114]

But it was not just the public from whom Johnson concealed crucial information or suppressed alternative perspectives; he also did so within his own administration and between the executive and legislative branches. The Tonkin Gulf incident illustrates the elite-centered nature of this deception. There is significant evidence that Johnson and other key officials rushed their assessments of the evidence and misrepresented the facts for political purposes.[115] On the evening of August 4, Johnson, Rusk, McNamara, McCone, and Wheeler met with sixteen congressional leaders. Johnson asked not only for support for retaliation but also for a congressional resolution, telling the group, "I have told you what I want from you."[116] Johnson had assured key senators, including Fulbright, that he would come back to Congress for further authorization and did not plan to escalate. Fulbright himself did not have access to key information about the Tonkin incident.[117] Nor did deception of doves in Congress stop after Tonkin had given Johnson blanket authority to act. Downes cites Johnson's January 1965 "whopper," in which he assured legislators that the Vietnamese must do the fighting, three weeks after he had cabled Saigon for options on introducing US ground troops.[118]

Within the administration, Johnson also preempted debate and limited the distribution of alternative perspectives, most famously with the State Department's George Ball.[119] James Thomson called this process the "domestication of dissenters," where "internal doubters and dissenters . . . were effectively neutralized." Thus "once Mr. Ball began to express doubts, he was warmly institutionalized: he was encouraged to become the inhouse devil's advocate on Vietnam."[120] Providing a forum for Ball and then sidelining his perspective can be considered a side payment of continued prestige and access to Ball—as in the case of Fulbright—in return for keeping dissent within the inner circle. For example, on July 1, 1965, as Johnson made the final decisions about US ground involvement in Vietnam, there was a high-level discussion of several key memoranda including a paper by Ball urging a compromise that would allow the United States to cut its losses. McGeorge Bundy wrote to Johnson that "both [Dean] Rusk and [Robert] McNamara feel strongly that the George Ball paper should not be argued with you in front of any audience larger than yourself, Rusk, McNamara, Ball, and me. They feel that it is exceedingly dangerous to have this possibility reported in a wider circle."[121] Johnson acceded to the hawks' request to limit discussion even inside the administration.

Johnson also worked to keep the military from voicing its displeasure with the gradual escalation strategy in Congress, where military complaints could damage the president politically. McNamara took steps to limit JCS testimony before Congress.[122] Johnson's secrecy and even deception extended to his own administration as the war escalated. As David Kaiser describes, even in June 1965, "Johnson was now practicing deception upon dissenters within his own administration, as well as on the public. Not only did the policymakers continue to make only the minimum necessary decisions to go forward, but their deliberations apparently allowed the few remaining skeptics to believe that policy might still stop short of large-scale war." Kaiser cites meetings in early June in which McNamara referred to more limited options and downplayed the potential size of deployments.[123] As McMaster summarizes, "because he continued to deceive the Congress and the public, the president could ill afford dissention within his own administration that might reveal his actual policy decisions."[124]

The management of information channels within and among elite groups undermines the marketplace of ideas, as Downes notes.[125] But particular patterns of information suppression favored hawks, because Johnson wanted to disrupt the development of a consolidated dovish alternative. If Johnson was trying to give the public the "free lunch" it wanted, and there had been a shared mind-set inside the government that Vietnam should not be lost but need not necessarily be won, then deception behind the Washington curtain might not have been necessary.

To be sure, Johnson could not stop some of these cues from making it into public debate. Nor could he suppress the relatively open secret in Washington that many in Congress had doubts or at least felt uncertainty about the war. But the problem for Johnson was not to cut off each cue; rather, it was to maintain consensus and disrupt the coordination of opposition that would split that consensus. As a Democratic president, the dovish dissent was not negligible, particularly since it came from within his own party. But as historian Robert Divine notes in assessing the memoir of longtime Johnson aide Harry McPherson, Johnson took hawkish stances on national security, dating back to his congressional career, because "it was the price the Democrats had to pay during the Cold War to achieve their social welfare measures in Congress."[126] The master of congressional power, Johnson went for the "whales" like Russell and taught McPherson to "to avoid wasting time on minnows."[127] He worried less about critiques from those pressing him to do whatever it would take to win, as long as he had some key hawks on board, putting the others on the back foot and painting them as extremists.

It is also notable that as the theory predicts, Johnson did not really attempt to affect perceptions of the probability of success, at least not in terms of outright victory. His strategy was not to trumpet the war as a likely win for the United States but rather to keep it out of the headlines as much as possible. Although he could not avoid speaking about the war or dealing with it as a public political issue as the level of US involvement increased dramatically, his approach was not that of a president seeking to build a rallying point.

War Escalation: Papering Over Cracks in the Coalition

As Johnson escalated the war, cracks began to form in his elite coalition. As Berinsky notes, Johnson's escalation of Vietnam was very unusual in that divisions over the war emerged within the Democratic Party, before Nixon's election shifted the fault line to a more familiar division along party lines.[128] What is notable, however, is that even as public doubts emerged from the dovish side of his party and from within his administration, Johnson was able to maintain the facade of elite consensus, and at times seemed much more concerned about the hawks.

This period of the war is challenging for the theory. On the one hand, it clearly shows the limits of the insiders' game, in the sense that Johnson began to lose his grip on dissent and began to engage in active efforts to contain rising dovish sentiment. Johnson began an effort to shape perceptions of the probability of success, for example, to shore up domestic support for continuing the war. On the other hand, scholars have demonstrated that the elite consensus did not fracture fully until 1968 and remained intact for most of 1967.[129] The Tet Offensive, like the MacArthur hearings, was a dramatic event that shattered White House attempts to continue on its existing course. But by 1967 Johnson had sent nearly half a million troops to Vietnam. We would not expect that Johnson could still shore up the appearance of elite consensus in this period. Yet he managed to do just that, through both information management aimed at doves, and continued, if different, side payments to hawks, resulting in policy spillovers as Johnson struggled to manage other national security issues.

Fulbright Goes Public

Fulbright, on whom Johnson had relied to get the overwhelming Tonkin Gulf vote, was one of the first credible voices to express doubts about the war. While he valued his role as behind-the-scenes counselor to Johnson and tried to use that channel as much as possible, by the middle of 1965 he was frustrated. He made two speeches in June and September of that year criticizing Johnson's foreign policy, mainly through the prism of the president's military intervention in the Dominican Republican that year. After the September speech, Johnson was incensed and "removed him from the White House's intimate guest list after this point."[130] Fulbright's defection, less than a year into the major Johnson administration escalation, indicates that Johnson could not contain dissent from spilling into the public domain. But as Fulbright escalated his opposition to the war, Johnson, though displeased, seems to have been less concerned about it than with potential opposition from hawks.

Fulbright took further action via hearings in early 1966. Long a believer in the "legislator as educator,"[131] Fulbright explicitly saw the hearings as an opportunity to educate the public about the war—and they were televised nationally, with witnesses that included the architect of containment, George F. Kennan.[132] Fulbright was far from the only dovish voice on the Foreign Relations Committee—Tennessee Democrat Albert Gore Sr. and Idaho Democrat Frank Church also joined in the criticism. As Joseph Fry notes, for Fulbright and Gore, calling for a negotiated settlement short of victory entailed taking a position unpopular with their hawkish constituents in the South.[133] Indeed, Zaller argues that antiwar politicians like Fulbright were hardly following public opinion, since "it was at the high tide of popular *support* for the war in 1966" that they turned on it publicly. He notes that "the evidence indicates that he took his antiwar position in spite of the best advice of his political staff."[134] Although formal congressional action to repeal the Tonkin Gulf Resolution or cut off funding for the war failed overwhelmingly in this early period of dissent, the flow of antiwar messages began to increase, giving the dovish view voice at the elite level and activating some receptive public sentiment.[135]

Although Fulbright would continue to hold more hearings, he also used other tools to impose costs on the president. He did so with great reluctance, however. In January 1966, before the hearings, UN ambassador Arthur Goldberg reported on a recent talk with Fulbright, noting that the senator was "highly approving of the President's peace initiative and anxious to 'make up' with the President. He is obviously disturbed about the recent flurry of stories that he and the President have had a falling-out."[136] But Johnson continued with the escalation, and Fulbright continued to speak out through both public and private channels. In a July 1967 meeting with Senate committee chairmen, during which the fiscal strain of Vietnam and domestic programs was a main topic of discussion, Fulbright was blunt, telling Johnson:

> Mr. President, what you really need to do is to stop the war. That will solve all your problems. . . . The Vietnam war is a hopeless venture. Nobody likes it. There was a very serious outbreak on your stand in the Congo situation in the [Foreign Relations] Committee. Vietnam is the root of many of your troubles. . . . Vietnam is ruining our domestic and our foreign policy. I will not support it any longer.

Fulbright then said, "I expect that for the first time in 20 years I may vote against foreign assistance and may try to bottle the whole bill up in the Committee." Johnson responded that "if the Congress wants to tell the rest of the world to go to hell, that's their prerogative." When others raised the prospect that backing off aid would hurt efforts to shore up anticommunist positions elsewhere, Fulbright responded, "my position is that Vietnam is central to the whole problem." Johnson finally responded with a dare: "If you want me to get out of Vietnam, then you have the perogative [*sic*] of taking the resolution under which we are out there now. You can repeal it tomorrow. You can tell the troops to come home. You can tell General Westmoreland that he doesn't know what he is doing." At that point, with the room presumably silenced, Mansfield "suggested that the discussion might proceed to governmental operations."[137] Fulbright's move against the foreign aid bill was not news here, as he had already taken this position publicly and linked the aid program to US involvement in Vietnam.[138] The tense discussion with committee chairmen reminded Johnson of individual senators' power. But Johnson felt able to absorb and redirect Fulbright's anger nonetheless.

Johnson remained focused on the hawks. At his "Tuesday luncheon" with top aides barely two weeks after the Senate committee chairmen meeting, McNamara reported the JCS's latest bombing recommendations but said "he favored no additional action around Hanoi and Haiphong," because among other reasons, it would "compound the problems with the doves in this country." Johnson ignored this concern, responding, "it doesn't look as though we have escalated enough to win." Later in the meeting, he "said Secretary McNamara should worry about the heat he has to take on the Hill about bombing limitations."[139] The hawks, not the doves, still preoccupied Johnson. Many Southern Democrats believed that once the United States was committed, it should follow through with an all-out effort, leading even initial skeptics like Russell to oppose Johnson's limited war approach and join calls by other Southerners like John Stennis to increase the war effort.[140]

Managing Information and Policy Spillover: The Order of Battle Controversy

As the number of US troops in Vietnam, as well as US casualties, climbed higher and higher, the task of maintaining elite consensus and preventing fire alarms grew more difficult for the president. Johnson's initial concern may have been preventing a relatively unified elite consensus that he was weak and had allowed Vietnam to fall to communism. Even if the public was not disposed to be hawkish, a chorus of criticism—including some hawks in his own party— might have been credible and informative to voters. But by 1967, he recognized he could not ignore rising dovish voices, particularly in Congress. As Joshua Rovner describes, in 1967 the administration began a campaign to shape perceptions that the war was going well and its strategy was working.[141]

This campaign resulted in a particularly egregious example of information management: the 1967 order of battle controversy. After years of inconclusive goals, the administration had chosen a strategy of attrition, whose central

principle was, as Rovner summarizes, to "defeat the enemy by killing or cap-
turing its forces faster than it could put new troops in place." The military and
the administration called this the "crossover point," when the rate of enemy
attrition was greater than its ability to reinforce its forces, and this idea became
central to the administration's ability to sell progress on the war.[142] The term was
used at the highest levels: for example, Westmoreland specifically referenced
reaching the "crossover point" in a meeting with the president in April 1967.[143]
Johnson, no fool, immediately asked his general, "When we add divisions, can't
the enemy add divisions? If so, where does it all end?" Despite the president's
evident doubt, elite consensus that the war was reaching the crossover point
remained essential to the White House message that the war was succeeding.

The CIA, however, was a crucial dissenter, because it insisted that the
Vietcong irregulars should be counted in the overall enemy strength along
with members of the regular North Vietnamese Army. As Rovner describes,
CIA and the military command in Saigon argued over several months about
whether to count the Vietcong, a choice that made an enormous difference
in whether one concluded the crossover point was near. Eventually CIA director Richard Helms ordered his officials to stop arguing. Rovner concludes
it was because of White House pressure, so that "by the end of the year, it
appeared to Congress and the public that all of the relevant national security
agencies, including the CIA, agreed that the enemy was withering."[144] This
search for consensus in how to count the enemy and measure victory further
damaged Johnson's standing within his own administration. But it allowed
Johnson to continue the war and avoid another moment of reckoning.

Johnson had one last pre-Tet test of his ability to manage elite dissent:
McNamara's turn against the war. A hawk like McNamara airing opposition
publicly would be especially damaging. But the other threat Johnson faced
was from the military's displeasure at limitations on bombing. Eventually, as
Herring notes, the suppression of a real debate over strategy inside the administration led to the "surreal" spectacle of the August 1967 hearings led by
Senator John Stennis, a hawkish Democrat from Mississippi who chaired the
Preparedness Investigating Subcommittee of the Armed Services Committee
and who had been calling for the administration to widen the war in search
of victory. Herring argues that the Stennis hearings "became the forum for
a debate that could not take place within the inner councils of the executive
branch."[145] The battle lines were between the military, which wanted the re-
straints Johnson had imposed removed, and McNamara, who by this point had
turned against the war and argued against an expanded air campaign.

With the JCS in near revolt following McNamara's testimony against expanded bombing, Johnson again moved to shore up the hawkish consensus.
As Herring puts it, "the Stennis hearings represented what Johnson had most

feared since the start of the war, division within his own administration and the threat of a military revolt backed by hawks in Congress."[146] His strategy to manage the opposing dissents was telling: he managed McNamara's exit from the administration by providing the secretary with a soft landing at the World Bank, while simultaneously recommitting to the military's side. He made "major concessions" to the military on bombing policy, over McNamara's objections.[147]

As Vietnam began to affect other policy areas because of its strain on the US budget, Johnson made another fiscally costly concession to the military: approving a limited version of an antiballistic missile system (ABM), which McNamara (and many others in the administration) opposed as unworkable.[148] Herring sees this concession as a way to "appease the military and the right wing in Congress" in the wake of the Stennis hearings.[149] Despite all the dovish cues emerging, therefore, Johnson conceded to hawks until his consensus reached its breaking point the following year.

Postscript: From Johnson to Nixon

Ultimately, Tet turned elite and popular support firmly against Johnson, who pulled out of the presidential race. Given how deeply involved the United States was in a failing war by 1968, it is unsurprising that the war had an impact on the election. A more complicated pattern emerges with examination of individual voting behavior, however. Page and Brody demonstrate that in the 1968 election, Vietnam did not shape individuals' votes significantly, largely because the two presidential candidates had nearly indistinguishable positions. Indeed, many of those who perceived a difference between the two candidates were "projecting" their own views onto the candidates so that "their perceptions were the result of intended vote, not the cause."[150] Furthermore, as noted, Democrats who chose McCarthy in the New Hampshire primary were more likely to want to expand the war, rather than end it.[151] Johnson thus felt hawkish pressure until the very end.

Richard Nixon campaigned in part on what the media dubbed a "secret plan" to end the war, and his positioning denied voters a real choice on Vietnam in 1968.[152] Indeed, Page and Brody find that despite its high salience in that election year, Vietnam was not the basis of most voters' choices, because the candidates took such similar positions on Vietnam.[153] But unlike Eisenhower, who inherited the Korean War and committed, haltingly, to find a truce, Nixon made the war his own, ultimately leading to polarization of views on the war along party lines.[154]

Nixon's simultaneous pursuit of "Vietnamization," or withdrawing American forces and leaving more combat to the Vietnamese, and escalation through steps like the bombing and invasion of Cambodia, illustrates that as a Republican president, he looked to maintain his reputation as he pursued other foreign policy goals. Johns argues that the 1970 Cambodian incursion, which Nixon announced with an address to the nation, was straightforwardly an "attempt to win the war and assure his reelection."[155] Designed to attack the sanctuaries from which the North Vietnamese launched attacks into South Vietnam, the incursion illustrates the cross-pressure from insider hawks and advisers advocating greater restraint that Republican presidents can face. Secretary of State William Rogers and Secretary of Defense Melvin Laird both objected to the plan to attack the Cambodian sanctuaries, although Laird's concern was mainly about its effect on Vietnamization, his main policy goal, and he put pressure on Nixon to further reduce US troops. But hawks, like Vice President Spiro Agnew, argued for dealing with the sanctuaries, and many Republicans in Congress still supported a more vigorous prosecution of the war.[156]

Nixon's strategy in Vietnam is an important reminder that the adage "it takes a Nixon to go to China" requires that the leader going to China have a hawkish reputation. John Lewis Gaddis notes that one of the reasons Nixon could approach the Cold War in the early 1970s with some "ideological flexibility" was his "earlier inflexibility so consistent in its anti-communism that critics could now hardly accuse him of 'softness' or 'naivete.'"[157] For Nixon to preside over a loss in Vietnam would threaten this image—as his search, with Henry Kissinger, for a solution that would keep South Vietnam viable for a "decent interval" after US forces left illustrates.[158] As Johns argues, "more than perhaps any politician in the country, [Nixon] understood the consequences he would face if he could not demonstrate progress toward an honorable (victorious) peace by 1972." Johns posits that Nixon "feared just as much as Kennedy" a debate over "who lost Vietnam," and thus Nixon "actually displayed more concern about conservative reactions to his policies than about antiwar forces throughout his presidency."[159] Nixon and Kissinger eventually abandoned hope that military pressure might bring something like actual victory, but they prolonged the war—at great human cost—in search of something they could frame as "peace with honor," blaming Saigon's collapse on Congress.[160]

Nixon's approach brings us back to Gelb and Betts's argument that successive presidents chose the "minimum necessary" to not lose the Vietnam War. In some respects, Nixon was just the latest in a long line stretching as far back to Eisenhower, if not Truman. They note that Nixon chose a different military strategy, however, while pursuing diplomacy with the Soviets and Chinese that limited the risk of a major counterintervention.[161] While they conclude that it is not clear if Nixon's strategy was actually successful in military or international terms, they note that it "worked politically in 1972," because it contained the antiwar movement by shifting its basic argument from the war's unwinnability to its immorality.[162]

As a Republican president, Nixon was able to use more hawkish policies that held out vague promises of victory, and thus he "captured the support of most Americans in the middle and on the right."[163] Additionally, he divided and disrupted the antiwar elites just at the time their power seemed to be "growing irresistibly."[164] While this approach was not really a true pursuit of victory, it was not quite the same as "not losing," at least until Nixon and Kissinger decided to pursue a negotiated settlement. While this conclusion may seem like a distinction without a difference, the high cost of Nixon's pursuit of "peace with honor," and the contrast with Eisenhower's studied avoidance of making the Korean War his own in 1953, suggest otherwise.

Conclusion

Like Korea, Vietnam was a limited war fought far from the United States in places unfamiliar to most Americans. Snyder argues that eventually the median voter constrained both Truman and Johnson,[165] but this chapter has shown that this process took a long time, and that to varying degrees, playing the insiders' game allowed Johnson, like Truman, to escalate to remarkably high levels, to delay fire alarms, and to prolong the war after significant elite dissent emerged. Johnson was acutely aware of the political challenges Truman faced as a Democrat open to charges of weakness, and the costs of Truman's actions in Korea. Johnson was able to pass his domestic agenda, partly thanks to Truman's effort to settle the rearmament question. But ultimately, Johnson, like Truman, trapped himself in a "dove's curse."

6

The Lebanon Intervention

ELITE CONSTRAINTS ON A SMALL WAR

THE PREVIOUS TWO CHAPTERS addressed large-scale wars initiated by Democratic presidents during the Cold War. In the next two chapters, I turn to two cases of Republican presidents who found it relatively easy to get into wars that would become "hawks' misadventures," and then faced elite constraints as the war unfolded. First, I examine Reagan's intervention in Lebanon in 1982–84, when a Republican president faced elite constraint that ended a small US military operation despite Reagan's wish to continue. In chapter 7, I examine George W. Bush's invasion of Iraq in 2003 and his decision to "surge" troops in 2007, despite the antiwar message of the 2006 midterm elections.

These cases show Republican presidents find it easier than Democratic ones to maneuver around constraints at the outset of wars both large and small, because it is easier for them to co-opt those who oppose hawkish policies. But these cases also show that elites can impose constraints on the conduct, scope, and duration of war. These constraints do not necessarily mean deescalation: indeed, Bush's escalation of the Iraq War despite clear signals after 2006 shows that the constraints can push hawks to gamble for a decision. But the Lebanon case shows that these constraints can bring troops home, even when the president wants to continue an operation and the public is reasonably permissive.

These cases are also useful in comparing against the alternative of public-oriented constraints, that is, the faithful intermediaries model. One case in which public and elite opinion may be separable is a relatively small intervention in which the public is either largely ignorant or indifferent, because the conflict is not especially salient. In such a case, the president should have a relatively easy time shaping (or ignoring) public opinion. Furthermore, a small deployment force should attract fewer elite constraints than would a large military operation, as Howell and Pevehouse argue in the context of congressional constraint.[1] Reagan undertook a "hawk's misadventure" with relative ease but

TABLE 6-1. Comparing Within-Case Expectations for Republican Presidents

	Faithful Intermediaries Model	Insiders' Game Model
Side payments	None; careful selection of conflict; insiders act in concert to seek victory if not too risky	Procedural or patronage benefits to insider doves; political pressure or benefits to opposition doves War policy concessions to insider doves (if escalation)
Information	Open flow within government Fire alarm when appropriate	Limited flow to those who could damage war plans or national security agenda (insider doves) Manage/limit discussion of war success Avoid/delay dovish fire alarm
Expectations	Send forces only if not too risky; commit necessary effort; do not prolong war unnecessarily	Seek decisive outcome via escalation or withdrawal (short or long war) Delayed dovish fire alarm

ran into significant elite constraints even before the Marine barracks bombing in October 1983, and those constraints led him to terminate US involvement against his preferences.

Another useful case in which elite and public opinion are somewhat distinguishable is the opposite scenario: an ongoing, significant, and failing war, because there is likely a secular downward trend in public opinion as the conflict drags on.[2] Given public war weariness, this scenario presents a difficult test for an argument that the president can arrest or reverse this trend in the short term by bargaining with elites, allowing him to continue or even escalate the war. To illustrate this scenario, in chapter 7 I discuss George W. Bush's "surge" in Iraq, when he chose escalation in search of a more decisive outcome, in the face of public opposition and even opposition from many elites, including within the military itself, as Peter Feaver describes.[3] Table 6-1 compares expectations for cases under Republican presidents across the faithful intermediaries and insiders' game models.

These cases also allow me to explore how Republican presidents bargain with elites. In the case of Reagan and Lebanon, as public support remained relatively steady in the face of casualties, the president faced internal divisions that constrained military strategy. He also faced skepticism in Congress. In the face of rising elite opposition and internal resistance to changes in strategy that would improve the odds of success, Reagan reluctantly withdrew US forces.

Reagan and Domestic Constraints: A Hawk's Misadventure

From the perspective of the theory, the Lebanon case is especially useful because it shows a Republican president bargaining with elites—particularly with Congress—over a small deployment. In terms of public opinion, at the outset of the second US deployment in Lebanon Reagan had a relatively free hand. As Kriner notes, public support for the new deployment was "tepid," averaging 47 percent (with a range of 40 percent to 56 percent) in polls.[4] But it is unlikely that public attitudes were firm at this early stage of the intervention. Another important feature of the intervention is that public opinion remained relatively steady. Public support did not decline appreciably even as conditions on the ground became more difficult and the United States began taking casualties in dramatic events like the embassy attack and the barracks bombing; in the wake of the barracks bombing, public support even temporarily increased.[5] Douglas Foyle likewise argues that Reagan was not constrained by public opinion.[6] Reagan's withdrawal was thus not the result of a direct public outcry.

Several studies point to the role of Congress in constraining Reagan, and legislative constraints are certainly important to the story. Howell and Pevehouse, as well as Kriner, argue that Congress constrained Reagan, and as Kriner puts it, "Congressional challenges to the administration's policies were not mere proxies for shifts in public opinion or changes in the situation on the ground in Lebanon."[7] Kriner also shows that Congress imposed direct costs on the Reagan administration, by raising "both the political and the military costs that administrations officials perceived they would have to pay if they continued the Lebanon deployment."[8] Not only might "virulent, sustained congressional opposition" damage the president and his copartisans at the polls in November 1984, but "top administration officials believed that congressional opposition . . . emboldened the Syrians and their allies in Lebanon," altering the military requirements for a continued US operation.[9] Other scholars point to Congress as an enabling factor: for example, Eric Larson concludes that despite the public's lack of enthusiasm, "the Reagan administration was able to continue the operation largely on the basis of conditional support from the Congress."[10]

The analysis in this chapter, while confirming the role of congressional constraint, goes several steps further. On the congressional front, it is somewhat peculiar that Reagan bargained with congressional leaders to extend the operation under the War Powers Resolution given the small size of the deployment. Indeed, Howell and Pevehouse argue that Congress is expected to exert greater constraints on larger deployments.[11] Perhaps Republican presidents, who tend to be more hawkish, undertake larger-scale military operations and therefore seek congressional support simply because they take bigger risks. The politics of the Lebanon operation show that congressional constraint operates as the theory

TABLE 6-2. Within-Case Evidence for Lebanon Intervention

	Side Payments	Information
War initiation (second MNF, Aug. 1982)	To insider doves (Weinberger/ JCS): limits on deployment To opposition doves (Tip O'Neill, other Democrats): procedural concession to avoid War Powers hostility clause; face time	Shape perceptions of probability of success (poorly done for second MNF)
Escalation (summer– fall 1983)	Limited rules of engagement and deployment scope War Powers compromise to extend operation	Cut insider doves out of the loop Manage testimony; limit distribution of possible escalation plans
Duration/termination (late 1983 to early 1984)	Rejection of insider hawks' push for escalation Reluctant withdrawal, Feb. 1984	Fire alarm from elites after Oct. 1983 barracks bombing

predicts for even a small use of force initiated by a Republican. This chapter shows that the administration sought and relied on help from Democratic leaders in the House, obtained with relative ease. Despite the procedural compromises, however, internal divisions within Reagan's own party—particularly the misgivings of Republican leaders in the Senate—weighed on the president.

Congressional concerns, however, were only one source of constraint on Reagan. Constraints from within his administration limited the scope and duration of the intervention, much to the president's displeasure. Given the small size of the deployment and Reagan's own preferences, these constraints are somewhat surprising. Internal administration divisions surfaced in the initial phase of US military operations in 1982, when Congress was more easily mollified, and continued to influence White House decision making even in the period in early 1983 when Lebanon faded from the news.

Additionally, the evidence suggests that although Reagan could get into the Lebanon battle easily, he was politically sensitive to the outcome in terms of how it affected his standing on national security and his other defense-related priorities, which were central to his agenda. He therefore sought a resolution and considered escalating before reluctantly choosing withdrawal. Using archival documents from the White House and other sources, this chapter thus illuminates an important set of within-case expectations for Republican presidents at war.[12] Table 6-2 summarizes the within-case evidence for the Lebanon case.

Reagan's Domestic Political Landscape

As Keren Yarhi-Milo demonstrates, Reagan not only was consistently hawkish but also—unsurprisingly for an actor—belonged to the category of "high self-monitors," who can "present themselves differently to suit the desires of their audience."[13] Reagan was therefore overwhelmingly inclined to fight for reputation, and we would not expect him to back down from a military operation he believed was important to demonstrating US resolve.[14]

Reagan's foreign policy and national security advisers were divided from the start, but the lines of conflict evolved in somewhat unusual ways. Reagan's first secretary of state, Alexander Haig, resigned in June 1982 after repeated clashes with Secretary of Defense Caspar Weinberger, ostensibly over US policy in the wake of the Israeli invasion of Lebanon. George Shultz replaced Haig, but the clashes between his State Department and Weinberger's Pentagon only continued. As Yarhi-Milo notes in her study of fighting for reputation—clearly one of Reagan's motives in Lebanon—"it was the more hawkish Weinberger who was reluctant to use military force in places like Lebanon, Grenada, and Libya, whereas the more pragmatic Shultz warned of the risks of backing down."[15] She concludes that "hawkishness is not determinative of concerns about reputation for resolve, or the selection of policies to enhance US reputation through the use of military instruments."[16] Indeed, in a February 1984 editorial titled "Failure in Lebanon," after the announcement of the impending US withdrawal, the *Washington Post* noted that

> President Reagan let run to the end an argument between State Department "hawks" who saw an opening to apply military power for both small (in Lebanon) and large (in respect to Syria and the Soviet Union) political purposes, and Pentagon "doves" who saw no such opening, only uncertainty and trouble.[17]

Given that the two distinct camps on this issue were documented in news sources at the time, we can reasonably designate Shultz and his State Department as "hawks" and the Pentagon as "doves." As noted in chapter 2, however, the distance between officials inside Republican administrations is expected to be smaller than that between officials inside Democratic administrations, because Republican presidents do not face the same selection pressures to include truly dovish voices. Despite their repeated clashes, both Weinberger and Shultz were firmly committed to the Reagan administration's Cold War approach.

There was an important third group of insiders in the Reagan administration: the National Security Council (NSC) staff, led by National Security Advisor William "Judge" Clark, a Reagan loyalist. As John Gans notes, the NSC staff was more hawkish and assertive about the use of force and pushed hard to use American military power to influence the Middle East and demonstrate resolve.[18] These hawks, close to the White House, played a significant role and both reflected and influenced Reagan's preferences and decisions throughout the Lebanon intervention.

In Congress, Republicans controlled the Senate, and Democrats controlled the house, but party control was not the only thing that mattered. Key leaders, like Senate majority leader Howard Baker, had serious reservations about using military force in Lebanon. Divisions within Reagan's own party would be a significant constraint on Reagan's actions. Additionally, the War Powers Resolution, a 1973 law enacted in response to Vietnam, had not faced a significant test yet, and Reagan sought to break the country out of the "Vietnam Syndrome," as he himself described it in a campaign speech in 1980.[19]

Mechanisms of Hawkish Bias

It is simpler to characterize the mechanisms of hawkish bias in the case of Republican presidents, because these mechanisms are less about pushing reluctant leaders into war than about lowering the barriers to following hawkish inclinations, if Republican presidents have them. The selection pressures on Reagan, while reflecting the usual demands to appoint those with experience and connections to prior administrations, did not include pressure to appoint doves. While Reagan had a domestic agenda, one of its primary aims was government retrenchment. My claim is not that Republican presidents have no domestic agenda, but their agenda exposure in terms of the use of force is lower than for Democratic presidents. Reagan had a significant national security agenda, however, that did require congressional backing. While initially Reagan may have seen a tough stance in Lebanon as furthering those aims—and arguably, he did take this perspective even after the withdrawal—his advisers began to see it as a threat to this national security agenda, and to Reagan's larger goals of a defense buildup and negotiations with the Soviets. Finally, as this chapter shows, Reagan was able to use procedural side payments like the War Powers Resolution to co-opt doves, including Democrats.

All three mechanisms did not so much push Reagan into war as allow him to send troops with relative ease when he was inclined to do so. Under a faithful intermediaries model, we would expect greater scrutiny up front of a hawk's war plans rather than mere acceptance of Reagan's promises that the intervention would be short and limited, without hostilities. While Reagan may have had a hawk's advantage in diplomacy with Mikhail Gorbachev, he also had leeway for hawkish misadventures. His decisions to initiate US involvement in the Lebanon conflict, however, embedded constraints on how hawkish his misadventure could be and how long it could last.

War Initiation(s): Summer 1982

The First Deployment to Lebanon

Lebanon had become a battleground in the conflict between Israel and the Palestine Liberation Organization (PLO), which used southern Lebanon as a base from which to launch attacks into Israel. Conflict also simmered between Israel and Syria, both of which backed factions inside Lebanon. In 1981, Israel attacked Syrian forces in Lebanon from the air, and in response, Syria placed surface-to-air missiles in Lebanon.[20] In the summer of 1982, as Israel contemplated invading Lebanon to eject the PLO, tensions boiled over when the PLO was allegedly involved in the attempted assassination of Israel's ambassador in London. Israel invaded Lebanon three days later, prompting divisions within Reagan's national security team, some of whom urged him to pressure the Israelis to halt the assault. Reagan's special envoy Philip Habib pushed for an American commitment to participate in a multinational force (MNF), as a tool to bring the Israelis and Syrians to the bargaining table and ultimately achieve the withdrawal of PLO fighters, and Israeli and Syrian forces. In July 1982 Reagan agreed in principle, and in August Reagan pressured Israel. Habib brokered a fragile agreement whose terms included a small contingent of eight hundred US troops to aid in the evacuation of PLO fighters from Lebanon. US Marines arrived on August 25 and returned to their ships less than three weeks later with the mission deemed complete.[21]

While Reagan pursued this initial deployment relatively unfettered, even prior to the deployment, divisions within the administration and within the two parties made it into news reports. On July 6, Israeli radio broadcast news that Reagan had agreed "in principle" to contribute US forces to a peacekeeping plan, forcing a vacationing Reagan to confirm publicly that he had agreed to a request via Habib to offer a small contribution of US forces as a bargaining tool, with administration officials stressing the limited scope of potential US involvement in time, deployment size, and mission.[22] The following day, Bernard Gwertzman of the *New York Times* reported in a front-page story that members of Congress, hurriedly briefed by the White House during a recess, "voiced deep concern" over sending US forces to Beirut. Gwertzman noted that Senate majority leader Howard Baker Jr., "who in the past has opposed American involvement in a permanent peacekeeping force in southern Lebanon, repeated his view today, saying 'It is not wise to introduce American fighting men in the Lebanese conflict.'" The article also cited other members of Congress, including Representative Clement J. Zablocki (D-WI), chairman of the House Foreign Affairs Committee, and other senators from both parties, who expressed reservations. The article also noted the Pentagon's lack of support for sending US forces, noting that "Defense Secretary Caspar W. Weinberger warned last month against sending troops into such a 'volatile area.'"[23]

Weinberger's opposition to a deployment was already fodder for newspaper commentary. On July 8, *Washington Post* columnist Mary McGrory described the almost physical discomfort Weinberger displayed at a meeting with reporters in discussing the potential US mission. McGrory noted the "tonelessness" of Weinberger's voice and his "noncommittal and vague" discussion, such as his description of the upside as "not wanting to be the cause of the thing not working out," or the moment when he "closed his eyes and seemed to be reading from some TelePromTer inside his head" when asserting the US commitment to Israel. As she summarized, "It wasn't so much what Caspar W. Weinberger said as the way he said it that left the impression he is not a total team player on U.S.-Israeli policy toward Lebanon."[24]

Reagan was able to diffuse the trouble already brewing in Congress without much difficulty. In the debate over a potential US role, Howard Baker, the leader of the president's party in the Senate, had made clear to Reagan his strong objections. Most other objections centered on consultation with Congress via the War Powers Resolution. Zablocki, the Democratic House Foreign Affairs Committee chair, sent Reagan a letter on July 6 about the technicalities of reporting under the War Powers Resolution, with which Reagan said he would comply but not necessarily under the provision notifying Congress of deployment into "imminent involvement in hostilities." Zablocki complained that this approach "would not constitute full compliance with the War Powers Resolution in these circumstances. Rather, it could only be interpreted as an attempt to avoid capriciously the subsequent requirements" triggered by reporting under the hostilities provisions. Zablocki closed by warning that "such an action would have incalculable effects on executive-legislative relations on a variety of foreign policy issues."[25] White House Legislative Affairs director Ken Duberstein flagged the letter for the NSC's "immediate attention," copying Reagan's political staff and asking the NSC for guidance.[26] Reagan discussed the issue with Zablocki in person. Though the State Department drafted a reply to Zablocki, the NSC and Duberstein recommended not sending the letter since "the President successfully defused this issue with Zablocki in person last week. . . . I would think the less said and written about this matter the better."[27] Some presidential face time to discuss procedures had apparently been enough to mollify Zablocki, for now.

Reagan had also repeatedly assured Congress that the intervention would be brief and succeed in its limited aims. These assertions seemed to be enough to convince members of Congress of the probability of success, or at least the unlikelihood of a protracted failure. As Howell and Pevehouse put it, "Duly informed about the engagements and assured that troops would return home before long . . . members said and did little to complicate either the president's military planning or his negotiations with the various combatants in Lebanon."[28] Reagan completed the first deployment without significant political problems.

Notably, however, there was some negative press coverage. Figure 6-1 shows newspaper coverage of Lebanon from July 1982 to March 1984, spanning both MNF deployments, in the *New York Times* and the *Washington Post*. Pure news coverage is excluded; coverage that reports pro- or anti-intervention views, as well as that which presents both stances, are coded for administration viewpoints (left panel) and congressional viewpoints (right panel). For the first MNF, most administration viewpoints are pro-intervention, reflecting the president's position, but there is some dissent. Of the congressional views expressed in July 1982, most contain either anti-intervention viewpoints or both stances. While these stories are relatively few in number, they reflect latent elite concern as the first MNF ended.

Return to Lebanon: Elite Politics and the Second MNF

In September, Lebanon's president-elect was assassinated, prompting Israel to return to Lebanon. The ensuing fighting, which included the massacres at the Sabra and Shatila refugee camps, once again prompted discussions of an American deployment. The Reagan administration was divided along now-familiar lines, with Shultz and the NSC favoring intervention, and Weinberger and the JCS opposed (unless there was a firm agreement already in place). In late September 1982, Reagan again dispatched troops, this time sending approximately twelve hundred Marines to protect Beirut International Airport. As the situation on the ground deteriorated, the mission gradually expanded, with US forces becoming more and more involved in the fighting. Over the next few months US forces suffered significant attacks, including the bombing of the US Embassy in Beirut in April 1983 and the bombing of the Marine barracks in October 1983, which killed 241 US servicemen. By February 1984, Reagan had decided to withdraw.[29]

As Kriner convincingly demonstrates, Reagan felt constraints from Congress more directly than from the public, which was not especially supportive but gave the president a small rally after the barracks bombing.[30] At the elite level, in light of Reagan's assurances that the mission would again be limited, Kriner notes that congressional reaction was initially muted, with dissent mostly limited to urging the president to invoke the War Powers Resolution (WPR). The "defining character of the initial congressional reaction to the second MNF deployment was neither one of enthusiastic support nor of acrimonious opposition."[31] From this point, most accounts note the mounting unease in Congress; the pressure on Reagan for some sort of War Powers

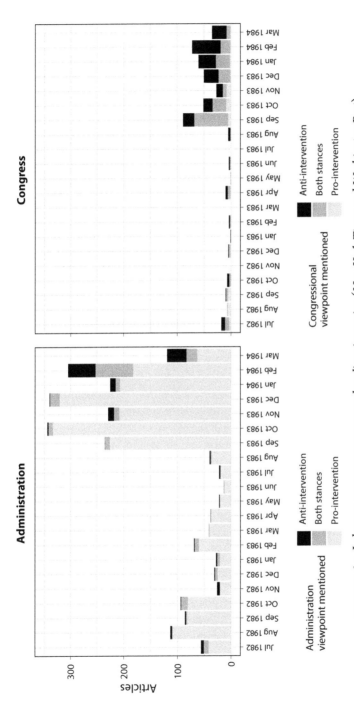

FIGURE 6-1. Lebanon newspaper coverage by elite viewpoint (*New York Times* and *Washington Post*)

compromise, culminating in a September 1983 deal with Congress to extend
the operation for another eighteen months; and the unraveling of congressional (but not public) support after the barracks bombing in October.[32]

But this general story of elite constraint masks elite politics that ultimately
led Reagan, a "reputation crusader" in Yarhi-Milo's parlance, to withdraw US
forces in early 1984 with extreme reluctance.[33] That Reagan could redeploy the
Marines again so soon after the end of the first MNF, which had resulted in
publicly aired concerns, reflects the leeway he had to initiate military action,
consistent with a hawk's misadventure. Reagan did, however, feel the pinch
of elite constraints from within his own administration almost immediately.

There were significant divisions within the administration over the decision
to deploy troops as well as the size and scope of the mission. Shultz and many
on the NSC favored a larger force whose presence could help create conditions
for diplomacy, and they continued to press for expanding the mission almost
from the moment the second Marine landing began. The White House and
Reagan generally backed those like Shultz who favored intervention with a
larger force. But Weinberger and the JCS chairman, John Vessey, consistently
opposed the deployment and pushed for a limited force.[34]

Weinberger made little effort to hide his opposition to the mission. Press coverage of the second deployment repeatedly noted his opposition and his concern about the Marines being drawn into combat. As the new deployment was
announced, Weinberger told reporters that he did not believe the prior mission
could have prevented the massacres of Palestinian civilians and reiterated that
the new deployment would not be a combat mission.[35] Another article noted
that Weinberger "insisted today that the marines would not be a police force and
would be withdrawn if they encountered combat."[36] Several days later, the *Post*
reported Weinberger statements about the limited nature of the mission, as well
as anonymous administration "officials" who said that Weinberger "has been the
most wary member of the administration about committing American units to
Beirut, both during the withdrawal of Palestinian forces last month and now during the Israeli pullback." The officials also said Weinberger would have preferred
acting through an existing UN force already operating in southern Lebanon.[37]
Reagan, however, was more open-ended in his language about the length of the
deployment, saying on September 28, when Marines began landing, "I can't tell
you what the time element will be," and stating that the Marines would stay "until
all foreign forces are withdrawn."[38] Reagan would publicly maintain this line for
several months.[39] Yet Weinberger continued to be publicly reluctant to endorse
a long stay for the Marines or enlarging the deployment.[40] Shultz, in contrast,
had made his support of using troops in Lebanon clear in his confirmation hearings. While the *Times* and the *Post* data show that mentions of Shultz dwarfed
mentions of Weinberger (consistent with the generally greater news coverage of
secretaries of state), Weinberger's opposition was a consistent theme.[41]

Behind the scenes, advocates of an expanded mission for the Marines were well aware they had to go through Weinberger's opposition. In October 1982, as the administration debated the scope and limits of the second deployment, Deputy Secretary of State Kenneth Dam noted after one weekly State-Defense breakfast that Weinberger was "less opinionated on the subject of the use of American troops in a multi-national force than he had been before, although he [made] clear his opposition to the use of American troops. Perhaps the reason was that Secretary Shultz also was rather negative about the use of such an American force, particularly in the Bekaa Valley."[42] At the following week's State-Defense breakfast, Dam gave an overview, "backing rather gently into the question of an extension of the multinational force to include the Beirut and Damascus Highway." He reported that "it became clear that Secretary Weinberger would probably accept a multinational force, given that the President is leaning that way, but he is still, I'm sure, going to argue against it."[43]

While Reagan sided with those who favored the second MNF, the actual force remained small and initially highly restricted in its rules of engagement, essentially confined to the Beirut airport with peacetime rules limiting them to self-defense. These restrictions represented a policy concession to the Weinberger and JCS view and helped to head off a challenge from Congress that the Marines were involved in active hostilities, triggering the clock under the WPR. In a way, it was another attempt to shape perceptions of the probability of success, by defining "success" as avoiding hostilities. But it left the Marines in an uncertain and vulnerable position, making it easier for critics to claim that the administration had not done enough to protect them or ensure the mission's security.

The degree of dovish constraint at the outset of the second MNF is somewhat surprising from the perspective of the theory. Given the small size of the deployment and Reagan's apparent commitment to it, the president's concessions to the civilian and military leadership at the Pentagon, along with his failure to resolve the internal tension that clearly affected the mission, are puzzling. The theory does suggest that hawks may be pulled somewhat in a dovish direction, but the war policy concessions at the outset were significant. One explanation may be the odd lineup of advisers, with Weinberger playing the role of "dove" and aligned with the JCS, and therefore in a position to extract concessions very directly.

War Escalation: Straining at Limits

As the violence worsened and the Marines remained at the Beirut airport, officials at the State Department and the NSC began pushing to expand the mission to include training of the Lebanese Armed Forces, and to give them the ability to undertake surveillance and patrolling in the south. But internal opposition from the Pentagon continued to limit Reagan's options over the winter of 1982–83, and he could not enlist his own party leadership in Congress to help. These tensions would come to a head later in 1983, with a compromise in Congress over War Powers. Although Reagan did not change his view of the need to stand firm in Lebanon after the bombing of the Marine barracks in October 1983, his political advisers questioned how much more political capital the operation in Lebanon was worth.

Debating and Limiting Escalation, Winter 1982–83

There was certainly a faction within the Reagan administration that favored using the Marines for more than just guarding the Beirut airport. The hawks' idea was to offer an expanded MNF to the Israelis as a way to provide enough security assurance on their northern border that they would withdraw. The State Department's Kenneth Dam provided Reagan with an update on February 3, mentioning the US preference that the UN peacekeeping mission could handle security in the south but if the Israelis object, "to offer as a fallback the MNF with U.S. participation in the security zone. . . . Although such an offer entails high risks with Congress and the public, it will demonstrate the extent of our commitment to Israeli security, may yield trade-offs on normalization, and may attract Begin while isolating Sharon."[44] In the National Security Planning Group meeting on February 4, Reagan authorized Habib to offer the expanded MNF to the Israelis, and the State Department was "requested to forward proposals for discreet consultations with Congress no later than noon, February 5." Reagan also asked for "worse case" planning in the event negotiations failed, to "bring a speedy withdrawal of all foreign forces."[45]

As Dam's warning about "high risks" and the request for "discreet consultations" indicated, supporters of the expanded MNF offer were acutely aware of the need not only to avoid direct congressional opposition, but also to limit information. On February 5, 1983, the State Department's L. Paul Bremer outlined options for these consultations in a memo to Clark at the NSC. Bremer described "two dilemmas in deciding how best to handle briefings on the Hill" in the event that negotiations required the US to offer an expanded MNF. "Both dilemmas," Bremer noted, were "related to the need to avoid premature leaks, while meeting most effectively the Congressional opposition to U.S. participation in an expanded MNF," raised by majority leader Baker earlier that week. The first dilemma was to "explain our rationale in advance to as many members as possible in order to acquire maximum support. However, the larger the group . . . the greater the likelihood of a leak." The second dilemma was one of timing and information management: "to avoid the charge of confronting Congress with a fait accompli," earlier would be better, but "too much advance notice . . . again increases the chance of a leak." Bremer attached two lists, both bipartisan, "one showing the members we would brief if leakage were not an issue and the other a smaller list containing the minimum number we could brief and still make a valid claim to prior consultation." Bremer concluded with the recommendation that "we brief the smallest number of members at the last possible moment."[46] The proposed talking points anticipated the War Powers problem and stated that the proposed expansion still would not mean introducing US forces into "hostilities," and that "legislation in advance of deliberations on these issues would impose inflexible constraints on U.S. negotiators."[47]

Armed with these talking points, Assistant Secretary of State Richard Fairbanks flew to Knoxville, Tennessee, a few days later to brief Howard Baker on the possibility that Habib might be forced to offer an expanded MNF in the south of Lebanon as the only way to reassure the Israelis on their northern border. The personal briefing evidently aimed to impress on Baker the need for secrecy, and he "understood the need for confidentiality and concurred in the procedural plans for early but limited Congressional consultation." But, in his memo reporting on the trip, Fairbanks noted that Baker "wanted me to deliver to you and the President his strong reservations about the wisdom of such a larger and longer commitment of U.S. troops in Lebanon. . . . He wanted it to be recorded that he reserves the right to oppose such an introduction of U.S. forces even if the President were to deem it necessary." Baker's aide told Fairbanks that "the Senator also feels that Phil [Habib] 'snookered the President' into the present circumstance which argues for a U.S. troop commitment to solve the Lebanon impasse."[48] The expanded MNF idea didn't get far, with Habib reporting in late March that the idea was a "total non-starter" with the Israelis.[49]

Even as State Department officials tended to talk about an expanded MNF in terms of a bargaining chip with Israel, the NSC hawks pushed their own version of the plan on other bureaucratic fronts in Washington. In March 1983, the NSC's senior director for Near East and South Asian affairs, Geoffrey Kemp, along with two staffers, Philip Dur and Howard Teicher, all of whom favored greater action in Lebanon, prepared talking points for Clark for a potential conversation with Weinberger. They noted that they "tried to anticipate his stated concerns and to provide points you could use to persuade him."[50] The talking points urged Clark to impress on Weinberger that "we are running out of time," and the question is "what to do which will get Israelis out, give Lebanon confidence, and allow Syrians, PLO to quit Lebanon." To get the Israelis out, it would be necessary to "make them a 'security arrangements' offer they can't refuse," and the "only way I know of to *assure* Israeli security without direct Israeli participation is for *us* to do it." Clark would recommend "a package of specialized military forces with the stress on surveillance, mobility and quick reaction," to "convince the Israelis we will *see* infiltration and that acting on our intelligence we can put the *Lebanese* Army in position to arrest infiltrators or terrorists." The talking points went on to stress that the United States would be training the Lebanese Army, rather than participating in counterinsurgency. The document ended with a near plea: "Cap, I'm convinced we could do it. . . . The President is very determined to see this Lebanon withdrawal through. He needs your help, Cap, and I think that a solid, well designed US military presence may prove to be the only solution."[51]

In the copy marked "seen" by Clark, handwritten notes, presumably Clark's, added that they needed to get "George [presumably Shultz] and Jack Vessey on board," noting that Shultz had said the "Israelis have turned down MNF in South" but that meant a "Beirut-style MNF," that is, a highly restricted force simply designed to show a US presence, "not what we are proposing here."[52] Indeed, Clark also sent a memo around this same time to Shultz, recommending a demarche to the Israelis from Reagan, making clear that the United States recognized Israeli's concerns on its northern border but reiterating the need to get foreign forces out of Lebanon as soon as possible and to respect Lebanese sovereignty.[53] "To this end," the demarche concluded, "the President is prepared to use U.S. resources to do whatever is necessary to enhance Israel's security until the [Lebanese government] is prepared—and seen as prepared—to assume unilateral responsibility." Additional points of clarification stressed that US forces would have an "*active* mission," not the "largely passive 'deter by presence' role we have undertaken in Beirut." Conjuring Weinberger's shadow, the document also noted that "the President recognizes that this expression of the US 'commitment' to the security of Israel will be very unpopular in some quarters of the US Government."[54]

Despite this hawkish pressure and his own inclinations, Reagan accommodated the preferences of Weinberger and the JCS and resisted repeated attempts to expand the Marines' mission or loosen the rules of engagement. Although Weinberger was known for favoring a tough stance against the Soviets, he advocated restraint in using force, particularly in peacekeeping or internal political missions. Thus while not a traditional "dove," he was on the more restrained end of the spectrum in situations like Lebanon. As Gans notes, there were intense interpersonal conflicts across the Reagan administration, but the NSC hawks seemed to attract ire from multiple directions, including not only the Pentagon but also Habib, the special envoy struggling to work out a diplomatic solution. Reagan seemed aligned in spirit with the hawks, but unwilling to grant them the more decisive American role they sought.[55]

Although Reagan placated Weinberger with war policy concessions, and the secretary of defense dutifully made supportive statements about the

Marines' mission, he was not a particularly effective candidate for an against-type statement that would reassure skeptical members of Congress that the mission in Lebanon was wise and worth continuing. As McFarlane discovered, Weinberger did not have much respect among defense-minded members of Congress. In December 1982, McFarlane sent Clark a memo marked "Sensitive/Exclusively Eyes Only" about "Problems Ahead," reporting a surprising conversation with Georgia Democratic senator Sam Nunn, widely regarded as a leading expert on defense issues. The topic was the controversial MX missile. Nunn said "as a friend and one concerned for the outcome" of the MX debate, he wanted to convey his view that "the entire basis for Senate and House opposition was their lack of confidence in Cap Weinberger; he simply is not credible on Defense issues and his protestations of thoroughness in looking at alternative modes were transparently false." McFarlane professed to be "shocked" that it had reached the level of Nunn, "surely the most intelligent member of the Committee." McFarlane went on to report a meeting with William Cohen of Maine, a "young and thoughtful Republican," who also volunteered that the administration "had better put together a bipartisan team of respected analysts to study this issue for you in the next two months because if the new plan is sent up here in March by Cap Weinberger, it will definitely fail."[56] Although these conversations concerned the issue Weinberger cared most about—the defense buildup—they reflected a lack of respect for his expertise.

A second reason to appease the Pentagon more generally was its ability to impose costs on other administration priorities. Some of these costs related to Lebanon at least indirectly. Weinberger, who took a harder line against Israel than did most in the administration, engaged in some bureaucratic freelancing that angered those who were trying to manage the situation in Lebanon. For example, in late April 1983, Dam had "quite a fight" with Weinberger at the weekly State-Defense breakfast after "what clearly was an attempt by Cap to welch on the agreement" related to Pentagon licenses for aircraft production. "This is another example," Dam noted in his diary, "of where Cap Weinberger is attempting unilaterally to pursue a very tough policy against Israel, even in the face of a Presidential decision in principle. He also is angry because he was not involved in the meeting in which the decision to issue the licenses was taken by the President."[57]

Other costs were related to Reagan's national security priorities in other areas, particularly nuclear weapons. During the period of the Lebanon crisis, the administration was on the defensive in pursuing its preferred policies on nuclear weapons and arms control and found itself confronting liberal members of Congress several times on these issues in 1983 at the same time it was struggling to manage the second MNF.[58] In the period during which the NSC was pressing for an expanded deployment, the administration was making a major push on legislation to approve the MX missile and its controversial basing concept. The administration was struggling to gain ground with the moderates in the Senate even as hard-liners' testimony gave those moderates pause; for example, in late June, White House legislative affairs warned chief of staff James Baker of "slippage" with crucial moderates, one of whom, Senator Warren Rudman (R-NH), warned that "we may have given MX opponents some leverage to argue that the Administration is less than totally sincere in its commitment to a viable arms agreement."[59] Reagan was concerned about the "warmonger" image as he tried to strike a balance between eliminating "Vietnam Syndrome" and an aggressive military buildup, with his pragmatic and hopeful views about the trajectory of the Cold War. The administration began to recognize the Lebanon operation as a hawk's misadventure that might endanger Reagan's hawkish advantage in later negotiations. Thus it did not want a second front erupting in Congress, not only because it would eat up valuable time, but also because it would reinforce the risk that Reagan's policies would seem too bellicose.

In addition to agenda costs on national security issues, Congress could impose costs on the US effort in Lebanon itself. For example, in April 1983, a few days before the bombing of the US embassy in Beirut that significantly raised concern in Congress, a House Foreign Affairs subcommittee, chaired by Lee Hamilton, added an amendment to the FY 84 Security Assistance budget "that would require the President to seek positive legislative authority for the use of U.S. troops as part of any expanded MNF." The NSC's Robert Lilac alerted Clark to this "disturbing" amendment.[60] Even after the embassy bombing, however, the administration continued to maintain the line that it would not seek authority from Congress until after it had "negotiated the role, function, size and location of any deployments of the Multinational Force in Lebanon."[61]

Wavering on Escalation: Spring–Fall 1983

As the negotiations to get foreign forces out of Lebanon dragged on and the war became increasingly dangerous to the Marines in the spring of 1983, the tension between wanting to stay in Lebanon to prove US staying power and appeasing those advocating for restraint only grew more acute. In the summer, McFarlane replaced Habib as special envoy, and as Gans notes, for a time, the NSC took control of Lebanon policy.[62] In February, McFarlane scrawled heated comments on a cable from Habib—writing, "All of this is absolutely bunk!" and mocking the lengthy timetable Habib set out—and sent it to Clark with a strongly worded cover note, writing that "it's almost as if Phil had not been in the room when the President met with him before he left," and that "this cable reflects that Phil is still chipping at the margins. This will never work. We have to go for a final arrangement and soon."[63] Consistent with the theory, Reagan also recognized the approaching fork in the road. In early September, when McFarlane, in his new role as special envoy, cabled a "Worst Case Strategy for Lebanon" that assessed the current incremental US approach was insufficient, Reagan added a handwritten note on the cable: "I consider this very important."[64] The same week, Reagan wrote in his diary, "we have to show the flag for those Marines. I can't get the idea out of my head that some F14s off the Eisenhower coming in at about 200 ft. over the Marines & blowing hell out of a couple of artillery emplacements would be a tonic for the Marines & at the same time would deliver a message to those gun happy middle east terrorists."[65] After developments a few days later that resulted in Reagan ordering some increased force (discussed shortly), he wrote, "if it doesn't work then we'll have to decide between pulling out or going to the Congress & making a case for greater involvement."[66] Elite pressure forced Reagan to choose some kind of definitive outcome, rather than settling for kicking the can further down the road.

The administration was already well aware that Congress was alarmed, however. In late August, after a new round of violence in Lebanon resulted in the deaths of two Marines from hostile fire, more prominent senators from both parties joined the call for WPR review. Shultz gave a news conference, with the *Post* reporting that "in what appeared to be a move to deal with congressional concerns, Shultz, who is widely respected on Capitol Hill, yesterday took over as principal administration spokesman," though he continued to brush aside calls to invoke the hostilities provision of the WPR.[67] The White House gathered the bipartisan congressional leadership over Labor Day weekend, just days after the shoot-down of Korean Air Lines 007, to discuss both that tragedy and the situation in Lebanon. In advance of the meeting, Duberstein warned that "Congress has become increasingly concerned" and that "calls have been made ... for the President to report to Congress" under the "imminent hostilities" provision of the War Powers Resolution, triggering the sixty-day timeline in the absence of legislation; Reagan's most recent report had been on August 30, "specifically avoiding mention" of that provision. But "Senator Baker and others believe that pressure will quickly build in Congress for a vote," which "could lead to an Executive-Legislative confrontation."[68] The talking points for Reagan urged him to note that "we need broad bipartisan support ... [and we] know there is concern in the Congress about the Marine presence in Lebanon and the casualties last week." The talking points ended with an instruction to Reagan: "FYI, Mr. President—look first to Howard Baker for response."[69] In his diary entry for that day, Reagan noted, "I believe we have Dem. support for what we're doing there. We may be on the verge of showing the world a truly united front."[70]

With the deaths of four Marines over a two-week period, however, congressional concern only grew. Democratic congressman Clarence Long, chair of the House Appropriations Subcommittee on Foreign Operations, announced he would try to block funds for US forces unless Reagan invoked the War Powers Resolution.[71] In the White House, where the administration was concerned about securing a continuing resolution (CR) to fund the government, James Baker's staff asked in early September what would happen if Reagan did not report under the hostilities provision of the WPR. In a memo, Baker aide Richard Darman asked, "will we lose Congressional support—and if so, what specific cost is likely to be associated with that loss? What are the risks of, *e.g.*, negative language on appropriations/CR? Would we wish to veto on grounds of such language?" In the margin, Baker wrote, one assumes derisively, "Shut Gov't down in order to allow yourself to continue to wage war in Leb."[72] Ten days later, on September 19, Baker scrawled notes for "RR," presumably to discuss with Reagan, on the bottom of his copy of the White House senior staff meeting agenda. Baker noted that "RR [would] have to make phone calls to hold 18 mos," that is, to keep the resolution at the eighteen-month limit under negotiation, and "RR could disclaim that it was a [hostilities] circumstance but still say desirable to have a Resolution." Just after this, however, Baker seemed to acknowledge that the White House was defending an untenable position, noting, "We're firing live shells + taking casualties—How can we claim not in hostilities."[73]

As figure 6-1 shows, news coverage reporting prowar or antiwar opinions spiked in September, with articles containing anti-intervention or both standpoints dominating congressional coverage, while the administration continued to put out reliably pro-intervention views. In the search for a decisive outcome, however, the basic problem Reagan never really confronted was how to define success. A memo from the State Department's Jonathan Howe, in the Bureau of Politico-Military Affairs, to Dam illustrated this fundamental point in January 1983. Titled "Alternative Scenarios for Departure of the MNF from Lebanon," the memo opened with the "need to address again the *role* which an expanded MNF would play during and after withdrawal of foreign forces from Lebanon and the *timing* of the MNF's departure." Making the obvious point that decisions about these crucial aspects "should flow from our objectives in Lebanon," Howe noted that US objectives were "derivative: One measure of the success of our Lebanon policy would be the extent to which it facilitates the Mideast peace process. Conversely, a policy which resulted in the US becoming politically and militarily tied down in Lebanon could be judged a failure." Howe cited a dilemma in defining the duration of a deployment: "On the one hand, there are good reasons to withdraw US forces from Lebanon as soon as possible. On the other hand, there are strong arguments in favor of remaining longer in Lebanon to enhance the possibility of the LAF" being able to provide stability.[74]

The administration's strategy for influencing congressional views of the likelihood of success was to avoid reporting under the "hostilities" requirement of the War Powers Resolution—if there were no hostilities, there could be no failure. Ominously, some hawkish promilitary stalwarts from both parties who had opposed the deployment initially, including Barry Goldwater, advocated withdrawing the Marines.[75] Reacting to news from White House pollster Dick Wirthlin that his handling of foreign policy was "way down" over Lebanon, Reagan wrote in his diary that "the people just don't know why we're there," and he blamed a "deeply buried isolationist sentiment in our land."[76] In his diary and in the available documentary record more generally, Reagan did not seem particularly bothered or constrained by public sentiment, perhaps reflecting his view that public opinion should not play a major role in foreign policy.[77] But Reagan did not resolve the tension within the administration over what the Marines' mission should be, leaving the impression that they were there for the sake of being there. The effort to placate all sides by leaving them in a position of "aggressive self-defense" left the Marines vulnerable to attack, and the military was increasingly vocal about the risks. To take one of many examples from the news coverage, the *New York Times* reported in early September, after four Marines were killed in a two-week period, that "just sitting in a bunker and taking fire is not what marines are trained to do, and many of the 1,200 members of the peacekeeping force find their work less than fully satisfying." One Marine said, "You feel helpless. . . . We're guinea pigs. What are we doing here?"[78]

War Powers Compromise: September 1983

This context is important for understanding how the crucial months of September and October 1983 unfolded. As Alexandra Evans and Bradley Potter demonstrate, senior American officials reacted to the October 1983 bombing of the Marine barracks in Beirut through the lens of their existing views, particularly their "theories of success," and thus the bombing only hardened attitudes and deepened divisions, rather than leading to a fundamental reassessment of the mission.[79] With so little ground laid in Congress, however, what limited elite support the administration could muster outside the White House crumbled, even as the public gave Reagan a small bump in approval.

In September 1983, the NSC hawks continued to push for a greater US role and expanded rules of engagement but continued to face resistance inside the administration. Matters came to a head when McFarlane sent an urgent message from Beirut that became known as the "sky is falling" cable, prompting an urgent meeting that seemingly expanded the rules of engagement to allow the Marines to call in airstrikes.[80] In calling for US forces to essentially become combatants, McFarlane's cable again invoked domestic politics, telling the White House, "I am very conscious of the difficulty of taking such a decision in a climate of public and congressional ignorance such as exists in the US today."[81] One immediate consequence was that the apparent change in the rules of engagement leaked within hours, appearing in the *Washington Post* with the headline, "Reagan Authorizes Marines to Call In Beirut Air Strikes."[82] As the White House news summary noted, the major TV networks reported versions of the air strike news. In the lead report on NBC, anchor Tom Brokaw asked correspondent Chris Wallace, "Within the Administration, who's for this idea of going after the Syrians and who's against it?" Wallace reported that "there are some interesting coalitions, unusual coalitions. Our sources say McFarlane, the NSC staff and the State Department are all calling for more military force. On the other hand, [CIA director William] Casey, some defense officials like Gen. Vessey and the political types at the White House are all worried about deeper U.S. involvement."[83] As Gans describes, there were conflicting interpretations in the Pentagon of just how much the rules of engagement had changed.[84]

The leak of Reagan's order, however, had several significant consequences for both politics and policy. First, Reagan referred the leak to the Justice Department with a list of attendees at the urgent meeting, asking the attorney general to investigate and explicitly authorizing polygraphs, prompting both Baker and Shultz to threaten to resign if forced to submit to the tests.[85] Second, the long-simmering tension on Capitol Hill became impossible to ignore, and in September the administration finally decided it was time to reach a compromise to gain some political cover. In the same summary report of the evening news for September 12, CBS and ABC each raised War Powers concerns in Congress, even as both reports also noted that the downing of the Korean airliner had created a sense of unity and diminished opposition to other Reagan defense policies like the MX. CBS declared, "the President was in trouble with his Mideast policy," noting Speaker Tip O'Neill's call for War Powers action even as "James Baker came to argue with O'Neill against invoking" the WPR. ABC noted that O'Neill also said "This is not the time for us to run." Notably, Brit Hume also reported that "Senior Administration sources tell ABC that while the President will not himself invoke the act, he would not veto a congressional decision to do so."[86]

Indeed, the White House was already signaling it would seek a War Powers compromise through a joint resolution, but not necessarily one that would tie the administration's hands through the hostilities provision that members had long complained the administration was avoiding.[87] On September 9, before the "sky is falling" cable, a US warship fired at an artillery emplacement, and in a partial fulfillment of Reagan's idea, two "F-14 fighters from the carrier Eisenhower had streaked over the embattled village of Deir al Qamar," as the *New York Times* reported but the administration would not confirm.[88]

Members of Congress from both parties, long irked by the administration's tactics on the WPR, became increasingly vocal. Amid debate over the safety of the Marines and the new phase of American involvement, the administration began to meet with congressional leaders to work out a compromise, since the White House continued to oppose invoking the hostilities section and its sixty-to-ninety-day timeline on the grounds that it would be excessively constraining. Although White House critics included many prominent Republicans, the initial round of talks was between the White House political team, led by James Baker, and Tip O'Neill and several other senior House Democrats. A White House official told the *Post*, "We're seeking bipartisan support, not a Tonkin Gulf resolution." The *Post* also noted that the White House and some members of Congress were "most anxious to prevent . . . a free-for-all debate in Congress that would be interpreted as a sign of U.S. weakness."[89] Part of the administration's calculus in compromising was the likelihood that Congress would support extending the Marines' mission, though Howard Baker and others clearly signaled uncertainty and qualifications to their support.[90] The administration was adamant that its hands not be tied on duration but negotiated on limits for the size and scope of the deployment.

There were undoubtedly sincere concerns both in the White House and in Congress about projecting weakness, particularly to the Syrians, widely seen as a crucial outside actor in the conflict.[91] But all sides also had their own policy and political preferences. O'Neill had serious reservations about the Marines' mission but also did not want to withdraw prematurely. Politically, he was torn between the natural opposition of his partisan and institutional position vis-à-vis the White House, and his desire to see Congress properly involved in war decisions. Similarly, Zablocki, the House foreign affairs chairman whose letter about the first MNF and the War Powers hostility clause had set down the congressional marker a year earlier, wanted to make sure the WPR survived. O'Neill was crucial to White House strategy, not only because he was willing to expend political effort to wrangle his own very reluctant caucus, but also because negotiations with Senate Democrats broke down after they introduced a resolution that would lead to a direct vote on War Powers. In negotiations between Baker and House Democrats, the White House agreed to an eighteen-month time limit (which many members of O'Neill's caucus opposed as too long), while Reagan preserved the right to sign the resolution but declare in writing his view that the War Powers Resolution was unconstitutional and that he retained the right to deploy US forces. Shultz, handling the testimony on Capitol Hill, reinforced Reagan's position that the president had the ultimate power to decide when to deploy US forces.[92]

The actual passage of the compromise was complicated by continuing opposition in both chambers. As Kriner recounts, O'Neill made "the vote a matter of party loyalty" and successfully engineered passage; ironically, the Republican Senate proved more difficult.[93] At Shultz's urging, majority leader Howard Baker agreed to "carry the banner for the president," although he had expressed doubts about the operation from the beginning.[94] Reagan's own party barely passed the compromise in the Senate Foreign Relations Committee when Charles Mathias, who objected to the eighteen-month limit as too long, agreed to vote for it nonetheless under pressure from Howard Baker. Senate Foreign Relations Committee (SFRC) chairman Charles Percy, echoing other concerns from Republicans on the committee, said, "I don't think any of us knows where this is leading." Baker engaged in "last-minute arm twisting" to get it cleared on the Senate floor but said he continued to have "grave doubts."[95] In the House, O'Neill beat back several challenges including an amendment to the main 1984 fiscal funding bill that passed the House Appropriations Committee before O'Neill had it killed by the House Foreign Affairs Committee. The speaker had even more work to do to get the bill passed, resorting to a restrictive rule on amendments, and making a speech defending the War Powers Resolution before the final vote. Although the measure passed both chambers with an eighteen-month authorization, James Baker warned Shultz that if the mission faltered, "we've written the script for the Democrats."[96]

Several points that bear on the theory emerge from the congressional compromise. First, Reagan had clearly failed to convince even members of his own party or traditional supporters of military action and instead had to expend significant political effort to maintain his policy, at a time when he had many other national security priorities. In the run-up to the vote, the White House political operation ramped up. At the end of September, during the run-up to final passage of the War Powers compromise, the vote had a prominent place in the Republican leadership meeting at the White House, which also covered the need for a continuing resolution to fund the government (and would ultimately be the target of a House amendment on Lebanon).[97] Reagan gave precious presidential face time to Republican senator Larry Pressler of South Dakota, who had indicated "strong reservations" about the compromise but agreed to vote with the Republicans provided "he be allowed to meet personally with the President to discuss this issue." Howard Baker and SFRC chairman Percy asked that Reagan grant the request and joined the meeting in the Oval Office.[98] That evening, he also met with a select group of GOP representatives because, as Duberstein noted, beyond the House GOP leadership, support for the Lebanon resolution was "shaky and the GOP leadership believes that the President must become more visible on the issue."[99] Reagan thus had to draw on not only his own scarce political resources but also those of his party's congressional leaders, including in the Senate, where the GOP held the majority.

Second, the pattern of elite consultation, side payments, and information management reflects a "hawk's misadventure." Reagan had a relatively easy time at the outset of the operation, and the constraints of maneuvering around the WPR seemed manageable at the beginning of the second MNF. The costs rose as the dangers became more visible. When Senate Democrats balked, the White House cut them out of negotiations and focused on House Democrats. Yet even the side payments required to obtain Democratic support and keep Republicans onside primarily took the form of prestige and procedural concessions, and with his written declaration that he regarded the WPR to be unconstitutional, Reagan reserved the right to slip the constraint on the duration of the deployment should he deem it necessary. The concerns of his Republican copartisans in Congress, however, threatened other national security and foreign policy priorities dear to the White House.

Third, however, the administration did not manage the insiders' game well enough to avoid the WPR fight in September 1983, and the result left what elite consensus there was hanging by a thread. As figure 6-1 shows, news articles that reported either mixed or anti-intervention views dominated congressional coverage after September 1983 despite many more articles reporting the administration's public pro-intervention statements. The outreach to Democrats to gain bipartisan support came so late that it could not effectively paper over widespread misgivings. That so many members kept asking basic questions about the mission right up until the vote illustrated that the White House strategy of avoiding a WPR report under the hostilities provision had left Congress feeling in the dark. Of course, the problem was the administration's own lack of clarity about the mission. Fourth, in its concern about information management and avoiding debate, as well securing elite support, the White House was more concerned about pressure from moderates and doves.

Fifth, public opinion was not the driving factor in the congressional compromise. At the time of the congressional debate, O'Neill's office had the results of a Harris Survey poll, conducted September 9–14, which showed that a "razor-thin 48–47 percent plurality" of Americans thought the Marines should be withdrawn. Americans were solidly against increasing the number of Marines (55 percent opposed), and 61 percent had a negative view of Reagan's handling of the situation. But tellingly, when presented with two statements about Lebanon, the results pointed in contradictory directions. As shown in table 6-3, nearly the same majority agreed with the statement that it was "both impossible

TABLE 6-3. Public Opinion on Situation in Lebanon, Harris Survey, September 1983

"Now let me read you some statements about the situation in Lebanon. For each, tell me if you agree or disagree."	Agree	Disagree	Not Sure
With Syria refusing to get out of Lebanon and with civil war breaking out among the Lebanese, it is both impossible and foolish to keep U.S. Marines in Lebanon on a peacekeeping mission	56%	38%	6%
After being occupied for a long time by Syria, Israel, and the PLO, Lebanon needs help from the U.S., including the presence of U.S. Marines, to help Lebanon re-establish control of its own country	55%	39%	6%

Source: Louis Harris, "Doubts Arise over U.S. Military Involvement in Lebanon," Harris Survey, September 22, 1983, copy in Tip O'Neill Papers, box 29, folder 7: "War Powers Act—Drafts and Correspondence, 1982–1983," John J. Burns Library, Boston College.

and foolish to keep U.S. Marines in Lebanon on a peacekeeping mission" as agreed with the statement "Lebanon needs help from the U.S., including the presence of U.S. Marines, to help Lebanon re-establish control of its own country."[100] The results suggest that public opinion was still quite malleable and that clearer elite messaging—one way or the other—could shape public attitudes.

Finally, none of the congressional maneuvering helped with the still-deep divisions within the administration, where Weinberger continued to press for redeploying the Marines offshore. For example, on October 21 (prior to the Marine barracks bombing), Weinberger argued in a memo to McFarlane that "it might be necessary and desirable to reduce or perhaps eliminate US ground presence in Beirut and keep our forces offshore, perhaps bolstered by additional naval gunfire support. . . . Any expansion in the employment of the MNF or their Rules of Engagement at this stage would be premature."[101]

War Termination: Fall-Winter 1983–84

Against all this backdrop, the bombing of the Marine barracks on October 23 snapped the thin thread of elite consensus. Consistent with the theory's prediction that Republicans face *ex post* scrutiny from opposition Democrats and insider doves—and that those "last in" will be "first out"—Democratic pressure mounted, and Tip O'Neill switched his position publicly, arguing against continuing with the intervention. O'Neill had formed an ad hoc monitoring group consisting of House Democrats just prior to the bombing, and the group immediately prepared to ask difficult questions in a briefing on October 24.[102] Congressional Republicans—including majority leader Baker—also questioned the mission and warned the administration of "fragile" Republican support and potential damage in the 1984 elections.[103] After the barracks bombing, an aide to the Senate Republican leadership told the *New York Times* that many in Congress reluctantly supported the operation but that "a lot of people have been waiting for something to happen so they can say what they really feel."[104] Members of Congress from both parties thus had more cover to express their concerns about the operation.

Yet as congressional criticism grew louder, Reagan took steps to signal his continuing commitment publicly. He sent both Shultz and, notably, Weinberger, to Capitol Hill to "try to calm the revolt brewing among many members of Congress," with both men arguing "strenuously that the presence of American troops in Lebanon is necessary to preserve stability not only in that country but throughout the Middle East."[105] Reagan reaffirmed his intention to continue the mission in Lebanon in a meeting with reporters and several days later, in a prime-time television address to the nation. As Kriner describes, Reagan "upped the political ante" and "had clearly thrown down the gauntlet at the feet of any political opponents who would countenance withdrawal."[106] Reagan thus tried to signal to elites who opposed the mission that he planned to press ahead.[107]

As Evans and Potter argue, most in the administration reacted to the bombing by deepening their commitment to prior positions, rather than changing them.[108] The bombing did not generate unity inside the administration but rather continued and even deepened the divisions. A diary entry from the State Department's Kenneth Dam in December 1983 underscored the dynamic:

> Most of the time was spent on Lebanon, and there was a certain amount of recrimination involved, especially after Secretary Shultz raised the question of whether it was really true, as has been rumored in the press, that the Chiefs had been opposed to the deployment of the Marines in Lebanon. Weinberger said that they had been opposed, but Shultz kept asking whether they had made any formal statement to that effect to the President. The most that Weinberger would say was that Chairman Vessey had said something in the NSC meeting. Shultz said that he did not recall that. Later in talking to Admiral Howe, our director of Politico-Military Affairs, it came back to me that the Chiefs had been very much involved in the planning, under State Department auspices, of the second deployment of the Marines in Lebanon after the events at the Palestinian camps in Beirut. I do not recall that they had any opposition at that time. I also made the point to Weinberger that the Marines were exactly where DOD had wanted them to be, namely, at the airport.[109]

Given the well-documented opposition of Weinberger and the military—some of it in the press—these recollections are somewhat surprising but also indicate that insider elites who oppose the use of force but nonetheless have responsibility for planning it may appear to be more supportive just by dint of carrying out their duties.

Amid the internal disagreement, the president's advisers recognized the political threat. In December, the *Times* quoted a "high official" saying, "It's going to be a problem how much longer Congress will let the Marines stay."[110] The administration also had other things to do. James Baker's senior staff meeting notes from December 1983 listed, as "RR" items, potentially combining the "START + INF" and the development of "arms control options" and then listed below that, "Relocate the Marines?"[111] In advance of a meeting set for January 3, 1984, National Security Advisor Robert McFarlane warned Reagan in a memorandum that he should "expect a growing crescendo of criticism from both liberals and conservatives when Congress reassembles on January 23. The growth in domestic opposition comes at a time when the situation on the ground in Lebanon has not deteriorated significantly." The meeting would be geared specifically to "agree on milestones to be reached before Congress reassembles on January 23," and McFarlane argued for a "legislative strategy for dealing with the Congress."[112] An NSC document prepared for the same meeting also highlighted the need to show "fresh progress and the emergence of milestones of success" specifically in advance of Congress's return on January 23, and it noted that "ironically, we find our domestic support unraveling . . . at the very moment certain conditions on the ground [in Lebanon] begin to improve." The paper noted that "the public understands our basic goals," and that "further casualties to the [multinational force] will only accelerate demands in the Congress and the European capitals to bring home the MNF."[113] Though the undercurrent of these comments was declining domestic support, the near-term emphasis was on convincing Congress.

White House staff with politics on their minds took an even dimmer view of the situation. M. B. Oglesby, who had recently taken over from Duberstein as White House director of legislative affairs, also sounded the alarm on January 3 in a memo to James Baker, whose job was to think about the big picture—including politics. Leading with O'Neill, Oglesby noted that the Speaker's ad hoc monitoring group would be meeting, and "the general attitude . . . will be negative—and news coverage will be negative."[114] Indeed, members of O'Neill's committee started sending outraged letters to both the speaker and the White House.[115] Many House Republicans also wanted the Marines out; Oglesby reported that minority leader Bob Michel had said, "You can't keep going on forever and ever." Democratic foreign affairs leaders like Dante Fascell and Lee Hamilton, who had been crucial negotiators of the congressional compromise, "are setting stage for changing their position." Oglesby's memo concluded: "support for the Marines presence has *not just eroded*—it has basically *vanished*." In his handwritten comments on Oglesby's memo, Baker not only triple underlined "not just eroded" and "vanished" in the memo itself, but also wrote out this part of the sentence by hand at the top of the page, and then added "Worst thing in world will be to act *following* Cong'l disapproval. Terrible indictment of our inability to conduct for. pol. *Lead*—not follow. We have 4 *wks* or so."[116] With national security central to Reagan's agenda—including his desire to negotiate with the Soviets, presumably taking advantage of the hawk's advantage in diplomacy—the hawk's misadventure in Lebanon was a liability.

Baker's sense that the administration could not allow Congress to act first, through a new vote after hearings that Oglesby warned would be coming, reflects the political danger for a Republican president in being seen as losing a war to which elites from both parties object. Despite the deployment's small size, a GOP president could not "keep going on forever and ever." Baker also had Reagan's very hawkish reputation on his mind. In mid-December 1983, with the reelection campaign year looming, Baker wrote at the bottom of the senior staff meeting agenda several agenda items for "RR" that included notes on a "draft speech on U.S.-Soviet relations." The final item was a "Time Inc poll—most imp[ortant] prob[lem] is 'war'—1st time since early 70's," and below that, "ability to keep country out of war—the one thing RR gets a negative rating on."[117]

The divisions within the administration also continued to plague the decision making and even the conduct of the war. The administration continued to battle over military strategy and the rules of engagement, again pitting Shultz's expansive view against Weinberger's drive for limits. Even after the bombing in October 1983, Reagan had approved expanded rules of engagement, over the objections of Weinberger and the JCS but with accommodations to their views on interpreting the new rules.[118] But as Gans describes, "the breakdown in trust grew so severe" that the NSC "believed that Pentagon leaders, particularly Weinberger, were taking deliberate steps to ensure that Reagan's decisions were not implemented."[119] As Philip Taubman details, there was a predictable split between those serving on the NSC and Shultz, on the one hand, who wanted forceful retaliatory action after the bombing, and Weinberger, on the other hand, who not only opposed further action but may have directly undermined the president's orders for airstrikes. While the "available historical record leaves unclear" whether these attacks had been approved by Reagan, many White House officials, including McFarlane and Baker, accused Weinberger of failing to carry out presidential decisions.[120] Talking points for McFarlane in early December outline the fault lines, with Shultz and others taking a more aggressive line and Weinberger and Vessey pushing for restraint.[121] By early January 1984, Reagan approved talking points, drafted by McFarlane for Reagan, to address press leaks about Lebanon with his top advisers. The talking points, for Reagan to use in an upcoming National Security

Planning Group meeting in the Situation Room, called for the president to say that he was "pretty mad . . . that we are reduced to considering redeployment of our forces in Lebanon in *response* to a public debate stimulated by leaks from within our government."[122]

Eventually, the balance shifted at the White House, as James Baker and Vice President George H. W. Bush began to advocate ending the mission. As can be seen in figure 6-1, in January and February 1984, articles mentioning internal dissent began to seriously impinge on coverage of the administration's pro-intervention stance. As Kriner summarizes, the administration was concerned about "the effects of congressional criticism on anticipated changes in public opinion, as well as the tangible electoral consequences such a shift would have for the president himself and for his party in congressional races."[123] But with the risks and costs of the mission, as well as the administration's internal dissension, now plainly visible, elites could constrain Reagan: there was little the administration could do to hold or rebuild its congressional support and stave off the effects of congressional criticism of a failing war on public opinion. McFarlane and Shultz, however, still favored an even more expanded mission to deal with the mounting attacks on US forces. Reagan approved expanded rules of engagement as late as February 1, 1984. Reagan proclaimed his intention to stay in Lebanon almost until the last moment.[124] But on February 7, 1984, he bowed to elite pressure and approved the withdrawal.

Conclusion

Thus the Lebanon case illustrates that fear of an elite backlash—even as public opinion remains steady—can constrain the escalation of a military operation, and even lead to withdrawal. As an unnamed Reagan aide put it in the *New York Times*, "Except for the marines, Lebanon is an inside-the-beltway story."[125] Congress may have smoothed the path for Reagan to initiate a hawk's misadventure, but administration divisions constrained the president from the first and contributed to confusion and indecision over strategy. Reagan was not able to push the mission as far as he, Shultz, and the NSC preferred, in part because of the need to accommodate the preferences of Weinberger and the JCS, as well as to avoid congressional scrutiny. Ultimately, the political costs of keeping the operation going rose so much that Reagan chose to abandon the operation, which had little chance of succeeding within the parameters its internal opponents would tolerate. Pressure from his own party and administration helped convince officials that the intervention was no longer politically tenable. Although the concerns of election-year politics loomed, the path to electoral consequences ran first through elites.[126]

7

Iraq, Afghanistan, and the Forever Insiders' Game

IF LEBANON WAS A LIMITED "hawk's misadventure," the 2003 Iraq War was its opposite: a large-scale invasion of a sovereign country for the purpose of regime change, undertaken over the known objections of many inside and outside the administration, with disastrous results. Analyses of the "forever wars" of the post-9/11 era often paint a picture of elite consensus—of officialdom in Washington, and to a lesser but important extent, in London, in the grip of a kind of shared liberalizing impulse, given free rein after the shock of 9/11, and reinforced by the need to conform to Washington establishment thinking.[1] This consensus-driven narrative is by no means the only explanation in the literature on the Iraq War. Others have focused on psychological biases,[2] or what Ahsan Butt has called "performative war" to demonstrate American military dominance.[3] But the consensus narrative, in its various forms, is especially relevant to this book, and to arguments about the importance of elite leadership of mass opinion.

In this chapter, I highlight a significant missing piece of the consensus-driven arguments: the elite politics that produced and maintained the consensus. It is certainly true that some high-profile elites unexpectedly supported the war out of conviction. Others, like Secretary of State Colin Powell, were deeply skeptical but stayed inside the administration to try to steer the course of the war. A third group held serious misgivings or even private opposition to the war but nonetheless supported it or, in the case of members of Congress, voted for it anyway. Analyzing this group's motives and choices does not absolve them of their responsibility for the war. But such an analysis is important for what these motives and choices tell us about the domestic politics of war. Elite politics are at the root of why they lent George W. Bush their support.

This chapter examines how the post-9/11 wars fit into the pattern of the insiders' game. The chapter concentrates primarily on the Iraq War, but I conclude the chapter with a brief discussion of what different presidents' approaches to the twenty-year war in Afghanistan tells us about the evolution of the insiders' game. What we are looking for in these cases is evidence that it is easier to co-opt dovish elites than hawkish elites, enabling war initiation with fewer *ex ante* constraints than we would expect under the faithful intermediaries model. The 2003 Iraq War was the ultimate hawk's misadventure: a large-scale invasion with few checks on war initiation despite widespread misgivings. The pattern of side payments and policy concessions at the outset of the war shows the less costly co-optation of relatively dovish elites—for example, the procedural concessions obtained by Colin Powell, who then became the skeptic-turned-supporter that made the administration's case at the United Nations. The escalation in the form of Bush's "surge," after the rare, clear signal sent by voters in the 2006 midterm elections, illustrates how hawkish leaders face elite constraints when wars are underway—although these constraints may take a long time to kick in—and why they seek resolution rather than pushing off losing.

The war in Afghanistan provides an opportunity to compare how presidents approached what began as a politically uncontroversial war over time. The Bush administration treated the war as essentially over in late 2001.[4] The politics of Afghanistan came to the fore later, during the 2008 presidential campaign and especially after Barack Obama took office in 2009. The renewed US effort in Afghanistan is best described as a "dove's curse" for Obama, who escalated the war reluctantly but in part out of a desire to protect his political capital. For Obama, co-opting hawks proved politically vexing, even though public approval of the war in Afghanistan had dipped below 50 percent by the time he made his major decisions.[5] His choice to nonetheless "surge" troops into Afghanistan in December 2009, at levels just enough to keep his more hawkish advisers happy and push the war off the agenda, is a telling example of a dove's curse. Donald Trump aimed to end the war, and while he struggled to get the military to implement his policy, he steadily reduced troops and made a deal with the Taliban in February 2020. The long-sought and yet still-tragic end of US involvement in August 2021 during the Biden administration reflects evolving political incentives and the effects of partisan polarization on the insiders' game.

The chapter serves two functions in terms of theory testing. First, the Iraq case, and to a lesser extent, the Bush administration's treatment of the Afghanistan War as won at the end of 2001, provide more examples of a Republican president's choices, this time to undertake a war far larger than Reagan's ill-fated intervention in Lebanon. The Iraq case also shows how Republican presidents, who can escape *ex ante* constraints more easily, face *ex post* constraints once war is underway, in part because they have reluctant doves in their coalition and Democrats eventually will want to hold Republican presidents to account.

Elite constraint was much slower to manifest than it had been for Reagan's intervention in Lebanon, partly because Bush had successfully implicated many Democrats in the original authorization to use force. But Bush paid political costs in his second term as elites challenged the rationale and conduct of the war.

This chapter also helps address additional facets of the comparison between the faithful intermediaries model and the insiders' game. In the wake of the 9/11 attacks, a fearful public was more inclined to support hawkish policies.[6] Indeed, John Mueller argues that public opinion was a driving force behind the hawkish policies of the Bush administration.[7] That Bush still felt the need to generate an elite consensus for invading Iraq is an important test for the theory. Conversely, by the time of Obama's decision to "surge" into Afghanistan, public opinion was far more skeptical of military force, and yet Obama still accommodated hawkish elite preferences.

It is important to note what this chapter cannot do. It cannot explain why the United States invaded Iraq—precisely because there are some motivations that remain unknowable, or so opaque that no empirical record can clarify them. The Bush administration's decision to invade Iraq in 2003 puzzled many observers at the time and continues to puzzle those who have attempted to make sense of it. Even some participants in the decision remain baffled: Richard Haass, director of policy planning in the run-up to the war, told the journalist George Packer that "he will go to his grave not knowing the answer."[8] Nor can this chapter add to the explanation of why the United States attacked Afghanistan in 2001—because the reason was so clearly retaliation for an attack on US soil. Given that these events do not yet have the kind of documentary record that we have for more distant cases, the chapter cannot draw on primary sources to the same extent. The goal of this chapter is not to provide a complete account of either war but rather is more modest: to show how the theory and its predictions for elite politics illuminate the choices made by the world's most powerful democracy after an attack on its own territory.

Bush's Domestic Political Landscape

The elite politics of the initiation of the Iraq War present a puzzle: why did a Republican president who had a highly experienced and respected national security team, who enjoyed significant deference on national security matters in the wake of the 9/11 attacks, and who by most accounts was convinced of the rightness of his course, feel the need to build an elite consensus that included congressional Democrats and insider skeptics like Colin Powell? Why did his administration try to emphasize that the war would be a "cakewalk," in the words of Ken Adelman?[9] That George W. Bush expended considerable

TABLE 7-1. Within-Case Evidence for Iraq War

	Side Payments	Information
War initiation (fall 2002 to Mar. 2003)	To insider doves (Powell): UN authorization To opposition doves: political pressure; procedural/ political benefits (Gephardt, other presidential hopefuls)	Shape perceptions of probability of success (intelligence, "cakewalk") Cut insider doves out of the loop Limit discussion of planning
Escalation (mid-2003 to 2006)	Shift to nation-building strategy; replace Rumsfeld after 2006 midterms	Information on "victory strategy"
Duration/ termination (surge, late 2006 to early 2007)	Promote surge opponents (e.g., General Casey) Budget increases for military	Petraeus/Crocker testimony (coordinated focal point for highlighting progress)

effort to secure the public backing of enough Democrats and insider skeptics like Powell, despite high approval ratings and a generally more favorable climate for hawkish policies after 9/11, illustrates the incentives for Republican presidents. As discussed in chapter 2, it is helpful for any president to have some degree of consensus for war, and for Republicans, *ex ante* consensus provides some protection against their biggest downside political risk: a failed war. All leaders would like to have such protection, but for leaders from the party associated with hawkishness, it is less costly to co-opt dovish elites, at least up front. Table 7-1 summarizes the within-case evidence for the Iraq War.

Public Opinion and the 2003 Iraq War

As with other cases, it is difficult to assess the "true" nature of what the public wanted, not only because the public has diverse preferences, but also because we cannot entirely separate expressed public attitudes from the elite cues that have already reached voters' eyes and ears. But scholarship on public opinion and the Iraq War shows several broad trends.

First, despite the post-9/11 increase in salience for national security and general acceptance of a more militarized footing for US foreign policy, the public was not clamoring for war in Iraq. John Mueller notes that despite a jump after the 9/11 attacks in support for invading Iraq—with Gallup polling showing it reaching nearly 75 percent in November 2001—it faded back to pre-9/11 levels by

August 2002.[10] As Caroline Smith and James Lindsay note, although a majority of Americans favored the war, they would also have accepted Bush's decision had he not sent troops.[11] In polling from mid-February 2003, for example, 59 percent favored going to war in Iraq, but nearly half of those who supported war said they would not be "upset" if Bush decided not to send troops. Gallup analysis reveals 38 percent who leaned one way but would not be upset if Bush decided the opposite, with 30 percent of these respondents favoring war and 8 percent opposing—meaning that those opposed to war had more intense beliefs, while support for war was less solidified.[12] These polarized camps left a substantial plurality in what Smith and Lindsay call the "movable middle."[13] Summarizing Gallup polling in February 2003, Frank Newport noted that despite nearly two-thirds of Americans supporting military action against Iraq, that support was "soft and subject to fairly quick change," including when respondents were asked about UN authorization, or were provided alternatives like waiting for weapons inspectors, or not fighting at all.[14] There was also already a partisan split in support before the invasion began, with Democrats far less supportive than Republicans.[15] This picture of public opinion is consistent with a generally moderate view that had shifted in a somewhat more hawkish direction after 9/11 but not so much that it endorsed the case for war unreservedly.

Second, Bush's direct efforts to move public opinion were not especially successful in raising the absolute level of public support. As Mueller notes, from the point in August 2002 when Bush started a public campaign for war, "with one exception, approval for sending the troops never ranged more than 4 percentage points higher (or lower) than the 55 percent figure tallied shortly after George W. Bush came into office in 2001, nine months before 9/11."[16] What mattered more was the relative dearth of antiwar opinion in the press, which might have galvanized opposition among Democrats.[17] Indeed, Stanley Feldman, Leonie Huddy, and George E. Marcus show that Democratic and independent voters were responsive to these arguments when they could find them—which they sometimes could, especially in regional print media— an effect they argue drove down support for the war among Democrats and independents even during Bush's public campaign in the fall of 2002.[18] But the press largely followed the administration's line or declined to offer an alternative frame. In an analysis of coverage in the *New York Times*, Amy Gershkoff and Shana Kushner find that "the administration's frame was not countered by intense, sustained criticism by either the press or the Democratic Party."[19] The pattern echoes Berinsky's finding that doves in the early years of the Vietnam War lacked dovish cues to latch onto, and instead chose "don't know" in surveys about the war.[20] It also accords with Baum and Potter's argument that countries with more opposition parties and greater media penetration are more effective at transmitting information, including antiwar cues.[21]

Third, the pattern was relatively similar in Britain, albeit with one major difference: the Labour Party was in government, while the more naturally hawkish Conservatives were in opposition. The Conservative opposition supported the war more strongly in parliamentary debates than did Prime Minister Tony Blair's own backbenchers, and important and well-circulated parts of the media, particularly on the conservative side, also voiced prowar sentiments.[22] Blair thus had insulation built in to his Iraq policy up front and could afford to wait for a rally effect, which did arrive once the war began. Still, Blair and many other European heads of state faced massive protests in the run-up to the war.

Given these patterns, what would we expect to observe under the faithful intermediaries model, in which elites transmit public sentiment to leaders and provide information to voters? The moderate voter assumption that underpins the theory is challenged by the post-9/11 environment, although by the time of the Iraq invasion, there were signs the hawkish trend in public attitudes required stoking to maintain. Still, even if we assume the public was more hawkish or accepting of hawkish policies than usual, we would expect that a democratic leader contemplating war would scrutinize all available evidence and plans, and do everything reasonably possible to ensure victory.

That Bush did neither represents a problem for public opinion arguments premised on delivering the public good of victory. There were, of course, many individual and collective reasons for the planning failures, most beyond the scope of this theory—notably, psychological biases and Bush's inexperience, which empowered his subordinates with little oversight to check those biases.[23] But Bush's father had prosecuted a war in Iraq with more than twice the number of troops and many of the same top advisers as his son would employ, and he kept the war aims limited despite pressure to overthrow Saddam Hussein.[24] Of course, the younger Bush's war aim was very different from the start, but the potential problems and requirements for regime change and occupation were hardly unknown to many on his team.[25]

Additionally, under the faithful intermediaries hypothesis, we would expect that elites would have pulled the fire alarm much earlier. As discussed below, there were a few crucial antiwar voices, including from those who served in the administration of Bush's father, George H. W. Bush, and from academics, including many international security scholars who collectively paid for an antiwar ad in the *New York Times*.[26] And as Feldman, Huddy, and Marcus argue, there were pockets of antiwar news coverage, particularly in regional print newspapers, which did sway Democratic and independent voters who were exposed to those arguments.[27] But the story of elites and the Iraq War is largely one of silent doubters, who did not fully turn against the war for several years. The faithful intermediaries model has difficulty accounting for this malfunctioning fire alarm.

Lastly, the faithful intermediaries model would expect that the 2006 midterm elections, which emphatically informed Bush of public displeasure with his Iraq policy, would bring about an accelerated drawdown of US forces. Indeed, Bush's own commanding general, George W. Casey Jr., recommended such a drawdown, as did the Iraq Study Group, a bipartisan panel led by former secretary of state James Baker and former representative Lee Hamilton.[28] As Andrew Payne argues, Bush delayed the surge until after the midterms.[29] But Bush chose to surge troops into Iraq after the midterms, not to withdraw them.

Mechanisms of Hawkish Bias

The relative ease with which hawks can maneuver around elite constraints allowed Bush to take the United States into Iraq, a tragic hawk's misadventure. When considering whether to invade, he faced few up-front agenda costs, especially since his post-9/11 agenda focused directly on national security. Unlike dovish leaders, Bush did not face much in the way of selection pressures, except to install an experienced team, and was able to first sideline and then co-opt crucial opponents like Colin Powell at relatively low cost. He took full advantage of the private benefits that doves who reluctantly supported the war could earn, putting political pressure on Democrats in Congress to vote before the 2002 midterm elections.

In some cases, not even a reluctant vote to authorize the use of force in Iraq was enough for Democrats to escape the charge of weakness, as illustrated by the fate of Georgia senator Max Cleland, a decorated veteran who had lost both legs and an arm in Vietnam. Cleland, running for reelection in 2002, voted for the Iraq authorization with great reluctance, later saying that it was "the worst vote I cast," but that "it was obvious that if I voted against the resolution that I would be dead meat in the race, just handing them a victory."[30] As it happened, Cleland's Republican opponent, Saxby Chambliss, made an issue of Cleland's toughness on national security anyway, running an attack ad with images of Osama bin Laden and Saddam Hussein and listing other votes on Bush homeland security measures that Cleland had opposed. Cleland lost the race for reasons probably more related to domestic politics, notably the Democratic governor's effort to remove the Confederate battle emblem from the state flag, which mobilized rural male Republican voters. But for Democratic elites, Cleland's fate became associated with the infamous ad and reminded them of the risks of opposing a hawkish leader on national security issues.[31]

War Initiation: Bush's Path into Iraq

The path to war in Iraq is both well covered in other accounts and still shrouded in fog more than two decades later.[32] I focus on two features of elite politics that smoothed Bush's path to a hawk's misadventure: his effort to secure the support of Democratic members of Congress for a resolution in support of war, and the role of Colin Powell in making the administration's case for war at the United Nations. In both cases, Bush and prowar members of his administration used side payments and information management, especially managing expectations about the probability of success. What stands out is the relative ease with which Bush could co-opt both dovish Democrats and the relatively dovish Powell using political threats and concessions and procedural compromises that did not significantly impede the march to war. The lack of *ex ante* scrutiny, purchased at a relatively low price, enabled a hawk's misadventure.

In early September 2002, it was by no means assured that Congress would give Bush the authorization he wanted. Members could read the polls and see that the public would support their commander in chief but were not clamoring for war. When Bush met with a bipartisan group of twenty congressional leaders on September 4 and told them he planned to ask for a resolution, he heard skepticism from voices like Carl Levin, a Democrat who chaired the Senate Armed Services Committee.[33] Democrats also raised alarms at the lack of intelligence in a briefing with Secretary of Defense Donald Rumsfeld on the same day.[34] But as the midterm election campaign swung into high gear, both the effort and the ease of Bush's path to a resolution are what stand out.

As noted, Bush's campaign in the fall of 2002 did not meaningfully increase overall public support for the war. But to see this effort as a failed use of the bully pulpit misses the elite politics dimension. Despite all his advantages and the anticipation of a rally effect once he sent in troops, Bush still wanted a resolution he could claim had bipartisan support in Congress.

While many Democrats felt pressure to support Bush in the post-9/11 era, the group with presidential ambitions had a special set of concerns. The role that House minority leader Dick Gephardt played in the authorization for the use of force against Iraq in 2002 illustrates the power of personal political incentives. Gephardt, who had presidential ambitions and had voted against the 1991 Gulf War, saw the damage to Democratic presidential aspirants who did not support the elder Bush (such as Georgia senator Sam Nunn).[35] In 2002, there were several proposals in the works for a congressional resolution, varying in their degree of constraint and requirements. Gephardt held his own negotiations with Bush, undercutting not only other proposals but also Senate majority leader Tom Daschle. Gephardt made a deal with Bush and went to the White House with House Speaker Dennis Hastert and Senate minority leader Trent Lott, but without Daschle, to announce the deal in the Rose Garden.[36]

The Gephardt resolution differed from other Democratic proposals largely in what it did not do—impose further requirements on the president, like securing a UN resolution or returning to Congress for authorization if the UN effort failed. As Democratic representative Charlie Rangel put it, "The most positive thing to say is that he softened up a resolution that would have been much more repugnant to Democrats."[37] The *New York Times* highlighted Gephardt's public break with Daschle and led by noting that Gephardt had given "the White House some cherished high-level Democratic support in its drive to move against Iraq.[38] The *Los Angeles Times* report, headlined "Liberal Gephardt Sides with Bush on Iraq War Resolution," called Gephardt's support a "coup" for Bush, especially given Gephardt's opposition to the 1991 Gulf War.[39]

Gephardt may have been the one who got what he saw then as the prized photo in the Rose Garden, but he was far from alone. In September 2002, over a dozen Democrats told the *Washington Post* (anonymously) that "many members who oppose the president's strategy to confront Iraq are going to nonetheless support it because they fear a backlash from voters."[40] Underscoring the private benefits and individual calculations, Gary Hart, a former defense-oriented Democratic senator, wrote in a 2002 *New York Times* op-ed, "once again, Democrats are responding to a Republican president as individual entrepreneurs trying to protect themselves against the traditional conservative charge of being 'soft on defense.'"[41] As Robert Draper notes, the presidential aspirants—including John Kerry, John Edwards, Hillary Clinton, and Joe Biden, as well as Gephardt—had personal reasons to fear Bush painting war opponents as unpatriotic or worse and wanted to avoid being on the wrong side of a war that a majority of Americans supported and the administration insisted would be successful.[42] The price for Bush was to lend Gephardt the political shine of the Rose Garden and the seemingly great prize of being the Democrat who brokered the deal with the president. Considering that the other proposals would have imposed more constraints, Bush likely considered this a bargain.

Bush also defused the potentially explosive opposition of Secretary of State Colin Powell. The president obtained not only Powell's public support, but also his presentation and endorsement of the administration's case at the United Nations, for remarkably little up-front cost. Powell had served as chairman of the JCS during the 1991 Gulf War and had been strongly in favor of limiting the US military effort to eject Saddam Hussein from Kuwait rather than overthrowing his regime. The younger Bush's initial appointment of Powell as secretary of state was designed to borrow Powell's standing and experience for the administration of a foreign policy novice. After the press reaction to the appointment, however, Bush worried that Powell would be too powerful and overshadow him. As a counterweight to Powell, Bush chose Rumsfeld, known for his bureaucratic politics prowess, as his secretary of defense, despite old tensions between Rumsfeld and the Bush family.[43]

Once inside the younger Bush's administration, Powell became increasingly frustrated. In the summer of 2002, when outside voices like former national security advisor Brent Scowcroft (who served in George H. W. Bush's administration) began publicly questioning the wisdom of going to war in Iraq,[44] Powell asked to meet privately with Bush. The secretary of state explained his now-famous "Pottery Barn" principle: "If you break it, you are going to own it," meaning the difficult problem of managing postinvasion Iraq.[45] Powell told Bush that "we should take the problem to the United Nations. . . . Even if the UN doesn't solve it, making the effort, if you have to go to war, gives you the ability to ask for allies or ask for help."[46] Bush took Powell's advice, over the objections of the hawkish Vice President Dick Cheney.

But accounts of the decision make clear that Bush used Powell's stature strategically rather than listening to the substance of his advice. Powell had been frozen out of much of the decision making, but Bush ensured he would play a visible role in backing the decisions. First, he made sure that Powell would not dissent and would stand with the administration. In January 2003, Bush met privately with Powell, "the one person in government with stature rivaling the president's."[47] Bush asked Powell directly, "Are you with me on this? I think I have to do this. I want you with me." After Powell said yes, Bush told him, "Time to put your war uniform on."[48]

After securing Powell's support, Bush went further, choosing Powell as the messenger for a crucial set of elite cues. When Bush decided to present the evidence about Iraq's weapons of mass destruction, he turned to Powell. As Peter Baker reports, a major reason was Bush's desire to borrow some of Powell's stature; as he told his secretary of state, "We've really got to make the case and I want you to make it. You have the credibility to do this. Maybe they'll believe you." Cheney was even more cynical, telling Powell, "You've got high poll ratings. You can afford to lose a few points."[49] Bob Woodward adds a second motive: Powell's status as a known skeptic of the Iraq War made his public presentation even more credible because it was surprising. Stephen Hadley, then Condoleezza Rice's deputy at the NSC, felt that "to have maximum credibility, it would be best to go counter to type and everyone knew that Powell was soft on Iraq, that he was the one who didn't want to go."[50] While making the presentation ultimately cost Powell far more than "a few points" in poll ratings, the entire UN effort was a relatively small procedural concession for Bush to keep both Powell and Tony Blair on board.

It is important to note that there were voices of dissent in the run-up to the war, some public, many private. Bush and Cheney relied on a mix of political threats and promises to contain much of this dissent. For example, House Republican majority leader Dick Armey, who was skeptical of the war, got a full-court press from Cheney in a private meeting, who asked him, "how would you feel if you voted no on this and the Iraqis brought in a bomb and blew up half the people of San Francisco?" Armey "felt he had no choice but to go along," and Baker argues it was a "fateful decision" because Armey's opposition "would have freed other nervous Republicans and given cover to Democrats to oppose it as well."[51]

A more public moment of tension that demonstrated the cost to insiders of speaking out came when Army Chief of Staff Eric Shinseki testified before the Senate Armed Services Committee that he estimated an occupation of Iraq after the war would require "something on the order of several hundred thousand soldiers." Shinseki warned that "we're talking about post-hostilities control over a piece of geography that's fairly significant, with the kinds of ethnic tensions that could lead to other problems."[52] Shinseki's comments were reported as a departure from official estimates—which they were—and attracted immediate anger from the administration, which had tried to downplay force estimates. Two days after Shinseki's comments, Deputy Secretary of Defense Paul Wolfowitz told the House Budget Committee that Shinseki's estimate was "wildly off the mark."[53] The "message to Shinseki," writes George Packer in his account of the run-up to the war, "was a message to everyone in and out of uniform at the Pentagon: The cost of dissent was humiliation and professional suicide."[54] This suppression of dissent required affirmative political effort, however, and was not the result of shared ideas leading to conformist thinking. The administration was willing to use political and career threats to make clear that it would not tolerate public questioning of its case for war.

Lastly, without diving too deeply into the well-known story of the administration's use and misuse of information, it is notable how much effort the Bush administration put into waving away concerns about the probability that the war would succeed, and emphasizing the "cakewalk" prediction.[55] When the skeptical Dick Armey told Cheney in their private meeting, "You're going to get mired down there," Cheney responded, "It'll be like the American troops going through Paris."[56] As in Lebanon, convincing Congress that the probability of success was high and the costs would be low was important to skipping scrutiny and going directly to congressional acquiescence. Perhaps it is understandable that Reagan could do so for a small deployment in the midst of an ongoing war, but it is remarkable that Bush succeeded with relative ease for an invasion on the scale of the Iraq War.

Thus the Iraq War's initiation—an invasion of a sovereign country undertaken with poor planning and intelligence—faced few *ex ante* constraints. Bush took steps to keep his hands untied, putting time and energy into securing elite support and preventing key dissent. But the side payments he made were relatively small and mainly of the political or procedural variety. As a result, he could claim bipartisan support and send his skeptical but well-respected secretary of state to try to convince the world of the administration's case for war.

The Grind of Elite Constraints:
From the "Murthquake" to the 2006 Midterms

Bush's unconstrained entry into Iraq was not the whole story of the elite politics of the Iraq War, however. Once the war turned out not to be a "cakewalk," the machinery of elite constraint slowly began to kick in. This machinery, admittedly, grinds exceedingly slowly, and Bush expended further political capital to further delay its workings. But he eventually had to face the consequences for his presidency of the failure to live up to his May 2003 declaration on the deck of the USS *Abraham Lincoln,* under a banner that read "Mission Accomplished," that "major combat operations in Iraq have ended. In the battle of Iraq, the United States and our allies have prevailed."[57]

Though much mocked, Bush's aircraft carrier speech underscored a continual theme of his view of the Iraq War: it had to end in victory, or in something he could declare as victory. During the years before the surge, when US strategy flailed and deaths and violence mounted, Bush refused to countenance anything other than "victory," even though it was difficult to say what victory would mean. In late 2005, the White House put forward the "National Strategy for Victory in Iraq" (NSVI), born of the sense that the strategy of strengthening Iraq's political institutions and training the Iraqi security forces to take over for American soldiers was working but not well communicated to the American people. The strategy stated that "victory in Iraq is a vital U.S. interest," that "failure is not an option," and that "our mission in Iraq is to win the war."[58] Bush gave a speech at the Naval Academy in December 2005 that used the word "victory" 15 times.[59] As one of the officials who worked on the NSVI, Peter Feaver (then serving in the NSC), put it, "at that time I thought we didn't have a strategy problem, we had a failure-to-explain-our-strategy problem."[60]

Yet as the violence only intensified and Iraq seemed to be sliding into civil war, and as his advisers began to question the strategy itself rather than simply its communication, Bush clung to the idea of "victory." By mid-2006, reviews were percolating in the administration. As Woodward reports, some officials, including Secretary of State Condoleezza Rice, "began a quiet effort to persuade President Bush to tone down his lofty rhetoric about the stakes in Iraq," not linking Iraq's fate to the national interest of the United States quite so directly.[61] Even Republican members of Congress asked the White House to tone it down, telling Hadley, "Don't talk about winning!" and "Stop talking about success!" But despite these efforts, Bush would put "win" and "victory" back into speeches.[62] Another Republican told Bush, "The American people don't believe that we're going to win, or that there is victory."[63] Still, Bush was able to keep elite dissent contained, partly because he had co-opted so many

Democrats up front, and partly because he continued to paint those criticizing the war as unpatriotic or soft on terrorism.

A turning point came in November 2005, when Democratic congressman John Murtha, a Vietnam veteran known for his support of the military, who had voted to authorize the war in 2002, spoke out forcefully against it and called for an immediate withdrawal of US forces. Murtha's message triggered what one analyst called the "Murthquake."[64] Murtha's call for a withdrawal was front-page news and emphasized both his institutional position and his prior hawkishness. For example, the front-page *Times* story reporting Murtha's speech noted in its opening sentence that Murtha was an "influential House Democrat on military matters" and quoted Republican representative John McHugh, who said, "When he talks, I listen."[65] Murtha's action "stunned many Republicans" and led the White House to respond harshly in an effort to paint the call for immediate withdrawal as cowardly.[66] While Murtha's call did not result in immediate action, Murtha provided cover for other Democrats that existing critics could not, "elevating Iraq on the Democratic platform and in turn putting the party in a position to benefit from the wave of anti-war sentiment that swept the 2006 elections."[67]

Murtha had long had misgivings, as the Pentagon was already well aware. Woodward reports that Army Chief of Staff Peter Schoomaker went to see Murtha in September 2006, hoping to convince him to support more funding for the Army. Instead, Murtha "launched into a diatribe against the president and the Iraq War," ultimately shouting at Schoomaker, "This meeting is over!"[68] When Murtha went public, those in the White House recognized that it was not just any Democrat speaking out against the war. In an oral history of the surge decision, Feaver recalls that the speech from Murtha, who was "no lefty" and was known as "hawkish on defense," had a significant effect. It "dramatically moved the Iraq debate leftward, because it created safe political space for a 'get out of Iraq now' wing which previously had been just the hard left, but now there's political cover."[69] Murtha also got Bush's attention while the president was traveling in Asia, "because he was known as one of the most pro-military members of his party."[70] While the initial administration response was to paint Murtha as a liberal who was soft on terrorism, Bush felt compelled to walk back that stance a few days later while in Beijing, telling reporters in an unprompted set of remarks that Murtha was a "strong supporter of the United States military" and showing respect for the congressman's decision to speak out.[71] Murtha's status as an opposition hawk gave his defection more credibility than the opposition of other, more dovish Democrats who had supported the war and later aired misgivings publicly.

It is notable that public sentiment about the Iraq War had already turned sharply negative, with a majority calling the war a "mistake" in many 2005 polls.[72]

There had been a sharp partisan divide on the Iraq War from the beginning, indicating that Democratic voters had given their representatives cover to oppose the war. But the public did not have a clear signal to send on how fast to reduce the US presence.[73] Democratic politicians were still divided about their party's midterm position on a withdrawal timetable. They continued to look over their shoulders at the "soft on terrorism" charge, especially since the Republican strategy had been to attack Democrats for their weakness on Iraq, until finally at the end of July 2006, the Democratic leadership unified around a position of calling for a withdrawal by the end of the year.[74] The leap to taking a firm stance against the administration was not the obvious path for elected Democratic elites until well into the 2006 campaign. Murtha helped Democrats begin to solve their coordination problem, however, and the 2006 election ultimately offered the voters a clearer contrast on Iraq than had the 2004 presidential election. The 2006 midterm elections delivered a clear blow to Bush's Iraq approach and finally led to Rumsfeld's departure.

Gambling for a Decision: The Iraq Surge

Bush's remaining time in office was remarkable for his reaction to the clear electoral rebuke in 2006, the elite constraints he faced, and his gamble for something he could call a victory. Despite his famous declaration after winning reelection in 2004—that he had "earned capital in the campaign, political capital . . . and now I intend to spend it"—Bush faced headwinds in his second term.[75] After the January 2005 national elections in Iraq, as Baker reports, Bush was optimistic about the war, which "fed into a strategic calculation about how to frame his second term and spend that political capital he talked about."[76] His signature domestic policy initiative was to be an overhaul of social security, but that quickly foundered, as did an attempt at immigration reform, as he found he could not ignore Iraq in his second term the way he planned. He also began to sideline Cheney and other hawks in favor of Rice, newly installed as secretary of state, signaling what would become a new emphasis on diplomacy. As Douglas Kriner notes, the dramatic rise in congressional opposition ushered in by the 2006 midterms and Democratic control of both chambers "brought action on virtually every other issue on his domestic and international agendas to a grinding halt." His last two years in office were far less productive than those of his predecessors by "almost any standard," even accounting for his lame duck status, because he "was forced to expend every remaining bit of political energy in waging a rearguard action against Congress to preserve his policies in Iraq."[77]

Bush did indeed spend considerable political capital on Iraq after the midterms, not only to maintain his policy, but also to increase the US commitment, through the surge. Bush chose to surge troops into Iraq over the objections of most of his own advisers and of top military leaders (including his commander in Iraq, George Casey), and against the recommendations of the Baker-Hamilton Iraq Study Group. He also did so against the expressed wishes of the public, writing in his memoir that he knew it would be the "most unpopular decision of my presidency."[78] Bush had been considering a surge since well before the midterms but, as Payne argues, delayed the decision until after the election.[79]

In terms of the insiders' game, what is particularly notable about the surge decision is that even after the election freed Bush from his final set of electoral constraints, he still faced elite constraints, this time threatening his core priority to seek something like a successful outcome in Iraq. He used side payments to manage the many dissenters, particularly in the military, who opposed the surge and favored withdrawal. In his memoir, Bush describes the need to get all his advisers and then the Joint Chiefs of Staff (JCS) on board, because "Congress and the press would probe for any rift within the administration."[80] Since the surge had originated from the NSC, he had less to worry about from within the White House, but the military was opposed. Bush had already faced what the media called the "revolt of the generals" in April 2006, when several recently retired generals went public with criticism of Rumsfeld and called for his removal.[81]

Bush used side payments to generate outward unity. To ease the sting of removing them from Iraq, Bush promoted the ambassador to Iraq, Zalmay Khalilzad, and the commander of US forces, General George Casey, to new positions (Khalilzad as UN ambassador and Casey as Army chief of staff). These were soft landings directly related to the conflict, akin to Kennedy's tactic of shipping off Admiral Anderson to be ambassador to Portugal.[82] As Feaver reports, the appointment of the surge-skeptical Casey to a position essentially providing forces to his successor was controversial, but Bush "was determined to bring Casey along to his point of view to avoid creating damaging fissures with the team."[83] He also went personally to the Pentagon to meet with the JCS in the "Tank" conference room, a symbolic gesture but one Bush backed up with the promise of military budget increases and an increase to the size of the Army and Marine Corps, to put less stress on the force.[84] As Payne reports, these promises seem to have had the desired effect: the commander of US Central Command (CENTCOM), John Abizaid, told the still-frustrated Casey, "Look, this is all tied to decisions about increasing the size of the Army and the Marine Corps. . . . It's done, get out of the way."[85]

Opposition continued from the public and from both parties in Congress after Bush announced the surge. As Feaver notes, Bush "and his dwindling Republican allies in Congress mounted a vigorous counteroffensive to buy time for the new strategy to yield results," until the new ambassador, Ryan Crocker, and the new commander, David Petraeus, could report to Congress in September 2007 with news of some progress in Iraq and the beginning of a pullback of US forces.[86] The *New York Times* called Petraeus's testimony "the most eagerly awaited appearance in decades by a military leader on Capitol Hill."[87] Both men avoided promising success, but said they felt it was possible.

While violence in Iraq declined dramatically in 2007, whether the surge delivered success is a matter of debate, not only in terms of how much the surge contributed to the decline, but also in terms of how it fit with the Bush administration's overall goals in Iraq. In terms of its contributions to security, Stephen Biddle, Jeffrey Friedman, and Jacob Shapiro argue that the surge, "though necessary, was insufficient to explain 2007's sudden reversal in fortunes" in Iraq.[88] Rather, their analysis finds that the surge interacted with the so-called Anbar Awakening, in which Sunni insurgents accepted payments from the United States and realigned with coalition forces, to produce the drop in violence.[89] Others focus on the relative stability that followed the surge. As Andrew Preston notes in assessing an oral history project of the surge decision, those who participated in the decision-making process "all assume that the surge was an unqualified success," but it remains unclear whether the undeniable reduction in violence was a short-term tactical victory or a real success in terms of the Bush administration's standard of victory in Iraq.[90] Preston argues that according to the administration's own stated objectives, "victory in Iraq is still a long, long way off."[91] Still others argue the surge ultimately undermined many objectives in Iraq and contributed to the poor performance of the Iraqi Army and government against the Islamic State after the US withdrawal in 2011.[92]

A full assessment of the surge is well beyond the scope of this chapter and indeed this book, but the main point from the perspective of the theory is that for Bush, the surge and the reduction in violence allowed him to declare a kind of victory, or at least a positive inflection point in the war. As Preston notes, both Bush and Cheney clearly viewed the surge as a victory of sorts.[93] In their view, gambling for a decision paid off, even if it left Iraq ill prepared to withstand the challenges it faced after the US withdrawal.

Overall, the war that had been so easy for Bush to start quickly ran aground. The public did not push the Bush administration into war, but those in Washington who serve and represent them did not put up much resistance, making it easier for the president to invade Iraq. Those elites eventually raised the cost of continuing the war for Bush and constrained him in many ways. Although many factors contributed to Bush's decision to invade Iraq—including many unique to Bush and his team—the Iraq War was also the product of elite politics. There were plenty of dissenters, including some who went public, but the elite political incentives favored letting Bush press ahead. Only when those on the inside recognized reality, and those elected elites who could credibly make the case went public with their doubts, did effective opposition to the president's policy consolidate—and even then, the president gambled for something he could call a decision. Given elite incentives—for Republicans to paint the Democratic Party as soft on terrorism, for individual Democrats to latch onto what they believed would be a winning project, and for a hawkish president to use side payments and information management to quiet the more restrained voices in his administration and threaten doubters in Congress and the military—it was difficult for elites to coordinate constraint and for the public, uncertain about the war, to hear a well-timed and properly pitched fire alarm.

The Afghanistan War and the Evolution
of the Insiders' Game

The United States responded to the 9/11 attacks with an attack on Afghanistan that most agree was inevitable. Only one member of Congress voted against authorization: Democratic representative Barbara Lee of California, who objected to the open-ended, blank-check nature of the authority Congress granted to the president, and received death threats and hate mail in the aftermath of the vote.[94] Yet the war lasted twenty years, ending in August 2021 with a combination of consensus in favor of withdrawal and anger over the rapid and bloody exit of US forces, seemingly with little planning in advance.

Four presidents presided over the war in Afghanistan, two Republican, and two Democratic. The progression of the war coincided with a rise in partisan polarization, and the effects, particularly on the two Democratic presidents, are interesting from the perspective of the theory. In this discussion, I focus mainly on the Obama and Biden decisions, in part because of this comparison. The two Republican presidents, Bush and Trump, made important but more truncated decisions that set the stage for their successors.

From Bush to Obama's Surge in Afghanistan

The Bush administration's treatment of the war as essentially over by the end of 2001 reflected many relevant factors. For one thing, declaring the war over ignored messy questions about what would follow, in an administration that prized victory and had come to office explicitly disdaining nation building. A stronger claim, made by Ahsan Butt, is that Afghanistan was too small a target to demonstrate the resolve and toughness required after 9/11, and thus the Bush administration sought a bigger target from the start: Iraq.[95] Afghanistan was, in this view, a logical target for retaliation for 9/11, but not a sufficient demonstration of American military power to deter future attacks.

Afghanistan therefore receded from view for years before Barack Obama made it an issue in the 2008 campaign, criticizing Bush not only for the invasion of Iraq but also for his neglect of Afghanistan.[96] Although Obama campaigned on giving Afghanistan more attention, his decision to deploy thirty thousand additional troops in December 2009 increased the US effort at a time of significant economic turmoil at home, as well as decreasing public support for the war in the wake of years of fighting in both Afghanistan and Iraq.

Mechanisms of Hawkish Bias

By the time of the debates inside the administration in the fall of 2009, Obama had become skeptical of committing further in Afghanistan. But the mechanisms of hawkish bias in the insiders' game worked strongly against his inclination. These mechanisms pulled his decision in a more hawkish direction than he would have preferred—and than we would expect under the faithful intermediaries model.

First, as a Democratic president with little foreign policy experience, and one who had campaigned against the Iraq War, Obama faced significant selection pressures that pointed in a hawkish direction. He retained Bush's secretary of defense, Robert Gates, a well-respected Republican. He also appointed his defeated 2008 primary rival Hillary Clinton as secretary of state, putting in that position someone with high visibility, presidential ambitions, and more hawkish preferences than his own. The military was pushing for more troops than Obama wanted to send and to use them in a counterinsurgency strategy about which he was ambivalent, but Gates and Clinton tended to side with the military.

Second, Obama faced large domestic agenda costs. He had ambitions to pass major healthcare legislation that had eluded Democrats for decades, coming to office at a time of great domestic economic hardship after the 2008 financial crisis. If he took ownership of the war and increased the US effort knowing it was unlikely to work, he endangered that agenda. But he also clearly feared losing the support of the military and of Gates, which could also cost him much-needed political capital for his domestic agenda. Third, Democrats in Congress, though clearly displeased, stayed loyal to the president and accepted the concession of a timetable for withdrawal. In this case, the benefits included not only helping a president of their own party, but also neutralizing the issue to the benefit of the party as a whole, allowing them to focus instead on the domestic agenda. Kriner, writing in 2010, notes that although many congressional Democrats expressed skepticism toward an expanded US mission in Afghanistan, "immediately after the president's speech" in December 2009, they "publicly fell in line behind their party leader and his new strategy." Republicans continued to criticize the president despite the fact that "Obama's announcement fit their policy preferences better than those of many Democrats."[97] House Speaker Nancy Pelosi also blocked efforts from some

Democratic members to offer legislation designed to rein in the war effort.[98] These pressures played out in the debate over what to do in Afghanistan and ultimately trapped Obama in a dove's curse.

Afghanistan as a Dove's Curse

At the outset of his term, with little debate, Obama authorized an additional twenty-one thousand troops to be sent to Afghanistan. He also replaced the US commander, David McKiernan, with Stanley McChrystal, an advocate of a troop-intensive counterinsurgency strategy and a close ally of CENTCOM commander David Petraeus, who had led the counterinsurgency effort in Iraq and presided over the "surge" there. Amid continuing difficulties on the ground and in the wake of a fraud-ridden election in Afghanistan in August 2009, a major debate ensued in the fall of 2009 over whether Obama should dispatch additional troops, perhaps as many as forty thousand, as the military ultimately requested.[99] Available accounts suggest that there was a significant deliberation component to this fall 2009 debate, as Obama grappled with his own position; the initial decision to send twenty-one thousand extra troops did not resolve the already-emerging internal administration debate over what strategy to choose for Afghanistan.[100] But there was also an element of bargaining and concern about political feasibility, aspects of which I focus on here.

As Gary Jacobson demonstrates, although the public heavily favored intervening in Afghanistan at the outset of the war in 2001, public opinion on the war had been in steady decline by the time Obama made his surge decision and fell to under 50 percent by fall 2009. Two polls, for example, put overall support for the war at 40 percent in October 2009.[101] Furthermore, while partisan differences on the war were never as great as they were during the Iraq War, Democrats supported the war at significantly lower rates than did Republicans, especially after Democrats turned against the Iraq War.[102] On the question of sending more troops, over the course of 2009 support for a troop increase hovered between 30 and 40 percent in most polls. One poll conducted in November 2009 showed 27 percent of Democrats supporting sending additional troops, while 61 percent of Republicans and 41 percent of independents were in favor.[103] Additionally, by 2009 the conflict had risen in salience in the media. Media attention to Afghanistan increased from 126 total minutes of weekday network nightly news coverage in 2008 to 556 minutes in 2009, when it was the third-most-covered story, in part because of the debate over troop increases.[104]

In terms of elite opinion prior to Obama's surge decision, Democratic leaders in Congress deferred to the new president and recognized that a commitment to Afghanistan was an Obama campaign promise. But they also made clear their displeasure at increased troop levels. When Obama quickly authorized twenty-one thousand additional troops at the outset of his term, House Speaker Nancy Pelosi instructed Democrats to line up behind the president but later recalled, "I have to admit that this wasn't what we had in mind."[105] Still, Obama's real promise to copartisan doves was to bring US troops home from Iraq, which may have given him more flexibility with this group on Afghanistan. On the other side of the aisle, congressional Republicans put pressure on Obama to listen to military requests for more troops and generally favored a more aggressive approach.[106]

After the initial troop increases totaling twenty-one thousand and as the debate over further increases began in earnest, the military itself also began to put pressure on the president to authorize more troops and employ a counterinsurgency strategy, which required the United States to engage in nation building and governance reform. In September 2009, to the consternation of the White House, both Petraeus and JCS chairman Mike Mullen made public statements essentially endorsing a counterinsurgency strategy with more troops, even as the internal administration debate was just getting under way.[107] Petraeus presented a challenging complication for Obama, given that his success in Iraq yielded him a higher public profile than most military commanders had.

Later in September, the public pressure on Obama ratcheted up when McChrystal's classified assessment of the war leaked to Bob Woodward of the *Washington Post*. The bleak assessment suggested the war might fail without more troops. Soon after, McChrystal further antagonized the White House by publicly calling a more limited counterterrorism strategy in Afghanistan "shortsighted."[108] Mindful that the military might appear to be tugging on the fire alarm prematurely, Obama met with Gates and Mullen in the Oval Office in early October and expressed his displeasure with the military's public pronouncements.[109]

In the ensuing internal administration debate, Obama asked his national security team to question the assumptions underlying the US effort and clearly articulate US goals and interests. The fault lines quickly became apparent. One side adhered to the counterinsurgency approach favored by McChrystal and Petraeus, as well as Mullen; Gates and Clinton generally supported the military's approach. The other view, held most prominently by Vice President Joe Biden, favored a more limited counterterrorism approach that would not involve nation building but would focus on Al Qaeda through the use of drones and other less troop-intensive measures.

In addition to the military's view, Gates's views in particular loomed large for Obama. As Fred Kaplan describes, Gates's views on Afghanistan had shifted over time toward a more escalatory policy featuring a counterinsurgency strategy.[110] On the day before Thanksgiving, with most of the debate behind him, Obama noted that it would be politically much easier to say no to a surge of thirty thousand. The military, however, "would be upset about it," he noted. When Deputy National Security Advisor Thomas Donilon suggested that Gates might resign if Obama chose an option to send only ten thousand military trainers to work with Afghan security forces, Obama said, "That would be the difficult part, because Bob Gates is . . . there's no stronger member of my national security team."[111] While Gates undoubtedly influenced Obama's substantive views of the debate, the need to maintain the support of Gates, and the Pentagon more generally, was also a significant concern.

Ultimately, Obama chose what James Mann calls a "lawyerly solution," but in reality, the outcome balanced political interests.[112] Obama decided to send thirty thousand troops—not as high as the forty thousand McChrystal originally requested, but enough to make the military feel it had gotten a significant portion of what it wanted. Most accounts suggest that Obama was reluctant to send a substantial new contingent of troops. As Woodward notes, during the pre-Thanksgiving White House meeting when Obama mused about how easy it would be to give a speech saying he would only send ten thousand trainers, "it was apparent that a part—perhaps a large part—of Obama wanted to give precisely that speech. He seemed to be road-testing it."[113]

Perhaps even more importantly, Obama compromised on the military strategy. Souring on the idea of a long-term commitment to counterinsurgency and nation building in Afghanistan, he seemed to favor a more limited approach, though perhaps not the full Biden counterterrorism option. From the first major strategy session of the internal debate, held at the White House on September 13, 2009, Obama probed the assumptions underlying the US effort, asking questions like, "Does America need to defeat the Taliban to defeat Al Qaeda? Can a counterinsurgency strategy work in Afghanistan given the problems with its government?"[114] Obama repeatedly made clear that he did not want to undertake a fully resourced counterinsurgency. When he met with his team, including Biden, Gates, Mullen, and Petraeus, on November 29, 2009, he told them his decision was "neither counterinsurgency nor nation-building," but he later said the strategy "obviously has many elements of a counterinsurgency strategy." Echoing the counterinsurgency imperative to "clear, hold, and build," he warned Petraeus, "Don't clear and hold what you cannot transfer [to the Afghans]. Don't overextend us." He made clear that his approach was a departure from the previous emphasis on counterinsurgency, but he had nodded just enough to "elements of a counterinsurgency strategy" to mollify the military. As Woodward recounts, Petraeus said he would support the president and "shifted into cheerleading mode."[115]

Thus the need to keep the military on board led Obama to shift off his ideal point, which was most likely closer to Biden's counterterrorism approach, but not so far as to endorse a full-fledged counterinsurgency and nation-building effort. As Peter Feaver summarizes, Obama "worried about . . . [a] military revolt, decided against imposing what he seemed to indicate was his most preferred solution, and instead went to extraordinary lengths to hem in the military and bring it along to a compromise that was markedly less than what it wanted."[116]

In terms of Congress, Obama did not expend much effort persuading hawkish Republicans, who were predisposed to support an increased effort in Afghanistan. The White House had a back channel to Senator Lindsey Graham, a leading Republican hawk, who suggested to Obama's chief of staff, Rahm Emanuel, that a troop number "that began with 3" would be enough to garner Republican support. Graham told Emanuel, "As long as the generals are O.K. and there is a meaningful number, you will be O.K."[117]

But on the Democratic side, Pelosi stated publicly that there was "serious unrest" over voting for new appropriations for the war.[118] Despite Republican and military opposition, Obama's final decision included a timetable for withdrawing the troops he was sending—the drawdown would begin in July 2011—so that the effect would be a surge rather than a permanent increase. He also ordered that the timeline for getting the surge troops in (and then out) be accelerated. In a meeting with Graham in the Oval Office, Obama said his policy meant "'We're going to start leaving.' I have to say that. I can't let this be a war without end, and I can't lose the whole Democratic Party."[119] In reality, however, Obama extended the US presence in Afghanistan for an effectively indefinite period. Kevin Marsh sees the withdrawal timetable as part of the "logrolling" politics of Obama's overall compromise, offering the side payment of a timetable to avoid a rift with "his liberal base within the Democratic Party in 2009, particularly as difficult votes loomed for the centerpiece of the president's domestic policy agenda, healthcare reform."[120] Consistent with the theory, the timetable can be seen as a procedural side payment to copartisan doves; additionally, the doves gained the (perhaps unacknowledged) benefit of neutralizing the issue and preserving Obama's attention to domestic policy.

Thus Obama engineered a compromise that allowed him to temporarily escalate the war, without really having to pay the political costs of ending it. As he rolled out his long-awaited decision, unity among his military and civilian advisers—both in private but especially in public—was a significant concern. As Woodward recounts, "in an unusual move" the president said at one point, "I want everybody to sign on to this. . . . We should get this on paper and on the record."[121] Obama went so far as to dictate a "terms sheet" with his directive. The president had all the key players read and agree to it in the

final round of meetings, where he emphasized that everyone had to voice disagreement at that moment, after which their "wholehearted support" would
be expected.[122] Key members of the national security team appeared together
at the December 1, 2009, speech at West Point in which Obama announced
the policy; officials also went to Capitol Hill to testify before Congress on
the new plan. Overall reaction was sufficiently muted that among the public,
71 percent of Republicans and about 50 percent of Democrats supported the
troop increase.[123] Obama kept his elite coalition intact enough to push through
his preference—a temporary escalation—while managing the risk of a public
backlash.

Importantly, however, the need to accommodate his more hawkish
advisers—who had unusually high public profiles—shifted his strategy in a
more assertive direction and forced changes to the final form of the policy, but
within limits and constraints that helped protect his flank in Congress and his
own party. Though ultimately Gates did publicly criticize the administration
in his much-discussed memoir, Obama succeeded in keeping Gates on board
long enough to push Afghanistan into the background as an issue, and to get
past the 2012 election.[124]

From Trump's Deal to Biden's Withdrawal

When Donald Trump unexpectedly succeeded Obama as president, his long-
standing skepticism of the war in Afghanistan led to expectations that he might
try to end the war. Initially, however, his appointment of the recently retired
general James Mattis as secretary of defense, partly to bolster Trump's credibility with the military, led to more, not less, American effort in Afghanistan.
Initially Trump announced he would delegate authority for troop decisions to
Mattis, who proposed adding three thousand to five thousand troops, and then
seemed to go along with yet another new strategy for the US effort.[125] But Trump
ultimately turned on Mattis and on his generals' tendency to recommend
more troops. He reduced troops further and further, and in February 2020, the
Trump administration concluded a deal with the Taliban that outlined a withdrawal of all US troops by May 2021.

The deal, which divided Trump's own administration, nonetheless reflected
the widely held desire to end what had become America's longest war. It came
with a side of Trump-fueled drama, when it emerged that Trump had wanted
to invite the Taliban to Camp David to broker the final deal with the Afghan
government—just days before the anniversary of the 9/11 attacks.[126] Trump
called off that plan, and the deal between only the United States and the Taliban
was signed by Zalmay Khalilzad in Doha, Qatar, in late February.[127] The deal was
not universally well received, with hawks in Congress, and others uncomfortable

about cutting a deal with those who harbored the 9/11 terrorists, criticizing it. Drawing on their research on the hawk's advantage, Weeks and Mattes argued, however, that Trump could weather domestic criticism of this particularly difficult and awkward agreement.[128] By the time Trump left office, there were approximately twenty-five hundred US troops still in Afghanistan.

That left incoming president Joe Biden with a choice about whether and when to bring home the remaining troops. While it is difficult to assess decisions within administrations so soon after they occur, Biden made no secret of his preferences in Afghanistan. As vice president, he had opposed getting more deeply involved in Afghanistan, favoring a counterterrorism approach, and felt Obama had been backed into a corner by the military and insider hawks.

What is especially interesting about Biden's approach to Afghanistan is that once elected, he made what appear to be concerted efforts to avoid at least one mechanism of hawkish bias: selection pressures. He made his top national security appointments seemingly to avoid the pull of insider hawks, perhaps specifically on Afghanistan. Notably, news reports suggest that one reason he chose Lloyd Austin rather than the widely expected Michèle Flournoy to be secretary of defense is that Austin had helped implement the US drawdown in Iraq, and had views more aligned with Biden's.[129] Notably, however, he could not avoid the other two mechanisms: he had a large domestic agenda and, despite Trump's deal, likely faced high costs to get hawkish endorsements for withdrawal. Indeed, when he announced that he planned to bring all US troops home before the twentieth anniversary of the 9/11 attacks, he faced criticism from Senate minority leader Mitch McConnell, among others.[130]

The tragic events of August 2021 brought Afghanistan back to the front pages and the evening news. As the Taliban takeover unfolded, Biden made clear that he was committed to withdrawal—that he was making a dove's choice. Biden could reasonably think the political costs would be manageable. Republicans had some responsibility for the war and the peace agreement, putting a ceiling on how far they could go in criticizing him. The surprising speed of the Afghan government's collapse and the chaos surrounding the fall of Kabul put the story in the news even without an elite "fire alarm," but the effect was mainly on perceptions of competence, not charges of weakness, as reflected in the many polls showing Americans supported the withdrawal but not how the Biden administration handled it.[131] By selecting advisers whom he knew would support his decision to end the war, he avoided internal hawkish pressure. The Biden administration received much criticism for the underplanned and costly circumstances of the withdrawal, but the absence of recriminations from senior national security civilians in the administration was notable.[132]

Did Biden pay a price politically? By one measure, yes: in tracking presidential approval, the events of August 2021 in Afghanistan were clearly an inflection point, before which Biden's net approval was positive, and after which it went underwater, where it remains.[133] On the other hand, Biden did not seem nearly as concerned as his predecessors about the effects of his wartime decision making on his domestic agenda (at a time well before Russia's invasion of Ukraine put him in a wartime leadership role, even if US troops were not involved). His administration passed several major pieces of legislation, including the Inflation Reduction Act, (IRA) widely seen as a bill to address climate change. The IRA passed only after one of the two holdout Democratic senators, Joe Manchin of West Virginia, made a deal with Senate majority leader Chuck Schumer. Biden signed the bill into law in August 2022, a year after the Afghanistan tragedy.[134]

One interpretation of Biden's actions is that as a president with long experience working on Afghanistan and other national security issues, having seen up close Obama's choices, he simply committed to withdrawal and was prepared to absorb the costs. Another interpretation is that he believed public opinion would support the withdrawal, and the circumstances were an unwelcome surprise but not one that would derail his decision—to avoid a dove's curse by making a conscious dove's choice.

Regardless of what Biden anticipated would happen, it seems clear he was determined to follow through on his decision to withdraw. Once the withdrawal turned into a series of dramatic events that garnered widespread news coverage—the collapse of the Afghan military, the fall of Kabul, the refugee crisis, chaotic scenes at the airport in Kabul, and the deaths of thirteen US servicemembers after a suicide bombing near the airport—one could imagine that Biden would feel pressure to reverse course and keep a small deployment in the country, even if only to extend evacuation operations.[135] But his defiant statements during and after the withdrawal suggest he did not consider such a reversal. On August 14, in the midst of the crisis, Biden made a televised statement defending his decision, ending with a defiant tone: "I was the fourth President to preside over an American troop presence in Afghanistan: two Republicans, two Democrats. I would not, and will not, pass this war onto a fifth."[136] Two days later, after the fall of Kabul, Biden made another set of televised remarks, stating bluntly, "I stand squarely behind my decision." Toward the end of his remarks, he reiterated that he stood by his decision: "I am deeply saddened by the facts we now face. But I do not regret my decision to end America's warfighting in Afghanistan and maintain a laser focus on our counterterrorism missions there and other parts of the world." Acknowledging the criticism already from many different quarters, Biden concluded, "I know my decision will be criticized, but I would rather take all that criticism than pass this decision on to another President of the United States—yet another one—a fifth one."[137]

It is true that Trump had somewhat altered the politics of military force. One of Trump's consistent views was opposition to military interventions in the Middle East, a stance that led to frequent, often-public clashes with the military leadership and with Secretary of Defense Jim Mattis over his desire to withdraw from Syria and Afghanistan, ultimately leading to Mattis's resignation over Syria policy in December 2018.[138] As Michael Tesler notes, this push for withdrawal brought Republican voters along, but through their loyalty to Trump, not because they selected him based on this policy stance. In fact, as Tesler shows, Trump voters originally expressed more hawkish views on interventions in the Middle East than voters who chose other candidates in the 2016 Republican primary, and they held more hawkish views than Clinton voters in the 2016 general election.[139] In 2019, Senate Republicans, who tended to represent the more traditionally hawkish internationalist stance of the GOP, pushed through a nonbinding measure drafted by majority leader McConnell criticizing Trump for his actions to withdraw troops from Syria and Afghanistan. But many Democratic senators—including nearly all those considering a presidential run in 2020—voted against McConnell's effort. In part, these Democrats had more cover to express their support for withdrawal because their naturally more dovish views interacted with the politics of opposing Trump and a growing sense in Washington that the war in Afghanistan had gone on too long. Still, by the time Biden executed his withdrawal in August 2021, after Trump's deal with the Taliban and after reports of Trump's order, just days after the November 2020 election, to withdraw all remaining troops—later rescinded in favor of a slower timeline—Biden surely had more political cover than the average Democratic president to finish what his predecessor had started and so clearly wanted to finish.[140]

Still, when Biden's August 2021 withdrawal resulted in the swift collapse of the Afghan military and the fall of Kabul, the media had no shortage of sharply critical cues to transmit, as would quickly be reflected in Biden's approval ratings. Republican criticism came swiftly, if in somewhat confused fashion. At a rally in August 2021, Trump criticized the chaos as "the greatest foreign policy humiliation" in US history and told his supporters that "Biden's botched exit from Afghanistan is the most astonishing display of gross incompetence by a nation's leader, perhaps at any time."[141] Congressional Republicans, some of whom had been calling for an end to the US war in Afghanistan, turned their fire on Biden as the collapse of the Afghan government and military unfolded, though they, like Trump, focused on the administration's handling of the situation given their prior stances.[142] Some former Trump officials, who had been part of Trump's effort to make withdrawal from Afghanistan happen before his term ended, cheered Biden's decision publicly, proudly claiming it as the "Trump-Biden withdrawal."[143] But there was a sustained flow of critical elite cues that lasted beyond the end of the evacuation mission. In a Senate hearing at the end of September, for example, military officials, including JCS chairman Mark Milley, stated that they had argued against Biden's withdrawal plan.[144] Indeed, in the spring of 2021 the media reported that US intelligence officials, along with some military commanders and civilian officials, were pressuring Biden to reconsider his withdrawal plan, using an assessment that the Taliban would take over Afghanistan again if the United States withdrew.[145] His cabinet appointments may have been chosen to avoid hawkish pressure, but Biden did not avoid such pressure before the withdrawal, nor hawkish criticism afterward.

Though Biden's belief in and commitment to withdrawal are clear, what is somewhat remarkable, at least in political terms, is his very public and defiant defense of his decision, during and after the tragic turn of events that unfolded so prominently in the media. It is also notable that Biden publicly referred to the unpopularity of his decision, as Bush had when he decided to send more troops to Iraq after the 2006 midterms. Both these actions were true to type, in the sense that they followed what presidents from each party would be expected to do (escalation for Republicans, withdrawal for Democrats). But the theory predicts that the costs of acting true to type are higher for leaders from dovish parties. Despite the perilous timing for his ambitious domestic agenda, Biden was seemingly unconcerned about the political optics and not tempted to reverse or slow his course (as Obama had done in 2015).[146]

Did Biden view the politics of making a "dove's choice" in Afghanistan differently than, say, Obama had in 2009, or Carter had in South Korea in 1977, or Kennedy or Johnson had at many points during the Vietnam War, or Truman had in Korea? To be sure, by 2021 Republicans had shifted their views of using military force somewhat, as noted above, partly thanks to Trump. But there is an interesting additional factor that may have influenced Biden's view of the politics of withdrawing from Afghanistan: partisan polarization. In Biden's view, perhaps polarization weakened the perceived connection between the political costs of withdrawal and the political capital he needed for his domestic agenda. If legislation passes only along party lines, then Biden's legislative priorities would come down to the views of those like Manchin, regardless of the president's choices in Afghanistan.

It is too early to assess how much these different interpretations influenced Biden's decision making in Afghanistan. But the weakening of agenda costs as a mechanism of hawkish bias offers an intriguing possibility for how we should understand the insiders' game in a highly polarized era. Perhaps one result of polarization is to reduce the asymmetry between the parties in terms of pressure to act against type, that is, to make it somewhat easier for doves to be doves. I explore this implication in the book's conclusion.

8

Conclusion

THIS BOOK HAS MADE A theoretical and empirical case that understanding when and how the United States uses military force requires a focus on elites. Scholars of American political behavior have long stressed that the public takes its cues from elites, who therefore play a critical role in leading and shaping public opinion. This elite-centric account is at odds with prevailing voter-driven theories of how democracies operate in the international system, because it suggests elites are often the primary domestic audience for foreign policy decisions, and that elites have more leverage than the mass public to shape policy choices and to hold leaders accountable.

In this concluding chapter, I explore the book's implications for broader debates about democracies and war. The chapter first summarizes the main findings and implications in the US context. The findings give rise to two sets of questions, which I address in the remainder of the chapter. First, if this account is right, what does it mean for democracies and war, and in particular, theories that posit a "democratic advantage" in crises and conflicts? Second, from a normative perspective, is an elite-driven foreign policy really democratic?

Summary

The heart of the book addresses elite constraints on presidential decisions about the use of force. The theory makes predictions about how insider and congressional elites generate constraints on presidents different from those imposed by voters, leading presidents to use side payments and information management to pursue their preferred policies at reasonable political cost. It is a major empirical challenge to separate the influence of public and elite opinion, so the strategy in this book is multipronged, using a theoretically motivated combination of survey experiments and case studies to show not only the costs presidents pay but also those they try to avoid—often paying other, elite-driven costs in the process.

TABLE 8-1. Summary of Findings (Main Cases)

	Findings of Insiders' Game Model	Departure(s) from Faithful Intermediaries Model	Mixed or Unexpected Findings
Korean War	*Dove's curse:* concessions to insider hawks with policy spillover to Taiwan and internal security program; delayed hawkish fire alarm	Lack of risk assessment; delegation of risky choices to hawk; policy spillover; delayed fire alarm	Dramatic public fire alarm over MacArthur's firing
Vietnam War	*Dove's curse:* repeated concessions to insider hawks; minimum necessary effort/strategy; delayed hawkish fire alarm	Escalation to high levels with inconclusive strategy; restricted debate and information flow; delayed fire alarm	Early Fulbright defection, hearings
Lebanon intervention	*Hawk's misadventure:* concessions to insider doves; limited but hamstrung mission	Limited, indecisive war; withdrawal before public clamor	Dovish constraints on war strategy at initiation phase (limited scope to appease Weinberger/JCS); failure to resolve internal tensions given small deployment
Iraq War	*Hawk's misadventure:* easy co-opting of insider and opposition doves for large-scale invasion, via procedural and political side payments; gamble for decision via surge	Poor planning and inflated probability of success before invasion; surge after 2006 midterm rebuke	Long delay in elite constraints given magnitude of war

Table 8-1 summarizes the findings from the four main cases. The theory finds strong support in the evidence. We observe presidents placating crucial elites from the outset of conflicts, seeking to build and maintain elite consensus. Presidents from the two parties do so differently, however, given their political incentives. Democratic presidents find it easier to fight than to stay out of conflicts given the cost of obtaining consensus. One dimension of this problem is that even if they could obtain congressional buy-in for staying out, there is no guarantee that hawks, especially Republican hawks, would not use this caution against them in the future—a fear that motivated Lyndon Johnson in Vietnam. More recently, it is notable that Barack Obama chose not to intervene in Syria after securing reelection. Republican presidents have more room to maneuver at the outset of conflicts. They can act "true to type" if they wish, because they can more easily co-opt members of the opposition or insiders within their administrations that are inclined toward restraint. Republicans may have a "hawk's advantage" in making conciliatory moves, as several studies have demonstrated.[1] Their incentive to act against type is weaker than we might expect if public opinion were the main source of constraint, however.[2] The result is a hawkish bias in US decisions to use force because of the asymmetric elite politics of war.

After war begins, elites are an important source of accountability and constraint. Again, however, there are partisan asymmetries. Democratic presidents get credit for fighting but not necessarily for winning. Not only are they often less willing to escalate as much as hawks would like them too, but they also can use hawkish pressure as a foil once involved in a conflict, claiming a moderate stance, as Johnson did in the 1964 elections. Democrats are more likely to kick the proverbial can down the road, prolonging indecisive conflicts. Republicans are by no means immune to this tendency but have political incentives to seek a decision.

Implications for US Foreign Policy

It is tempting to conclude from all this that elite politics pushes the United States into wars, or to find fault in the parties for failing to check this hawkish bias. Both parties bear some responsibility. Democratic presidents have often trapped themselves in the "dove's curse." Democrats can also be quick to sign on to Republican military ventures, and Republicans have used the deference afforded to their party to short-circuit accountability and undertake military misadventures. The lack of *ex ante* constraints on Republican presidents' initiation of war shifts the burden of prudence to the individual decision maker, with uneven results. Some Republican presidents since World War II have imposed strict limits on the use of force, as in Eisenhower's decisions in Lebanon in 1958 or George H. W. Bush's approach to both Somalia and the 1991 Gulf War. Other Republican presidents with less foreign policy experience have gone down far riskier paths, as George W. Bush did in the Iraq War, and as Donald Trump seemed willing to do with repeated nuclear saber rattling.[3]

Still, both parties can point to strengths. Republican presidents have used their "hawk's advantage" to make peace or arms control agreements. Democratic opposition can often be more effective at constraining Republican leaders than the reverse. Indeed, given the role Democratic members of Congress have played in constraining not only Republican presidents but also presidents of their own party, it is notable that constraint in war often runs through the Democratic Party.

The Insiders' Game and Partisan Polarization

The cases in this book span different eras in US politics and different configurations of partisan competition. It is also important to note that partisan competition over the use of force can benefit the public—which makes the current environment of partisan polarization all the more dangerous.[4] When the parties take different positions, the public can see the choices available more clearly. When there is elite consensus, it can signal necessary national security steps, as long as at least some in the party are willing to cross the aisle. What happens, then, when willingness to cross the aisle all but disappears?

While there was no mythical age of bipartisanship on foreign policy, the Cold War was less polarized than the post–Cold War era. Furthermore, the political environment changed over the decades of US-Soviet competition. As discussed in chapter 4, the early Cold War saw the Republican Party split between internationalists and isolationists, while the Democratic Party had a contingent of hawks. This political configuration both influenced the Korean War and shifted as a result of it, helping to bring about the Republican Party of internationalist anti-Communism we associate with the Eisenhower, Nixon, and Reagan administrations.[5] The Democratic Party's hawkish wing diminished after the party's southern contingent realigned in response to Johnson's Great Society. While foreign policy was not the driving force of this shift, the sorting of conservative legislators into the Republican Party and liberals into the Democratic Party put the hawks and doves more neatly into partisan camps, reducing the potential for crossover votes. Research shows that at the elite level, polarization began to increase significantly in the 1970s.[6] Notably, mass polarization did not catch up until the 1990s.[7] While bipartisanship was by no means guaranteed in the less polarized era, there was a greater likelihood of building a bipartisan coalition, whereas more polarization at the elite level translates into more party-line votes.

It is important to note that even in a polarized world, both parties retain a diversity of views on international affairs. In the 2008 Democratic primary, for example, Hillary Clinton represented the more hawkish wing of the Democratic Party, while Barack Obama represented a more dovish or restrained view of the use of force. In 2020, candidates like Elizabeth Warren advocated more explicitly for reducing the size of the military, while Joe Biden represented a more traditional, centrist stance. It may be difficult to classify each individual candidate, but what matters is that they are all Democrats, and they represent different views on building military capabilities and using military force.

The Republican Party also has a range of views, with its libertarian and neo-isolationist wing, always present but marginalized since the Korean War, on the rise in the post-2016 era. In May 2022, a few months after the Russian invasion of Ukraine, the Republican Senate leader, Mitch McConnell, felt compelled to speak publicly after a secret trip to Ukraine's capital, Kyiv. In an interview with the *New York Times*, McConnell said that he made the trip "to try to convey to the Europeans that skepticism about NATO itself, expressed by the previous president [Trump], was not the view of Republicans in the Senate," and that he "was trying to minimize the vote against the [Ukraine aid] package in my own party."[8] That McConnell felt he needed to make this clear as a leader of the party that prided itself on its anticommunist and hawkish credentials for decades shows that the distribution of views inside the Republican Party has widened in a politically relevant way. Thus the parties still house what we can call hawkish and dovish wings—a diversity that is essential to generating the uncertainty required for the kind of credibility signaling that underpins Nixon-to-China logic.[9]

But polarization has complex effects, many of which, scholars have concluded, are detrimental to the conduct of national security. Polarization means there is much less likelihood of bipartisan cover and much more likelihood of knee-jerk opposition from the other party. As Schultz argues, partisan polarization makes beneficial partisan competition more difficult, because presidents can no longer obtain political cover for risky ventures that may well be fraught with uncertainty but worth the gamble for national security reasons.[10] Furthermore, polarization may prevent many beneficial agreements, simply by making them more costly, particularly for doves. As Kreps, Saunders, and Schultz show, polarization acts as a kind of penalty, increasing the size of side payments required to get hawks to endorse the same international agreement.[11] A further problem exacerbated by polarization is the decline of foreign policy and national security expertise in Congress.[12] If there is no caucus with informed views on these issues, then the crucial mechanism of "anticipated reactions," in which presidents try to craft policies they know Congress will accept, ceases to function.[13] The insiders' game itself, however, is not inherently the problem. Polarization can affect intra-elite bargaining and information flow as well as public opinion.

What this book shows is that the kind of back-room deals and implicit bargaining that characterize the insiders' game are an important part of what is lost in a highly polarized environment, particularly when the polarization is at the elite level. Difficult national security decisions, especially those involving the potential use of military force, frequently require elites to balance their policy views with loyalty to party, agency, or president, whether they are elected members of Congress or insiders. Choosing party loyalty over policy is not inherently a problem as long as the potential for crossover exists and can be an informative signal to voters and adversaries, as Schultz's work on democracies and coercive diplomacy showed.[14] The question is what the effect of a shift to near-automatic out-party criticism means for decisions about war and peace.

The effects of this shift are an important avenue for future research. When party loyalty becomes automatic, and crossover on policy grounds virtually impossible, the insiders' game becomes a game played almost entirely within the executive branch. Perhaps this retreat even further behind the curtain reinforces old tendencies, making Democrats more likely to accommodate insider hawks and Republicans less likely to bother seeking cover for military operations. On the other hand, the Biden experience in Afghanistan hints at a different effect of polarization: could it lead to less pressure, particularly on Democratic presidents, to act "against type"—and greater leeway for doves to be themselves? If leaders no longer worry as much about agenda costs, perhaps they can take more advantage of a diversity of views within their administrations, since they will expect their party to back them and have no hope of winning much support from the other side. We would still expect incentives to act against type, but much more symmetrically, with both sides able to choose to follow their preferences more easily. Some scholars have argued that polarization can best represent specific voter preferences.[15] Perhaps on foreign policy, it can allow both hawks and doves to represent distinctly different viewpoints that have support among democratic citizens. This potential upside is by no means an unvarnished good, however. It would be only one of many implications of polarization, and much more research is required to assess how these effects interact and influence national security and foreign policy choices.

It is also tempting to see the findings in this book as another indictment of the mythical group of "elites," sometimes called the "blob" in American national security debates.[16] The book highlights the career and private benefits elites can obtain from participating in decisions about the use of force. Diagnosing the problem correctly is crucial, however. In the cases covered in this book, elites did not have a shared mind-set that emphasized war, or a need for camaraderie that generated "groupthink."[17] On the contrary, many administrations saw bitter and acrimonious fights over the use of force. It is also striking the number of elites from both parties and from both inside and outside different administrations who believed, and said at the time, that the use of force was ill advised or that the United States should end an ongoing war. Political and institutional incentives were more important than the lack of diversity in policy views. Nor is the problem the cycle of elites moving into and out of administrations via positions outside government. If foreign policy professionals had expectations of career-ending punishment for perceived mistakes or policy differences, there would be little incentive to go into government in the first place, much less build expertise and experience over time. Those who hold powerful positions might also have incentives to gamble or double-down on poor policy choices if they did not have future prospects.

This argument does not mean that expertise or experience should be accepted uncritically—we know from decades of research that expertise brings its own biases—or that we should not scrutinize the track record of elites.[18] But we must also consider the alternative, which would significantly weaken the "bench" of foreign policy, where professionals climb the ladder of experience. As Robert Jervis has argued, experience and the biases that come with it are essential to efficient and effective decision making.[19] Decisions about the use of force are usually very challenging on both political and policy grounds. There is no escaping elite input into those decisions.

Implications for International Relations Theory

Although this book has focused on the United States, the theory has implications for many debates about domestic politics and war. These implications require further elaboration in other democratic settings, but the theory offers several paths for future research on elites and democratic accountability, credibility, and war.

Democracies and Accountability

An important conclusion of the book that bears further exploration is the challenge elites have in sanctioning democratic leaders for poor performance. Some of this difficulty stems from democratic leaders' ability to disrupt elite coordination, for example by dividing opposition or raising the costs of coordinating on war as a wedge issue. There are also structural reasons to expect elites to be slow to challenge their leaders' choices about the use of force. Even elites who disagree with or disapprove of the leader may not be quick to pull the fire alarm. Legislators with their own electoral concerns may prefer private bargains with the president to making political hay out of international crises. Bureaucrats or military leaders can leak, publicly criticize the president, or resign, but these strategies carry significant personal risk with only a relatively small and indirect chance of leading to sanctions on the leader. Bargaining within the Beltway may be preferable to many elites, especially if they can satisfy other goals. If Baum and Potter are right that the public relies on opposition parties for information it can use to constrain democratic leaders, then those same leaders' ability to tame coordination introduces significant friction into processes of democratic constraint.[20]

Thus while recent research on accountability in authoritarian regimes expands our understanding of the effective size of autocratic audiences, my argument suggests a shrinking of the effective size of democratic audiences, or at least interposing a smaller audience of elites between democratic leaders and the voters. Theorizing a smaller domestic audience for decisions about war in democracies is the mirror image of the important work scholars of autocracies and war have done to theorize a larger domestic audience for decisions about the use of force in some autocratic states. While it was natural for the scholarly pendulum to swing away from the "democratic advantage" given the black-box treatment of autocracies, it also seems unsatisfying to conclude that there are few if any differences in how autocracies and democracies wage war.

Exploring the elite politics of war in democracies offers a fresh avenue through which to explore comparisons across regime type for a number of topics that have preoccupied IR scholars in recent decades. Although this book examines a single democracy, its findings have general implications for several aspects of democracies in crises and conflicts.

Democracies and Credibility

Consider the credibility of democratic threats in crises. Since Fearon's research suggested democracies might have an advantage in generating audience costs—that is, that leaders could tie their hands by going public with threats from which it would be costly to back down—an enormous body of work has investigated whether democracies are more effective in crisis bargaining.[21]

Elite political dynamics may make it more difficult for democracies to signal credibility in crises compared to a voter-driven model. As Schultz argues, informed opposition can play both a "restraining" role, keeping democratic leaders from initiating unpopular wars, and a "confirmatory" role, since opposition-party support is informative to adversaries when the opposition has access to the same information.[22] But if leaders can buy off or punish opponents, use side payments to climb down from threats, or undermine opposition parties' access to high-quality information, these selectivity and credibility advantages decrease, increasing the possibility of ill-advised threats and deterrence failure.

Of course, credibility effects ultimately depend on the ability of a foreign adversary to observe domestic politics in the democracy.[23] But the information requirements of an elite audience may be effectively quite low. If the adversary believes that democratic foreign policy is made through real or implicit elite deals, then the details of those deals—while of interest just as democratic intelligence services take interest in the inner workings of autocracies—may be less important than knowledge that accountability for foreign policy may reside mainly with elites. Weeks makes a comparable argument for autocracies that "visibility requirements" for accountability are low and involve only credible sanctioning by elite groups, not knowledge of elite preferences themselves.[24] Thus foreign actors may need to engage in a certain degree of "Kremlinology" when dealing with democratic states in crises, just as they would if their opponent were an autocracy.

If democratic leaders use bargaining and accommodation to untie their hands—and foreign adversaries know such bargaining is possible—then democratic signals may be weaker.[25] If the leader can persuade other elites that backing down was the right decision, he or she can avoid paying audience costs precisely because the public will follow the unified elite cue.[26] If such mechanisms operate, it is more difficult for the media and the public to distinguish between sincere elite support and support generated through bargaining.

It is important to note that the theory—like several other related studies—allows for the possibility that the elite bargaining and side payments may become public knowledge.[27] As long as the nature and size of these side payments remains within reasonable bounds, however, they are unlikely to trigger public attention and can be informative in their own way by signaling that skeptics felt the bargain was worth making. Furthermore, for democratic leaders who want to "go public," the process of generating traditional public audience costs may be more cumbersome and slow. The point is not that elite politics put everything behind a veil of secrecy or corrupt the practices of democratic politics. Nor does this argument mean that democratic leaders are not motivated by the fear of public audience costs at all. Yet the ability to maneuver around them through an intermediate audience may reduce their utility as a signaling device.

War Initiation

The book's findings also have implications for how democracies choose and fight wars. At the initiation stage, elite politics can undermine the information gathering and planning that other theories expect will help democracies make more careful decisions about which wars to fight. Again, the argument is not that elites necessarily push for war; rather, the theory points to democratic wars we would not necessarily expect in a voter-driven model, and less selectivity or compromised effort in some of the wars we observe. The theory expects that many of these unexpected wars will be initiated by dovish leaders pulled in a hawkish direction, because the costs of obtaining hawkish support for staying out of conflicts is higher for dovish leaders. In general, the lower the cost to democratic leaders to secure elite support for fighting—as it often is for hawkish leaders—the greater the likelihood of initiating a war that a leader would not choose if the cost of evading constraint were higher. The ability to use relatively "cheap" side payments undermines the democratic selectivity mechanisms and makes it easier for elites to slip the constraints that come with public scrutiny.[28]

Even if elites cannot stop a war, they can shape how democracies fight—which can affect the likelihood of war initiation itself. For a hawkish leader, making policy concessions to reluctant elites on war strategy may dampen or eliminate crucial elite dissent, but also significantly affect military strategy. For leaders who are on the fence or reluctant to fight, but face hawkish elites or political upsides to using force, limited military options could make force more appealing or reduce the downsides of supporting a war.

Military Effectiveness and the Probability of War Success

Once war begins, the effect of elite politics becomes more uncertain. Elite bargaining and information management can compromise military strategy, undermining military effectiveness, reducing the probability of success, and possibly prolonging war—whether the leader prefers war, or fights reluctantly using a more limited strategy. The theory suggests two ways in which elite bargaining can affect war success. First, as mentioned, relatively cheap side payments or informational shortcuts can allow leaders to initiate ill-advised wars. Second, the larger the actual side payment or information distortion leaders make to gain support for war, the greater the potential compromising effect on military strategy and the lower the probability of victory.[29] This larger reduction in effectiveness stems not only from the direct effect on military effort and strategy, but also from the depletion of a leader's future political and material resources.[30] Side payments reduce the pool of resources available to leaders if they need to make politically challenging adjustments to strategy as the war goes on.

These compromises, however, also contain the seeds of elite constraints as wars unfold over time. The challenge for leaders to maintain their coalition rises as wars continue, and the pace of elite scrutiny increases. Time acts to loosen the bonds of coalitions, as Mueller noted in his study of presidents, war, and public opinion.[31] Time also gives elites and the public more opportunity to gain information as "reality asserts itself."[32] How leaders play the insiders' game can affect constraint after conflicts begin, however. The Iraq War offers a dramatic example: the lack of postwar planning in order to maintain the narrative that the war would be a "cakewalk"[33] contributed to the debacle after the fall of Saddam Hussein. Compromised military effectiveness can hasten elite scrutiny and put pressure on elite consensus, raising the price for leaders to maintain it.

War Duration and Termination

The effect of elite politics on war duration is the most dependent on context, as well as how successfully leaders play the increasingly challenging insiders' game. For example, in a military operation that is going poorly, some leaders seek to postpone defeat if not achieve outright victory.[34] Escalation is possible, as both Bush and Obama demonstrated with the "surge" of troops into Iraq and Afghanistan, respectively. Bush's effort was made easier, of course, by waiting until after the 2006 midterms, and then bargaining with surge skeptics.[35] But as Reagan's abrupt pullout from Lebanon in 1984 illustrates, elite politics can also end wars. Although it was a small intervention, elite-driven limits on military strategy and political costs to legislators put pressure on Reagan before public opinion fully turned against the operation.

The theory suggests some hypotheses about how hawkish and dovish leaders face different incentives for war termination. Dovish leaders can reap some potential benefits of fighting irrespective of victory, suggesting that once they start wars, doves will stay in at lower levels, for longer. Hawks, in contrast, are more sensitive to war outcomes and may therefore seek war outcomes at either end of the spectrum: ending wars sooner, or fighting longer in search of an outcome they can declare as a victory.[36]

It is important to note that leaders can fail at the insiders' game, at any stage. Observed failure at the initiation stage is much less likely given leaders' informational and procedural advantages. Cameron's shock defeat in the 2013 Syria vote in the House of Commons illustrates that public failure at the initiation stage is rare. But failure can happen at the escalation stage, as when Truman could no longer tolerate MacArthur's policy sabotage as a price for containing his dissent. Failure can also occur much earlier, as Reagan discovered in his ill-fated attempt to continue and slightly escalate the Lebanon intervention. Not all examples of a fracture in elite consensus are the result of leadership failure—exogenous events and forces can strain the insiders' game to the breaking point, as Johnson found in Vietnam. Throughout the book, I have attempted to recognize the limits of the insiders' game, but the pathways to fractured elite consensus and public spillover are areas ripe for future research, especially in an era of populism and polarization, when leaders and elites have more incentives to take extreme positions.

The above discussion is theoretical, and testing these arguments across regime type remains for future research. Even if these conjectures are right, it is not clear how much they undermine or weaken the mechanisms underpinning theories of democratic advantage, such as credibility in crises or selectivity in wars. Since we know that elite politics are very different in democracies and autocracies, it could be that democracies have other sources of advantages at the elite level. The book suggests that these are fruitful avenues for further research and testing, at a time when the differences between democracies and autocracies in the international arena—including on the battlefield—are only growing in relevance.

Is an Elite-Centric Foreign Policy Democratic?

It seems normatively unappealing to conclude that in democracies, war is the domain of elites. But an elite-centered approach is consistent with some "minimalist" conceptions of democracy in political theory. International relations scholars who draw on democratic theory have tended to focus on popular accountability. Indeed, one of Kant's arguments about war making posits that

> if . . . the consent of the citizens is required to decide whether or not war is to be declared, it is very natural that they will have great hesitation in embarking on so dangerous an enterprise. For this would mean calling down on themselves all the miseries of war. . . . But under a constitution where the subject is not a citizen, it is the simplest thing in the world to go to war. For the head of state is not a fellow citizen, but the owner of the state, and a war will not force him to make the slightest sacrifice.[37]

In contrast, an earlier generation of realist scholars of American foreign policy, including Walter Lippmann and Hans Morgenthau, took the malleability of public opinion for granted, arguing that elites could manipulate public opinion and the public would follow.[38]

The framework presented here, while elite centric, represents a middle ground between the elite-driven story of early realists, and more recent voter-driven accounts of democratic international relations. Even Kant stresses that direct popular sovereignty is not the source of institutional constraints on leaders' ability to make war.[39] Kant hints that it is really republics that are distinctive, with checks and balances presumably among elites. As John Ferejohn and Frances Rosenbluth note, Kant also saw republics as generating a "vertical check" through the delegation of decisions to elites, insulating decisions from the public, which might be "moved to take action based on momentary passions."[40] Domestic politics still matters significantly for understanding international relations—but even in democracies, much of the relevant domestic politics happens at the elite level.

Another line of argument highlights the inevitability and even desirability of elite leadership in democracies.[41] For example, Joseph Schumpeter highlights general voter ignorance and apathy, arguing that "groups," including politicians, are "able to fashion and, within very wide limits, even to create the will of the people," so that "what we are confronted with . . . is largely not a genuine but a manufactured will."[42] In place of a model that presumes individuals have preferences over issues and elect representatives who will follow those preferences, Schumpeter argues for defining democracy as "that institutional arrangement for arriving at political decisions in which individuals acquire the power to decide by means of a competitive struggle for the people's vote."[43] People elect a government, which then makes decisions that in some sense shape the people's notion of what they want, or at least what the options are. He argues that such a definition gives "proper recognition of the vital fact of leadership."[44] While the electorate retains the power to unseat the government at the polls, Schumpeter argues that these "spontaneous revulsions" are rare, and the public does not directly "control" government actions.[45] The public's role is vital but indirect.

Contemporary scholarship on democracy, particularly in comparative politics, has partly taken up the Schumpeterian view, at least on one side of a long-running debate over whether democracy should be defined minimally and dichotomously (a state is or is not a democracy), or continuously (a state can be more or less democratic). Alvarez and colleagues, for example, take a minimalist approach, defining democracy as "a system in which government offices are filled by contested elections."[46] This definition, as they explicitly note, does not include accountability, responsiveness, representation, or participation. Instead it is the contestation of elections between at least some conflicting interests that is foundational.[47]

These arguments put the spotlight on elites as the key actors entrusted with policy making, and with the selection of many policy makers themselves. They suggest that elite leadership is intrinsic to democracy, rather than antithetical to it. One element missing in this line of theory, however, is interaction among elites.[48] As I have argued, such interactions are an important part of democratic accountability on foreign policy.

Entrusting accountability on foreign policy to elites carries many risks. Most obviously, leaders may make poor judgments, take bad risks, or make policies that voters ultimately deem unpalatable. In the last case especially, leaders' ability to disrupt or co-opt opposition means decisions will take longer to correct, as occurred in Vietnam and Iraq. Leaders may also exploit their ability to bargain with other elites, for example by getting the opposition to support or at least tacitly acquiesce to the government's policies even if it is a bad risk. This tendency is exacerbated at times of high threat or war, when, as Tocqueville noted, state power becomes more centralized.[49] The deference shown to George W. Bush in the run-up to the Iraq War was one such instance.

Yet it is not clear that more public participation alleviates these risks. The public might also be deferential to the leader's judgment if voters played a more direct role in decision making. More generally, the need to bargain with and accommodate other elites with access to the media—including those outside the legislature such as military leaders—goes some way toward lessening these risks. Elite competition and a leader's need to accommodate elite preferences may be a healthy way to ensure that alternative options are aired and considered. Hamilton and Madison argued in the *Federalist* that representative democracy, with citizens electing representatives who then voted for laws, would protect against the dangers of majority rule and of "factions."[50] As Moravcsik points out, delegation and insulation from popular control can also benefit diffuse majorities, such as those favoring free trade, that are often overpowered by narrower, organized interest groups.[51] This competition—within the boundaries set by voters—ensures that different perspectives will be represented while providing the benefits of insulation and delegation. These arguments suggest that leaving policy making in the hands of elites need not lead to excessive politicizing of foreign affairs. Rather, elite competition is an intrinsic and healthy part of democratic foreign policy. Of course, as discussed above, polarization can have potentially negative consequences for the health of this process, although it may provide some benefit in terms of mitigating hawkish bias.

A final normative consideration is how substantive norms related to specific foreign policy issues might constrain democratic leaders. Such constraints may point to different normative outcomes: on the one hand, leaders may be so insulated from opprobrium that they can violate norms more easily; on the other hand, norms might limit their ability to make decisions or even conduct wars in ways they deem necessary for the national interest. For example, some have argued that democracies are ill equipped to conduct counterinsurgency wars, in part because public concerns about human rights render democratic leaders unwilling to use violent, coercive measures.[52] Yet empirically, Lyall shows that democracies seem to be as effective at counterinsurgency as autocracies; furthermore, as Downes has shown, democracies regularly target civilians in wartime.[53]

Here again, however, moving the spotlight from voters to elites has important consequences. With some exceptions, many aspects of war fighting remain out of public view. In the wake of 9/11, for example, the debate about torture had difficulty breaking through in the public debate, apart from major scandals like Abu Ghraib. Furthermore, to the extent that elites present a united front, the dynamics of public opinion suggest that the mass public will follow. During the Vietnam War, despite widespread devastation on the ground, the public remained largely supportive of government policy for several years, reflecting elite consensus.[54]

It seems more likely that foreign policy elites, rather than the public, can raise questions of morality and restraint that will get the president's attention. Again, entrusting elites to make judgments about the morality of foreign policy comes with risks, in this case either that policy will veer into territory morally incompatible with public wishes or democratic values, or, conversely, that the president will be unduly constrained by overly cautious advisers. But given voter inattention, debate and competition among informed elites may be the best available option for balancing moral and pragmatic concerns in foreign policy, and ensuring that gross violations reach voters' eyes and ears.

Even if the arguments here imply that an elite-driven foreign policy is consistent with democratic principles, they by no means guarantee good outcomes. Schumpeter noted that the typical voter's ignorance might, "at certain junctures . . . prove fatal to his nation."[55] There remains scope for leaders to manipulate the environment of elite cues so that they can pursue risky and poorly executed policies. Especially for larger military operations, the very insulation from public opinion that empowers leaders can become a liability in that it can take a long time for accountability mechanisms to kick in.

Yet from a theoretical and empirical perspective, the question is whether there is a realistic alternative to elite management of foreign policy. Voters have good reasons to delegate foreign policy. As I have stressed, this is not an indictment of citizens' inattention. As Michael Walzer puts it in an essay about socialism and participatory democracy, "surely there is something to be said for the irresponsible nonparticipant and something also for the part-time activist, the half-virtuous man (and the most scorned among the militants), who appears and disappears, thinking of Marx and then of his dinner?"[56] Elites specialize, too, across issues, regions, or bureaucracies. The record of elite stewardship of foreign policy and decisions for war is by no means pristine. But understanding the political incentives that drive elites, and how those political trade-offs can be mitigated, is more plausible than waiting for a public alternative.

In the end, then, mechanisms of accountability at the elite level are crucial to democratic decisions to use force. The decline of legislative expertise on national security, the frequent absence of foreign policy from the nominating process and general election campaign in the United States, and the rise of partisan polarization put these mechanisms at significant risk. Their frequent failures, however, do not change the basic centrality of elites in decisions about war and peace. Democratic elites enable the use of force and constrain the use of force. Changing the balance between these outcomes would require changes in elite selection and incentives. But war will remain an insiders' game.

NOTES

Chapter One: Introduction

1. A useful discussion of Kant's approach, in contrast to that of Thucydides, is Russett 2009.

2. Fearon 1994; Schultz 2001a; Reiter and Stam 2002; Bueno de Mesquita, Smith, Siverson, and Morrow 2003; Schultz and Weingast 2003.

3. For a useful overview, see Baum and Potter 2008.

4. The classic is Mueller 1973. For useful reviews of experimental approaches, see Kertzer and Tingley 2018; Hyde 2015; see also Hafner-Burton, Haggard, Lake, and Victor 2017 on the "behavioral revolution" in international relations.

5. Delli Carpini and Keeter 1996, 82–89; Guisinger 2009.

6. Edwards 2003.

7. Campbell, Converse, Miller, and Stokes 1960; Page and Brody 1972; Lenz 2009; Guisinger and Saunders 2017.

8. Scholars have found this to be true of not only war but also more "pocketbook" issues like trade policy. See Mansfield and Mutz 2009; Kertzer, Powers, Rathbun, and Iyer 2014; Rathbun, Kertzer, Reifler, Goren, and Scotto 2016; Guisinger 2017.

9. A. Downs 1957. See also Guisinger 2009, 536.

10. Guisinger 2009; Busby and Monten 2012, 118–20.

11. Zaller 1992; Berinsky 2009.

12. Berinsky 2009.

13. Charlie Cook, "Obama's bin Laden Polling Bounce Is Mostly Over," *Atlantic*, May 20, 2011, https://www.theatlantic.com/politics/archive/2011/05/obamas-bin-laden-polling-bounce-is -mostly-over/239214/. Trends in Obama's approval by week are available at Gallup, "Presiden-tial Approval Ratings—Barack Obama," https://news.gallup.com/poll/116479/barack-obama -presidential-job-approval.aspx.

14. On the "foreign policy disconnect," see Page and Bouton 2006.

15. Gravel 1971; Whitlock 2021.

16. On the irrelevance of public opposition to continued NATO operations in Afghanistan across alliance member states, see Kreps 2010; see also Auerswald and Saideman 2014.

17. Kahneman and Renshon 2007; see also Kahneman and Renshon 2009.

18. On the "democratic advantage," see Schultz and Weingast 2003. For related arguments on democracies and war, see, e.g., Lake 1992; Reiter and Stam 2002; Bueno de Mesquita, Smith, Siverson, and Morrow 2003.

19. Baum and Potter 2015.

20. On deception, see especially Schuessler 2015.

21. Kahneman and Renshon 2009; Lake 2010/2011; Hafner-Burton, Haggard, Lake, and Victor 2017.

22. For "holidays from democracy" arguments, see Snyder 1991, 257; Johnson 2004, 213.

23. See, respectively, Walt 2018; Dueck 2006; Gelb and Betts 1979.

24. Gelb and Betts 1979, 25–26.

25. Baum and Potter 2015; Baum and Groeling 2010.

26. See, e.g., Guisinger 2009; Busby and Monten 2012.

27. Edwards 2003.

28. Aldrich, Sullivan, and Borgida 1989, 123; Schultz 2001a, 78; see also Zaller 1994a.

29. Lupia and McCubbins 1998.

30. Zaller 1992; Berinsky 2009.

31. See Lippmann 1922; Morgenthau and Thompson 1985, 164–69.

32. Page and Shapiro 1992; Holsti 2004, ch. 3; Hurwitz and Peffley 1987; Gelpi 2010; Rathbun, Kertzer, Reifler, Goren, and Scotto 2016.

33. E.g., Aldrich, Sullivan, and Borgida 1989, 135–36.

34. Lupia and McCubbins 1998.

35. On stable collective public preferences, see especially Page and Shapiro 1992. Some rationalist models do examine systematic distortions in democratic decision making, as in the famous "gambling for resurrection" argument. See G. Downs and Rocke 1994. More generally, Page and Bouton (2006) find persistent gaps between elite and public opinion on foreign policy, leading to what they call the "foreign policy disconnect."

36. See, respectively, Bueno de Mesquita, Smith, Siverson, and Morrow 2003; Weeks 2014.

37. Svolik 2012.

38. On the selection and responsiveness mechanisms, see Tomz, Weeks, and Yarhi-Milo 2020.

39. See, in particular, Fearon 1994; Reiter and Stam 2002; Bueno de Mesquita, Smith, Siverson, and Morrow 2003.

40. For definitions and discussions of the selectorate and winning coalitions, see Bueno de Mesquita, Smith, Siverson, and Morrow 2003, 41–57.

41. On the possibility of doling out spoils of war and the implications in selectorate theory, see especially ibid., ch. 6.

42. The "fire alarm" metaphor is associated with McCubbins and Schwartz 1984 in the context of congressional oversight; Zaller 2003b uses the term "burglar alarm" in the context of news media alerts for citizens hoping to monitor their leaders.

43. On selectorate theory, see Bueno de Mesquita, Smith, Siverson, and Morrow 2003. In the context of arms control, Kreps, Saunders, and Schultz (2018) show that side payments are crucial to domestic ratification.

44. Kernell 1986; see also Eshbaugh-Soha 2006 on intra-elite signaling.

45. Exceptions include Caverley 2014, focusing directly on the preferences of the median voter; others focusing on the shadow of upcoming elections include Gowa 1998; Marinov, Nomikos, and Robbins 2015; Lee 2015; Payne 2020 and 2023.

46. Petrocik 1996; Egan 2013.

47. Mattes and Weeks 2019; Schultz 2005; Trager and Vavreck 2011; but see Clare 2014.

48. Cukierman and Tommasi 1998.

49. In chapter 2, I argue the best argument for asymmetric constraints under a public model generates only a mild asymmetry, because of leaders' incentives to signal moderation.

50. Western 2002, 130–40.

51. Rhodes 2018, 235–37.

52. Fearon 1995; Powell 2002; Reiter 2003. Theoretically, if bargaining with elites requires the leader to pursue smaller gains or objectives, war could be less likely because a peaceful solution would be easier to find. But if a hawkish leader makes these accommodations in order to pursue war, then this effect might not be enough to constrain war initiation.

53. For a formal treatment, see Saunders and Wolford, n.d.

54. Schultz 2001a.

55. On avoiding public audiences, see Baum 2004; Brown and Marcum 2011; Carson 2018.

56. Katzenstein 1996.

57. Schultz 2005, 10–11.

58. Grossmann and Hopkins 2016.

59. Krasner 1978; Risse-Kappen 1991 (however, as Baum and Potter suggest, as a two-party system, the United States will not generate as much information from opposition parties as a multiparty system does). For evidence of elite leadership on mass opinion on the use of force in other countries, see Kreps 2010.

60. For commentary reflecting these political currents, see Katya Hoyer, "Germany's Green Foreign Minister Is Taking the Lead on Ukraine," *Washington Post*, January 12, 2023; Guy Chazan and Laura Pitel, "'Free the Leopards!': Tank Dispute Heightens Germany's Isolation over Ukraine," *Financial Times*, January 23, 2023.

61. Debs and Goemans 2010; Snyder and Borghard 2011; Downes and Sechser 2012; Trachtenberg 2012; Croco and Weeks 2016.

62. Kertzer and Brutger 2016.

63. Schattschneider 1960, 3.

64. Ibid., 4.

65. Ibid., 7.

66. See, respectively, Bueno de Mesquita, Smith, Siverson, and Morrow 2003; Reiter and Stam 2002.

67. Bueno de Mesquita, Smith, Siverson, and Morrow 2003.

68. Colgan 2013; Weeks 2014; Colgan and Weeks 2015; Talmadge 2015.

69. Weeks 2014; Weiss 2014.

70. Weeks 2008; Weiss 2013. For a review, see Hyde and Saunders 2020.

71. Weeks 2012, 333. See A. Downs 1957 on rational ignorance.

72. Lyall 2020; Talmadge 2015.

73. For example, leaders may "gamble for resurrection" rather than ending wars. G. Downs and Rocke 1994.

74. Baum and Potter 2015; Schultz 2001a.

75. On shared hawkishness, see Walt 2018; on "limited liability" liberalism, see Dueck 2006, 26–30; on force structure and casualty aversion, see Caverley 2014.

76. Jervis 1976; Johnson 2004.

77. Gelb and Betts 1979.

78. Ibid.

79. Grossmann and Hopkins 2016; see also Egan 2013.

80. On "issue ownership," see Egan 2013; see also Petrocik 1996.

81. On reinforcing the party's priorities, see Egan 2013; on candidate "trespassing" across issues, see D. Hayes 2005, 909.

82. On party ideology, see Rathbun 2004; on the importance of party heterogeneity for generating against-type logic, see Schultz 2005, 8–10; Cukierman and Tommasi 1998, 192.

83. Schultz 2017; Myrick 2021.

84. See, for example, Bueno de Mesquita, Smith, Siverson, and Morrow 2003; Chiozza and Goemans 2011.

85. Lindsay 1992–93; Howell and Pevehouse 2007; Kriner 2010. Baum and Groeling 2010 look at the effect of congressional party support and opposition on public opinion.

86. See, for example, Feaver 2003; Brooks 2013; Brooks 2020.

87. Allison and Zelikow 1999, 256. A summary of the model can be found in ibid., 296–313.

88. Neustadt 1990, 11.

89. Among other critiques, see especially, Krasner 1972; Art 1973; Bendor and Hammond 1992. For an exception, see Drezner 2000.

90. Milner and Tingley 2015.

91. Schultz 2001a, 80–81; see also Baum and Potter 2015.

92. Arena 2008, 137.

93. Brody 1991, ch. 3.

94. See especially Berinsky 2009; Baum and Groeling 2010; D. Hayes and Guardino 2013; Kertzer 2016.

95. Kernell 1986; Baum 2004; Schuessler 2015.

96. Schattschneider 1960, 6.

97. Ibid., 8.

98. Schultz 2001b, 33.

99. Among the first prominent studies in the security arena was Tomz 2007. On external validity, see Barabas and Jerit 2010. Recently, scholars have used elite samples; see, for example, Tomz, Weeks, and Yarhi-Milo 2020.

100. On the relationship between the military and the public in the postdraft era, see Schake and Mattis 2016; on drones and democracy, see Kaag and Kreps 2014, ch. 3; on improvements in military medicine and declining battle deaths, see Fazal 2014; on war and taxation, see Kreps 2018.

101. Fowler 2015; Fazal and Kreps 2018.

102. See, for example, Hibbs 2000, 149–80.

103. Mueller 1973; Zaller 1992; Berinsky 2009.

104. Mueller 1973, 228–29.

105. Beverly Gage, "How Elites Became One of the Nastiest Epithets in American Politics," *New York Times Magazine*, January 3, 2017.

106. C. Hayes 2012, 199–205. See also Nichols 2017; Drezner 2017.

107. See Andrew Prokop, "The Change in Republican Voters' Views of Putin since Trump's Rise Is Remarkable," *Vox*, December 14, 2016, http://www.vox.com/2016/9/9/12865678 /trump-putin-polls-republican.

108. Lenz 2012.

109. Binder 2017; Schultz 2017; Myrick 2021.

110. Achen and Bartels 2016. For a similar argument in the context of the EU's "democratic deficit," see Moravcsik 2004, 337.

111. Michels 1962, part 6, ch. 2.

112. Tocqueville 1969, 228–30.

113. See, for example, Svolik 2012, 16. In IR, see also Weeks 2014; Weiss 2014; Hyde and Saunders 2020.

Chapter Two: Why War Is an Insiders' Game

1. Svolik 2012; Greitens 2016; Hollyer, Rosendorff, and Vreeland 2018.

2. For example, Weeks 2014; Brown and Marcum 2011.

3. For further elaboration, see Hyde and Saunders 2020. Weeks (2014) uses a similar chain of accountability to demonstrate that autocratic elites can constrain dictators at war.

4. Of course, other elites will matter depending on the issue at stake or the countries involved, including think tanks, lobbying groups, and well-known experts. See Tama 2011; Guisinger and Saunders 2017.

5. Kriner 2010, ch. 2.

6. See Howell and Pevehouse 2007, ch. 6 (chapter coauthored by Douglas Kriner).

7. Bendor and Hammond 1992, 315.

8. Ibid., 315–16; see also Art 1973, 475.

9. See, e.g., P. Baker 2013.

10. On the Carter administration, see Glad 2009; on the Reagan administration, see Taubman 2023.

11. Fehrs 2014; Dyson 2007.

12. Entman 2004, 9.

13. Kriner 2010, 162 (table 4.1).

14. Hallin 1986, 10.

15. See, for example, Feaver 2003; Brooks 2013; Brooks 2020; Narang and Talmadge 2017; Recchia 2015.

16. Golby, Feaver, and Dropp 2018.

17. Brooks 2013, 372; see also Schake and Mattis 2016.

18. This argument also underpins the selectorate model, where democracies are more selective and try harder in wars they fight because their leaders are accountable to an large pool of voters, who cannot be bought off with targeted side payments. Bueno de Mesquita, Smith, Siverson, and Morrow 2003.

19. On voters' coordination problems in democracies, see Cox 1997.

20. Holsti 2004, 55. See also Delli Carpini and Keeter 1996, 82–89.

21. Lupia and McCubbins 1998.

22. E.g., Aldrich, Sullivan, and Borgida 1989, 135–36.

23. Schultz 2001a; Baum and Potter 2015.

24. Schultz 2001a, 88–89.

25. Levendusky and Horowitz 2012.

26. Baum and Groeling 2010, ch. 7.

27. Research on international cooperation has long recognized that well-informed elites can provide endorsements to other legislators, but the role of endorsers in war or security issues has been far less explored. In the context of trade policy, see Milner 1997; in the context of arms control, see Kreps, Saunders, and Schultz 2018.

28. Weeks 2014, 19.

29. Recent scholarship on elections and decisions about military force include Marinov, Nomikos, and Robbins 2015; Lee 2015; Payne 2020.

30. Reiter and Stam 2002, 9. Others focus on perceptions of a leader's competence: see Smith 1998; Bueno de Mesquita, Smith, Siverson, and Morrow 2003, 228–29; Ramsay 2004.

31. Fearon 1994, 581. For experimental evidence, see Tomz 2007.

32. Tomz, Weeks, and Yarhi-Milo 2020.

33. Guisinger 2009.

34. D. Hayes 2005, 909.

35. Page and Brody 1972.

36. Tomz, Weeks, and Yarhi-Milo 2020, 122.

37. Gelpi and Grieco 2015; see also Smith 1998.

38. Foyle 1999.

39. Zaller 1992; on the original concept of "latent public opinion," see Key 1961, ch. 11.

40. On democracies and repression, see Davenport 2007a and 2007b.

41. See Lake 1992, 26, on the cost of exercising "voice," though mainly in the context of voting in democracies.

42. Weeks 2008; Brown and Marcum 2011. Both explicitly compare autocratic elites to democratic voters, however. On group size and collective action, see also Olson 1965.

43. Kelley and Pevehouse 2015.

44. Kriner argues that this is one of Congress's main tools for imposing costs on the president after wars begin. Kriner 2010, ch. 2.

45. Many arguments linking crisis bargaining and domestic politics rest on voter perceptions of a leader's competence, but here I argue that elites can have powerful effects on policy that shape events on which domestic audiences judge competence. See Smith 1998; Ramsay 2004; Gelpi and Grieco 2015.

46. On anticipated reactions, see Lindsay 1992–93, 613–16; Howell and Pevehouse 2007, 115.

47. On narratives in US national security, see Krebs 2015; for a general argument about elites solving the coordination problem around the limits of democratic norms, see Weingast 1997.

48. Baum and Groeling 2010.

49. Ibid.; D. Hayes and Guardino 2013.

50. Calvert 1985; Lupia and McCubbins 1998.

51. Austin Scott, "President Fires Gen. Singlaub as Korea Staff Chief," *Washington Post*, May 22, 1977.

52. Kant 1970, 100.

53. See, respectively, Fazal and Kreps 2018; Walt 2018; Kahneman and Renshon 2009.

54. Kertzer and Zeitzoff 2017; Tomz, Weeks, and Yarhi-Milo 2020; Chu and Recchia 2022.

55. Zaller 1992; Berinsky 2009.

56. Key 1961, ch. 11; see also Zaller 2003a.

57. E.g., Zaller 1994a; Aldrich, Gelpi, Feaver, Reifler, and Sharp 2006.

58. Guisinger and Saunders 2017.

59. Berinsky 2004.

60. Rathbun, Kertzer, Reifler, Goren, and Scotto 2016; Herrmann 2017; Guisinger 2017; Hafner-Burton, Haggard, Lake, and Victor 2017.

61. Lenz 2009 and 2012.

62. See Andrew Prokop, "The Change in Republican Voters' Views of Putin since Trump's Rise Is Remarkable," *Vox*, December 14, 2016, http://www.vox.com/2016/9/9/12865678 /trump-putin-polls-republican; Michael Tesler, "Trump's Base Did Not Elect Him to Withdraw Troops from Syria and Afghanistan," *Washington Post, Monkey Cage* blog, January 4, 2019, https://www.washingtonpost.com/news/monkey-cage/wp/2019/01/04/no-trumps-base-did -not-elect-him-to-withdraw-troops-from-syria-and-afghanistan.

63. Russett 1990, 80–81.

64. On the "pretty prudent" public, see Jentleson 1992; see also Schultz 2005, 3.

65. Nincic 1988; on "thermostatic" tendencies in public opinion, see also Erikson, MacKuen, and Stimson 2002, 326–28.

66. Mattes and Weeks 2019; see also Brutger 2021, 151–53.

67. Schultz 2005, 9–10.

68. Johnson and Tierney 2006.

69. Mattes and Weeks 2019.

70. Calvert 1985; Lupia and McCubbins 1998.

71. On issue ownership, see Egan 2013; on trespassing, see D. Hayes 2005.

72. Trager and Vavreck 2011; see also Mattes and Weeks 2019.

73. Trager and Vavreck 2011, 532, 542.

74. See, respectively, Trager and Vavreck 2011; and Mattes and Weeks 2019. Mattes and Weeks also find that doves are less punished for maintaining the status quo, which is the more confrontational stance in their study. Their study examines status quo vs. peace initiatives and does not include military conflict.

75. For a recent variant of this argument emphasizing how voters use candidates' image of strong leadership and toughness as a "commander-in-chief test" that pushes policy in a more hawkish direction than voter preferences would otherwise predict, see Friedman 2023.

76. On the "who lost China" debate, see Kurtz-Phelan 2018, especially the epilogue; on the debate's long shadow over Democratic presidents, especially Lyndon Johnson, see Johns 2010, 45.

77. Schultz, n.d.; Mattes and Weeks 2019.

78. D. Hayes 2005.

79. Indeed, this is what Trager and Vavreck 2011 find for Republicans who fight wars.

80. Egan 2013, 35–38.

81. This breakdown is similar to that of Weeks 2014, 15, but includes the benefits of fighting irrespective of victory.

82. E.g., Schultz 2001a, 108–9.

83. Saunders 2011.

84. On "intense policy demanders" in the context of party nominations, see M. Cohen, Karol, Noel, and Zaller 2008, 30–31.

85. On diplomats and preferences toward host countries, see Lindsey 2017; Malis 2021.

86. Yarhi-Milo 2018.

87. Helene Cooper and Steven Lee Myers, "Obama Takes Hard Line with Libya after Shift by Clinton," *New York Times*, March 18, 2011.

88. Gelpi and Feaver 2002; Feaver and Gelpi 2004. See also Betts 1977.

89. Weeks 2014, 26–28; Sechser 2004.

90. Dempsey 2009; on gender preferences, see Barnhart, Trager, Saunders, and Dafoe 2020. This overrepresentation of hawkish views dovetails with Kertzer's observation that it is not always clear whether military preferences reflect demographic or socioeconomic characteristics that select people into military roles, or elite-related characteristics like knowledge or experience—but either can lead to a gap between elite and mass preferences. See Kertzer 2020.

91. See also Schultz 2005, 10, on the intraparty hawk-dove dynamics.

92. Many of these Southern Democrats fit the "Jacksonian" mold, which may not necessarily support war initiation, but once a war begins, they prefer committing maximum resources to achieve victory. Mead 1999. On honor and war in the context of the South, see also Dafoe and Caughey 2016; Stein 2019, ch. 3.

93. Ray 1980; Weingast and Marshall 1988; Krehbiel 1990. Whether these members are socialized after joining committees or are appointed because of their expertise is an interesting question but one I defer to future research.

94. Fowler 2015, 99.

95. Western 2005, 157.

96. Michael R. Gordon and Thom Shankar, "Bush to Name a New General to Oversee Iraq," *New York Times*, January 5, 2007.

97. On "pivotal politics," see Krehbiel 1998.

98. Binder 2015, 96–97.

99. Arena 2008.

100. Howell and Pevehouse 2007, 36–38; see also Gelpi and Grieco 2015.

101. Baum and Groeling 2010.

102. Arena 2008.

103. Howell and Pevehouse 2007, 38.

104. Kriner 2010, 276–83; for a discussion of the costs of cooperation in terms of loss of control, see Milner 1997, 46.

105. John Hudson, "Congress Privately Thrilled There's No Syria Vote," *Foreign Policy, The Cable* blog, September 11, 2013, https://foreignpolicy.com/2013/09/11/congress-privately -thrilled-theres-no-syria-vote/.

106. In theory, a leader might tolerate dissent to exploit an issue for electoral gain if the policy is successful (see Trubowitz 2011). But leaders are unlikely to deliberately court dissent, because war is a gamble that comes with domestic political risk, while elite consensus brings other benefits. More generally, Chiozza and Goemans (2004) and Debs and Goemans (2010) find that victory does not extend the tenure of democratic leaders.

107. Schultz 2001a, 62–64.

108. See also Bueno de Mesquita, Smith, Siverson, and Morrow 2003, 236; Slantchev 2006, 454. Snyder 1991 is an exception. For discussions of side payments in the realm of international cooperation, see Milner 1997 (on trade); Kreps, Saunders, and Schultz 2018 (on arms control); Vreeland and Dreher 2014 (on the UN).

109. Edwards 2003.

110. Riker 1962, 109; see also Milner 1997, 111.

111. Milner 1997, 111.

112. Ibid., 109.

113. Ibid., 110.

114. On this point, see Kreps, Saunders, and Schultz 2018, 491; Vreeland and Dreher 2014, 56–57.

115. Vreeland and Dreher 2014; Fordham 1998.

116. Betts 1977, 71.

117. Schultz 2003; Chapman and Reiter 2004; Voeten 2005; Grieco, Gelpi, Reifler, and Feaver 2011; Vreeland and Dreher 2014; Recchia 2015.

118. Riker 1962. Weeks makes a similar point in the context of authoritarian audience costs. Weeks 2008, 41.

119. Feaver 2011, 107.

120. E.g., Schultz 2001a, 62–65; Reiter and Stam 2002.

121. Kaufmann 2004; Downes 2009; Downes 2011; Schuessler 2015; Baum and Groeling 2010; Baum and Potter 2015.

122. On domain-specific knowledge, see Hafner-Burton, Hughes, and Victor 2013; see also Jervis 1976, ch. 4.

123. Schultz 2001a, 80–81.

124. Zaller 1994b, 262.

125. Rovner 2011.

126. Singh 2014; Talmadge 2015.

127. An important caveat is that the theory does not address the strategic behavior of adversaries; that is, it is decision theoretic. As Schultz (2001a) and others have demonstrated, strategic domestic political behavior by opposition parties can affect the adversary's reaction to threats: for example, adversaries may not resist a coercive threat if the opposition can credibly signal the government's threat is genuine, decreasing the probability of war. In many modern conflicts, however, the decision to use military force is one-sided, even if resistance materializes later, as in the 2003 Iraq War. I bracket the strategic response of the adversary to concentrate on the dynamics inside democracies, as well as misperceptions or biases that lead the intervening state to miscalculate the likelihood that target states will resist (see Lake 2010/2011).

128. Lyndon B. Johnson quoted in David Halberstam, review of *The Vantage Point, New York Times*, October 31, 1971, 10.

129. George 1980, 193.

130. On Bryan, see Fenno 1959, 190–92.

131. Schultz 2005, 10.

132. Ibid., 8–10; Cukierman and Tommasi 1998, 192.

133. Malis, n.d.

134. Golby 2011.

135. Betts 1977, 71.

136. Ibid.

137. Grossmann and Hopkins 2016; J. Cohen 2012; Bertoli, Dafoe, and Trager 2019.

138. In the European context there is debate over the strength of the association between left governments and the welfare state, but scholars have found the relationship to be durable across changing international economic contexts. See, for example, Garrett and Lange 1991; Iversen and Cusack 2000; Korpi and Palme 2003.

139. Grossmann and Hopkins 2016.

140. Ibid., 256.

141. On intense policy demanders, see M. Cohen, Karol, Noel, and Zaller 2008, 30–31.

142. As reported in John W. Finney, "Nixon Wins Broad Approval of Congress on China Talks but Some Criticism Arises; Conservatives in G.O.P. Voice Doubts on Taiwan," *New York Times*, February 29, 1972.

143. Kreps, Saunders, and Schultz 2018.

144. In the context of endorsements from opposition parties, Trager and Vavreck argue that "endorsements that run contrary to the perceived biases of the parties will be more informative to voters." Trager and Vavreck 2011, 532.

145. For a discussion, see Schulhofer-Wohl 2021, 526–28.

146. See Guisinger and Saunders 2017 on war weariness and its effects on willingness to use force in Syria in 2013.

147. Calvert 1985; Schultz 2001a, 105–7.

148. In a series of votes in spring 2022 on aid to Ukraine and other measures related to the war, progressive Democrats showed remarkably unified backing for President Biden's support for Ukraine and praised his approach. In October 2022, a group of progressives released a letter calling on Biden to pursue more diplomacy to end the war but withdrew the letter and reiterated their support for the administration after a strong and swift backlash. On the early unity, see Olivier Knox, "Progressives (Mostly) Line Up behind Biden's Ukraine Policy," The Daily 202, *Washington Post*, May 16, 2022; on the progressive letter, see Marianna Sotomayor and Yasmeen Abutaleb, "Jayapal Draws Ire of Fellow Democrats over Bungled Ukraine Letter," *Washington Post*, October 27, 2022.

149. Schultz 2001a, 103–7.

150. Howell and Pevehouse 2007, 72–73, 99; see also Gowa 1998.

151. Gelb and Betts 1979, 25.

152. Grieco, Gelpi, Reifler, and Feaver 2011.

153. On avoiding hawkish pressure through secrecy, see Carson 2018.

154. On presidential experience, see Saunders 2017; on the Eisenhower cases and nonintervention decisions generally, see Saunders 2011.

155. In the Iraq case, Jervis argues that confirmation bias and motivated reasoning led some within the Bush administration to sincerely estimate an easy path. Jervis 2006.

156. Baum and Groeling 2010, ch. 7.

157. Mueller 1973, 205–8.

158. Berinsky 2009; on elites relying on preexisting views as wars drag on, see Evans and Potter 2019.

159. Fowler 2015, 141.

160. G. Downs and Rocke 1994.

161. Tomz 2007, 822.

162. Ibid., 825. Elites may also behave differently in interviews, or not include political factors when weighing responses to hypothetical scenarios.

163. Baum and Groeling argue that as conflicts unfold, "reality assert[s] itself." Baum and Groeling 2010, ch. 7.

164. Croco 2015; Croco and Weeks 2016.

165. Saunders 2011, ch. 1.

166. Gelb and Betts 1979, chs. 4, 5.

Chapter Three: Evidence from Public Opinion

1. Data and replication materials for all experiments are available in appendix B, "Supplementary Information and Replication Data for *The Insiders' Game: How Elites Make War and Peace*," Harvard Dataverse, https://doi.org/10.7910/DVN/FHQYWF.

2. Entman 2004; Kriner 2010, 162; Hallin 1986, ch. 5.

3. See, for example, Howell and Kriner 2007; Trager and Vavreck 2011; Golby, Feaver, and Dropp 2018.

4. Erikson, MacKuen, and Stimson 2002; on baseline public attitudes, see Guisinger and Saunders 2017.

5. Ansolabehere, Schaffner, Luks, and Shih, 2008–22. The CCES, since 2022 known as the Cooperative Election Study (CES), is a multi-university, national stratified sample survey with a set of common questions asked across all university teams, with each participating team designing its own survey questions on a team module given to a subset of 1,000 respondents. The survey is administered by the survey firm YouGov. In 2012, I asked the same questions on two modules, as described in Guisinger and Saunders 2017, resulting in a sample of 2,000 for that year. The survey has two waves, one conducted before the election, in late September to late October of the election year, and one conducted in November after the election is over; and team questions can be on either wave. The CCES/CES aims to have a nationally representative sample of US adults; the results reported here use weights provided by YouGov for each module.

6. Deering and Sigelman 2011.

7. Although omitted for brevity, in 2008 respondents did well on identifying countries with which the United States has friendly or unfriendly relations, with over 80 percent answering correctly for Venezuela, Great Britain, Syria, and North Korea. The lowest scores were for countries less frequently in the news, such as Brazil (62 percent) and Kuwait (55 percent).

8. In the 2016 and 2022 versions, I added, "Please choose the closest number."

9. Similarly, support from members of the president's party in Congress is expected; see, e.g., Baum and Groeling 2010, 25.

10. These hypotheses build on Trager and Vavreck 2011, who focus on congressional opposition support.

11. Feaver 2011. Future research could refine the predictions to reflect different missions (such as peacekeeping).

12. SSI recruits participants and then randomly selects those who are invited to participate in a particular survey. For this survey, the aim was to have a sample that mirrored the census distribution (for those over eighteen years old), in terms of demographics such as race, age,

household income, and education. The sample is thus a diverse national sample, although not a probability sample. For an IR-related experiment using SSI data, see Kertzer and Brutger 2016.

13. E.g., Tomz 2007; Trager and Vavreck 2011; Herrmann, Tetlock, and Visser 1999; Kertzer and Brutger 2016.

14. A portion of these results was published in Saunders 2018; reprinted with permission.

15. Full vignette text is available in appendix B, "Supplementary Information and Replication Data for *The Insiders' Game: How Elites Make War and Peace*," Harvard Dataverse, https://doi .org/10.7910/DVN/FHQYWF.

16. E.g., Tomz 2007; Trager and Vavreck 2011.

17. Gelpi, Feaver, and Reifler 2009.

18. It is important to note that all the combinations of support and opposition—including the ones less likely to occur in the real world—are necessary to calculate the effects of interest.

19. See Kertzer and Brutger 2016 for a similar design.

20. Balance tests indicate successful randomization irrespective of age, gender, race, education, and party identification.

21. For similar reasoning, see Mattes and Weeks 2019, 60.

22. Here, an adviser's support has a discernible effect: acting in accordance with an adviser's statement increases approval compared to when the adviser says nothing, though the effect is smaller (4 percentage points) and just barely significant ($p = .09$, two tailed).

23. This difference appears to be driven by self-reported Democrats in the sample who, in the baseline no-speech condition, strongly support using force under a Democratic president (60 percent) compared to under a Republican president (48 percent, difference significant at $p = .04$); Republican respondents overwhelmingly support using force regardless of the president's party (77 percent support under Democratic president; 76 percent support under Republican president). We see similar results in the full sample.

24. Although this scenario is rarer than a hawk giving a Democrat cover for staying out, defense secretary Robert Gates's opposition to the 2011 Libya intervention is one example.

25. Smith 1998; Ramsay 2004.

26. The direction of the scale was randomized, to ensure bias from response order was randomly distributed.

27. This result does not hold between hawkish adviser support and opposition, because hawkish support pushes up the value of sending troops just enough compared to baseline. A dovish adviser's support for the use of force leads to a weakly significant difference in favor of sending troops, but not compared to baseline or a dove's opposition.

28. Gelpi, Feaver, and Reifler 2005/2006; Berinsky and Druckman 2007.

29. Johnson and Tierney 2006.

30. On the costs of hypothetical scenarios, see Croco, Hanmer, and McDonald 2021; see also Brutger, Kertzer, Renshon, and Weiss 2022.

31. The "Successful" and "Unsuccessful" options were randomized as the top two options, with "Neither" fixed as the third option, since respondents might see the outcome as truly "neither" rather than a middle option. Regressions using all three choices therefore use multinomial logit so as not to impose an ordering assumption.

32. The one significant exception is that in the control condition of no adviser speech, there is a sharp drop in the probability of viewing the outcome as "neither successful nor unsuccessful" for

Democratic presidents who send troops, while there is no drop at all for Republican presidents, leading to a significant difference in differences.

33. Republican presidents also see a decrease of about 7 percentage points in the probability of seeing the outcome as inconclusive (p = .003), but the difference in differences with Democratic presidents is not significant.

34. In terms of differences across parties, the only significant differences are in the probability of answering "neither," although these differences are substantial (18–20 percentage point swings) and for the effect of adviser opposition versus control on the effect of fighting, significant at p = .04. This reflects the much larger effects of adviser support on Democratic presidents and of adviser opposition for Republican presidents. All results in this section are from multinomial logit models.

35. Montgomery, Nyhan, and Torres 2018.

36. Eggers, Tuñón, and Dafoe, n.d.

37. Full question wording: "Some people believe the United States should solve international problems by using diplomacy and other forms of international pressure, and use military force only if absolutely necessary. Suppose we put such people on a scale that goes from 1 to 7, placing them at the end of the scale numbered '1.' Other people believe that diplomacy and pressure often fail and the U.S. must be more willing to use military force. Suppose these people are at the other end of the scale, at point number '7.' And of course, other people fall into positions in-between, at points 2, 3, 4, 5, and 6. Where would you place yourself and the two major political parties on this scale?" Respondents then placed themselves and the two parties on a sliding scale (the order of the scales for the parties was randomized). The American National Election Study (ANES) asked this question in 2004 (see American National Election Studies 2004, 217–18).

38. Relatedly, Brutger 2021 finds that the "match" between the respondents' partisanship and the leader's party is important for whether respondents support a compromise peace proposal, and that Republican respondents are not supportive of Democratic presidents who proposes a compromise. Democratic respondents, in contrast, tend to view most compromises, even those proposed by Republican presidents, favorably. See Brutger 2021, 151–53.

39. Egan 2013.

40. Appendix B, "Supplementary Information and Replication Data for *The Insiders' Game: How Elites Make War and Peace*," Harvard Dataverse, https://doi.org/10.7910/DVN/FHQYWF.

41. Kertzer and Brutger 2016.

42. Berinsky, Huber, and Lenz 2012.

43. Evidence in Governance and Politics (EGAP) Registration ID: 20220120AA (registered January 20, 2022), https://osf.io/9uemf.

44. Jeffrey M. Jones, "Biden Year One Approval Ratings Subpar, Extremely Polarized," Gallup, January 18, 2022, https://news.gallup.com/poll/389033/biden-year-one-approval-ratings-subpar-extremely-polarized.aspx.

45. There is an approximately 5 percent increase in opposition to the war from the expected cue swings for presidents of both parties; i.e., hawkish opposition versus support increases war opposition for Democratic presidents, although this misses conventional levels of significance; dovish opposition versus support increases war opposition for Republican presidents, p = .07 one-tailed. But these effects are substantively small, and support is consistently around 60 percent.

46. Another possibility is that partisan polarization has hardened views so that countertype cues are more likely to move attitudes, particularly among the president's copartisans. But this sample does not allow for examining these effects, and thus I leave this possibility for future research.

47. This vignette is one of three from a planned experiment that I planned before the events of August 2021 in Afghanistan and then delayed. It received IRB approval in July 2021 and was preregistered at the EGAP Registry (EGAP Registration ID 20210926AB) on September 26, 2021, https://osf.io/kcbxs.

48. This experiment contained only one of three planned vignettes because of the timing with respect to the August 2021 US withdrawal from Afghanistan; cell sizes are thus too small for the purposes of examining the effect of adviser type.

49. This approach is similar to Mattes and Weeks (2019), who ask approval questions at different stages.

50. Following Herrmann, Tetlock, and Visser 1999. In all three experiments, the basic scenario was the same: "For several years, the United States has been engaged in a military intervention in a foreign country that fell into a civil war. The war-torn foreign country is important to U.S. economic and security interests. The U.S. currently has 30,000 troops deployed in the foreign country, and there have been 1,000 U.S. casualties to date. The U.S. president, who is a [Democrat | Republican], faced a decision about whether to send additional troops and extend the United States' involvement in the intervention." In one version, casualties varied. The first study was conducted via SSI in July 2014 (n = 1,846); the second in late October / early November 2014 via MTurk (n = 1,792); and the third on both the prewaves and the postwaves of the 2014 CCES (via YouGov), shortly before and after the 2014 congressional election. In the 2014 CCES, I repeated the experiment in both waves, rerandomizing between the waves, and pooled the data to yield n = 1,815 responses.

51. Jentleson 1992; Jentleson and Britton 1998.

52. Guisinger and Saunders 2017.

53. Indeed, Howell and Pevehouse argue that Congress pays more attention and exerts more constraint over larger deployments. Howell and Pevehouse 2007, 40–42.

54. The difference in differences is weakly significant at p = .09.

55. Herrmann, Tetlock, and Visser find that when US interests are at stake, respondents are more willing to use force against a strong aggressor than against a weak aggressor. Herrmann, Tetlock, and Visser 1999, 562–63.

56. A 9 percentage point drop in approval (p = .05) and a 6 point increase in disapproval (p = .04). These effects are larger for the higher troop condition, again indicating that the troop level may be a proxy for stakes.

Chapter Four: The Korean War: Defining the Insiders' Game

1. See, for example, Ellis 2002, ch. 4; Kagan 2006, ch. 4.

2. On the war's influence on the entire direction of the Cold War, see Jervis 1980.

3. Supplementary information on the archival data for this chapter, as well as archival data in chapters 5, 6, and 7, is available in appendix A, "Qualitative Data for *The Insiders' Game: How Elites Make War and Peace*," Qualitative Data Repository (QDR) Main Collection, https://doi.org/10.5064/F6XUBRAQ.

4. Mueller 1973, 229.

5. Neustadt 1990, 25.

6. Casey 2008.

7. Snyder 1991, 256.

8. See, for example, Christensen 1996.

9. Quoted in Kernell 1986, 22.

10. Casey 2008, 4–5, 366.

11. See, for example, Christensen 1996 on public opinion; for an exception that looks at shifting domestic coalitions and the end of the war, see Stanley 2009.

12. Mueller 1973; see also, Mack 1975; Merom 2003.

13. Mueller 1973, 50–51.

14. Casey 2008, 366–67.

15. Cha 2016, ch. 5.

16. Snyder 1991, 256.

17. Ibid., 257–58.

18. Fordham 1998.

19. Snyder 1991, 264–68.

20. Casey 2008, 23.

21. Tucker 1983, 154.

22. Neustadt 1974, 17.

23. Snyder 1991, 295.

24. On this point, see Fordham 1998.

25. Snyder 1991, 268; on the continued Republican attacks during the Korean War, see Casey 2008, 216. On the politics of China policy in this period, see also Christensen 1996, ch. 4.

26. See, for example, Carson 2018, 148–49; Casey 2005.

27. Casey 2008, 32.

28. Carson 2018, 148.

29. Casey 2005, 662.

30. See Vandenberg to Acheson, March 29, 1950, Acheson MemCon file, Acheson Papers, Harry S. Truman Library (HSTL).

31. Vandenberg to Acheson, March 31, 1950, John Foster Dulles Papers, MC016, 1950, Public Policy Papers, Department of Special Collections, Princeton University Library.

32. Snyder 1991, 294.

33. Memorandum of Telephone Conversation, Acheson with Truman, April 4, 1950, Acheson MemCon file, Acheson Papers, HSTL.

34. Memorandum of Telephone Conversation, Acheson with Dulles, April 6, 1950, Acheson MemCon file, Acheson Papers, HSTL, 1; see also Memorandum of Telephone Conversation, Acheson with Dulles, April 5, 1950, Acheson MemCon file, Acheson Papers, HSTL. Dulles had indeed contacted Vandenberg's office in the midst of the senator's illness, to seek approval (and perhaps get Vandenberg to intercede) on the issue of the ambassador-at-large title. See Memorandum of Conversation between Dulles and G. Creagan, Secretary to Senator Vandenberg, March 31, 1950, John Foster Dulles Papers, MC016, 1950, Public Policy Papers, Department of Special Collections, Princeton University Library.

35. Memorandum of Conversation, Dulles with Truman, April 28, 1950, Acheson MemCon file, Acheson Papers, HSTL.

36. Ayers diary, July 1, 1950, Eben A. Ayers Papers, Diary, 1941–53, box 20, "January 1, 1950–July 31, 1950" folder, HSTL. Many Ayers diary entries also reprinted in Ferrell 1991.

37. Ibid.

38. Casey 2008, 44.

39. Dulles to Acheson, July 7, 1950, *FRUS 1950*, vol. 7, doc. 237.

40. Casey 2008, 72–74.

41. Ibid., 7.

42. Ibid., 86.

43. Mayhew 2005, 480, 488n79.

44. Ibid., 480.

45. Neustadt 1974, 41–42.

46. Ibid., 40, quoting journalist Elmer Davis.

47. Fordham 1998, 2.

48. Tucker 1983, 165.

49. "The President's News Conference," January 5, 1950, Harry S. Truman Library, https://www.trumanlibrary.gov/library/public-papers/3/presidents-news-conference.

50. Cha 2016, 72–73.

51. On the Taiwan recognition debate, see Christensen 1996, 106–9; Tucker 1983. On Johnson, see Casey 2005, 667. The military did not advocate military intervention in Taiwan, however. See Finkelstein 1993.

52. See Memorandum of Conversation, by Acheson, January 5, 1950, *FRUS 1950*, vol. 6, doc. 127.

53. James Reston, "Truman Decision against Occupying Formosa Reported," *New York Times*, January 1, 1950; see also the discussion in Christensen 1996, 111–12.

54. Christensen 1996, 112.

55. Senator Smith diary quoted in Gaddis 1987, 85.

56. Extract, Draft Memo from Rusk to Acheson, May 30, 1950, *FRUS 1950*, vol. 6, doc. 183 (annex). The original memo from Dulles to Acheson on May 18, identically worded, is in *FRUS 1950*, vol 1, doc. 94.

57. Howe to Armstrong, May 31, 1950, *FRUS 1950*, vol. 6, doc. 182 (reporting meeting of May 30).

58. Tucker 1990, 237.

59. The relevant portion of Acheson's remarks are excerpted in "Secretary Acheson and the Defense of Korea," January 12, 1950, Truman Papers, Korean War and Its Origins Collection, "Remarks by Dean Acheson before the National Press Club" folder, HSTL, https://www.trumanlibrary.gov/library/research-files/remarks-dean-acheson-national-press-club?documentid=NA&pagenumber=1.

60. Memorandum of Conversation, June 25, 1950, *FRUS 1950*, vol. 7, doc. 86. See also MacArthur Memorandum on Formosa, June 25, 1950, *FRUS 1950*, vol. 7, doc. 86 (annex).

61. Acheson 1987, 405–6.

62. Snyder 1991, 293–95.

63. Memorandum of Conversation, June 25, 1950, *FRUS 1950*, vol. 7, doc. 86.

64. Cha 2016, 73.

65. Snyder 1991, 295.

66. Memorandum of Conversation, June 26, 1950, *FRUS 1950*, vol. 7, doc. 105.

67. Foot 1985, 64–65.

68. Chen 2001, 87.

69. Christensen 1996, 175; see also Stanley 2009, 136. Christensen's view of the Seventh Fleet move is also reflected in Christensen 2011, 87–89.

70. Stueck 1981, 197–98.

71. Tucker 1983, 156.

72. Ibid., 157.

73. Ibid., 161.

74. Foot 1985, 67.

75. Ibid., 65.

76. Schoenbaum 1988, 224; NSC 48/5 (slightly revised version of NSC 48/4), May 17, 1951, *FRUS 1951*, vol. 7, part 1, doc. 12.

77. Fordham 1998, 10–11.

78. Ibid., ch. 3, ch. 5.

79. Ibid., 117–18. Dulles's initial communication after the invasion, while he was still in Tokyo, called for "US force" to be used "even though this risks Russian counter moves." Dulles and Allison to Acheson and Rusk, in Sebald to State, June 25, 1950, *FRUS 1950*, vol. 7, doc. 73.

80. Others stress the international environment; see, for example, Leffler 1992.

81. Fordham 1998, ch. 6.

82. Ibid., 130.

83. Ibid.; see also 179.

84. Ibid., 141–50, 167–74.

85. Kreps, Saunders, and Schultz 2018.

86. Blomstedt 2016.

87. Casey 2005, 33–35; Brands 2016, 76–77; for the discussion of whether to go to Congress, see Memorandum of Conversation, Truman with Acheson, Johnson, et al., July 3, 1950, *FRUS 1950*, vol. 7, doc. 205.

88. Casey 2008; Craig and Logevall 2009, 118.

89. Memorandum of Conversation, Truman with Acheson, Johnson, et al., July 3, 1950, *FRUS 1950*, vol. 7, doc. 205.

90. Carson 2018, 153–57.

91. Elsey Memorandum, "Blair House Meeting—June 27, 1950," June 30, 1951, 7–8.

92. Casey 2008, 85, 35–40.

93. Hamby 1995, 539.

94. Blomstedt 2016, 52.

95. Hamby 1995, 538.

96. As reported by Webb to Elsey in 1951; see Elsey Memorandum, "Blair House Meeting—June 27, 1950," June 30, 1951, Elsey Papers, box 71, "Korea—June 27, 1950" folder, HSTL.

97. Casey 2008, 85; see also Brands 2016, 151–52.

98. Memorandum for file "Preparation of President's Message to Congress on Korea," Elsey Papers, "July 19, 1950, Korea—July 19, 1950—Message to Congress on Korean Situation [1 of 3] Folder," HSTL, 3.

99. Ayers diary, June 29, 1950, Ayers Papers, Diary, 1941–53, box 20, "January 1, 1950—July 31, 1950" folder, HSTL.

100. Ayers diary, July 3, 1950.

101. Draft Memorandum of Conversation, NSC meeting, June 29, 1950, 5 p.m., Elsey Papers, box 71, Korea—June 29, 1950, White House, State, Defense Meeting folder, HSTL, 1–2. Truman did agree to air strikes against North Korean bases north of the thirty-eighth parallel so long as US planes did not go beyond North Korea.

102. Draft Memorandum of Conversation, NSC meeting, June 29, 1950, 5 p.m., 6. This is the meeting mentioned in "Editorial Note," *FRUS 1950* vol. 7, doc. 160.

103. Leffler 1992, 369.

104. For a recent account of the Truman-MacArthur interactions, see Brands 2016.

105. Cumings 2011, 73.

106. Stueck 2002, 97.

107. Ibid. This book also provides a useful and nuanced summary of the historiographical debates.

108. Truman quoted in Memorandum, "Wake Island," Ayers Papers, box 9, "Korea—MacArthur, Wake Island" folder, HSTL, 3.

109. Boykin to Sidney Souers, December 5, 1950, Souers Papers, Subject file, "White House Counsel" folder, HSTL, 2–3.

110. MacArthur to Boykin, December 13, 1950, Souers Papers, Subject file, "White House Counsel" folder, HSTL, 1.

111. On the bureaucratic consensus surrounding the crossing of the thirty-eighth parallel, see Foot 1985, 70–72; see also NSC 81, "United States Courses of Action with Respect to Korea," September 1, 1950, *FRUS 1950*, vol. 7, doc. 486.

112. Reiter 2009, 75, 79.

113. Dulles to Nitze, July 14, 1950, *FRUS 1950*, vol. 7, doc. 287.

114. Reference to the July 5 memo is in Allison to Rusk, July 15, 1950, *FRUS 1950*, vol. 7, doc. 295.

115. Allison to Rusk, July 15, 1950. Allison registered an "emphatic dissent" to a Policy Planning draft of July 22. See Allison to Nitze, July 24, 1950, *FRUS 1950*, vol. 7, doc. 349; for the Policy Planning draft, see Draft Memorandum Prepared by the Policy Planning Staff, July 22, 1950, *FRUS 1950*, vol. 7, doc. 344.

116. Allison to Rusk, July 27, 1950, *FRUS 1950*, vol. 7, doc. 361. See also Draft Memorandum Prepared by the Policy Planning Staff [revised draft], July 25, 1950, *FRUS 1950*, vol. 7, doc. 354.

117. Dulles to Nitze, August 1, 1950, *FRUS 1950*, vol. 7, doc. 385.

118. See, for example, Minutes of the Fourth Meeting of the United States Delegation to the United Nations General Assembly, September 21, 1950, *FRUS 1950*, vol. 7, doc. 525.

119. See Foot 1985, 67–69.

120. Stueck 2002, 98; see also Casey 2008, 97–98. On pressure from Congress to cross the thirty-eighth parallel, see Foot 1985, 69–70.

121. Casey 2008, 100.

122. Ibid.

123. Craig and Logevall 2009, 134.

124. Ibid., 135.

125. Ibid., 129. On Kennan and containment, see Gaddis 2005, ch. 2.

126. Truman to MacArthur, August 29, 1950, Elsey Papers, box 72, "Korea—Truman-MacArthur-Matthews Statements, August, 1950" folder, HSTL.

127. Casey 2008, 113.

128. On the Wake Island trip, see ibid., 113–16; Brands 2016, 172–84.

129. For discussions of the debate, see Foot 1985, 95–105; Stueck 2002, 111–17.

130. Christensen 1996, 153–76.

131. Stueck 2002, 111.

132. JCS to MacArthur, November 24, 1950, *FRUS 1950*, vol. 7, doc. 878. For the discussion with civilians at which stopping short of the Yalu was discussed, see Memorandum of Conversation, November 21, 1950, *FRUS 1950*, vol. 7, doc. 864. On this meeting and instructions, see Foot 1985, 99–100.

133. MacArthur to JCS, November 25, 1950, *FRUS 1950*, vol. 7, doc. 883.

134. Draft Policy Planning Paper, July 22, 1950.

135. Draft Memorandum Prepared by the Policy Planning Staff, *FRUS 1950*, vol. 7, doc. 354.

136. Allison to Rusk, July 27, 1950, *FRUS 1950*, vol. 7, doc. 361.

137. Memorandum, July 28, 1950, *FRUS 1950*, vol. 7, doc. 365.

138. Revisions included in Butler to Bishop, August 1, 1950, *FRUS 1950*, vol. 7, doc. 386.

139. Casey 2008, 100.

140. Foyle 1999, 179–80.

141. Steve Crabtree, "The Gallup Brain: Americans and the Korean War," Gallup, February 4, 2003, https://news.gallup.com/poll/7741/gallup-brain-americans-korean-war.aspx.

142. Neustadt 1990, 109–17.

143. Ibid., 105–6.

144. Ibid., 108.

145. Ibid., 121.

146. Feaver rightly calls the MacArthur firing "the pivotal experience in modern American civil-military relations." Feaver 2003, 128–29.

147. MacArthur VFW letter, copy reprinted in *US News & World Report*, 29, September 1, 1950, 32–34, and in Elsey Papers, box 72, "Korea—Truman-MacArthur-Matthews Statements, August, 1950" folder, HSTL, 6. See also the discussion in Brands 2016, 133–35.

148. See, for example, Brands 2016, 229–30.

149. Reiter 2009, 82.

150. MacArthur's statement is reported in Acheson to Certain Diplomatic Offices, *FRUS 1951*, vol. 7, part 1, doc. 184; see also Stueck 2002, 130; Brands 2016, 285–86.

151. See "Editorial Note," *FRUS 1951*, vol. 7, part 1, doc. 206 (which reprints MacArthur's letter).

152. JCS to Marshall, in Memorandum of Conversation, April 6, 1951, *FRUS 1951*, vol. 7, part 1, doc. 211 (annex).

153. Quoted in Brands 2016, 292.

154. Cumings 2011, 156–57.

155. Dingman 1998/1989, 72–74; see also Casey and Stueck 2011, 37–38. Cumings also hints that "Truman had used this extraordinary crisis to get the JCS to approve MacArthur's removal." Cumings 2011, 157.

156. Belknap and Campbell 1951, 608.

157. Mueller 1973, 227–29.

158. Casey 2008, ch. 9.

159. Ibid., 240, 246.

160. Ibid., 246–57.

161. Foot 1985, 136.

162. Quoted in Casey 2008, 251.

163. Ibid., 261–62. See also Casey and Stueck 2011.

164. Casey and Stueck 2011.

165. Casey 2008, 366.

166. Casey and Stueck 2011, 40.

167. Christensen 1996, 115; Reiter 2009, 87.

168. Reiter 2009, ch. 5.

169. Stanley 2009, 10.

170. Croco 2015 (on Eisenhower and Korea, see 191–92).

171. Stueck 1997, 317–18.

172. Dingman 1998/1989, 79–91; Hitchcock 2018, 106.

173. Stueck 1997, 306, 310; Foot 1985, 220–23.

174. Stueck 1997, ch. 9; Casey 2008, ch. 12.

175. Casey 2008, 349.

176. See, for example, Dulles's requesting some "public reinforcing statement" from Knowland following the secretary's letter to Rhee, in Dulles to Knowland, June 25, 1953, "Knowland, William F., 1953" folder, Dulles Papers, MC016, Princeton University; see also Robertson to Dulles, July 1, 1953, and "Editorial Note," *FRUS 1952–1954*, vol. 15, part 2, docs. 649 and 650.

177. Foot 1985, 220, 239.

178. Steve Crabtree, "The Gallup Brain: Americans and the Korean War," Gallup, February 4, 2003, https://news.gallup.com/poll/7741/gallup-brain-americans-korean-war.aspx.

179. See Saunders 2011, ch. 3.

180. Berinsky 2009, 111.

181. Snyder 1991, 257.

Chapter Five: The Vietnam War as an Insiders' Game

1. Gelb and Betts 1979.

2. See Zaller 1992, 102–4, 186–211; Berinsky 2009, 111–18.

3. VanDeMark 1991, 75. Robert Dallek also notes that "in the winter of 1964–65, Johnson felt pressured much more by hawks than doves." Dallek 1998, 244.

4. Logevall 1999, xiii. On Kennedy's decisions, see Saunders 2011, ch. 4.

5. Saunders 2011, ch. 5.

6. A notable and very useful exception is Johns 1997.

7. Among others, see Logevall 1999; Yarhi-Milo 2018, 2.

8. Gelb and Betts 1979.

9. On Eisenhower and the Dien Bien Phu decision, see Billings-Yun 1988; Saunders 2011, ch. 3.

10. Gelb and Betts 1979.

11. See especially Berinsky 2004, ch. 5.

12. Zaller 1992; Lunch and Sperlich 1979.

13. Converse, Miller, Rusk, and Wolfe 1969, 1092.

14. Gelb and Betts 1979; see also Thomson 1973.

15. Zaller 2003a, 317.

16. Caverley makes a different voter-driven argument: that the voters prefer strategies that shelter labor (troops) with capital (firepower) and thus have an affirmative preference for fighting insurgencies like the one in Vietnam with strategically dubious firepower-intensive strategies. See Caverley 2014. For a contrary view deemphasizing the role of public opinion, see McAllister 2010/2011 (taking on an earlier version of Caverley's argument).

17. Zaller 2003a, 313–14.

18. Converse, Miller, Rusk, and Wolfe 1969, 1092.

19. Casey 2008, 261–62.

20. Walter Russell Mead calls this reluctance to intervene, but to have all-in commitment once war starts, the "Jacksonian" tradition in US foreign policy, citing Southern Democrats in the Vietnam War as an exemplar. Mead 1999.

21. Johns 2010; see also Johns 2006.

22. Figures from "Vietnam Conflict—U.S. Military Forces in Vietnam and Casualties Incurred: 1961 to 1972," table 590, *Statistical Abstract of the United States*, 1977, 369.

23. Zaller 1992, 102, 204; Berinsky 2009, 111–18. See also Hallin 1986.

24. Lunch and Sperlich 1979, 30–31.

25. Mueller 1973, 227–31.

26. Jacobs and Shapiro 1999, 600. On Johnson's view of public opinion, see also Foyle 1999, 182–84.

27. Herring 1996, ch. 5.

28. On the Kennedy-Johnson National Security Council (NSC) and advisers, see Preston 2006.

29. Schlesinger 1965, 989. On the political motive, see also Freedman 2000, 367–68.

30. Johns 2010, 32.

31. Quoted in Johns 2010, 46.

32. Ibid., 34–35; on the US consideration of the coup against Diệm, see Freedman 2000, ch. 39.

33. Quoted in Freedman 2000, 393.

34. Downes 2009, 44.

35. Humphrey to LBJ, February 17, 1965, *FRUS 1964–1968*, vol. 2, doc. 134; see also Logevall 2008, 358.

36. See especially Berman 1982; VanDeMark 1991, 1–18; Downes 2009, 45.

37. Bator 2008, 309 (emphasis omitted).

38. Ibid., 329.

39. Logevall 1999; Logevall 2004.

40. Logevall 2008, 359.

41. Logevall 1999, 391. For a discussion of the historical consensus, see Downes 2009, 44–45.

42. McMaster 1997, 309.

43. Telephone conversation, Johnson with Russell, May 27, 1964, in Beschloss 1997, 369. Beschloss notes that "they tell you to get out" refers to the senators Johnson was concerned about. See ibid., 369n3.

44. Quoted in VanDeMark 1991, 60; see also Halberstam 1969, 530.

45. Johns 2010, 7. See also Stone 2007.

46. Woods 2008, 344; see also VanDeMark 1991, 60. On the South and Vietnam, see also Fry 2002, ch. 8.

47. Johns 2010, 60–61.

48. Downes 2011, 94–97.

49. Berinsky 2004, 105–8.

50. Telephone conversation, Johnson with Russell, May 27, 1964, in Beschloss 1997, 365.

51. For an important account of the NSC and Bundy's influence in particular, see Preston 2006.

52. Logevall 1999, 115.

53. McNamara to LBJ, November 23, 1963, *FRUS 1961–1963*, vol. 4, doc. 324; Situation Report (transmitted by Rusk), November 23, 1963, *FRUS 1961–1963*, vol. 4, doc. 325.

54. Quoted in Dallek 1998, 99.

55. McCone Memorandum, November 24, 1963, *FRUS 1961–1963*, vol. 4, doc. 330.

56. Memorandum of Telephone Conversation, Harriman with Bundy, December 4, 1963, *FRUS 1961–1963*, vol. 4, doc. 346.

57. Telephone conversation, Johnson with Cook, November 30, 1963, in Beschloss 1997, 74.

58. Telephone conversation, Johnson with Russell, May 27, 1964, in Beschloss 1997, 366 (emphasis in original).

59. Forrestal to Bundy, February 4, 1964, *FRUS 1964–1968*, vol. 1, doc. 33.

60. Lodge to LBJ, February 19, 1964, *FRUS 1964–1968*, vol. 1, doc. 53 (Johnson's request is mentioned in note 2, and Johnson's reply is mentioned in note 3).

61. Nes to Hillsman, February 19, 1964, *FRUS 1964–1968*, vol. 1, doc. 52.

62. Forrestal Memorandum, February 20, 1964, *FRUS 1964–1968*, vol. 1, doc. 54.

63. Lodge to LBJ, February 20, 1964, *FRUS 1964–1968*, vol. 1, doc. 55.

64. LBJ to Lodge (with cover note from Bundy), February 22, 1964, *FRUS 1964–1968*, vol. 1, doc. 56 (Bundy comments in note 1).

65. Telephone conversation, Johnson with McNamara, March 2, 1964, in Beschloss 1997, 259.

66. Telephone conversation, Johnson with Rusk, March 2, 1964, in Beschloss 1997, 261–62.

67. Johns 2010, 46–47. On Eisenhower's urging of Lodge to run, see Felix Belair Jr., "Eisenhower Urges Lodge to Pursue G.O.P. Nomination," *New York Times*, December 8, 1963.

68. Summary Record, NSC Meeting, March 5, 1964, *FRUS 1964–1968*, vol. 1, doc. 71. Johnson followed up with a note to McNamara stating, "I particularly want your opinions and recommendations to be framed in the light of your discussions with Ambassador Lodge and his colleagues." LBJ to McNamara, March 5, 1964, *FRUS 1964–1968*, vol. 1, doc. 72.

69. Johns 2010, 34–35.

70. Arthur Krock, "New Hampshire: Lodge Victory in Primary Is Traced to Special Circumstances," *New York Times*, March 14, 1964.

71. Beschloss 1997, 406.

72. Telephone conversation, Johnson with McNamara, June 16, 1964, in Beschloss 1997, 410.

73. Beschloss 2001, 348n2.

74. Memorandum of Conversation, JCS and Johnson, March 4, 1964, *FRUS 1964–1968*, vol. 1, doc. 70.

75. Valenti to LBJ, November 14, 1964, Confidential file, box 71, "ND 19/CO 312 VIETNAM (Situation in) (1964–1965) [4 of 4]" folder, Lyndon B. Johnson Library (LBJL).

76. McMaster 1997.

77. For a useful discussion, see Downes 2011, 88–93.

78. Herring 1996, 40; see also McMaster 1997; Downes 2011, 88–93.

79. Goldstein 2008, 219.

80. Berman 1982, 126.

81. Herring 1996, 33, 44.

82. The classic account, which concludes the administration did not manufacture but certainly used the incident for its own purposes, is Moïse 1996.

83. Schultz 2003; see also Kreps 2019 on alternative sources of legitimacy for US military interventions.

84. Hendrickson 2002.

85. Rhodes 2018, 235–37.

86. Pressman 2001.

87. Mansfield to JFK, September 12, 1962, President's Office files. "Mansfield, Mike, April 1962–September 1963," folder, JFKPOF-031-023, John F. Kennedy Library (digital collection).

88. Kennedy call with McCormack, Morgan, and Vinson, September 13, 1962, *Presidential Recordings Digital Edition*, http://prde.upress.virginia.edu/conversations/802001. On the politics of the months before the Cuban Missile Crisis and pressure on Kennedy, see Pressman 2001; McKercher 2014.

89. On the domestic politics of the resolution, see especially Johns 1997.

90. Telcon, Johnson with Bundy, March 2, 1964, tape WH6403.01, citation 2309, *Presidential Recordings Digital Edition*, http://prde.upress.virginia.edu/conversations/9040278.

91. Rostow to Rusk, "Southeast Asia," February 13, 1964, *FRUS 1964–1968*, vol. 1, doc. 43.

92. Karnow 1983, 373–77.

93. For planning for congressional consultations and perhaps ultimately a resolution as part of an overall strategy for Vietnam, see, for example, "Political Scenario in Support of Pressures on the North (Third Draft)," attachment to Forrestal to Bundy, March 31, 1964, *FRUS 1964–1968*, vol. 1, doc. 102.

94. Telcon, Johnson with Rostow, March 4, 1964, tape WH6403.03, citation 2346, *Presidential Recordings Digital Edition*, http://prde.upress.virginia.edu/conversations/9040306.

95. Telcon, Johnson with Ball, March 2, 1964, tape WH6403.01, citations 2306 and 2307, *Presidential Recordings Digital Edition*, http://prde.upress.virginia.edu/conversations/9040277. Johnson discussed the senators' statements in his calls that week with Rusk and McNamara in which he pushed to back Lodge's requests, as discussed above.

96. On Johnson's speech, in which he called North Vietnamese aggression a "deeply dangerous game," see Logevall 1999, 115.

97. Quoted in Johns 1997, 184.

98. In early December 1963, for example, Mansfield sent Johnson some of the documents he had sent Kennedy, adding, "What national interests in Asia would steel the American people for the massive costs of an ever-deepening involvement of that kind? It may be that we are confronted with a dilemma not unlike that which faced us in Korea a decade ago." Mansfield to

LBJ, "Southeast Asia and Vietnam," December 7, 1963, *FRUS 1961–1963*, vol. 4, doc. 355. See also Mansfield to LBJ, "Viet Namese Situation," January 6, 1964, *FRUS 1964–1968*, vol. 1, doc. 2. On doubts from the Democratic caucus in general in this period, see Johns 1997, 198–99.

99. Johns 1997, 197.

100. Bundy to LBJ, "Planning Actions on Southeast Asia," May 22, 1964, *FRUS 1964–1968*, vol. 1, doc. 167.

101. Bundy to LBJ, "Basic Recommendation and Projected Course of Action on Southeast Asia," May 25, 1964, *FRUS 1964–1968*, vol. 1, doc. 173.

102. Johns 1997, 192.

103. Bundy to LBJ, "Alternative Public Positions for U.S. on Southeast Asia for the Period July 1–November 15," June 10, 1964, *FRUS 1964–1968*, vol. 1, doc. 211.

104. Summary Record of Meeting, June 10, 1964, *FRUS 1964–1968*, vol. 1, doc. 210.

105. Bundy memo, "Elements of a Southeast Asian Policy That Does Not Include a Congressional Resolution," June 15, 1964, *FRUS 1964–1968*, vol. 1, doc. 215. For the draft resolution and other planning documents to be discussed at the June 15 meeting, see Bundy to McNamara, June 15, 1954, *FRUS 1964–1968*, vol. 1, doc. 214.

106. Johns 1997, 201.

107. Logevall 1999, 203.

108. Halberstam 1969, 415; Woods 1995, 353.

109. Johns 1997, 205.

110. Bundy consistently argued that the value of a resolution was its international signal. In his memo to Johnson on June 10, for example, he noted that "the great advantages of an early Congressional resolution are international." Bundy to LBJ, "Alternative Public Positions for U.S. on Southeast Asia for the Period July 1–November 15," June 10, 1964.

111. Berinsky 2004, ch. 5.

112. Lerner 1995.

113. Johnson to Rusk, McNamara, and McCone, December 7, 1964, *FRUS 1964–1968*, vol. 1, doc. 440.

114. Schuessler 2015, ch. 3; see also Downes 2011, 81–88.

115. See the discussion in Logevall 1999, 196–203; see also Moïse 1996.

116. Quoted in Logevall 1999, 199.

117. Woods 1995, 348, 353.

118. Downes 2011, 85.

119. On Johnson's attempt to manage consensus in July 1965, see, especially, Berman 1982, ch. 4.

120. Thomson 1973, 102.

121. Bundy to Johnson, July 1, 1965, *FRUS 1964–1968*, vol. 3, doc. 42. David Kaiser notes that while there were other reasons to restrict the meeting, one of them was to keep key Rusk and McNamara subordinates from expressing skepticism in front of Johnson. Kaiser 2000, 460–61.

122. Herring 1996, 27–29.

123. Kaiser 2000, 444–45.

124. McMaster 1997, 275.

125. Downes 2011, 81.

126. Divine 1987, 11.

127. Ibid.

128. Berinsky 2009, 111–12.

129. See, for example, Hallin 1986, 133; Zaller 1992, 189.

130. Small 1988, 53.

131. Fulbright 1979. On the hearings and their minimal effects in the short term, see Small 1988, 78–81.

132. Gaddis 2005.

133. Fry 2010.

134. Zaller 1992, 270–71.

135. Berinsky 2004, ch. 5.

136. Goldberg to Douglas MacArthur II (Assistant Secretary, Congressional Relations, State Department), January 16, 1966, Confidential files, box 71 [1 of 2], "ND 19/CO 312 VIETNAM (Situation in) (January–March 1966)" folder, LBJL, 2.

137. Meeting Notes (prepared by Tom Johnson), Meeting of the President on July 25, 1967, with Senate Committee Chairmen, Tom Johnson's Notes of Meetings file, box 1, "July 25, 1967— 6:10 p.m. Senate Committee Chairmen" folder, LBJL.

138. See, for example, "Fulbright Doubts If He Will Back Aid," Associated Press reprinted in *New York Times,* June 13, 1967.

139. Notes of the President's Meeting with McNamara, Katzenbach, Christian, Rostow, Califano, August 8, 1967, Tom Johnson's Notes of Meetings file, box 1, "August 8, 1967—1:25 p.m. Tuesday Luncheon Group" folder, LBJL, 2–3.

140. See Fry 2002, 283–87.

141. Rovner 2011.

142. Ibid., 66.

143. Ibid., 66. See also Notes on Discussions with President Johnson, April 27, 1967, *FRUS 1964–1968,* vol. 5, doc. 149.

144. Rovner 2011, 67. On the White House pressure, Rovner concludes that Johnson probably did not apply pressure directly, but was aware of the controversy and "probably influenced Helms' judgment by seeking only good news from the field." See ibid., 73–74.

145. Herring 1996, 55.

146. Ibid., 56.

147. Ibid., 57.

148. On the ABM debate in the context of the budget and Vietnam in the final period of the Johnson administration, see Cameron 2018, ch. 3.

149. Herring 1996, 57.

150. Page and Brody 1972, 987.

151. Converse, Miller, Rusk, and Wolfe 1969, 1092.

152. As Johns notes, Nixon never actually said he had a "secret plan," but once it became a political talking point, "he never officially denied having one." Johns 2010, 197–98.

153. Page and Brody 1972, 993–95.

154. Berinsky 2009, 115–18.

155. Johns 2010, 282.

156. On the internal administration debate, as well as GOP divisions in Congress, see ibid., 281–82.

157. Gaddis 2005, 282.

158. Hanhimaki 2003.

159. Johns 2010, 235.

160. Berman 2001, 7–9.

161. Gelb and Betts 1979, 356.

162. Ibid., 356–57.

163. Ibid., 357.

164. Ibid.

165. Snyder 1991, 257.

Chapter Six: The Lebanon Intervention: Elite Constraints on a Small War

1. Howell and Pevehouse 2007, 40–42.

2. Gartner and Segura 1998; see also Mueller 1973, 205–8, on the downward trend in presidential popularity as time goes on.

3. Feaver 2011.

4. Kriner 2010, 200; see also Jentleson 1992, 55–56.

5. Kriner 2010, 203, 213; see also Burk 1999, 66.

6. Foyle 1999, 210.

7. Kriner 2010, 195; see also Howell and Pevehouse 2007, 126–34.

8. Kriner 2010, 195.

9. Ibid.

10. Larson 1996, 48.

11. Howell and Pevehouse 2007.

12. The archival record of the Lebanon case at the Reagan Presidential Library was still only partially opened as of the time of writing. Where possible, I have supplemented with additional material in the James Baker Papers at Princeton University; the Tip O'Neill Papers at Boston College; and material available via the State Department's Virtual Reading Room.

13. Yarhi-Milo 2018, 173.

14. On Reagan and reputation, see Ibid., ch. 7.

15. Ibid., 180.

16. Ibid., 183.

17. "Failure in Lebanon," *Washington Post*, February 17, 1984.

18. Gans 2019, 67–73.

19. Ronald Reagan, "Address to the Veterans of Foreign Wars Convention in Chicago," August 18, 1980, available at Peters and Woolley, The American Presidency Project, https://www.presidency.ucsb.edu/documents/address-the-veterans-foreign-wars-convention-chicago; see also Gans 2019, 71.

20. For a useful overview, see "The Reagan Administration and Lebanon, 1981–1984," *Milestones in the History of U.S. Foreign Relations, 1981–1988*, Office of the Historian, State Department, https://history.state.gov/milestones/1981-1988/lebanon.

21. For an account of the US Marines' missions in Lebanon (1982–84), see Frank 1987.

22. Howell Raines, "Reagan Agrees 'in Principle' to Troops for P.L.O. Escort," *New York Times*, July 6, 1982.

23. Bernard Gwertzman, "Key Lawmakers Express Doubts about the Plan," *New York Times,* July 7, 1982.

24. Mary McGrory, "Playing Rodney Dangerfield in the Mideast Has Its Hazards," *Washington Post,* July 8, 1982.

25. Zablocki to Reagan, July 6, 1982, White House Office of Records Management (WHORM) Subject file ND (National Security–Defense), box ND 006 (274760)—ND 007 (09239), "ND007 092397" folder, Ronald Reagan Presidential Library (RRPL).

26. Duberstein to Clark, July 8, 1982, WHORM Subject file ND, box ND 006 (274760)—ND 007 (09239), "ND007 092397" folder, RRPL.

27. Kimmitt to Clark, "Zablocki Letter on War Powers," July 19, 1982, WHORM Subject file ND, box ND 006 (274760)—ND 007 (09239), "ND007 092397" folder, RRPL. Duberstein concurred that "we wish to say as little on this subject as possible." Duberstein to Clark, "Zablocki Letter on War Powers," July 21, 1982, WHORM Subject file ND, box ND 006 (274760)—ND 007 (09239), "ND007 092397" folder, RRPL.

28. Howell and Pevehouse 2007, 128.

29. For useful overviews, see Howell and Pevehouse 2007, 126–34; Kriner 2010, ch. 5.

30. Kriner 2010, 203, 213.

31. Ibid., 201–2; see also Howell and Pevehouse 2007, 129.

32. This is the general picture in both Kriner 2010 and Howell and Pevehouse 2007.

33. Yarhi-Milo 2018, 118–19.

34. Cannon 2000, 391–92.

35. George C. Wilson, "Even If Marines Had Stayed, Weinberger Doubts Killings Could Have Been Prevented," *Washington Post,* September 21, 1982.

36. Bernard Gwertzman, "U.S. Irked as Israel Seems to Balk at Pullout of Troops from Beirut," *New York Times,* September 22, 1982.

37. Michael Getler and John M. Goshko, "Britain and Netherlands Express Interest in Sending Troops to Join Force in Beirut," *Washington Post,* September 25, 1982.

38. "The President's News Conference," September 28, 1982, RRPL, https://www.reaganlibrary.gov/archives/speech/presidents-news-conference-3.

39. See, for example, Bernard Weinraub, "Reagan Decides to Send Habib Back to Mideast," *New York Times,* November 12, 1982.

40. "Weinberger Reluctant on Bigger Beirut Force," *New York Times,* October 29, 1982.

41. Deering and Sigelman 2011.

42. Kenneth Dam diary, October 13, 1982, State Department Virtual Reading Room (SDVRR), doc. no. C05180935.

43. Dam diary, October 21, 1982, SDVRR, doc. no. C05182933.

44. Dam to Reagan, "Lebanon Negotiations: Next Steps," February 3, 1983, SDVRR (no document number available).

45. National Security Planning Group (NSPG) 51 Summary of Decisions, February 4, 1983, reprinted in Saltoun-Ebin 2012, 183–84.

46. Bremer to Clark, "Offering Israel an Expanded MNF: Briefing Members of Congress," February 5, 1983, Robert Lilac files, box 6, "AT Lebanon (January 1983–April 1983)" folder, RRPL.

47. Talking Points, attachment to Bremer to Clark, February 5, 1983, 2.

48. Fairbanks to Shultz, "Briefing of Senator Baker," February 9, 1983, Robert Lilac files, box 6, "AT Lebanon (January 1983–April 1983)" folder, RRPL.

49. Draper/Habib to Shultz, March 31, 1983, SDVRR, doc. 83TELAV04377.

50. Kemp, Dur, and Teicher to Clark, "Lebanon: Telephone Call to Secretary Weinberger," March 30, 1983, Near East and South Asia Affairs Directorate, NSC: Records files, RAC box 8, "Lebanon: March 1983–April 1983 (03/30/1983–04/06/1983)" folder, RRPL.

51. "Talking Points for Judge Clark's Call to Secretary Weinberger," March 30, 1982, NSC: Records files, RAC box 8, "Lebanon: March 1983–April 1983 (03/30/1983–04/06/1983)" folder, RRPL (emphasis in original).

52. Handwritten addendum on "Talking Points for Judge Clark's Call to Secretary Weinberger," March 30, 1982, Near East and South Asia Affairs Directorate, NSC: Records files, RAC box 8, "Lebanon: March 1983–April 1983 (03/30/1983–04/06/1983)" folder, RRPL.

53. Clark to Shultz, "Lebanon: Next Steps," undated memorandum, Near East and South Asia Affairs Directorate, NSC: Records files, RAC box 8, "Lebanon: March 1983–April 1983 (03/30/1983–04/06/1983)" folder, RRPL.

54. Draft Demarche, undated, Near East and South Asia Affairs Directorate, NSC: Records files, RAC box 8, "Lebanon: March 1983–April 1983 (03/30/1983–04/06/1983)" folder, RRPL.

55. Gans 2019, 71–74.

56. McFarlane to Clark, "Problems Ahead," December 17, 1982, Robert McFarlane files, RAC box 12, "Sensitive Chron—1982 (2)" folder, RRPL.

57. Dam diary, April 28, 1983, SDVRR, doc. C05181867.

58. "Defense, 1983 Overview," *CQ Almanac 1983*, 39th ed., Congressional Quarterly, 1984, 171–75. CQ Almanac Online Edition, library.cqpress.com/cqalmanac/cqal83-1198573.

59. Turner to Baker, "Senator Warren Rudman's (R-New Hampshire) Comments on the MX," June 29, 1983, James A. Baker files, box 4, "White House Staff Memoranda—Legislative Affairs January 1983–June 1983 (1)" folder, RRPL.

60. Lilac to Clark, "Weekly Report," Robert Lilac files, box 6, "AT Lebanon (January 1983–April 1983)" folder, RRPL.

61. See "Agreed Language on MNF," attachment to McFarlane to Hill, April 20, 1983, Robert Lilac files, box 6, "AT Lebanon (January 1983–April 1983)" folder, RRPL.

62. Gans 2019, 74–75.

63. McFarlane to Clark, undated cover note, with copy of Habib to State, "Habib/Draper Mission: Where We Stand after Initial Rounds in Lebanon and Israel," February 15, 1983, William Clark files, box 4, "Lebanon: Middle East" folder, RRPL.

64. Reagan note on copy of McFarlane to Clark, September 5, 1983, "McFarlane/Fairbanks Mission—Worst Case Strategy for Lebanon," William Clark files, box 4, "Lebanon" folder, RRPL; see also Gans 2019, 75.

65. Reagan diary entry, September 7, 1983, in Brinkley 2007, 177.

66. Reagan diary entry, September 11, 1983, in Brinkley 2007, 179.

67. John M. Goshko and Helen Dewar, "U.S. Rules Out Any Expansion of Marine Force; Questions on Hill Review Turned Aside by Shultz," *Washington Post*, September 1, 1983.

68. Duberstein, "Meeting with Bipartisan Congressional Leadership," September 3, 1983, Richard G. Darman files, box 28, "[Presidential Briefing Papers: 08/15/1983–09/05/1983]" folder, RRPL.

69. "Talking Points on Lebanon," attachment to Duberstein, "Meeting with Bipartisan Congressional Leadership."

70. Reagan diary entry, September 4, 1983, in Brinkley 2007, 176.

71. "A Reluctant Congress Adopts Lebanon Policy." *CQ Almanac 1983*, 39th ed., Congressional Quarterly, 1984, 113–23. CQ Almanac Online Edition, library.cqpress.com/cqalmanac /cqal83-1198422. See also Richard Halloran, "U.S. Weighing Policy Options in Beirut Clash," *New York Times*, September 8, 1983.

72. Darman, "LSG Agenda: Lebanon," September 9, 1983, Baker Papers, MC197, box 60, folder 4: "Legis. Strat—Gen., 1983," Mudd Manuscript Library, Princeton University. On the back of this document, Baker wrote extensive handwritten notes about the various options, including that if the administration didn't report under the hostilities provision, "they'll force it on you."

73. Baker notes on Senior Staff Meeting Agenda, September 19, 1983, Baker Papers, MC197, box 74, folder 3: "Agendas, 1983 (2 of 2)," Mudd Manuscript Library, Princeton University.

74. Howe to Dam, "Alternative Scenarios for Departure of the MNF from Lebanon," January 5, 1983, SDVRR, doc. 9302566.

75. "Reluctant Congress Adopts Lebanon Policy."

76. Reagan diary entry, September 30, 1983, in Brinkley 2007, 184.

77. Foyle 1999, 206; Brinkley 2007.

78. E. J. Dionne Jr., "Some Marines 'Feel Helpless,'" *New York Times*, September 7, 1983.

79. Evans and Potter 2019.

80. Gans 2019, 78.

81. McFarlane to White House, September 11, 1983, William Clark Papers, box 4, "Lebanon" folder, RRPL.

82. Lou Cannon and George C. Wilson, "Reagan Authorizes Marines to Call In Beirut Air Strikes," *Washington Post*, September 13, 1983.

83. White House News Summary, September 13, 1983 (summarizing evening news of September 12), William Clark Papers, box 4, "Lebanon" folder, RRPL.

84. Gans 2019, 78.

85. Reagan to William French Smith, September 14, 1983, William Clark Papers, box 4, "Lebanon" folder, RRPL. Shultz and Baker's threats to resign reported in Don Oberdorfer and David Hoffman, "Shultz Sparked Shift on Polygraph Policy," *Washington Post*, December 22, 1985. Reagan noted the leak in his diary on September 14 as "the latest violation of classified info" that he'd "ordered Justice to investigate." Reagan diary entry, in in Brinkley 2007, 179.

86. White House News Summary, September 13, 1983.

87. Halloran, "U.S. Weighing Policy Options in Beirut Clash."

88. Eric Pace, "U.S. Ships Enter Lebanon Fighting Shelling Hill Site," *New York Times*, September 9, 1983, https://timesmachine.nytimes.com/timesmachine/1983/09/09/154025.html ?pageNumber=8.

89. Cannon and Wilson, "Reagan Authorizes Marines to Call In Beirut Air Strikes."

90. See Baker's comments in Hedrick Smith, "Reagan Upgrading Lebanon Presence." *New York Times*, September 13, 1983.

91. James Baker's handwritten notes on the back of the September 9 Darman memo noted that the "uncertainty this created would encourage Syrians to move + prevent negotiated a negotiated settlement." Darman, "LSG Agenda: Lebanon," September 9, 1983.

92. "Reluctant Congress Adopts Lebanon Policy."

93. Kriner 2010, 205–8.

94. Shultz 1993, 226; see also Cannon 2000, 348.

95. "Reluctant Congress Adopts Lebanon Policy."

96. Shultz 1993, 226.

97. Duberstein briefing memo, "Meeting with Republican Congressional Leadership," September 28, 1983, Office of the President, Presidential Briefing Papers, box 35, "09/28/1983 (case file 189128)" folder, RRPL.

98. Duberstein briefing memo, "Meeting with Senators Howard Baker (R-Tennessee), Charles Percy (R-Illinois), and Larry Pressler (R–South Dakota)," September 28, 1983, Office of the President, Presidential Briefing Papers, box 35, "09/28/1983 (case file 189128)" folder, RRPL.

99. Duberstein briefing memo, "Meeting with Select Republican House Members," September 28, 1983, Office of the President, Presidential Briefing Papers, box 35, "09/28/1983 (case file 189128)" folder, RRPL.

100. Louis Harris, "Doubts Arise over U.S. Military Involvement in Lebanon," Harris Survey, September 22, 1983, copy in Tip O'Neill Papers, box 29, folder 7: "War Powers Act—Drafts and Correspondence, 1982–1983," John J. Burns Library, Boston College, 2.

101. Weinberger to McFarlane, October 21, 1983, Executive Secretariat, NSC: Country file, box 41, "Lebanon Chronology (1)" folder, RRPL, 1.

102. O'Donnell to O'Neill, "Questions for Ad Hoc Committee Briefing, Lebanon," October 24, 1983, Tip O'Neill Papers, box 30, folder 3: "Lebanon Resolution, 1983–1984," John J. Burns Library, Boston College.

103. David Rogers, "Congress Warns Reagan to Show Progress on Lebanon or Face Crumbling Support," *Wall Street Journal*, December 14, 1983; see also Howell and Pevehouse 2007, 132; Reeves 2005, 198, 202.

104. Quoted in Steven V. Roberts, "Legislators Say Reagan Must Reassess U.S. Role," *New York Times*, October 24, 1983.

105. Steven V. Roberts, "Some Democrats Want Marines Out," *New York Times*, October 25, 1983.

106. Kriner 2010, 209–10.

107. Notably, Weinberger himself used Lebanon as a bargaining chip, raising the need to "stay the course" in White House meetings in which he faced resistance to his plans for a larger military budget (see James F. Clarity and Warren Weaver Jr., "Briefing," *New York Times*, October 27, 1983). This bargaining suggests the possibility of a side payment to keep Weinberger on board, however reluctantly, with White House policy.

108. Evans and Potter 2019.

109. Dam diary entry, December 21, 1983, SDVRR, doc. no. C05182977.

110. Hedrick Smith, "Lebanon Rekindles U.S. Foreign Policy Troubles," *New York Times*, December 11, 1983.

111. The meeting agenda noted that "news stories say the Administration is thinking [of] moving the Marines to a new, more defensible location." Baker notes on Senior Staff Meeting Agenda, December 8, 1983, Baker Papers, MC197, box 74, folder 3: "Agendas, 1983 (2 of 2)," Mudd Manuscript Library, Princeton University.

112. McFarlane to Reagan, undated memorandum in advance of January 3, 1984, NSPG meeting on Next Steps in Lebanon, Executive Secretariat, NSC: Country file, box 41, "Lebanon Chronology (2)" folder, RRPL.

113. NSC Non Paper: "Next Steps in Lebanon," undated paper prepared in advance of January 3, 1984, NSPG meeting on Next Steps in Lebanon, Executive Secretariat, NSC: Country file, box 41, "Lebanon Chronology (2)" folder, RRPL, 1.

114. Oglesby to Baker, "Hill Attitude Regarding Lebanon," January 3, 1984, James Baker files, box 8, "Legislative Affairs (7)" folder, RRPL, 1 (emphasis in Baker's original handwritten comments).

115. See correspondence in "Folder 1: Speaker's Ad Hoc Lebanon Monitoring Group, 1983–84," box 30, Tip O'Neill Papers.

116. Oglesby to Baker, "Hill Attitude Regarding Lebanon," January 3, 1984, 1 (emphasis in Baker's original handwritten comments).

117. Baker notes on Senior Staff Meeting Agenda, December 19, 1983, Baker Papers, MC197, box 74, folder 3: "Agendas, 1983 (2 of 2)," Mudd Manuscript Library, Princeton University.

118. See National Security Decision Directive (NSDD) 111, "Next Steps towards Progress in Lebanon and the Middle East," October 28, 1983, White House and Staff and Office files, Executive Secretariat, NSC Records, NSDDs, box 91291, "NSDD 111 (1)" folder, RRPL; for the JCS objections and proposed amendments to the rules of engagement, see Vessey to McFarlane, "Draft NSDD on Lebanon," December 3, 1983, Executive Secretariat, NSC: Country file, box 41, "Lebanon Chronology (2)" folder, RRPL.

119. Gans 2019, 81.

120. Taubman 2023, 245; see also 246–48.

121. Talking Points for Robert McFarlane, National Security Planning Group Meeting, December 1, 1983, Executive Secretariat, NSC: Country file, box 41, "Lebanon Chronology (2)" folder, RRPL, 5.

122. McFarlane to Reagan, Talking Points for NSPG on the Next Steps in Lebanon, January 3, 1984 (with inclusion of draft talking points for Reagan's use at Tab A), Executive Secretariat, NSC: Country file, box 41, "Lebanon Chronology (2)" folder, RRPL (emphasis in original). McFarlane's cover note sharing the proposed talking points for the president to use indicates that Reagan approved them.

123. Kriner 2010, 224.

124. Cannon 2000, 397–99.

125. Quoted in Steven R. Weisman, "The White House: Dealing with a Period of Foreign Policy Reverses," *New York Times*, February 20, 1984.

126. Jentleson 1992, 58.

Chapter Seven: Iraq, Afghanistan, and the Forever Insiders' Game

1. See, respectively, Mearsheimer 2018; Miller 2010; Walt 2018. For a different assessment that nonetheless focuses on the shared views of a few policy makers as central to the Bush administration's choice to intervene in Iraq, see Flibbert 2006.

2. Lake 2010/2011; Johnson 2004.

3. Butt 2019, 251.

4. Lebovic 2019, 129–32.

5. Jacobson 2010.

6. Gadarian 2010.

7. Mueller 2021.

8. Packer 2005, 46.

9. Ken Adelman, "Cakewalk in Iraq," *Washington Post*, February 13, 2002.

10. Mueller 2021.

11. Caroline Smith and James M. Lindsay, "Rally 'round the Flag: Opinion in the United States before and after the Iraq War," Brookings, June 1, 2003, https://www.brookings.edu /articles/rally-round-the-flag-opinion-in-the-united-states-before-and-after-the-iraq-war/.

12. David W. Moore and Frank Newport, "Powell 'Bounce' Fades," Gallup News, February 21, 2003, https://news.gallup.com/poll/7843/powell-bounce-fades.aspx.

13. Smith and Lindsay, "Rally 'round the Flag."

14. Frank Newport, "International Opinion on War in Iraq, American Public Opinion on Iraq," Gallup News, February 18, 2003, https://news.gallup.com/poll/7834/international -opinion-war-iraq-american-public-opinion-iraq.aspx.

15. Berinsky 2009.

16. Mueller 2021, 12, referencing data from Gallup, "In Depth: Iraq," https://news.gallup.com /poll/1633/iraq.aspx.

17. Mueller 2021; Gershkoff and Kushner 2005.

18. Feldman, Huddy, and Marcus 2015.

19. Gershkoff and Kushner 2005, 529.

20. Berinsky 2004, ch. 5. In later work on the Iraq War, however, Berinsky argues that that the war's association with Bush was enough to turn Democratic voters against it, even without cues. See Berinsky 2009, 109.

21. Baum and Potter 2015.

22. Strong 2017, 38–42.

23. Lake 2010/2011; Saunders 2017.

24. I explore this comparison in Saunders 2017.

25. On the hazards of occupation, see especially Edelstein 2008.

26. The ad, titled "War with Iraq Is *Not* in America's National Interest," appeared on the op-ed page of the *New York Times* on September 26, 2002. Thirty-three scholars of international relations signed. For a copy, see the website of Shibley Telhami, one of the ad's organizers, https://sadat.umd.edu/sites/sadat.umd.edu/files/iraq_war_ad_2002_2.pdf.

27. Feldman, Huddy, and Marcus 2015.

28. J. Baker, Hamilton, Eagleburger, Jordan, Meese, O'Connor, Panetta, Perry, Robb, and Simpson 2006.

29. Payne 2020, 180–85.

30. Quoted in Ricks 2007, 63.

31. On the long shadow of Cleland's electoral defeat and the Chambliss attack ad, see Katharine Q. Seelye, "Max Cleland, Vietnam Veteran and Former Senator, Dies at 79," *New York Times*, November 9, 2021.

32. See, among many others, Packer 2005; P. Baker 2013; Draper 2020.

33. Draper 2020, 222.

34. Ibid., 222–23.

35. On Nunn's regret over his vote, see David Pace, "Nunn Regrets Vote on Gulf War," *Washington Post*, December 26, 1996; see also Ricks 2007, 62.

36. On the sequence of events, see Draper 2020, 227–28.

37. Quoted in Carl Hulse, "Endorsement by Gephardt Helps Propel Resolution," *New York Times*, October 3, 2002.

38. Ibid. See also Western 2005, 207–8.

39. Nick Anderson, "Liberal Gephardt Sides with Bush on Iraq War Resolution," *Los Angeles Times*, October 3, 2002. On costly congressional signals, see Howell and Kriner 2007, 122–31.

40. Jim VandeHei, "Daschle Angered by Bush Statement," *Washington Post*, September 26, 2002.

41. Gary Hart, "Note to Democrats: Get a Defense Policy," *New York Times*, October 3, 2002.

42. Draper 2020, 225–30.

43. Mann 2004, 264–70.

44. Steven Mufson, "Scowcroft Urges Restraint against Iraq," *Washington Post*, August 5, 2002.

45. Quoted in P. Baker 2013, 208.

46. Ibid.

47. Ibid., 241.

48. Quoted in ibid.

49. Quoted in ibid., 242.

50. Woodward 2004, 291.

51. P. Baker 2013, 220–21.

52. Eric Schmitt, "Army Chief Raises Estimate of G.I.'s Needed in Postwar Iraq," *New York Times*, February 25, 2003.

53. Quoted in Packer 2005, 117.

54. Ibid., 117. Shinseki was not the only one: Lawrence Lindsey, a White House economic adviser, was forced out after predicting that the war would cost far more than the administration's estimates. Ibid., 116.

55. A particularly useful account of the politicization of the Iraq intelligence is Rovner 2011, ch. 7.

56. Quoted in P. Baker 2013, 221.

57. "Factbox: Iraq War; Quotes from the Conflict and Its Aftermath," Reuters, March 15, 2023, https://www.reuters.com/world/middle-east/iraq-war-quotes-conflict-its-aftermath-2023-03-15/.

58. "National Strategy for Victory in Iraq," National Security Council, November 2005, 1–2, https://permanent.fdlp.gov/lps65388/ADA442621.pdf.

59. Scott Shane, "Bush's Speech on Iraq War Echoes Voice of an Analyst," *New York Times*, December 4, 2005.

60. Quoted in Sayle, Engel, Brands, and Inboden 2019, 33.

61. Woodward 2008, 189–90.

62. Ibid., 193.

63. Ibid.

64. Sam Stein, "Remembering the 'Murthquake': When John Murtha Took On the Iraq War," *Huffington Post*, April 10, 2010, https://www.huffpost.com/entry/remembering-the-murthquak_n_454182.

65. Eric Schmitt, "Fast Withdrawal of G.I.'s Is Urged by Key Democrat," *New York Times*, November 18, 2005.

66. Ibid.

67. Stein, "Remembering the 'Murthquake.'"

68. Woodward 2008, 125–27.

69. Quoted in Sayle, Engel, Brands, and Inboden, 36.

70. P. Baker 2013, 430.

71. Ibid., 430–31.

72. Jeffrey M. Jones, "Basic Attitudes toward Iraq War Slightly More Positive," Gallup, December 14, 2005, https://news.gallup.com/poll/20455/basic-attitudes-toward-iraq-war-slightly-more-positive.aspx.

73. Ibid.

74. Adam Nagourney, "Democratic Leaders Ask Bush to Redeploy Troops to Iraq," *New York Times*, August 1, 2006; Adam Nagourney and Jim Rutenberg, "Tables Turned for the G.O.P. over Iraq Issue," *New York Times*, October 19, 2006.

75. Quoted in P. Baker 2013, 360.

76. Ibid., 380.

77. Kriner 2010, 282–83.

78. Bush 2010, 355. On the surge decision, see Ricks 2009; Lebovic 2019, 93–104; Sayle, Engel, Brands, and Inboden 2019.

79. Payne 2020, 180–85.

80. Bush 2010, 375.

81. See, for example, David S. Cloud, Eric Schmitt, and Thom Shanker, "Rumsfeld Faces Growing Revolt by Retired Generals," *New York Times*, April 13, 2006; see also Michael Duffy, "The Revolt of the Generals," *Time*, April 16, 2006. On the "revolt of the generals" as an echo of a prior incident, the "revolt of the admirals" during the Truman administration, see Feaver 2011, 90n7.

82. Betts 1977, 71.

83. Feaver 2011, 113.

84. Woodward 2008, 286–89; Feaver 2011, 107. Three NSC officials who were instrumental in the "surge," Hadley, Meghan O'Sullivan, and Feaver, later wrote that this increase in "end strength" of the Army and Marine Corps had already been analyzed "months earlier" as a possibility to offer to the service chiefs. See Hadley, O'Sullivan, and Feaver 2019, 222.

85. Payne interview with Casey, in Payne 2020, 187.

86. Feaver 2011, 88.

87. David Stout, "Slow Progress Being Made in Iraq, Petraeus Tells Congress," *New York Times*, September 10, 2007.

88. Biddle, Friedman, and Shapiro 2012, 10.

89. Ibid., 23–35.

90. Preston 2019, 257.

91. Ibid., 258.

92. Rovner 2019, 297.

93. Preston 2019, 257.

94. Gillian Brockell, "She was the Only Member of Congress to Vote against War in Afghanistan. Some Called Her a Traitor," *Washington Post*, August 17, 2021.

95. Butt 2019, 270–72.

96. Lebovic 2019, 145.

97. Kriner 2010, 34.

98. Ibid.

99. For an overview of the 2009 Afghanistan debate and decision see Lebovic 2019, 145–58; see also Woodward 2010; Mann 2012, chs. 9–10; Sanger 2012, ch. 2; Marsh 2014.

100. Kaplan 2013, 300–302.

101. Jacobson 2010, fig. 5; see also CNN/ORC Poll and AP-GfK Poll data, http://www.pollingreport.com/afghan.htm.

102. Jacobson 2010, 592–94.

103. Polling data at http://www.pollingreport.com/afghan2.htm, especially FOX / Opinion Dynamics Poll, November 17–18, 2009.

104. Tyndall Report Year in Review 2009, http://tyndallreport.com/yearinreview2009/.

105. Quoted in Mann 2012, 127. On the troop increases in spring 2009, see Jim Garamone, "Press Secretary Cites Candor on Afghan Troops Levels," American Forces Press Service, October 15, 2009, https://www.army.mil/article/28781/press_secretary_cites_candor_on_afghan_troop_levels.

106. See, for example, Bob Dreyfuss, "The Generals' Revolt," *Rolling Stone*, October 28, 2009.

107. Woodward 2010, 157–58, 172–73.

108. Woodward 2010, chs. 15–16.

109. Mann 2012, 135.

110. Kaplan 2013, 309.

111. Quoted in Woodward 2010, 304.

112. Mann 2012, 138.

113. Woodward 2010, 304.

114. Peter Baker, "How Obama Came to Plan for 'Surge' in Afghanistan," *New York Times*, December 5, 2009.

115. Woodward 2010, 229, 325–27.

116. Feaver 2011, 123.

117. Quoted in P. Baker, "How Obama Came to Plan for 'Surge' in Afghanistan."

118. Michael D. Shear and Paul Kane, "Obama and Fellow Democrats at Odds about Troop Increase for Afghanistan," *Washington Post*, November 26, 2009.

119. Woodward 2010, 336.

120. Marsh 2014, 283–84.

121. Woodward 2010, 302.

122. Ibid., 326.

123. Jacobson 2010, 603.

124. Gates 2014.

125. Michael R. Gordon, Eric Schmitt, and Maggie Haberman, "Trump Settles on Afghan Strategy Expected to Raise Troop Levels," *New York Times*, August 20, 2017.

126. Peter Baker, Mujib Mashal, and Michael Crowley, "How Trump's Plan to Secretly Meet with the Taliban Came Together, and Fell Apart," *New York Times*, September 8, 2019.

127. Lindsay Maizland, "U.S.-Taliban Peace Deal: What to Know," Council on Foreign Relations Backgrounder, March 2, 2020, https://www.cfr.org/backgrounder/us-taliban-peace-deal-agreement-afghanistan-war.

128. Jessica L. P. Weeks and Michaela Mattes, "Trump Wants a Deal with the Taliban. Will It Hurt Him at Home?," *Washington Post, Monkey Cage* blog, February 29, 2020, https://www.washingtonpost.com/politics/2020/02/29/trump-wants-deal-with-taliban-will-it-hurt-him-home/.

129. Jennifer Steinhauer, "Michèle Flournoy Again Finds Her Shot at the Top Pentagon Job Elusive," *New York Times*, December 8, 2020.

130. Missy Ryan and Karen DeYoung, "Biden Will Withdraw All U.S. Forces from Afghanistan by Sept. 11, 2021," *Washington Post*, April 13, 2021.

131. Paul Staniland, "US Public Opinion on the Afghanistan Withdrawal?," September 7, 2021, https://paulstaniland.com/2021/09/07/us-public-opinion-on-the-afghanistan-withdrawal/.

132. Daniel Drezner, "Biden's Team of Non-rivals," *Washington Post*, September 1, 2021.

133. Gallup Presidential Approval Ratings—Joe Biden, https://news.gallup.com/poll/329384/presidential-approval-ratings-joe-biden.aspx.

134. Amy B. Wang, "Biden Signs Sweeping Bill to Tackle Climate Change, Lower Health-Care Costs," *Washington Post*, August 16, 2022.

135. Biden authorized six thousand troops for the specific purpose of assisting in securing the airport and facilitating the evacuation mission, but did not extend the mission past August 31.

136. Joseph R. Biden, Statement on the Situation in Afghanistan, August 14, 2021, available at Peters and Woolley, The American Presidency Project, https://www.presidency.ucsb.edu/node/352031.

137. Joseph R. Biden, Remarks on the Situation in Afghanistan, August 16, 2021, available at Peters and Woolley, The American Presidency Project, https://www.presidency.ucsb.edu/node/352279.

138. For an overview, see Jonathan Swan and Zachary Basu, "Trump's War with His Generals," *Axios*, May 16, 2021, https://www.axios.com/2021/05/16/off-the-rails-trump-military-withdraw-afghanistan.

139. Michael Tesler, "Trump's Base Did Not Elect Him to Withdraw Troops from Syria and Afghanistan," *Washington Post, Monkey Cage* blog, January 4, 2019, https://www.washingtonpost.com/news/monkey-cage/wp/2019/01/04/no-trumps-base-did-not-elect-him-to-withdraw-troops-from-syria-and-afghanistan.

140. For an overview of these events, including Trump's November 2020 order that broke in the press at the time and was later confirmed by the January 6 committee, see Swan and Basu, "Trump's War with His Generals"; see also Zachary Basu, "Jan. 6 Panel: Trump Ordered Large-Scale U.S. Troops Withdrawals after Election," *Axios*, October 13, 2022, https://www.axios.com/2022/10/13/january-6-trump-us-troops-withdrawal.

141. Lawrence Hurley and David Morgan, "Trump Assails Biden for Afghanistan 'Humiliation,'" Reuters, August 22, 2021, https://www.reuters.com/world/us/trump-assails-biden-afghanistan-humiliation-2021-08-22/.

142. Reid J. Epstein and Catie Edmondson, "On Afghanistan, G.O.P. Assails the Pullout It Had Supported under Trump," *New York Times*, September 1, 2021.

143. Jonathan Karl, "Former Trump Officials Praise Biden for Carrying Out 'Trump-Biden Withdrawal' from Afghanistan," ABC News, September 3, 2021, https://abcnews.go.com/Politics/trump-officials-praise-biden-carrying-trump-biden-withdrawal/story?id=79794652.

144. Helene Cooper and Eric Schmitt, "Military Officials Say They Urged Biden against Afghanistan Withdrawal," *New York Times*, September 28, 2021.

145. Julian E. Barnes, Thomas Gibbons-Neff, and Eric Schmitt, "Officials Try to Sway Biden Using Intelligence on Potential for Taliban Takeover of Afghanistan," *New York Times*, March 26, 2021.

146. On Obama's 2015 reversal on withdrawing troops from Afghanistan, see Matthew Rosenberg and Michael D. Shear, "In Reversal, Obama Says U.S. Soldiers Will Stay in Afghanistan to 2017," *New York Times*, October 15, 2015.

Chapter Eight: Conclusion

1. Schultz 2005; Trager and Vavreck 2011; Mattes and Weeks 2019.

2. Trager and Vavreck 2011.

3. On the role of experience, see Saunders 2017.

4. On polarization and US foreign policy, see Schultz 2017; Myrick 2021.

5. Jervis 1980.

6. McCarty 2019, 25–31.

7. Ibid., 17–18.

8. Catie Edmondson, "On Ukraine, McConnell Tries to Show the World This Isn't Trump's G.O.P.," *New York Times*, May 20, 2022.

9. Schultz 2005, 8–10; Cukierman and Tommasi 1998, 192.

10. Schultz 2017.

11. Kreps, Saunders, and Schultz 2018.

12. Goldgeier and Saunders 2018.

13. Lindsay 1992–93, 613–16; Howell and Pevehouse 2007, 115.

14. Schultz 2001a.

15. Ahler and Broockman 2018.

16. On the "blob," see Rhodes 2018, 366–67; Porter 2018; Walt 2018.

17. Groupthink, while often used as a shorthand for shared ideas, refers to a specific set of pressures for acceptance in a group. See Hart 1991.

18. Tetlock 2005.

19. Jervis 1976, ch. 4; see also Hafner-Burton, Hughes, and Victor 2013; Saunders 2022.

20. Baum and Potter 2015.

21. Fearon 1994.

22. See Schultz 2001a, 7–10.

23. Schultz 2001a, 18–19.

24. Weeks 2008, 43–44.

25. Slantchev's model of democratic audience costs, for example, assumes that "information is decisive" and that "no group of citizens can be bought off by selective disbursement of private or public goods." Slantchev 2006, 454.

26. Levendusky and Horowitz 2012.

27. Vreeland and Dreher 2014, 56–57; Kreps, Saunders, and Schultz 2018, 491.

28. For a formal treatment, see Saunders and Wolford, n.d.

29. Large side payments can signal how serious the leader is about fighting, reassuring those who doubt the leader's motives; but such arguments depend on the free flow of information

among relevant elites. For a discussion in the context of treaty ratification, see Kreps, Saunders, and Schultz 2018, 491.

30. Leaders may or may not prefer the theoretically optimal military strategy. If they do, they may have to compromise on a suboptimal strategy; if they are inclined to support suboptimal strategies (to keep costs down, for example), they may compromise with elites who are pushing for a better strategy, but still end up with a suboptimal approach.

31. Mueller 1973, 205–8.

32. Baum and Groeling 2010, ch. 7.

33. Ken Adelman, "Cakewalk in Iraq," *Washington Post*, February 13, 2002.

34. See especially Gelb and Betts 1979.

35. Feaver 2011.

36. Although some arguments suggest right-leaning governments fight longer (Koch and Sullivan 2010), this prediction is that war duration will be u-shaped for hawks, i.e., shorter or longer wars.

37. Kant 1970, 100.

38. Lippmann 1922; Morgenthau and Thompson 1985, 164–69.

39. Kant 1970, 101.

40. Ferejohn and Rosenbluth 2008, 7.

41. Kane and Patapan 2012, 14–19.

42. Schumpeter 1942, 263.

43. Ibid., 269.

44. Ibid., 270.

45. Ibid., 272.

46. Alvarez, Cheibub, Limongi, and Przeworksi 1996, 7.

47. Ibid., 18–19.

48. For an extended discussion, see Saunders 2022.

49. Tocqueville 1969, 677.

50. Rossiter 1961 (nos. 9 and 10).

51. Moravcsik 2004, 346.

52. Merom 2003.

53. See, respectively, Lyall 2010; Downes 2008.

54. Zaller 1992, ch. 6; Berinsky 2009, 111–18.

55. Schumpeter 1942, 262.

56. Walzer 1970, 234.

BIBLIOGRAPHY

Appendixes

Appendix A. "Qualitative Data for *The Insiders' Game: How Elites Make War and Peace.*" Qualitative Data Repository (QDR) Main Collection. https://doi.org/10.5064/F6XUBRAQ.

Appendix B. "Supplementary Information and Replication Data for *The Insiders' Game: How Elites Make War and Peace.*" Harvard Dataverse. https://doi.org/10.7910/DVN /FHQYWF.

Archival Collections

James A. Baker III Papers, Mudd Manuscript Library, Princeton University

John Foster Dulles Papers, Mudd Manuscript Library, Princeton University

John F. Kennedy Library, Boston, Massachusetts (JFKL)

Lyndon B. Johnson Library, Austin, Texas (LBJL)

Tip O'Neill Papers, Burns Library, Boston College

Ronald Reagan Presidential Library, Simi Valley, California (RRPL)

Harry S. Truman Library, Independence, Missouri (HSTL)

Published Document Collections

Beschloss, Michael R., ed. 1997. *Taking Charge: The Johnson White House Tapes, 1963–1964.* New York: Simon and Schuster.

———. 2001. *Reaching for Glory: Lyndon Johnson's Secret White House Tapes, 1964–1965.* New York: Simon and Schuster.

Ferrell, Robert H. 1991. *Truman in the White House: The Diary of Eben A. Ayers, 1890–1977.* Columbia: University of Missouri Press.

Gravel, Mike, ed. 1971. *The Pentagon Papers: The Defense Department History of United States Decisionmaking on Vietnam,* vols. 1, 2, and 3. Boston: Beacon.

Peters, Gerhard, and John T. Woolley, eds. The American Presidency Project. University of California–Santa Barbara. https://www.presidency.ucsb.edu/.

Presidential Recordings Digital Edition, Miller Center, University of Virginia. https://prde.upress .virginia.edu/.

Statistical Abstract of the United States. Washington, DC: US Department of Commerce, Bureau of the Census.

US Department of State. Various Years. *Foreign Relations of the United States* (*FRUS*). Washington: US Government Printing Office.

US Department of State. Virtual Reading Room. https://foia.state.gov/Search/Search.aspx.

Whitlock, Craig. 2021. *The Afghanistan Papers: A Secret History of the War*. New York: Simon and Schuster.

Books and Articles

Achen, Christopher H., and Larry M. Bartels. 2016. *Democracy for Realists: Why Elections Do Not Produce Responsive Government*. Princeton, NJ: Princeton University Press.

Acheson, Dean. 1987. *Present at the Creation: My Years in the State Department*. New York: W. W. Norton.

Ahler, Douglas J., and David E. Broockman. 2018. "The Delegate Paradox: Why Polarized Politicians Can Represent Citizens Best." *Journal of Politics* 80(4): 1117–33.

Aldrich, John H., Christopher Gelpi, Peter D. Feaver, Jason Reifler, and Kristin Thompson Sharp. 2006. "Foreign Policy and the Electoral Connection." *Annual Review of Political Science* 9:477–502.

Aldrich, John H., John L. Sullivan, and Eugene Borgida. 1989. "Foreign Affairs and Issue Voting: Do Presidential Candidates 'Waltz before a Blind Audience'?" *American Political Science Review* 83(1): 123–41.

Allison, Graham, and Philip Zelikow. 1999. *Essence of Decision: Explaining the Cuban Missile Crisis*. 2nd ed. New York: Longman.

Alvarez, Mike, José Antonio Cheibub, Fernando Limongi, and Adam Przeworksi. 1996. "Classifying Political Regimes." *Studies in Comparative International Development* 31(2): 3–36.

American National Election Studies. 2004 American National Election Study (2004). Codebook variable documentation file VERSION 20050816 (August 16, 2005). Ann Arbor: University of Michigan, Center for Political Studies (producer and distributor). https://electionstudies.org/wp-content/uploads/2018/03/anes_timeseries_2004_vardoc_codebook.pdf.

Ansolabehere, Stephen, Brian F. Schaffner, Samantha Luks, and Marissa Shih. 2008–22. Cooperative Congressional Election Study. Cambridge, MA: Harvard University (producer). http://cces.gov.harvard.edu.

Arena, Philip. 2008. "Success Breeds Success? War Outcomes, Domestic Opposition, and Elections." *Conflict Management and Peace Science* 25(2): 136–51.

Art, Robert J. 1973. "Bureaucratic Politics and American Foreign Policy: A Critique." *Policy Sciences* 4:467–90.

Auerswald, David P., and Stephen M. Saideman. 2014. *NATO in Afghanistan: Fighting Together, Fighting Alone*. Princeton, NJ: Princeton University Press.

Baker, James A., III, Lee H. Hamilton, Lawrence S. Eagleburger, Vernon E. Jordan Jr., Edwin Meese III, Sandra Day O'Connor, Leon F. Panetta, William J. Perry, Charles S. Robb, and Alan K. Simpson. 2006. *The Iraq Study Group Report*. New York: Vintage Books.

Baker, Peter. 2013. *Days of Fire: Bush and Cheney in the White House*. New York: Doubleday.

Barabas, Jason, and Jennifer Jerit. 2010. "Are Survey Experiments Externally Valid?" *American Political Science Review* 104(2): 226–42.

Barnhart, Joslyn N., Robert F. Trager, Elizabeth N. Saunders, and Allan Dafoe. 2020. "The Suffragist Peace." *International Organization* 74(4): 633–70.

Bator, Francis M. 2008. "No Good Choices: LBJ and the Vietnam / Great Society Connection." *Diplomatic History* 32(3): 309–40.

Baum, Matthew A. 2004. "Going Private: Public Opinion, Presidential Rhetoric, and the *Domestic* Politics of Audience Costs in U.S. Foreign Policy Crises." *Journal of Conflict Resolution* 48(5): 603–31.

Baum, Matthew A., and Tim J. Groeling. 2010. *War Stories: The Causes and Consequences of Public Views of War*. Princeton, NJ: Princeton University Press.

Baum, Matthew A., and Philip B. K. Potter. 2008. "The Relationships between Mass Media, Public Opinion, and Foreign Policy: Toward a Theoretical Synthesis." *Annual Review of Political Science* 11:39–65.

———. 2015. *War and Democratic Constraint: How the Public Influences Foreign Policy*. Princeton, NJ: Princeton University Press.

Belknap, George, and Angus Campbell. 1951. "Political Party Identification and Attitudes toward Foreign Policy." *Public Opinion Quarterly* 15(4): 601–23.

Bendor, Jonathan, and Thomas H. Hammond. 1992. "Rethinking Allison's Models." *American Political Science Review* 86(2): 301–22.

Berinsky, Adam J. 2004. *Silent Voices: Public Opinion and Political Participation in America*. Princeton, NJ: Princeton University Press.

———. 2009. *In Time of War: Understanding American Public Opinion from World War II to Iraq*. Chicago: University of Chicago Press.

Berinsky, Adam J., and James N. Druckman. 2007. "Review: Public Opinion Research and Support for the Iraq War." *Public Opinion Quarterly* 71(1): 126–41.

Berinsky, Adam J., Gregory A. Huber, and Gabriel S. Lenz. 2012. "Evaluating Online Labor Markets for Experimental Research: Amazon.com's Mechanical Turk." *Political Analysis* 20(3): 351–68.

Berman, Larry. 1982. *Planning a Tragedy: The Americanization of the War in Vietnam*. New York: W. W. Norton.

———. 2001. *No Peace, No Honor: Nixon, Kissinger, and Betrayal in Vietnam*. New York: Simon and Schuster.

Bertoli, Andrew, Allan Dafoe, and Robert F. Trager. 2019. "Is There a War Party? Party Change, the Left-Right Divide, and International Conflict." *Journal of Conflict Resolution* 63(4): 950–75.

Betts, Richard K. 1977. *Soldiers, Statesmen, and Cold War Crises*. Cambridge, MA: Harvard University Press.

Biddle, Stephen, Jeffrey A. Friedman, and Jacob N. Shapiro. 2012. "Testing the Surge: Why Did Violence Decline in Iraq in 2007?" *International Security* 37(1): 7–40.

Billings-Yun, Melanie. 1988. *Decision against War: Eisenhower and Dien Bien Phu, 1954*. New York: Columbia University Press.

Binder, Sarah. 2015. "The Dysfunctional Congress." *Annual Review of Political Science* 18:85–101.

———. 2017. "Congress and the President: Legislating in Polarized Times." In *Rivals for Power: Presidential-Congressional Relations*, edited by James A. Thurber and Jordan Tama, 23–35. Lanham, MD: Rowman and Littlefield.

Blomstedt, Larry. 2016. *Truman, Congress, and Korea: The Politics of America's First Undeclared War*. Lexington: University Press of Kentucky.

Brands, H. W. 2016. *The General vs. the President: MacArthur and Truman on the Brink of Nuclear War*. New York: Doubleday.

Brinkley, Douglas, ed. 2007. *The Reagan Diaries*. New York: Harper Collins.

Brody, Richard A. 1991. *Assessing the President: The Media, Elite Opinion, and Public Support*. Stanford, CA: Stanford University Press.

Brooks, Risa. 2013. "The Perils of Politics: Why Staying Apolitical Is Good for Both the U.S. Military and the Country." *Orbis* 57(3): 369–79.

———. 2020. "Paradoxes of Professionalism: Rethinking Civil-Military Relations in the United States." *International Security* 44(4): 7–44.

Brown, Jonathan N., and Anthony S. Marcum. 2011. "Avoiding Audience Costs: Domestic Political Accountability and Concessions in Crisis Diplomacy." *Security Studies* 20(2): 141–70.

Brutger, Ryan. 2021. "The Power of Compromise: Proposal Power, Partisanship, and Public Support in International Bargaining." *World Politics* 73(1): 128–66.

Brutger, Ryan, Joshua D. Kertzer, Jonathan Renshon, and Chagai M. Weiss. 2022. *Abstraction in Experimental Design: Testing the Tradeoffs*. Cambridge: Cambridge University Press.

Bueno de Mesquita, Bruce, Alastair Smith, Randolph M. Siverson, and James D. Morrow. 2003. *The Logic of Political Survival*. Cambridge, MA: MIT Press.

Burk, James. 1999. "Public Support for Peacekeeping in Lebanon and Somalia: Assessing the Casualties Hypothesis." *Political Science Quarterly* 114(1): 53–78.

Busby, Joshua W., and Jonathan Monten. 2012. "Republican Elites and Foreign Policy Attitudes." *Political Science Quarterly* 127(1): 105–42.

Bush, George W. 2010. *Decision Points*. New York: Crown.

Butt, Ahsan I. 2019. "Why Did the United States Invade Iraq in 2003?" *Security Studies* 28(2): 250–85.

Calvert, Randall L. 1985. "The Value of Biased Information: A Rational Choice Model of Political Advice." *Journal of Politics* 47(2): 530–55.

Cameron, James. 2018. *The Double Game: The Demise of America's First Missile Defense System and the Rise of Strategic Arms Limitation*. New York: Oxford University Press.

Campbell, Angus, Philip E. Converse, Warren E. Miller, and Donald E. Stokes. 1960. *The American Voter*. New York: Wiley.

Cannon, Lou. 2000. *President Reagan: The Role of a Lifetime*. New York: Public Affairs.

Carson, Austin. 2018. *Secret Wars: Covert Conflict in International Politics*. Princeton, NJ: Princeton University Press.

Casey, Steven. 2005. "Selling NSC-68: The Truman Administration, Public Opinion, and the Politics of Mobilization, 1950–51." *Diplomatic History* 29(4): 655–90.

———. 2008. *Selling the Korean War: Propaganda, Politics, and Public Opinion in the United States, 1950–1953*. New York: Oxford University Press.

Casey, Steven, and William Stueck. 2011. "Reflections on the MacArthur Controversy at Sixty." *Historically Speaking* 12(2): 37–40.

Caverley, Jonathan D. 2014. *Democratic Militarism: Voting, Wealth, and War*. Cambridge: Cambridge University Press.

Cha, Victor D. 2016. *Powerplay: The Origins of the American Alliance System in Asia*. Princeton, NJ: Princeton University Press.

Chapman, Terrence L., and Dan Reiter. 2004. "The United Nations Security Council and the Rally 'round the Flag Effect." *Journal of Conflict Resolution* 48(6): 886–909.

Chen Jian. 2001. *Mao's China and the Cold War*. Chapel Hill: University of North Carolina Press.

Chiozza, Giacomo, and H. E. Goemans. 2004. "International Conflict and the Tenure of Leaders: Is War Still *Ex Post* Inefficient?" *American Journal of Political Science* 48(3): 604–19.

———. 2011. *Leaders and International Conflict*. New York: Cambridge University Press.

Christensen, Thomas J. 1996. *Useful Adversaries: Grand Strategy, Domestic Mobilization, and Sino-American Conflict, 1947–1958*. Princeton, NJ: Princeton University Press.

———. 2011. *Worse Than a Monolith: Alliance Politics and Problems of Coercive Diplomacy in Asia*. Princeton, NJ: Princeton University Press.

Chu, Jonathan A., and Stefano Recchia. 2022. "Does Public Opinion Affect the Preferences of Foreign Policy Leaders? Experimental Evidence from the UK Parliament." *Journal of Politics* 84(3): 1874–77.

Clare, Joe. 2014. "Hawks, Doves, and International Cooperation." *Journal of Conflict Resolution* 58(7): 1311–37.

Cohen, Jeffrey E. 2012. *The President's Legislative Policy Agenda, 1789–2002*. New York: Cambridge University Press.

Cohen, Marty, David Karol, Hans Noel, and John Zaller. 2008. *The Party Decides: Presidential Nominations before and after Reform*. Chicago: University of Chicago Press.

Colgan, Jeff D. 2013. *Petro-Aggression: When Oil Causes War*. New York: Cambridge University Press.

Colgan, Jeff D., and Jessica L. P. Weeks. 2015. "Revolution, Personalist Dictatorships, and International Conflict." *International Organization* 69(1): 163–94.

Converse, Philip E., Warren E. Miller, Jerrold G. Rusk, and Arthur C. Wolfe. 1969. "Continuity and Change in American Politics: Parties and Issues in the 1968 Election." *American Political Science Review* 63(4): 1083–105.

Cox, Gary W. 1997. *Making Votes Count: Strategic Coordination in the World's Electoral Systems*. Cambridge: Cambridge University Press.

Craig, Campbell, and Fredrik Logevall. 2009. *America's Cold War: The Politics of Insecurity*. Cambridge, MA: Belknap Press of Harvard University Press.

Croco, Sarah E. 2015. *Peace at What Price? Leaders and the Domestic Politics of War Termination*. New York: Cambridge University Press.

Croco, Sarah E., Michael J. Hanmer, and Jared A. McDonald. 2021. "At What Cost? Reexamining Audience Costs in Realistic Settings." *Journal of Politics* 83(1): 8–22.

Croco, Sarah E., and Jessica L. P. Weeks. 2016. "War Outcomes and Leader Tenure." *World Politics* 68(4): 577–607.

Cukierman, Alex, and Mariano Tommasi. 1998. "When Does It Take a Nixon to Go to China?" *American Economic Review* 88(1): 180–97.

Cumings, Bruce. 2011. *The Korean War: A History*. New York: Modern Library.

Dafoe, Allan, and Devin Caughey. 2016. "Honor and War: Southern US Presidents and the Effects of Concern for Reputation." *World Politics* 68(2): 341–81.

Dallek, Robert. 1998. *Flawed Giant: Lyndon Johnson and His Times, 1961–1973*. New York: Oxford University Press.

Davenport, Christian. 2007a. *State Repression and the Domestic Democratic Peace*. New York: Cambridge University Press.

Davenport, Christian. 2007b. "State Repression and Political Order." *Annual Review of Political Science* 10:1–23.

Debs, Alexandre, and H. E. Goemans. 2010. "Regime Type, the Fate of Leaders, and War." *American Political Science Review* 104(3): 430–45.

Deering, Christopher J., and Lee Sigelman. 2011. "Who Makes the News? Cabinet Visibility from 1897 to 2006." *Brookings Issues in Governance Studies* 42:1–14.

Delli Carpini, Michael X., and Scott Keeter. 1996. *What Americans Know about Politics and Why It Matters*. New Haven, CT: Yale University Press.

Dempsey, Jason K. 2009. *Our Army: Soldiers, Politics, and American Civil-Military Relations*. Princeton, NJ: Princeton University Press.

Dingman, Roger. 1998/1989. "Atomic Diplomacy during the Korean War." *International Security* 13(3): 50–91.

Divine, Robert A. 1987. "The Johnson Literature." In *The Johnson Years*, vol. 1, *Foreign Policy, the Great Society, and the White House*, edited by Robert A. Divine, 3–23. Lawrence: University Press of Kansas.

Downes, Alexander B. 2008. *Targeting Civilians in War*. Ithaca, NY: Cornell University Press.

———. 2009. "How Smart and Tough Are Democracies? Reassessing Theories of Democratic Victory in War." *International Security* 33(4): 9–51.

———. 2011. "The Myth of Choosy Democracies: Examining the Selection Effects Theory of Democratic Victory in War." *H-Diplo–ISSF Roundtable* 2(12): 64–102.

Downes, Alexander B., and Todd S. Sechser. 2012. "The Illusion of Democratic Credibility." *International Organization* 66(3): 457–89.

Downs, Anthony. 1957. *An Economic Theory of Democracy*. New York: Harper and Row.

Downs, George W., and David M. Rocke. 1994. "Conflict, Agency, and Gambling for Resurrection: The Principal-Agent Problem Goes to War." *American Journal of Political Science* 38(2): 362–80.

Draper, Robert. 2020. *To Start a War: How the Bush Administration Took America into Iraq*. New York: Penguin.

Drezner, Daniel W. 2000. "Ideas, Bureaucratic Politics, and the Crafting of Foreign Policy." *American Journal of Political Science* 44(4): 733–49.

———. 2017. *The Ideas Industry: How Pessimists, Partisans, and Plutocrats Are Transforming the Marketplace of Ideas*. New York: Oxford University Press.

Dueck, Colin. 2006. *Reluctant Crusaders: Power, Culture, and Change in American Grand Strategy*. Princeton, NJ: Princeton University Press.

Dyson, Stephen Benedict. 2007. "Alliances, Domestic Politics, and Leader Psychology: Why Did Britain Stay Out of Vietnam and Go into Iraq?" *Political Psychology* 28(6): 647–66.

Edelstein, David M. 2008. *Occupational Hazards: Success and Failure in Military Occupation*. Ithaca, NY: Cornell University Press.

Edwards, George C. 2003. *On Deaf Ears: The Limits of the Bully Pulpit*. New Haven, CT: Yale University Press.

Egan, Patrick J. 2013. *Partisan Priorities: How Issue Ownership Drives and Distorts American Politics*. New York: Cambridge University Press.

Eggers, Andrew C., Guadalupe Tuñón, and Allan Dafoe. n.d. "Placebo Tests for Causal Inference." Working Paper, University of Chicago, Princeton University, and University of Oxford.

Ellis, Joseph J. 2002. *Founding Brothers: The Revolutionary Generation*. New York: Vintage.

Entman, Robert M. 2004. *Projections of Power: Framing News, Public Opinion, and U.S. Foreign Policy*. Chicago: University of Chicago Press.

Erikson, Robert S., Michael B. MacKuen, and James A. Stimson. 2002. *The Macro Polity*. New York: Cambridge University Press.

Eshbaugh-Soha, Matthew. 2006. *The President's Speeches: Beyond "Going Public."* Boulder, CO: Lynne Rienner.

Evans, Alexandra T., and A. Bradley Potter. 2019. "When Do Leaders Change Course? Theories of Success and the American Withdrawal from Beirut, 1983–1984." *Texas National Security Review* 2(2): 10–38.

Fazal, Tanisha M. 2014. "Dead Wrong? Battle Deaths, Military Medicine, and Exaggerated Reports of War's Demise." *International Security* 39(1): 95–125.

Fazal, Tanisha M., and Sarah Kreps. 2018. "The United States' Perpetual War in Afghanistan." *Foreign Affairs*, August 20. https://www.foreignaffairs.com/articles/north-america/2018-08 -20/united-states-perpetual-war-afghanistan.

Fearon, James D. 1994. "Domestic Political Audiences and the Escalation of International Disputes." *American Political Science Review* 88(3): 577–92.

———. 1995. "Rationalist Explanations for War." *International Organization* 49(3): 379–414.

Feaver, Peter D. 2003. *Armed Servants: Agency, Oversight, and Civil-Military Relations*. Cambridge, MA: Harvard University Press.

———. 2011. "The Right to Be Right: Civil-Military Relations and the Iraq Surge Decision." *International Security* 35(4): 87–125.

Feaver, Peter D., and Christopher Gelpi. 2004. *Choosing Your Battles: American Civil-Military Relations and the Use of Force*. Princeton, NJ: Princeton University Press.

Fehrs, Matthew. 2014. "Too Many Cooks in the Foreign Policy Kitchen: Confused British Signaling and the Falklands War." *Democracy and Security* 10(3): 225–50.

Feldman, Stanley, Leonie Huddy, and George E. Marcus. 2015. *Going to War in Iraq: When Citizens and the Press Matter*. Chicago: University of Chicago Press.

Fenno, Richard F. 1959. *The President's Cabinet: An Analysis in the Period from Wilson to Eisenhower*. Cambridge, MA: Harvard University Press.

Ferejohn, John, and Frances McCall Rosenbluth. 2008. "Warlike Democracies." *Journal of Conflict Resolution* 52(1): 3–38.

Finkelstein, David M. 1993. *Washington's Taiwan Dilemma, 1949–1950: From Abandonment to Salvation*. Annapolis, MD: Naval Institute Press.

Flibbert, Andrew. 2006. "The Road to Baghdad: Ideas and Intellectuals in Explanations of the Iraq War." *Security Studies* 15(2): 310–52.

Foot, Rosemary. 1985. *The Wrong War: American Policy and the Dimensions of the Korean Conflict, 1950–1953*. Ithaca, NY: Cornell University Press.

Fordham, Benjamin O. 1998. *Building the Cold War Consensus: The Political Economy of U.S. National Security Policy, 1949–51*. Ann Arbor: University of Michigan Press.

———. 2002a. "Another Look at 'Parties, Voters, and the Use of Force Abroad.'" *Journal of Conflict Resolution* 46(4): 572–96.

———. 2002b. "Domestic Politics, International Pressure, and the Allocation of American Cold War Military Spending." *Journal of Politics* 64(1): 63–68.

Fowler, Linda L. 2015. *Watchdogs on the Hill: The Decline of Congressional Oversight of U.S. Foreign Relations*. Princeton, NJ: Princeton University Press.

Foyle, Douglas C. 1999. *Counting the Public In: Presidents, Public Opinion, and Foreign Policy*. New York: Columbia University Press.

Frank, Benis M. 1987. *U.S. Marines in Lebanon: 1982–1984*. Washington DC: History and Museums Division Headquarters, US Marine Corps.

Freedman, Lawrence. 2000. *Kennedy's Wars: Berlin, Cuba, Laos, and Vietnam*. New York: Oxford University Press.

Friedman, Jeffrey A. 2023. *The Commander-in-Chief Test: Public Opinion and the Politics of Image-Making in US Foreign Policy*. Ithaca, NY: Cornell University Press.

Fry, Joseph A. 2002. *Dixie Looks Abroad: The South and U.S. Foreign Relations, 1789–1973*. Baton Rouge: Louisiana State University Press.

———. 2010. "To Negotiate or Bomb: Congressional Prescriptions for Withdrawing U.S. Troops from Vietnam." *Diplomatic History* 34(3): 517–28.

Fulbright, J. William. 1979. "The Legislator as Educator." *Foreign Affairs* 57(4): 719–32.

Gadarian, Shana Kushner. 2010. "The Politics of Threat: How Terrorism News Shapes Foreign Policy Attitudes." *Journal of Politics* 72(2): 469–83.

Gaddis, John Lewis. 1987. *The Long Peace: Inquiries into the History of the Cold War*. Oxford: Oxford University Press.

———. 2005. *Strategies of Containment: A Critical Appraisal of American National Security Policy during the Cold War*. Rev. and expanded ed. Oxford: Oxford University Press.

Gans, John. 2019. *White House Warriors: How the National Security Council Transformed the American Way of War*. New York: W. W. Norton.

Garrett, Geoffrey, and Peter Lange. 1991. "Political Responses to Interdependence: What's 'Left' for the Left?" *International Organization* 45(4): 539–64.

Gartner, Scott Sigmund, and Gary M. Segura. 1998. "War, Casualties, and Public Opinion." *Journal of Conflict Resolution* 42(3): 278–300.

Gates, Robert M. 2014. *Duty: Memoirs of a Secretary of War*. New York: Alfred A. Knopf.

Gelb, Leslie, and Richard K. Betts. 1979. *The Irony of Vietnam: The System Worked*. Washington, DC: Brookings Institution Press.

Gelpi, Christopher. 2010. "Performing on Cue? The Formation of Public Opinion toward War." *Journal of Conflict Resolution* 54(1): 88–116.

Gelpi, Christopher, and Peter D. Feaver. 2002. "Speak Softly and Carry a Big Stick? Veterans in the Political Elite and the American Use of Force." *American Political Science Review* 96(4): 779–93.

Gelpi, Christopher, Peter D. Feaver, and Jason Reifler. 2005/2006. "Success Matters: Casualty Sensitivity and the War in Iraq." *International Security* 30(3): 7–46.

———. 2009. *Paying the Human Costs of War: American Public Opinion and Casualties in Military Conflicts*. Princeton, NJ: Princeton University Press.

Gelpi, Christopher, and Joseph M. Grieco. 2015. "Competency Costs in Foreign Affairs: Presidential Performance in International Conflicts and Domestic Legislative Success, 1953–2001." *American Journal of Political Science* 59(2): 440–56.

George, Alexander. 1980. *Presidential Decisionmaking in Foreign Policy: The Effective Use of Information and Advice*. Boulder, CO: Westview.

Gershkoff, Amy, and Shana Kushner. 2005. "Shaping Public Opinion: The 9/11-Iraq Connection in the Bush Administration's Rhetoric." *Perspectives on Politics* 3(3): 525–37.

Glad, Betty. 2009. *An Outsider in the White House: Jimmy Carter, His Advisors, and the Making of American Foreign Policy*. Ithaca, NY: Cornell University Press.

Golby, James Thomas. 2011. "Duty, Honor . . . Party? Ideology, Institutions, and the Use of Military Force." PhD diss., Stanford University.

Golby, James, Peter Feaver, and Kyle Dropp. 2018. "Elite Military Cues and Public Opinion about the Use of Military Force." *Armed Forces and Society* 44(1): 44–71.

Goldgeier, James, and Elizabeth N. Saunders. 2018. "The Unconstrained Presidency: Checks and Balances Eroded Long before Trump." *Foreign Affairs* 97(5): 144–56.

Goldstein, Gordon M. 2008. *Lessons in Disaster: McGeorge Bundy and the Path to War in Vietnam*. New York: Holt.

Gowa, Joanne. 1998. "Politics at the Water's Edge: Parties, Voters, and the Use of Force Abroad." *International Organization* 52(2): 307–24.

Greitens, Sheena Chestnut. 2016. *Dictators and Their Secret Police: Coercive Institutions and State Violence*. New York: Cambridge University Press.

Grieco, Joseph M., Christopher Gelpi, Jason Reifler, and Peter D. Feaver. 2011. "Let's Get a Second Opinion: International Institutions and American Public Support for War." *International Studies Quarterly* 55(2): 563–83.

Grossmann, Matt, and David A Hopkins. 2016. *Asymmetric Politics: Ideological Republicans and Group Interest Democrats*. New York: Oxford University Press.

Guisinger, Alexandra. 2009. "Determining Trade Policy: Do Voters Hold Politicians Accountable?" *International Organization* 63(3): 533–57.

———. 2017. *American Opinion on Trade: Preferences without Politics*. New York: Oxford University Press.

Guisinger, Alexandra, and Elizabeth N. Saunders. 2017. "Mapping the Boundaries of Elite Cues: How Elites Shape Mass Opinion across International Issues." *International Studies Quarterly* 61(2): 425–41.

Hadley, Stephen, Meghan O'Sullivan, and Peter Feaver. 2019. "How the 'Surge' Came to Be." In *The Last Card: Inside George W. Bush's Decision to Surge in Iraq*, edited by Timothy Andrews Sayle, Jeffrey A. Engel, Hal Brands, and William Inboden, 207–38. Ithaca, NY: Cornell University Press.

Hafner-Burton, Emilie M., Stephan Haggard, David A. Lake, and David G. Victor. 2017. "The Behavioral Revolution and International Relations." *International Organization* 71(S1): S1–S31.

Hafner-Burton, Emilie M., D. Alex Hughes, and David G. Victor. 2013. "The Cognitive Revolution and the Political Psychology of Elite Decision Making." *Perspectives on Politics* 11(2): 368–86.

Halberstam, David. 1969. *The Best and the Brightest*. New York: Random House.

Hallin, Daniel C. 1986. *The "Uncensored War": The Media and Vietnam*. New York: Oxford University Press.

Hamby, Alonzo L. 1995. *Man of the People: A Life of Harry S. Truman*. New York: Oxford University Press.

Hanhimaki, Jussi. 2003. "Selling the 'Decent Interval': Kissinger, Triangular Diplomacy, and the End of the Vietnam War, 1971–73." *Diplomacy and Statecraft* 14(1): 159–94.

Hart, Paul 't. 1991. "Irving L. Janis' *Victims of Groupthink.*" *Political Psychology* 12(2): 247–78.

Hayes, Christopher. 2012. *Twilight of the Elites: America after Meritocracy.* New York: Crown.

Hayes, Danny. 2005. "Candidate Qualities through a Partisan Lens: A Theory of Trait Ownership." *American Journal of Political Science* 49(4): 908–23.

Hayes, Danny, and Matt Guardino. 2013. *Influence from Abroad: Foreign Voices, the Media, and U.S. Public Opinion.* New York: Cambridge University Press.

Hendrickson, Ryan C. 2002. *The Clinton Wars: The Constitution, Congress, and War Powers.* Nashville, TN: Vanderbilt University Press.

Herring, George C. 1996. *LBJ and Vietnam: A Different Kind of War.* Austin: University of Texas Press.

Herrmann, Richard K. 2017. "How Attachments to the Nation Shape Beliefs about the World: A Theory of Motivated Reasoning." *International Organization* 71(S1): S61–S84.

Herrmann, Richard K., Philip E. Tetlock, and Penny S. Visser. 1999. "Mass Public Decisions to Go to War: A Cognitive-Interactionist Framework." *American Political Science Review* 93(3): 553–73.

Hibbs, Douglas A., Jr. 2000. "Bread and Peace Voting in U.S. Presidential Elections." *Public Choice* 104:149–80.

Hitchcock, William I. 2018. *The Age of Eisenhower: America and the World in the 1950s.* New York: Simon and Schuster.

Hollyer, James R., B. Peter Rosendorff, and James Raymond Vreeland. 2018. *Information, Democracy, and Autocracy: Economic Transparency and Political (In)Stability.* New York: Cambridge University Press.

Holsti, Ole R. 2004. *Public Opinion and American Foreign Policy.* Ann Arbor: University of Michigan Press.

Howell, William G., and Douglas L. Kriner. 2007. "Bending So as Not to Break: What the Bush Presidency Reveals about the Politics of Unilateral Action." In *The Polarized Presidency of George W. Bush*, edited by George C. Edwards III and Desmond S. King, 96–142. New York: Oxford University Press.

Howell, William G., and Jon C. Pevehouse. 2007. *While Dangers Gather: Congressional Checks on Presidential War Powers.* Princeton, NJ: Princeton University Press.

Hurwitz, Jon, and Mark Peffley. 1987. "How Are Foreign Policy Attitudes Structured? A Hierarchical Model." *American Political Science Review* 81(4): 1099–120.

Hyde, Susan D. 2015. "Experiments in International Relations: Lab, Survey, and Field." *Annual Review of Political Science* 18:403–24.

Hyde, Susan D., and Elizabeth N. Saunders. 2020. "Recapturing Regime Type in International Relations: Leaders, Institutions, and Agency Space." *International Organization* 74(2): 363–95.

Iversen, Torben, and Thomas R. Cusack. 2000. "The Causes of Welfare State Expansion: Deindustrialization or Globalization?" *World Politics* 52(3): 313–49.

Jacobs, Lawrence R., and Robert Y. Shapiro. 1999. "Lyndon Johnson, Vietnam, and Public Opinion: Rethinking Realist Theory of Leadership." *Presidential Studies Quarterly* 29(3): 592–616.

Jacobson, Gary C. 2010. "A Tale of Two Wars: Public Opinion on the U.S. Military Interventions in Afghanistan and Iraq." *Presidential Studies Quarterly* 40(4): 585–610.

Jentleson, Bruce W. 1992. "The Pretty Prudent Public: Post Post-Vietnam American Opinion on the Use of Military Force." *International Studies Quarterly* 36(1): 49–74.

Jentleson, Bruce W., and Rebecca L. Britton. 1998. "Still Pretty Prudent: Post–Cold War American Public Opinion on the Use of Military Force." *Journal of Conflict Resolution* 42(4): 395–417.

Jervis, Robert. 1976. *Perception and Misperception in International Politics*. Princeton, NJ: Princeton University Press.

———. 1980. "The Impact of the Korean War on the Cold War." *Journal of Conflict Resolution* 24(4): 563–92.

———. 2006. "Reports, Politics, and Intelligence Failures: The Case of Iraq." *Journal of Strategic Studies* 29(1): 3–52.

Johns, Andrew L. 1997. "Opening Pandora's Box: The Genesis and Evolution of the 1964 Congressional Resolution on Vietnam." *Journal of American–East Asian Relations* 6(2/3): 175–206.

———. 2006. "Doves among Hawks: Republican Opposition to the Vietnam War, 1964–1968." *Peace and Change* 31(4): 585–628.

———. 2010. *Vietnam's Second Front: Domestic Politics, the Republican Party, and the War*. Lexington: University Press of Kentucky.

Johnson, Dominic D. P. 2004. *Overconfidence and War: The Havoc and Glory of Positive Illusions*. Cambridge, MA: Harvard University Press.

Johnson, Dominic D. P., and Dominic Tierney. 2006. *Failing to Win: Perceptions of Victory and Defeat in International Politics*. Cambridge, MA: Harvard University Press.

Kaag, John, and Sarah Kreps. 2014. *Drone Warfare*. Cambridge: Polity.

Kagan, Robert. 2006. *Dangerous Nation: America's Foreign Policy from Its Earliest Days to the Dawn of the Twentieth Century*. New York: Vintage Books.

Kahneman, Daniel, and Jonathan D. Renshon. 2007. "Why Hawks Win." *Foreign Policy* 158:34–38.

———. 2009. "Hawkish Biases." In *American Foreign Policy and the Politics of Fear: Threat Inflation since 9/11*, edited by A. Trevor Thrall and Jane K. Cramer, 79–96. New York: Routledge.

Kaiser, David E. 2000. *American Tragedy: Kennedy, Johnson, and the Origins of the Vietnam War*. Cambridge, MA: Belknap Press of Harvard University Press.

Kane, John, and Haig Patapan. 2012. *The Democratic Leader: How Democracy Defines, Empowers, and Limits Its Leaders*. Oxford: Oxford University Press.

Kant, Immanuel. 1970. "Perpetual Peace." In *Kant: Political Writings*, edited by H. S. Reiss, 93–130. Cambridge: Cambridge University Press.

Kaplan, Fred. 2013. *The Insurgents: David Petraeus and the Plot to Change the American Way of War*. New York: Simon and Schuster.

Karnow, Stanley. 1983. *Vietnam: A History*. New York: Viking.

Katzenstein, Peter J. 1996. *Cultural Norms and National Security: Policy and Military in Postwar Japan*. Ithaca, NY: Cornell University Press.

Kaufmann, Chaim. 2004. "Threat Inflation and the Failure of the Marketplace of Ideas: The Selling of the Iraq War." *International Security* 29(1): 5–48.

Kelley, Judith G., and Jon C. W. Pevehouse. 2015. "An Opportunity Cost Theory of US Treaty Behavior." *International Studies Quarterly* 59(3) 531–43.

Kernell, Samuel. 1986. *Going Public: New Strategies of Presidential Leadership*. Washington, DC: CQ Press.

Kertzer, Joshua D. 2016. *Resolve in International Politics*. Princeton, NJ: Princeton University Press.

———. 2020. "Re-assessing Elite-Public Gaps in Political Behavior." *American Journal of Political Science* 66(3): 539–53.

Kertzer, Joshua D., and Ryan Brutger. 2016. "Decomposing Audience Costs: Bringing the Audience Back into Audience Cost Theory." *American Journal of Political Science* 60(1): 234–49.

Kertzer, Joshua D., Kathleen E. Powers, Brian C. Rathbun, and Ravi Iyer. 2014. "Moral Support: How Moral Values Shape Foreign Policy Attitudes." *Journal of Politics* 76(3): 825–40.

Kertzer, Joshua D., and Dustin Tingley. 2018. "Political Psychology in International Relations: Beyond the Paradigms." *Annual Review of Political Science* 21:319–39.

Kertzer, Joshua D., and Thomas Zeitzoff. 2017. "A Bottom-Up Theory of Public Opinion about Foreign Policy." *American Journal of Political Science* 61(3): 543–58.

Key, V. O. 1961. *Public Opinion and American Democracy*. New York: Knopf.

Koch, Michael T., and Patricia Sullivan. 2010. "Should I Stay or Should I Go Now? Partisanship, Approval, and the Duration of Major Power Democratic Military Interventions." *Journal of Politics* 72(3): 616–29.

Korpi, Walter, and Joakim Palme. 2003. "New Politics and Class Politics in the Context of Austerity and Globalization: Welfare State Regress in 18 Countries, 1975–95." *American Political Science Review* 97(3): 425–46.

Krasner, Stephen D. 1972. "Are Bureaucracies Important? (or Allison Wonderland)." *Foreign Policy* 7:159–79.

———. 1978. *Defending the National Interest: Raw Materials Investments and U.S. Foreign Policy*. Princeton, NJ: Princeton University Press.

Krebs, Ronald R. 2015. *Narrative and the Making of US National Security*. New York: Cambridge University Press.

Krehbiel, Keith. 1990. "Are Congressional Committees Composed of Preference Outliers?" *American Political Science Review* 84(1): 149–63.

———. 1998. *Pivotal Politics: A Theory of U.S. Lawmaking*. Chicago: University of Chicago Press.

Kreps, Sarah. 2010. "Elite Consensus as a Determinant of Alliance Cohesion: Why Public Opinion Hardly Matters for NATO-Led Operations in Afghanistan." *Foreign Policy Analysis* 6(3): 191–215.

———. 2018. *Taxing Wars: The American Way of War Finance and the Decline of Democracy*. New York: Oxford University Press.

———. 2019. "Legality and Legitimacy in American Military Interventions." *Presidential Studies Quarterly* 49(3): 551–80.

Kreps, Sarah E., Elizabeth N. Saunders, and Kenneth A. Schultz. 2018. "The Ratification Premium: Hawks, Doves, and Arms Control." *World Politics* 70(4): 479–514.

Kriner, Douglas L. 2010. *After the Rubicon: Congress, Presidents, and the Politics of Waging War*. Chicago: University of Chicago Press.

Kurtz-Phelan, Daniel. 2018. *The China Mission: George Marshall's Unfinished War, 1945–1947*. New York: W. W. Norton.

Lake, David A. 1992. "Powerful Pacifists: Democratic States and War." *American Political Science Review* 86(1): 24–37.

———. 2010/2011. "Two Cheers for Bargaining Theory: Assessing Rationalist Explanations of the Iraq War." *International Security* 35(3): 7–52.

Larson, Eric V. 1996. *Casualties and Consensus: The Historical Role of Casualties in Domestic Support for U.S. Military Operations.* Santa Monica, CA: RAND.

Lebovic, James H. 2019. *Planning to Fail: The US Wars in Vietnam, Iraq, and Afghanistan.* New York: Oxford University Press.

Lee, Carrie A. 2015. "The Politics of Military Operations." PhD diss., Stanford University.

Leffler, Melvyn P. 1992. *A Preponderance of Power: National Security, the Truman Administration, and the Cold War.* Stanford, CA: Stanford University Press.

Lenz, Gabriel S. 2009. "Learning and Opinion Change, Not Priming: Reconsidering the Priming Hypothesis." *American Journal of Political Science* 53(4): 821–37.

———. 2012. *Follow the Leader? How Voters Respond to Politicians' Policies and Performance.* Chicago: University of Chicago Press.

Lerner, Mitchell. 1995. "Vietnam and the 1964 Election: A Defense of Lyndon Johnson." *Presidential Studies Quarterly* 25(4): 751–66.

Levendusky, Matthew S., and Michael C. Horowitz. 2012. "When Backing Down Is the Right Decision: Partisanship, New Information, and Audience Costs." *Journal of Politics* 74(2): 323–38.

Lindsay, James M. 1992–93. "Congress and Foreign Policy: Why the Hill Matters." *Political Science Quarterly* 107(4): 607–28.

Lindsey, David. 2017. "Diplomacy through Agents." *International Studies Quarterly* 61(3): 544–56.

Lippmann, Walter. 1922. *Public Opinion.* New York: Macmillan.

Logevall, Fredrik. 1999. *Choosing War: The Lost Chance for Peace and the Escalation of War in Vietnam.* Berkeley: University of California Press.

———. 2004. "Lyndon Johnson and Vietnam." *Presidential Studies Quarterly* 34(1): 100–112.

———. 2008. "Fredrik Logevall Comment on Francis M. Bator's 'No Good Choices: LBJ and the Vietnam / Great Society Connection.'" *Diplomatic History* 32(3): 355–59.

Lunch, William L., and Peter W. Sperlich. 1979. "American Public Opinion and the War in Vietnam." *Western Political Quarterly* 32(1): 21–44.

Lupia, Arthur, and Mathew D. McCubbins. 1998. *The Democratic Dilemma: Can Citizens Learn What They Need to Know?* New York: Cambridge University Press.

Lyall, Jason. 2010. "Do Democracies Make Inferior Counterinsurgents? Reassessing Democracy's Impact on War Outcomes and Duration." *International Organization* 64(1): 167–92.

———. 2020. *Divided Armies: Inequality and Battlefield Performance in Modern War.* Princeton, NJ: Princeton University Press.

Mack, Andrew. 1975. "Why Big Nations Lose Small Wars: The Politics of Asymmetric Conflict." *World Politics* 27(2): 175–200.

Malis, Matt. 2021. "Conflict, Cooperation, and Delegated Diplomacy." *International Organization* 75(4): 1018–57.

———. n.d. "Foreign Policy Appointments." Working Paper, Texas A&M University.

Mann, James. 2004. *Rise of the Vulcans: The History of Bush's War Cabinet.* New York: Penguin Books.

———. 2012. *The Obamians: The Struggle inside the White House to Redefine American Power.* New York: Viking.

Mansfield, Edward D., and Diana C. Mutz. 2009. "Support for Free Trade: Self-Interest, Socio-tropic Politics, and Out-Group Anxiety." *International Organization* 63(3): 425–57.

Marinov, Nikolay, William G. Nomikos, and Josh Robbins. 2015. "Does Electoral Proximity Affect Security Policy?" *Journal of Politics* 77(3): 762–73.

Marsh, Kevin. 2014. "Obama's Surge: A Bureaucratic Politics Analysis of the Decision to Order a Troop Surge in the Afghanistan War." *Foreign Policy Analysis* 10(3): 265–88.

Mattes, Michaela, and Jessica L. P. Weeks. 2019. "Hawks, Doves, and Peace: An Experimental Approach." *American Journal of Political Science* 63(1): 53–66.

Mayhew, David R. 2005. "Wars and American Politics." *Perspectives on Politics* 3(3): 473–93.

McAllister, James. 2010/2011. "Who Lost Vietnam? Soldiers, Civilians, and U.S. Military Strategy." *International Security* 35(3): 95–123.

McCarty, Nolan. 2019. *Polarization: What Everyone Needs to Know*. New York: Oxford University Press.

McCubbins, Mathew D., and Thomas Schwartz. 1984. "Congressional Oversight Overlooked: Police Patrols versus Fire Alarms." *American Journal of Political Science* 28(1): 165–79.

McKercher, Asa. 2014. "Steamed Up: Domestic Politics, Congress, and Cuba, 1959–1963." *Diplomatic History* 38(3): 599–627.

McMaster, H. R. 1997. *Dereliction of Duty: Lyndon Johnson, Robert McNamara, the Joint Chiefs of Staff, and the Lies That Led to Vietnam*. New York: Harper Collins.

Mead, Walter Russell. 1999. "The Jacksonian Tradition and American Foreign Policy." *National Interest*, no. 58:5–29.

Mearsheimer, John J. 2018. *The Great Delusion: Liberal Dreams and International Realities*. New Haven, CT: Yale University Press.

Merom, Gil. 2003. *How Democracies Lose Small Wars: State, Society, and the Failures of France in Algeria, Israel in Lebanon, and the United States in Vietnam*. Cambridge: Cambridge University Press.

Michels, Robert. 1962. *Political Parties: A Sociological Study of the Oligarchical Tendencies of Modern Democracy*. Translated by Eden Paul and Cedar Paul. New York: Free Press.

Miller, Benjamin. 2010. "Explaining Changes in U.S. Grand Strategy: 9/11, the Rise of Offensive Liberalism, and the War in Iraq." *Security Studies* 19(1): 26–65.

Milner, Helen V. 1997. *Interests, Institutions, and Information: Domestic Politics and International Relations*. Princeton, NJ: Princeton University Press.

Milner, Helen V., and Dustin Tingley. 2015. *Sailing the Water's Edge: The Domestic Politics of American Foreign Policy*. Princeton, NJ: Princeton University Press.

Moïse, Edwin E. 1996. *Tonkin Gulf and the Escalation of the Vietnam War*. Chapel Hill: University of North Carolina Press.

Montgomery, Jacob M., Brendan Nyhan, and Michelle Torres. 2018. "How Conditioning on Posttreatment Variables Can Ruin Your Experiment and What to Do about It." *American Journal of Political Science* 62(3): 760–75.

Moravcsik, Andrew. 2004. "Is There a 'Democratic Deficit' in World Politics? A Framework for Analysis." *Government and Opposition* 39(2): 336–63.

Morgenthau, Hans J., and Kenneth W. Thompson. 1985. *Politics among Nations: The Struggle for Power and Peace*. 6th ed. New York: Knopf.

Mueller, John E. 1973. *War, Presidents, and Public Opinion*. New York: John Wiley and Sons.

———. 2021. "Public Opinion on War and Terror: Manipulated or Manipulating?" White Paper, Cato Institute, Washington, DC, August 10. https://doi.org/10.36009/WP.20210810.

Myrick, Rachel. 2021. "Do External Threats Unite or Divide? Security Crises, Rivalries, and Polarization in American Foreign Policy." *International Organization* 75(4): 921–58.

Narang, Vipin, and Caitlin Talmadge. 2017. "Civil-Military Pathologies and Defeat in War: Tests Using New Data." *Journal of Conflict Resolution* 62(7): 1379–405.

Neustadt, Richard E. 1974. "Congress and the Fair Deal: A Legislative Balance Sheet." In *Harry S. Truman and the Fair Deal*, edited by Alonzo L. Hamby, 15–42. Lexington, MA: D. C. Heath.

———. 1990. *Presidential Power and the Modern Presidency: The Politics of Leadership from Roosevelt to Reagan*. New York: Free Press.

Nichols, Tom. 2017. *The Death of Expertise: The Campaign against Established Knowledge and Why It Matters*. New York: Oxford University Press.

Nincic, Miroslav. 1988. "The United States, the Soviet Union, and the Politics of Opposites." *World Politics* 40(4): 452–75.

Olson, Mancur. 1965. *The Logic of Collective Action: Public Goods and the Theory of Groups*. Cambridge, MA: Harvard University Press.

Packer, George. 2005. *The Assassins' Gate: America in Iraq*. New York: Farrar, Straus and Giroux.

Page, Benjamin I., with Marshall M. Bouton. 2006. *The Foreign Policy Disconnect: What Americans Want from Our Leaders but Don't Get*. Chicago: University of Chicago Press.

Page, Benjamin I., and Richard A. Brody. 1972. "Policy Voting and the Electoral Process: The Vietnam War Issue." *American Political Science Review* 66(3): 979–95.

Page, Benjamin I., and Robert Y. Shapiro. 1992. *The Rational Public: Fifty Years of Trends in Americans' Policy Preferences*. Chicago: University of Chicago Press.

Payne, Andrew. 2020. "Presidents, Politics, and Military Strategy: Electoral Constraints during the Iraq War." *International Security* 44(3): 163–203.

———. 2023. *War on the Ballot: How the Election Cycle Shapes Presidential Decision-Making in War*. New York: Columbia University Press.

Petrocik, John R. 1996. "Issue Ownership in Presidential Elections, with a 1980 Case Study." *American Journal of Political Science* 40(4): 825–50.

Porter, Patrick. 2018. "Why America's Grand Strategy Has Not Changed: Power, Habit, and the U.S. Foreign Policy Establishment." *International Security* 42(4): 9–46.

Powell, Robert. 2002. "Bargaining Theory and International Conflict." *Annual Review of Political Science* 5(1): 1–30.

Pressman, Jeremy. 2001. "September Statements, October Missiles, November Elections: Domestic Politics, Foreign Policy Making, and the Cuban Missile Crisis." *Security Studies* 10(3): 80–114.

Preston, Andrew. 2006. *The War Council: McGeorge Bundy, the NSC, and Vietnam*. Cambridge, MA: Harvard University Press.

———. 2019. "Iraq, Vietnam, and the Meaning of Victory." In *The Last Card: Inside George W. Bush's Decision to Surge in Iraq*, edited by Timothy Andrews Sayle, Jeffrey A. Engel, Hal Brands, and William Inboden, 239–59. Ithaca, NY: Cornell University Press.

Ramsay, Kristopher W. 2004. "Politics at the Water's Edge: Crisis Bargaining and Electoral Competition." *Journal of Conflict Resolution* 48(4): 459–86.

Rathbun, Brian C. 2004. *Partisan Interventions: European Party Politics and Peace Enforcement in the Balkans*. Ithaca, NY: Cornell University Press.

Rathbun, Brian C., Joshua D. Kertzer, Jason Reifler, Paul Goren, and Thomas J. Scotto. 2016. "Taking Foreign Policy Personally: Personal Values and Foreign Policy Attitudes." *International Studies Quarterly* 60(1): 124–37.

Ray, Bruce A. 1980. "The Responsiveness of the U.S. Congressional Armed Services Committees to Their Parent Bodies." *Legislative Studies Quarterly* 5(4): 501–15.

Recchia, Stefano. 2015. *Reassuring the Reluctant Warriors: U.S. Civil-Military Relations and Multilateral Intervention*. Ithaca, NY: Cornell University Press.

Reeves, Richard. 2005. *President Reagan: The Triumph of Imagination*. New York: Simon and Schuster.

Reiter, Dan. 2003. "Exploring the Bargaining Model of War." *Perspectives on Politics* 1(1): 27–43.

———. 2009. *How Wars End*. Princeton, NJ: Princeton University Press.

Reiter, Dan, and Allan C. Stam. 2002. *Democracies at War*. Princeton, NJ: Princeton University Press.

Rhodes, Ben. 2018. *The World as It Is: A Memoir of the Obama White House*. New York: Random House.

Ricks, Thomas E. 2007. *Fiasco: The American Military Adventure in Iraq, 2003 to 2005*. New York: Penguin.

———. 2009. *The Gamble: General David Petraeus and the American Military Adventure in Iraq, 2006–2008*. New York: Penguin.

Riker, William H. 1962. *The Theory of Political Coalitions*. New Haven, CT: Yale University Press.

Risse-Kappen, Thomas. 1991. "Public Opinion, Domestic Structure, and Foreign Policy in Liberal Democracies." *World Politics* 43(4): 479–512.

Rossiter, Clinton, ed. 1961. *The Federalist Papers*. New York: Penguin Books.

Rovner, Joshua. 2011. *Fixing the Facts: National Security and the Politics of Intelligence*. Ithaca, NY: Cornell University Press.

———. 2019. "Strategy and the Surge." In *The Last Card: Inside George W. Bush's Decision to Surge in Iraq*, edited by Timothy Andrews Sayle, Jeffrey A. Engel, Hal Brands, and William Inboden, 296–313. Ithaca, NY: Cornell University Press.

Russett, Bruce M. 1990. *Controlling the Sword: The Democratic Governance of National Security*. Cambridge, MA: Harvard University Press.

———. 2009. "Democracy, War and Expansion Through Historical Lenses." *European Journal of International Relations* 15(1): 9–36.

Saltoun-Ebin, Jason, ed. 2012. *The Reagan Files: Inside the National Security Council*. CreateSpace.

Sanger, David E. 2012. *Confront and Conceal: Obama's Secret Wars and Surprising Use of American Power*. New York: Crown.

Saunders, Elizabeth N. 2011. *Leaders at War: How Presidents Shape Military Interventions*. Ithaca, NY: Cornell University Press.

———. 2014. "Good Democratic Leadership in Foreign Affairs: An Elite-Centered Approach." In *Good Democratic Leadership: On Prudence and Judgment in Modern Democracies*, edited by John Kane and Haig Patapan, 158–77. Oxford: Oxford University Press.

———. 2015. "War and the Inner Circle: Democratic Elites and the Politics of Using Force." *Security Studies* 24(3): 466–501.

———. 2017. "No Substitute for Experience: Presidents, Advisers, and Information in Group Decision Making." *International Organization* 71(S1): S219–S247.

———. 2018. "Leaders, Advisers, and the Political Origins of Elite Support for War." *Journal of Conflict Resolution* 62(10): 2118–49.

———. 2022. "Elites in the Making and Breaking of Foreign Policy." *Annual Review of Political Science* 25:219–40.

Saunders, Elizabeth N., and Scott Wolford. n.d. "Elites, Voters, and Democracies at War." Working Paper, Georgetown University and the University of Texas at Austin.

Sayle, Timothy Andrews, Jeffrey A. Engel, Hal Brands, and William Inboden, eds. 2019. *The Last Card: Inside George W. Bush's Decision to Surge in Iraq.* Ithaca, NY: Cornell University Press.

Schake, Kori N., and Jim Mattis. 2016. *Warriors and Citizens: American Views of Our Military.* Stanford: Hoover Institution Press.

Schattschneider, E. E. 1960. *The Semi-sovereign People: A Realist's View of Democracy in America.* New York: Holt, Rinehart, and Winston.

Schlesinger, Arthur M. Jr. 1965. *A Thousand Days: John F. Kennedy in the White House.* Boston: Houghton Mifflin.

Schoenbaum, Thomas J. 1988. *Waging Peace and War: Dean Rusk in the Truman, Kennedy, and Johnson Years.* New York: Simon and Schuster.

Schuessler, John M. 2015. *Deceit on the Road to War: Presidents, Politics, and American Democracy.* Ithaca, NY: Cornell University Press.

Schulhofer-Wohl, Jonah. 2021. "The Obama Administration and Civil War in Syria, 2011–2016: US Presidential Foreign Policy Making as Political Risk Management." *Journal of Transatlantic Studies* 19(4): 517–47.

Schultz, Kenneth A. 2001a. *Democracy and Coercive Diplomacy.* New York: Cambridge University Press.

———. 2001b. "Looking for Audience Costs." *Journal of Conflict Resolution* 45(1): 32–60.

———. 2003. "Tying Hands and Washing Hands: The U.S. Congress and Multilateral Humanitarian Intervention." In *Locating the Proper Authorities: The Interaction of Domestic and International Institutions*, edited by Daniel W. Drezner, 105–42. Ann Arbor: University of Michigan Press.

———. 2005. "The Politics of Risking Peace: Do Hawks or Doves Deliver the Olive Branch?" *International Organization* 59(1): 1–38.

———. 2017. "Perils of Polarization for U.S. Foreign Policy." *Washington Quarterly* 40(4): 7–28.

———. n.d. "Could Humphrey Have Gone to China? Measuring the Electoral Costs and Benefits of Making Peace." Working paper, Stanford University.

Schultz, Kenneth A., and Barry R. Weingast. 2003. "The Democratic Advantage: Institutional Foundations of Financial Power in International Competition." *International Organization* 57(1): 3–42.

Schumpeter, Joseph. 1942. *Capitalism, Socialism and Democracy.* New York: Harper and Brothers.

Sechser, Todd S. 2004. "Are Soldiers Less War-Prone Than Statesmen?" *Journal of Conflict Resolution* 48(5): 746–74.

Shultz, George P. 1993. *Turmoil and Triumph: My Years as Secretary of State.* New York: Scribner's.

Singh, Naunihal. 2014. *Seizing Power: The Strategic Logic of Military Coups.* Baltimore: Johns Hopkins University Press.

Slantchev, Branislav L. 2006. "Politicians, the Media, and Domestic Audience Costs." *International Studies Quarterly* 50(2): 445–77.

Small, Melvin. 1988. *Johnson, Nixon, and the Doves*. New Brunswick, NJ: Rutgers University Press.

Smith, Alastair. 1998. "International Crises and Domestic Politics." *American Political Science Review* 92(3): 623–38.

Snyder, Jack L. 1991. *Myths of Empire: Domestic Politics and International Ambition*. Ithaca, NY: Cornell University Press.

Snyder, Jack, and Erica D. Borghard. 2011. "The Cost of Empty Threats: A Penny, Not a Pound." *American Political Science Review* 105(3): 437–56.

Stanley, Elizabeth A. 2009. *Paths to Peace: Domestic Coalition Shifts, War Termination, and the Korean War*. Stanford, CA: Stanford University Press.

Stein, Rachel M. 2019. *Vengeful Citizens, Violent States*. New York: Cambridge University Press.

Stone, Gary. 2007. *Elites for Peace: The Senate and the Vietnam War, 1964–1968*. Knoxville: University of Tennessee Press.

Strong, James. 2017. *Public Opinion, Legitimacy and Tony Blair's War in Iraq*. London: Routledge.

Stueck, William. 1997. *The Korean War: An International History*. Princeton: Princeton University Press.

———. 1981. *The Road to Confrontation: American Policy toward China and Korea, 1947–1950*. Chapel Hill: University of North Carolina Press.

———. 2002. *Rethinking the Korean War: A New Diplomatic and Strategic History*. Princeton, NJ: Princeton University Press.

Svolik, Milan W. 2012. *The Politics of Authoritarian Rule*. New York: Cambridge University Press.

Talmadge, Caitlin. 2015. *The Dictator's Army: Battlefield Effectiveness in Authoritarian Regimes*. Ithaca, NY: Cornell University Press.

Tama, Jordan. 2011. *Terrorism and National Security Reform: How Commissions Can Drive Change during Crises*. New York: Cambridge University Press.

Taubman, Philip. 2023. *In the Nation's Service: The Life and Times of George P. Shultz*. Stanford, CA: Stanford University Press.

Tetlock, Philip E. 2005. *Expert Political Judgment: How Good Is It? How Can We Know?* Princeton, NJ: Princeton University Press.

Thomson, James C. 1973. "How Could Vietnam Happen? An Autopsy." In *Readings in American Foreign Policy: A Bureaucratic Perspective*, edited by Morton H. Halperin and Arnold Kanter, 98–110. Boston: Little, Brown.

Tocqueville, Alexis de. 1969. *Democracy in America*. Translated by George Lawrence. New York: Harper Perennial.

Tomz, Michael. 2007. "Domestic Audience Costs in International Relations: An Experimental Approach." *International Organization* 61(4): 821–40.

Tomz, Michael, Jessica L. P. Weeks, and Keren Yarhi-Milo. 2020. "Public Opinion and Decisions about Military Force in Democracies." *International Organization* 74(1): 119–43.

Trachtenberg, Marc. 2012. "Audience Costs: An Historical Analysis." *Security Studies* 21(1): 3–42.

Trager, Robert F., and Lynn Vavreck. 2011. "The Political Costs of Crisis Bargaining: Presidential Rhetoric and the Role of Party." *American Journal of Political Science* 55(3): 526–45.

Trubowitz, Peter. 2011. *Politics and Strategy: Partisan Ambition and American Statecraft*. Princeton, NJ: Princeton University Press.

Tucker, Nancy Bernkopf. 1983. *Patterns in the Dust: Chinese-American Relations and the Recognition Controversy, 1949–1950*. New York: Columbia University Press.

———. 1990. "John Foster Dulles and the Taiwan Roots of the 'Two Chinas' Policy." In *John Foster Dulles and the Diplomacy of the Cold War*, edited by Richard H. Immerman, 235–62. Princeton, NJ: Princeton University Press.

VanDeMark, Brian. 1991. *Into the Quagmire: Lyndon Johnson and the Escalation of the Vietnam War*. New York: Oxford University Press.

Voeten, Erik. 2005. "The Political Origins of the UN Security Council's Ability to Legitimize the Use of Force." *International Organization* 59(3): 527–57.

Vreeland, James Raymond, and Axel Dreher. 2014. *The Political Economy of the United Nations Security Council: Money and Influence*. New York: Cambridge University Press.

Walt, Stephen M. 2018. *The Hell of Good Intentions: America's Foreign Policy Elite and the Decline of US Primacy*. New York: Farrar, Straus and Giroux.

Walzer, Michael. 1970. "A Day in the Life of a Socialist Citizen." In *Obligations: Essays on Disobedience, War, and Citizenship*, 229–38. New York: Clarion.

Weeks, Jessica L. [P.] 2008. "Autocratic Audience Costs: Regime Type and Signaling Resolve." *International Organization* 62(1): 35–64.

———. 2012. "Strongmen and Straw Men: Authoritarian Regimes and the Initiation of International Conflict." *American Political Science Review* 106(2): 325–47.

———. 2014. *Dictators at War and Peace*. Ithaca, NY: Cornell University Press.

Weingast, Barry R. 1997. "The Political Foundations of Democracy and the Rule of Law." *American Political Science Review* 91:245–63.

Weingast, Barry R., and William J. Marshall. 1988. "The Industrial Organization of Congress, or, Why Legislatures, Like Firms, Are Not Organized as Markets." *Journal of Political Economy* 96(1): 132–63.

Weiss, Jessica Chen. 2013. "Authoritarian Signaling, Mass Audiences, and Nationalist Protest in China." *International Organization* 67(1): 1–35.

———. 2014. *Powerful Patriots: Nationalist Protest in China's Foreign Relations*. Oxford: Oxford University Press.

Western, Jon. 2002. "Sources of Humanitarian Intervention: Beliefs, Information, and Advocacy in the U.S. Decisions on Somalia and Bosnia." *International Security* 26(4): 112–42.

———. 2005. *Selling Intervention and War: The Presidency, the Media, and the American Public*. Baltimore: Johns Hopkins University Press.

Woods, Randall Bennett. 1995. *Fulbright: A Biography*. Cambridge: Cambridge University Press.

———. 2008. "Randall B. Woods Comment on Francis M. Bator's 'No Good Choices: LBJ and the Vietnam / Great Society Connection.'" *Diplomatic History* 32(3): 343–45.

Woodward, Bob. 2004. *Plan of Attack*. New York: Simon and Schuster.

———. 2008. *The War Within: A Secret White House History 2006–2008*. New York: Simon and Schuster.

———. 2010. *Obama's Wars*. New York: Simon and Schuster.

Yarhi-Milo, Keren. 2018. *Who Fights for Reputation: The Psychology of Leaders in International Conflict*. Princeton, NJ: Princeton University Press.

Zaller, John R. 1992. *The Nature and Origins of Mass Opinion*. Cambridge: Cambridge University Press.

Zaller, John R. 1994a. "Elite Leadership of Mass Opinion: New Evidence from the Gulf War." In *Taken by Storm: The Media, Public Opinion, and U.S. Foreign Policy in the Gulf War*, edited by W. Lance Bennett and David L. Paletz, 186–209. Chicago: University of Chicago Press.

———. 1994b. "Strategic Politicians, Public Opinion, and the Gulf Crisis." In *Taken by Storm: The Media, Public Opinion, and U.S. Foreign Policy in the Gulf War*, edited by W. Lance Bennett and David L. Paletz, 250–76. Chicago: University of Chicago Press.

———. 2003a. "Coming to Grips with V. O. Key's Concept of Latent Opinion." In *Electoral Democracy*, edited by Michael B. MacKuen and George Rabinowitz, 311–36. Ann Arbor: University of Michigan Press.

———. 2003b. "A New Standard of News Quality: Burglar Alarms for the Monitorial Citizen." *Political Communication* 20(2): 109–30.

INDEX

Page numbers in *italics* indicate figures and tables

Nixon, Richard, 10, *66*; and Cambodian incursion (1970), 181–82; congressional authorization of, *170*; election of 1968 and, 36; inheriting Vietnam War, 153, 181–83; and trip to China, 10, 59, 62, 155, 182; Vietnamization strategy of, 72; Vietnam War and, 73, 155–56

Nixon-to-China logic, 10, 11, 41, 59, 62, 182, 244

North Korea, 14, 153; invasion of South Korea by, 119–20. *See also* Korean War

North Vietnamese Army, 180

Nunn, Sam: on MX missile debate, 199; on opposition to 1991 Gulf War, 220

Obama, Barack, *66*, 239; Afghanistan and, 3, 73, 113, 214; and Afghanistan as a dove's curse, 231–35; and Afghanistan surge, 229–35; and American troops, 79; appointment of Hillary Clinton under, 56, 230; and congressional authorization, *170*; as dovish wing of Democratic Party, 243; and killing of bin Laden, 3; Libya and, 45; McChrystal and Afghanistan report, effect on, 39, 60; and ratification negotiation for New START, 59; Syria and, 11, 242; using Congress on Syria crisis, 169. *See also* Afghanistan War

Oglesby, M. B., sounding alarm to Baker, 210–11

O'Neill, Thomas "Tip" Jr.: Baker and, 205; calling for War Powers action, 204; and deal extending Lebanon intervention, 70; letters from committee of, 210; switching positions, 208

Pace, Frank: and circumventing Secretary Johnson, 139; on directive to MacArthur, 140; on sending US ground forces to Korea, 135

Packer, George, on Haass and 2003 Iraq war, 215

Palestine Liberation Organization (PLO), 190, 197

Panetta, Leon, public identifying, *78*

partisan polarization, 13, 20, 26, 46, 214, 239, 268n46; insiders' game and, 243–46

peace: elite politics of, 62; terminology, 9

Pelosi, Nancy: on Afghanistan, 230, 234; on supporting Obama, 232

Pentagon Papers, 3

Percy, Charles, on compromise vote, 206

Petraeus, David: Crocker and, 227; endorsing more troops to Afghanistan, 232; and Iraq surge, 231; praise and promotion of, 46; supporting Obama, 233; testimony of, 228

policy costs, elites, 37–38

policy preferences, elites, 44–45

policy sabotage, elites, 38

policy spillover, 38

political preferences, elites, 43, 45–48

politics, of elites, 7–9

politics of opposites (Nincic's term), public engaging in, 40

post-9/11 wars, 1, 14, 213; insiders' game pattern of, 213–14

Potter, A. Bradley, on bombing of Marine Barracks, 203

Powell, Colin: Bush (G.W.) administration and, 60; as insider skeptic, 213, 215; and intervention in Somalia, 11; on Iraq War, 222; opponent of Iraq War, 219; procedural concessions to, 214, *216*; selection of, 57; at United Nations, 214, 220, 221

presidential power, post-Cold War and post–9/11, 24

Pressler, Larry, on compromise vote, 206

Preston, Andrew, on Iraq surge, 228

private benefits, 10–11, 245; asymmetric, 59; dovish elites and, 29, *55*, 58–59, 61; escalatory action and, 68; Gary Hart on, 221; leader's decisions and, 46; placating copartisan doves, 130; for supporting war, 19

protests, voters coordinating, 36–37

psychological bias, decision makers, 4

public opinion, 76; concept of latent, 36, 158, 260n39; and elite and leaders, 15–16;